Japan's Quiet Transformation

In the 1990s the phenomenal growth of the Japanese economy ground to a shuddering halt and the country was subsequently crippled by enormous and ongoing political, economic, and social problems. This accessible and engaging textbook for all students of Japanese studies is beautifully illustrated with striking images of turmoil and change in contemporary Japan. Kingston examines the transformation of Japan, evaluating the social, economic, and political challenges it has faced, as well as prospects for the future, addressing what is often missed by the media's relentlessly pessimistic coverage. Controversially, it argues that the Japan that emerges from these manifold problems may, in fact, be stronger than before. Areas covered include:

- the growth of nonprofit organizations;
- the erosion of bureaucratic power;
- information disclosure;
- judicial reform;
- the political economy of the construction industry;
- HIV, leprosy, and the struggle for human rights;
- food safety – BSE and whaling;
- nationalism and identity; and
- social transformation: family, gender, aging, and work.

Jeff Kingston is Professor of History and Director of Asian Studies at Temple University Japan, and is a regular contributor to *Japan Times*.

Asia's Transformations

Edited by Mark Selden

Binghamton University and Cornell University, USA

The books in this series explore the political, social, economic and cultural consequences of Asia's transformations in the twentieth and twenty-first centuries. The series emphasizes the tumultuous interplay of local, national, regional, and global forces as Asia bids to become the hub of the world economy. While focusing on the contemporary, it also looks back to analyze the antecedents of Asia's contested rise. This series comprises several strands:

Asia's Transformations aims to address the needs of students and teachers, and the titles will be published in hardback and paperback. Titles include:

Japan's Comfort Women
Sexual slavery and prostitution
during World War II and the US
occupation
Yuki Tanaka

Debating Human Rights
Critical essays from the United
States and Asia
Edited by Peter Van Ness

Hong Kong's History
State and society under colonial rule
Edited by Tak-Wing Ngo

Asia's Great Cities
Each volume aims to capture the heartbeat of the contemporary city from
multiple perspectives emblematic of the authors' own deep familiarity with
the distinctive faces of the city, its history, society, culture, politics and
economics, and its evolving position in national, regional and global frame-
works. While most volumes emphasize urban developments since the Second
World War, some pay close attention to the legacy of the longue durée in shaping the contemporary. Thematic and comparative volumes address such
themes as urbanization, economic and financial linkages, architecture and
space, wealth and power, gendered relationships, planning and anarchy, and
ethnographies in national and regional perspective. Titles include:

Hong Kong
Global city
Stephen Chiu and Tai-Lok Lui

Beijing in the Modern World
David Strand and Madeline Yue Dong

Bangkok
Place, practice and representation
Marc Askew

Shanghai
Global city
Jeff Wasserstrom

Singapore
Carl Trocki

Asia.com is a series which focuses on the ways in which new information and
communication technologies are influencing politics, society and culture in
Asia. Titles include:

Asia.com
Asia encounters the Internet
*Edited by K.C. Ho, Randolph Kluver
and Kenneth C.C. Yang*

Japanese Cybercultures
*Edited by Mark McLelland and Nanette
Gottlieb*

Literature and Society is a series that seeks to demonstrate the ways in which
Asian literature is influenced by the politics, society and culture in which it is
produced. Titles include:

Chinese Women Writers and the
Feminist Imagination
(1905–1945)
Haiping Yan

The Body in Postwar Japanese
Fiction
Edited by Douglas N. Slaymaker

RoutledgeCurzon Studies in Asia's Transformations is a forum for innovative new research intended for a high-level specialist readership, and the titles will be available in hardback only. Titles include:

1. Japanese Industrial Governance
Protectionism and the licensing state
Yul Sohn

2. Remaking Citizenship in Hong Kong
Community, nation and the global city
Edited by Agnes S. Ku and Ngai Pun

3. Chinese Media, Global Contexts
Edited by Chin-Chuan Lee

4. Imperialism in South East Asia
'A fleeting, passing phase'
Nicholas Tarling

5. Internationalizing the Pacific
The United States, Japan and the Institute of Pacific Relations in war and peace, 1919–1945
Tomoko Akami

6. Koreans in Japan
Critical voices from the margin
Edited by Sonia Ryang

7. The American Occupation of Japan and Okinawa*
Literature and memory
Michael Molasky

* Now available in paperback

Critical Asian Scholarship is a series intended to showcase the most important individual contributions to scholarship in Asian Studies. Each of the volumes presents a leading Asian scholar addressing themes that are central to his or her most significant and lasting contribution to Asian studies. The series is committed to the rich variety of research and writing on Asia, and is not restricted to any particular discipline, theoretical approach, or geographical expertise.

China's Past, China's Future
Energy, food, environment
Vaclav Smil

China Unbound
Evolving perspectives on the Chinese past
Paul A. Cohen

Women and the Family in Chinese History
Patricia Buckley Ebrey

Southeast Asia
A testament
George McT. Kahin

Japan's Quiet Transformation

Social change and civil society in the twenty-first century

Jeff Kingston

RoutledgeCurzon
Taylor & Francis Group
LONDON AND NEW YORK

First published 2004
by RoutledgeCurzon
2 Park Square, Milton Park, Abingdon, Oxon OX14 4RN

Simultaneously published in the USA and Canada
by RoutledgeCurzon
270 Madison Ave, New York, NY 10016

RoutledgeCurzon is an imprint of the Taylor & Francis Group

Reprinted 2005

© 2004 Jeff Kingston

Typeset in Baskerville by Bookcraft Ltd, Stroud, Gloucestershire

Printed and bound in Great Britain by TJ International Ltd, Padstow, Cornwall

British Library Cataloguing in Publication Data
A catalogue record for this book is available from the British Library

Library of Congress Cataloging in Publication Data
Kingston, Jeff, 1957–
 Japan's quiet transformation: social change and civil society in the
 21st century / by Jeff Kingston.
   p. cm. – (Routledge studies in Asia's transformation)
 Includes bibliographical references.
 1. Social change–Japan. 2. Civil society–Japan. 3. Japan–social
 conditions–1945– I. Title. II. Series.
HN723.5 .K537 2004
303.4'0952–dc22

                                                          2003024595

ISBN 0-415-27482-6 (hbk)
ISBN 0-415-27483-4 (pbk)

Contents

Figures

Acknowledgements

This book is dedicated to Greg Davis (1948–2003), friend, mentor, and renowned photojournalist. His sudden death from cancer was probably due to exposure to Agent Orange during the Vietnam War. We often discussed developments in Japan and elsewhere in Asia where he spent much of the last 35 years of his life. I learned a great deal from him about reconsidering dominant narratives and reading between the lines and on the margins. He was a truly kind and inspiring person and helped me better understand the meanings of time and friendship. Through his introduction I met Suzuki Koji, a longtime resident of a leprosy colony in Kusatsu, Gunma. This helpful gesture had a major influence on this book. As can happen in a writing project I was bogged down, getting nowhere fast in searching for the right approach, something that could somehow render coherent my inchoate thoughts and concerns. Interviewing Mr. Suzuki suddenly helped me to decide what I had long been considering; I threw out my original book proposal and decided to write about important developments in Japan that were largely being ignored or overlooked by other observers. I want to preserve and make some sense of Mr. Suzuki's grim story and place it in the larger context of contemporary social change. I credit Larry Repeta, advocate and scholar of information disclosure, with helping me figure out how the various pieces of the puzzle connected. Although he is not liable for the results, he played a key role in directing my focus to how Japanese are responding to socioeconomic turmoil and nurturing civil society.

Without the encouragement, advice, and feedback of Mark Selden and Laura Hein this book would never have seen the light of day. I have benefited from their patience and unstinting assistance and cannot properly express how deeply grateful I am for their contributions. They have guided and goaded me to improve my manuscript and along the way saved me from numerous errors and analytical lapses. Paul Sorrell provided excellent editorial assistance and pinned back my ears when needed.

Many others have contributed to this book in various ways and helped me in sharpening my ideas and in writing it. Naturally they are absolved of all responsibility for the outcome, but deserve kudos for their efforts and generosity. This book owes much to the help of: Tom Boardman, David Campbell,

In memory of Greg Davis (1948–2003).

Kyle Cleveland, Gerry Curtis, Howard French, Honna Jun, Andrew Horvat, Veli Kattoulas, Mataebara Yutaka, Sebastian Moffett, Jack Mosher, Lars and Henriette Myrup, Nagai Mariko, Ogawa Akihiro, Oshima Sakurako, Sakata Masako, Donald Richie, Sumitomo Emi, Suzuki Ayumi, Suzuki Koji, Watanabe Shinya, Bob Whiting, Charles Worthen, Yamamoto Akiko, and Hyun Sook Yun.

I am grateful to Greg Davis, Stuart Isett and Andreas Seibert for making their photos available and to Roger Dahl for his cartoons.

I wish to thank my students over the years and the Temple University administration, especially Robert Reinstein, Roman Cybriwsky, and Kirk Patterson, for giving me the time to complete this project.

Finally, I would like to express my deep gratitude to my wife Osawa Machiko. She and our dogs, Ochan, Rhubarb, and Goro, listened attentively and kept me in good spirits.

Notes

An exchange rate of ¥120 = $1 is used for calculations in the text.
Japanese names are cited with family name first as is the convention in Japan.

Preface

In the opening years of the twenty-first century, Japanese people, organizations, and policy makers are responding to the myriad challenges generated by the Lost Decade of the 1990s in thoughtful, significant, and diverse ways that are making possible sweeping social, economic, and cultural change. This book describes their efforts to lay the foundations for a more robust civil society and assesses the portents of this process. Japan's plunge from the giddying heights of the 1980s asset bubble – at a time when it was ostensibly the world's most successful economy – unleashed a social tsunami, forcing people to question and revise many assumptions and verities that lay at the heart of Japan following World War II.

Japan is widely portrayed by both the media and the academy as a nation adrift, doing too little too late to cope with its enduring economic malaise. Its sclerotic political system, tied to the status quo and mired in structural corruption, is rightly identified as a major obstacle to substantive reforms. While these issues tell important stories about twenty-first-century Japan, they are only part of the story.

I wrote this book because so much of what is happening in contemporary Japan is not accounted for in the relentlessly pessimistic prose and stagnant images that dominate media and academic writing, both domestic and international. The ongoing reinvention of Japan driven by creative responses to its admittedly immense problems reveals a far more dynamic polity. This book examines a variety of developments since the early 1990s that are contributing to this ongoing transformation. While Japan's problems are formidable, mine is a story that highlights substantive transformation rather than dismal prospects. Certainly, there are good reasons for pessimism about Japan's future, some of which I discuss in these pages, but there is also much to be learned from examining how a variety of groups and individuals are responding to adversity and coping with the nation's gathering problems.

The substantial and wide-ranging reforms detailed in the book demonstrate a building momentum in the renovation of Japan. The seeds of change are being planted and nurtured; small changes made in the 1980s are bearing fruit twenty years later. The national information disclosure law passed in 1999 is a prime example. Back in 1982 when the first local freedom of information ordinance was enacted in Kanagawa, advocates hardly imagined that they were initiating a chain reaction favoring greater transparency and accountability in governance that would sweep through the archipelago and culminate in national legislation. While other reform initiatives are already having some immediate impact, one can also anticipate broader consequences in the future. Throughout the book, I try to convey the growing sense of urgency that animates this quest towards a more robust civil society.

It is not what remains to be done but the magnitude of what has already been achieved that provides the most accurate barometer of change in contemporary Japan. If we assess the tectonic shifts in economic practices and policies over the past decade, the pace and breadth of transformation is astonishing. While the economic reforms have not yet cured what ails the nation, and may indeed fail, they are already transforming the once familiar landscape of Japan, Inc. Economic practices that were long taken for granted in Japan – full employment, secure jobs, seniority wages, strong banks guided and protected by the Ministry of Finance, and corporate-centered welfare – are now fading vestiges of a system that has soured. The loss of economic security and stability is influencing society in many ways, not least in the attitudes and assumptions of a people suddenly confronted with the loss of reassuring familiarity. Such dislocations, with threats of more to come, are percolating through society and transforming it. Once-staunch advocates of the system are now among its harshest critics while passive acceptance of the status quo is giving way to greater skepticism. At the same time, the gathering crisis of confidence is generating new levels of ambivalence as some cling to the familiar while searching for new answers. Thus, the Liberal Democratic Party, architects of the old system, continues to hold on to power while the ways and means of that system are widely seen to be significant factors in the current malaise.

Japan's quiet transformation is above all a story of the gradual and incremental reinvigoration of civil society. Since the mid-1990s a series of interlocking and mutually reinforcing reforms in government policies and corporate practices, coupled with legislative and institutional innovations, have been laying the foundations for a thorough renovation of civil society. Citizens are responding by using the new weapon of information disclosure and participating in nonprofit organizations (NPOs) to exercise political oversight and shape the national agenda. Popular support for open government and concerns about quality-of-life issues are increasingly reflected in politicians' campaigns. Greater transparency and accountability are evident and affecting relations between the people and those who govern. Volunteerism is rapidly expanding and the government is promoting expanded partnerships with NPOs. At the same time, a major fiscal crisis is forcing the government to curtail spending on public works and privatize at least some of the public corporations that are draining the treasury; the tangled skein of corruption in the construction sector is slowly, if only partially, unraveling. Bureaucratic scandals are alerting citizens to the need for greater scrutiny and spurring them to exercise their new powers of oversight. The courts are supporting citizens' rights to freedom of information far more vigorously than anyone anticipated and helping to shine a light onto dubious practices. Abuses of power that were once tolerated are now increasingly the subject of public disapprobation and criminal prosecution. An activist and accessible judiciary is being established with astonishing speed. Citizens are engaging in widespread acts of public defiance, demonstrating the crisis of faith in government and belying the meek and submissive stereotypes peddled by the media.

But despite these positive developments and the progress towards creating a more vibrant civil society, lingering problems remain. Naturally, social transformations do not happen on a fixed schedule. The quiet transformation discussed in these pages is fitful, gradual, and cumulative, meaning that subtle changes sit uncomfortably next to, and sometimes in the shadow of, prominent continuities. There is a lag between reform initiatives and substantive consequences, mirroring the gap between intentions and actual results. Progress is not measured in linear terms, onward and upward, indeed pragmatic compromises figure more prominently than grand gestures and sweeping measures. Yet Japan in 2004 is very different from the way it was in 1989; from a historical perspective fifteen years is a small blip of time and in this brief moment many of the seemingly ineradicable verities and practices of Japan have been unalterably transformed.

The reinvention of Japan is a work in progress. The quiet transformation in policies, practices, attitudes, values, and institutions gains little attention because it will not solve today's problems tomorrow and because it is a prolonged process rather than a 'big bang.' It is the result of myriad reforms and responses that considered on their own appear to be of little consequence. Here I try to show how they fit together in a larger mosaic and why they are both reflecting and propelling the contemporary transformation of Japan.

1 · The Lost Decade of the 1990s

> The so-called Lost Decade of the 1990s has been misunderstood because it really marks a watershed in Japan and has been a time of far reaching transformation.
>
> Gerald Curtis, Professor of Political Science,
> Columbia University, July 26, 2002

> During the Lost Decade the powerful and privileged lost while ordinary people benefited.
>
> Miyazaki Ikuko, founder of *Mail Magazine*, an internet
> job information service for working women, August 2002

> The final ten years of the twentieth century have been called a 'lost decade' for Japan, which continues to suffer woes from the burst of the late-1980s bubble economy. Japan's comeback as a globally competitive economic powerhouse will require fundamental reforms not only in the industrial and financial sectors but also in government administration, politics and social systems, including education, the judiciary and immigration.
>
> *Japan Times*, January 1, 2001

The 1990s in Japan have been dubbed the Lost Decade. This is a period when the economy imploded, the asset bubble collapsed, banks teetered on the edge of insolvency, unemployment skyrocketed, suicides increased and the leaders of Japan, Inc. were tarnished by exposés of pervasive corruption. The nation of the 'economic miracle' found itself looking into the abyss, lunging from the swaggering late 1980s, when commentators gushed about a Pax Nipponica, to the sobering realities of the turn of the century when analysts predicted systemic collapse. The nation's credit rating slumped to the level of junk bonds and zombie companies staggered towards bankruptcy. Everything seemed to go wrong at the same time, an inauspicious beginning to the Heisei era, a period that has virtually become synonymous with Japan's prolonged recession.[1]

What was lost in the Lost Decade? Mountains of money, a sense of security, stable families, and the credibility of the nation's leadership. To this standard list of debits one might add hubris and confidence about the future. The mighty have been brought low and the reputations of some have been dragged through the mud. Many topics that were once carefully avoided have now been brought into the open: subjects such as money politics, mob influence, and pervasive malfeasance are now regularly aired in a feistier national press. Also lost in the 1990s was an orchestrated innocence about the nation's shared past with Asia between 1931 and 1945.

But while Japan lost a system and a fortune, it found improved lifestyles and a greater acceptance of diversity. People also gained new insights into the shortcomings of the system and those who were running it. They began to question prevailing values and the stifling regimentation of many aspects of life in Japan. The popular phrase 'Not being #1, but being only 1' articulates a new humility and a new-found freedom of self-expression. Such affirmation of individuality and uniqueness is a new phenomenon for Japan. The 1990s was also a decade when cellular phones and internet connections became widespread, generating a revolution in communications that is not yet fully understood, but cannot be overlooked as one of the significant changes that are sweeping contemporary Japan.[2]

Crisis and turmoil have a way of defining a people and their society. Japan has experienced pervasive adversity in the recession-plagued 1990s, undermining longstanding beliefs, attitudes, relationships, and patterns of behavior. As Japan enters the twenty-first century, it is emerging from a decade of profound change driven in no small part by the wave of developments in the tumultuous 1990s that acted as a grim finale for the postwar era. Perhaps one of the most profound changes has occurred in the way that citizens view their government, as a series of scandals and exposés of negligence, incompetence, and mismanagement have undermined the credibility of the ruling elite. The rhetoric of deregulation and reform owes its popular appeal to widespread skepticism about the abilities of those who make the regulations and wield power. The reforms and dynamics unleashed during and since the 1990s are comparable with the social and political transformations associated with the Meiji restoration (1868) and the American Occupation (1945–52). The breadth and pace of change in this emerging third era of transformation is remarkable: the Japan that slunk out of the 1990s was very different from the Japan that entered the decade with smug confidence and heady optimism. There have been profound changes in the public face of the nation – in attitudes and expectations, patterns of relationships, institutions, and civil society. It is an era of growing irreverence towards, and subversion of, the powers that be.

The building blocks of Japan's quiet transformation are being put in place and the shape of this new foundation is slowly emerging. The rapidity of the social metamorphosis is testimony to the adaptability and pragmatism of a nation that has often been criticized for failing to embrace reform and viewing the challenges facing it with complacency. Under the best of conditions, reform is often a slow and unsatisfactory process marked by setbacks and diversions – but once underway it has a knack of spilling over the carefully prepared sluices and flowing in unanticipated directions with unintended consequences. What happens is not always planned and what is planned does not always work out as intended. This book sketches some of these plans and consequences and suggests what they may portend for Japan in the twenty-first century.

Japan's quiet transformation involves the gradual process of extending and reinvigorating its stunted civil society. Although the institutions, practices, and patterns of civil society atrophied over the course of the twentieth century, recent developments suggest that they are slowly and incrementally recovering. Ordinary citizens are demanding a more democratic society marked by more transparent governance, more public participation and oversight, and greater accountability based on the rule of law – a trend heightened by the economic nose-dive of the 1990s.[3] This debacle severely discredited Japan, Inc.,[4] and led many to reconsider existing social and political arrangements. There is a growing revolution in the way people perceive and interact with those who lead Japan and the institutions that govern the nation.

However, this revolution in perceptions involves only a partial repudiation of Japan, Inc. The captains of industry have not been demoted, the Liberal Democratic Party (LDP) still calls the shots and the bureaucrats still wield considerable power to shape political processes and outcomes. The iron triangle (big business, the LDP, and the bureaucracy) may be battered, rusty, and out of synch, but it has not yet been toppled or melted down for scrap. Ironically, some of the strongest momentum for change has been generated by powerful elements in this triumvirate who – albeit out of self-interest – have jumped on the reform train. The reform agenda thus far unveiled, involving half-measures and carefully calibrated change, reflects the natural instinct of these vested interests to preserve their advantages, and a fundamental distrust of a vibrant civil society. Despite the establishment's misgivings over the consequences of ongoing reforms, it is becoming more perilous to stand against reform in an age when the status quo is so badly tarnished.

The quiet transformation portrayed in the following pages is a transitional period where the discredited practices and institutions of the past persist alongside the slow emergence of a new paradigm. Thus there is a degree of continuity between Japan, Inc. and the new reality being shaped – or rather cobbled together – in these early years of the twenty-first century. The persistence of the old order has been taken as a sign of stagnation and paralysis, reflecting a deep resistance to meaningful reform. While the transition to a new Japan will certainly encounter opposition, it is remarkable just how thoroughly the assumptions of the past have been questioned and jettisoned since the early 1990s. Moreover, there are few voices calling for the old system to be preserved. There is consensus on the need for reform, and maintaining the existing system is not seen as a viable option. Some favor a faster pace of change while others prefer to muddle through and manage a soft landing. There are also disagreements over who will bear the pain of reform and

Figure 1.1 Bikers clash with police in Hiroshima. (Photo: Stuart Issett)

restructuring. Certainly the vested interests are not rolling over and meekly acquiescing to the logic of reform. But ongoing institutional, regulatory, and legal changes favoring a more robust civil society are creating a momentum for change and the means to achieve it. These dynamics of transformation explain why Japan's transformation is a process that will take a couple of decades rather than a few years.

Before exploring recent developments in detail, it is important to understand why Japan, Inc. became discredited so rapidly in the Lost Decade. There are many questions that might be asked. Why did a system that had apparently worked so well for so many for so long suddenly lose the trust of the public? What can the scandals and disasters that beset 1990s Japan tell us about the systemic problems that so rapidly felled Japan, Inc.? Why does the comfortable and predictable status quo seem to be less and less appealing to many – business leaders, bureaucrats, politicians, and citizens alike – who have benefited from it in the past? An examination of the final decade of the twentieth century shows why increasing numbers of people are rejecting the discredited ways of the past – seen as 'part of the problem' – and pinning their hopes on a social transformation.

Collective hysteria

Japan's 'bubble era' takes its name from the steep appreciation in asset prices that occurred during the late 1980s. Economic bubbles, and the crashes that inevitably follow them, have occurred throughout history; they are marked by a collective mania spurred on by a contagious optimism that what is bought today can be sold tomorrow for a higher price. In general, bubbles result from a combination of strong growth, low inflation, and rampant expansion of money supply and credit. At some point the crowd – or, more often, those with privileged positions in the market – realize that prices cannot be sustained at stratospheric levels, resulting in panic selling, an implosion in prices and economic crisis.

During the bubble, stock and urban land prices soared to unprecedented heights in Japan. The Nikkei 225 stock index tripled in the 45 months prior to the December 1989 stock market peak when Japanese stocks reached a value of $4 trillion, constituting 44 percent of the world's equity market. Meanwhile, the urban land-price index quadrupled between 1985 and 1989. Between 1987 and 1989 alone, the value of all property assets in Japan held by corporations rose by the equivalent of the nation's entire gross domestic product (GDP) in 1988.[5] By 1991, the value of Japan's property assets accounted for 20 percent of global wealth and was double the value of global equities. But just as suddenly as asset prices rose, they plummeted in the 1990s and have remained depressed into the twenty-first century. In 1990 property values in Tokyo, Osaka, and Nagoya fell between 40 percent and 60 percent from their bubble era peaks, while in 1991 alone the stock market average lost 36 percent of its value. This correction in asset prices constituted the bursting of the bubble. As of 2003, the Nikkei stock average was down 80 percent from its peak and urban residential land prices remain down by two-thirds.[6] For example, a 150 m^2 wooden house with 284 m^2 of land in a desirable residential area in western Tokyo that was valued at roughly ¥300 million in 1990 was worth approximately ¥130 million (just over $1 million) in 2002.[7]

Why did the asset bubble occur? There are a variety of theories, and many factors no doubt contributed to the dizzying spiral in asset prices. Like speculative spirals throughout history, price increases were fed by greed and a herd mentality, and made possible by excessive liquidity and easy credit. In addition, a continuing escalation in prices for both stocks and land became a matter of faith, and investors remained confident, even as prices dove, that there was still untapped upward momentum if only they remained patient and hung on to their investments.[8] A decade later, in the midst of a prolonged recession, it is hard to credit the leap of faith made by speculators and investors at that time. A powerful group psychology encouraged people to suspend their judgment and focus their anxieties on being left out of the boom.[9]

The asset bubble was not merely a result of this speculative frenzy – both international developments and domestic factors combined to pump it up. On the international front, Japan's agreements at the 1985 Plaza Accord to allow a sharp appreciation in the value of the yen and pursue monetary policies favoring high economic growth were aimed at reining in burgeoning trade surpluses with the USA; a more expensive yen was expected to dampen exports while imports would rise in tandem with growth and an appreciating yen.[10] In the wake of the US stock-market crash in 1987, there was considerable international pressure on Japan to stabilize world financial markets and act as an engine of global growth by stimulating its economy. As a consequence, the Bank of Japan acted to boost domestic demand by slashing the discount rate from 5 percent to 2.5 percent and increasing money supply growth between 1987 and 1989 by 9–12 percent per year.[11]

On the domestic front, surging monetary growth and easy credit fueled speculation. In the absence of alternative investment vehicles, and with extremely low interest rates on bank deposits and government bonds, surplus capital was funneled into stocks and land, driving an appreciation in asset prices. Due to corporate cross-holding of shares, the supply of stocks available for purchase was artificially limited, ensuring that the spike in stock buying would have an amplified effect on stock prices.[12] As a result, by 1989 the average price/earnings ratio on the Nikkei exceeded 65, more than quadruple the historic price/earnings ratio of the Dow Jones stock index in the US. Government plans to stimulate domestic demand by promoting urban redevelopment and making Tokyo into an international financial center sent a clear signal to bankers who promptly increased real estate lending from only 7 percent of their loan portfolios in 1985 to 17 percent by 1990. Zoning regulations on land use, development controls, taxation policies, and the myth of ever-rising land prices limited the supply of land for sale, thus ensuring a similarly amplified impact on real estate prices. At one point, the land in Tokyo alone was supposedly more valuable than all of the land in the USA.[13]

Decisions by the Japanese government, bankers, and corporate executives exacerbated the financial crisis. The government's interest-rate policy contributed to speculation by making it very cheap to borrow money, injecting huge sums into a system already awash in capital. The government was promoting expansion with cheap money and achieved growth rates averaging 5 percent per annum between 1986 and 1989, at a time when other leading economies languished in recession. Given low interest rates, bankers had to lend more money to turn a profit and aggressively expanded lending without careful risk assessment or a full appraisal of corporate balance sheets. In addition, neither bankers nor government banking authorities carefully monitored how the money was used. Since companies could easily raise vast sums on the soaring stock market, and cut their costs of capital by doing so, banks found little appetite for loans from blue-chip clients. As a consequence they increased lending to second- and third-tier companies and became more aggressive in lending linked to real estate, relying on land as collateral. With what seemed like a green light from bankers and government officials, companies borrowed vast sums of money to expand production facilities and also engaged in *zaitech*, asset speculation designed to boost company balance sheets. In this frenzied atmosphere, risks were dismissed as minimal and

Figure 1.2 Long hours of commuting, work, and after-work drinking with colleagues and clients take their toll on Japan's beleaguered salarymen. (Photo: Andreas Seibert/Lookat)

Figure 1.3 Urban sprawl and modern infrastructure encroaching on disappearing
ways of rural Japan. (Photo: Greg Davis)

megaprojects were launched without concern for returns or worst-case
scenarios.

Lavish corporate spending, excess liquidity, speculation, over-investment,
and an absence of risk assessment made for a volatile combination and an
overheated economy. These factors also lay at the roots of the still-lingering
problem of bad debts that continue to batter the financial sector. The government popped the bubble in 1989 by raising interest rates five times in that
year in an attempt to prevent asset inflation from spilling over into the rest of
the economy. Tight money policy continued until the end of 1990, with the
discount rate rising to 6 percent. Although the central bank's efforts to
contain inflation succeeded in popping the bubble, the house of cards built
by speculative fever was very fragile and it was only a matter of time before
some shock sent it crashing down. The government may have hoped for a
soft landing, but instead Japan was mired in recession throughout the 1990s.
In the wake of the bubble, Finance Ministry bureaucrats have been blamed
for mismanaging economic policy, causing the crash and failing to pursue
policies that would effectively address the problems that had accumulated
during the bubble era. Bankers have been accused of lax lending policies and
incompetent credit risk assessment, while the *yakuza* (gangsters) stand
accused of manipulating bankers and bureaucrats to secure huge loans for
speculative and illegal activities. Whiting (1999) argues that many of the *jusen*
– real-estate lending institutions tied to banks – had links with *yakuza* that
were known to both the bankers and government overseers. A significant
proportion of the loan default problem can be traced back to these *jusen*,

suggesting that the bubble may have been a giant con game that enriched the mob at public expense.

The collapse of land and stock prices sent shockwaves throughout the Japanese archipelago and brought the financial sector to its knees. Suddenly the land that served as collateral for most of the bank loans was worth less than the original loans, and bankers discovered that some unscrupulous borrowers had used the same land to secure multiple loans. Those who had borrowed money for stock speculation were also unable to repay their loans. Until the end of the 1990s the government tried to conceal the extent of loan defaults, fearing that revelations of the true scale of the problem would spark a panic and further worsen already straitened economic conditions. There was also hope that economic conditions would improve and that, with an upturn in the business cycle, bankers and lenders would be able to work their way out of the mess. However, business conditions in the 1990s remained depressed and the bad loan problems festered. The government could no longer stand by while the nation's entire financial system teetered on the edge of insolvency.

The bubble episode left a bitter taste in the public's mouth. Taxpayer-funded bailouts of the banks and related financial institutions restored stability to a wobbly financial system, but at the expense of public confidence in the credibility of government leaders and bankers. In addition, there is still a lingering sense that the explanations about the bad loan problems just don't add up and that the bailouts are unfair programs that benefit vested interests. Estimates of the total bad debt incurred range from a low of $600 billion to nearly four times as much. By comparison, the US Savings and Loan Bank crisis of the 1980s involved some $250 billion in an economy twice the size of Japan's.

During the bubble era, 1986–91, the domestic real estate market overheated, pricing affordable housing out of reach of the average salaryman. An apartment of 75 m^2 within ninety minutes' travel of the Tokyo central business district cost 8.5 times the average annual salary, more than double the housing-cost-to-salary ratio in other advanced industrialized nations. 'Reasonably' priced apartments in Tokyo's 23 wards cost ¥1 million per m^2, and more in the better neighborhoods. A million US dollars in Tokyo would buy a relatively small, shoddily built house with virtually no garden some thirty minutes by train from the central business district. But there was a pervasive faith that land prices could only rise – as had always been the case in the postwar era. So even when prices seemed astronomical, families mortgaged their futures to the hilt, confident that, twenty years on, their investment would be considered a shrewd coup. Second-home and resort communities sprouted up around the country, bringing the influence of the bubble to some rural areas. Even golf-club memberships became a field for speculation and astronomical valuations. It seemed as if the cult of Mammon had spread a mass hysteria among a people not traditionally inclined to crass materialism.

Disturbing new social realities emerged as a result of the crisis. The bubble created immense wealth for those who had bought land or stocks at the right time, suddenly creating significant socioeconomic differences among a people who see themselves as uniformly 'middle class.'[14] Japan had been enormously successful in spreading the fruits of the economic miracle and limiting income inequalities, but this achievement and the social cohesion it generated was tested by the sudden and sharp disparities fueled by the asset bubble.[15] Japan was suddenly made to face the reality of a society divided into 'haves' and 'have nots' in a nation that had always valued conformity and uniformity.

Hangover

The bubble-induced hangover persists and the consequences will be felt well into the twenty-first century. The human toll has been enormous. Observers remark that the postbubble experience in Japan has been relatively benign compared to the restructuring that swept through corporate America following the 1987 stock market crash. Visitors to Tokyo routinely comment that Japan does not look like a nation locked in deep recession, pointing to packed boutiques and bistros, a building boom, and well-attired pedestrians walking on clean streets amidst pulsating energy and activity. But while layoffs and unemployment have been relatively limited, the misery index can be measured by other means. Many families had assumed massive mortgages to acquire housing only to see the value of their property plummet below the level of their outstanding loan. This phenomenon of negative equity has helped depress consumption in Japan as families minimize their spending to compensate for the folly of bubble-era purchases. Some landowners who had pledged their land as collateral for loans have since lost it. Many families lost everything in the crash, having failed to hedge their heavily leveraged bets. The media carried numerous reports of debtors disappearing, with the assistance of 'specialist services' (*yonigei*), presumably to escape creditors and assume new identities. Families suffered a rising divorce rate and children were pulled out of university because tuition had become an unaffordable expense. The media focused on the rising number of heads of households committing suicide so that their families could collect on life insurance policies.[16] The growing cardboard-box communities of homeless men on train station sites bore testimony to a degree of hardship not reflected in official statistics on unemployment. So too did the shift of many young female university graduates into the sex industry and the rise in juvenile delinquency (see page 29).

Nor has the business sector gone unscathed. There has been a spate of high-profile bankruptcies involving major enterprises such as banks, security firms, real estate and construction companies, and large retailers. Much has changed from the days when it was assumed that the government would always act as the lender of last resort and that some companies were just too

Figure 1.4 Trendy boutiques like this are sprouting up in Japan's cities. (Photo: Jeff Kingston)

big to fail. The demise of Hokkaido Takushoku Bank (1997), Yamaichi Securities (1997), the Long-Term Credit Bank (1998), and the Nippon Credit Bank (1998), all large and venerable firms with well-established political connections, reflects the Ministry of Finance's new approach to managing the economy. The vaunted 'convoy' system of protecting the weakest at a cost to the strongest is abating. In the financial sector, links with foreign investors have generated pressures for a faster pace of deregulation. But the economic crisis has been the most effective force behind deregulation (including the aviation, retail, and communications sectors) as the mandarins belatedly recognize that the nation's high cost structure is dampening economic performance and leading industries to relocate overseas.

The aftermath of the bubble has also unleashed unprecedented criticism of Japan's corporate culture and its values of conformity, personal sacrifice, and unquestioning loyalty. The 1999 hit film, *Jubaku: Archipelago of Rotten Money*, carried a biting critique of the business world and the activities of *sokaiya*, corporate racketeers with mob ties who extort money from companies in exchange for protecting their image and insulating them from accountability to their stockholders.[17] The film depicts the 'redeeming' features of Japanese-style capitalism as the cause of the nation's decline and an impediment to recovery. In his satirical book *The Bubble: What Could That Money Have Bought?* (1999), popular novelist Murakami Ryu lampooned the taxpayer bailout of bankrupt financial institutions by listing 123 alternatives for spending the same $600 billion. Rather than paying the 'gambling debts' of profligate bankers, Murakami points out that Japan could have done something of lasting benefit with this huge sum of money. Such open challenging of the status quo, and the powers that be, is more evident in Japan as people demand greater government transparency and accountability. No one in public office is immune, and the media are leading the charge (see Chapter 2). Media exposés forced the once-revered officials of the Ministry of Finance, the most powerful institution in Japan, to curtail their patronage of *nopantsushabushabu* (Japanese beef restaurants featuring mirrored floors and waitresses wearing no panties) as guests of bankers and others under their purview. Such behavior is no longer considered acceptable, less out of prudishness than of concerns about collusion and violation of the public trust.

Disinterring the past

A further sign of Japan's social revolution is seen in the painful confrontation with its shared past with Asia since the 1930s. The death in 1989 of the Showa Emperor (Hirohito), the most prominent link with this period, opened this largely unexamined past to greater scrutiny and unleashed a flood of grim revelations about the Japanese military's wartime conduct. Already in the 1980s there was robust public debate over government censorship of school history textbooks, and criticism, both overseas and in Japan, of the failure to acknowledge Japan's victimization of its Asian neighbors in officially sanctioned narratives. Thus, although there were signs of a changing consciousness about Japan's war record before 1989, it was only with the death of Hirohito that the nation really began to face up to the bloody record of its rampage through Asia between 1931 and 1945.

The ghosts of this troubled past had effectively been buried by agreement between the victors (the USA) and the defeated (Japan's conservative elite) at a time when a full and frank accounting of past misdeeds seemed far less important than fighting the Cold War. The US government protected the Emperor from prosecution for war crimes.[18] During the occupation, the USA relied heavily on those who had wielded power in wartime Japan. It also retained existing bureaucratic institutions. The Americans made common cause with Japan's conservative political and business elite, overlooking whatever dubious dealings they may have been involved in; the USA was far more concerned with containing the Soviet threat in Asia than policing the Japanese elite.[19] For the USA, trying a handful of scapegoats at the Tokyo War Crimes Tribunal, and executing seven of them, was an expeditious way of turning the page and getting on with the next war for global influence with the Soviets. The US strategy involved building up Japan's economy as an example of the virtues of the American model and using its islands for forward basing of troops to counter the presumed threat of communist expansionism in the region. Thus, an accounting of Japan's wartime excesses in Asia was sacrificed in the service of the Cold War and proved convenient for those in Japan who had the most to lose from public exposure of the 'hidden horrors' of that period.[20]

The Cold War may have postponed the reckoning, but memories are long, witnesses survive, and even cleansed archives – burning incriminating documents was official policy in the wake of surrender in 1945 – can prove inconvenient. Over the ensuing decades, progressive scholars and radical social movements, especially those opposing the US–Japan Security Treaty and the Vietnam War in the 1960s, have challenged the orthodox narrative imposed by the government.[21] These efforts gained increasing momentum in the 1980s as the government's role in whitewashing secondary-school history textbooks became an international and domestic controversy. In one of those strange coincidences of history, Hirohito died just as the Cold War's denouement swept across what had been the Soviet empire in Eastern Europe. At the same time, repressive military-dominated governments that had been supported by the USA in Taiwan and Korea began the transition to democracy. Political liberalization and growing sensitivity to human rights issues sparked campaigns in these countries, supported by progressive groups in Japan, to lobby the Japanese government for official apologies and atonement. The combination of all these developments suddenly brought Japan's inglorious past into sharper focus than ever before.

With Hirohito's death absolving them of any risk of *lèse-majesté*, soldiers 'discovered' their diaries, witnesses stepped forward, the archives began to yield their secrets, collective amnesia began to recede, and Japanese society was forced to cope with a version of the past for which their educational system had left them ill-prepared. Suddenly, people were being asked to confront revelations about atrocities committed by the Imperial military forces that had been expunged from the approved narrative.[22] Following

World War II, a highly selective version of the nation's wartime record prevailed in Japan's textbooks. In this exculpatory narrative, Hirohito was a man of peace manipulated by militarists, the comfort women did not exist, biological and chemical warfare experiments and attacks did not occur, prisoners of war were not mistreated, the Rape of Nanking was a mere incident where 'many people died in the chaos,' slave labor was not enslaved, and more than 20 million Asians were not killed in the name of liberating Asia from Western colonialism. Japanese progressives, most notably Ienaga Saburo (died 2002), have long challenged this whitewashing of an unpleasant past. They continue to battle conservative historians and their supporters who cling to a vindicating version of Japan's conduct despite mounting contrary evidence. As discussed in Chapter 9, the issue of war memory at the heart of the textbook controversies is critical to understanding the nature of contemporary Japanese nationalism and identity.[23]

The unflattering portrait of Japan that has emerged from this debate has battered an already bruised national psyche and helps explain the popularity of the 'Dr. Feelgoods' of Japanese history who have responded by denying, mitigating, shifting responsibility, quibbling over details, and reasserting the exonerating narrative.[24] However, despite their best efforts, the barrage of media coverage and scholarly work in disinterring the past has made it a permanent part of contemporary Japan. This ongoing contesting of the past belies images of a slavishly conformist nation where everyone follows the same script. However, the battles over Japan's wartime record are far from over and will continue to play a significant role in shaping how the Japanese see themselves and their nation. Some Japanese have tried to come to terms with the past by shading the truth in a unilateral manner that has caused old animosities to fester and impeded regional reconciliation. In contrast to Germany's reintegration in Europe, Japan remains relatively estranged from its neighbors, notably China and Korea, largely as a result of these hasty attempts to bury an unexamined past.[25] The manner in which this past is now examined and how this is reflected in government actions, choices, and policies will affect the scope and pace of regional integration.

Since the early 1990s Japanese have been confronting their nation's brutal record in the 1930s and 1940s. Like many of the issues discussed below, this experience has been unsettling and unwelcome. For many it represents an indictment of the national educational system and the costs of government censorship. For those at the other end of the political spectrum, it represents a weak government continually kowtowing to foreign pressure and failing to acknowledge the sacrifices of heroic forbears, especially Emperor Showa. In addition to polarizing the nation, the war debate has been an alienating experience underscoring the failings of the ruling elite. It is part of the larger pattern of transformation in attitudes and realities that has swept through the archipelago with the intensity of a typhoon. The past is haunting Japan and refuses to go away quietly, adding yet another element to the constellation of forces favoring change and generating a debate that can only be good for the growth of civil society.

1995

In the 1990s, auguries of national collapse were everywhere. In 1995, people saw the powerful Hanshin earthquake in Kobe and the gassing of Tokyo commuters by religious fanatics as omens that things were very wrong in the realm. Turmoil, hardships, and natural disasters have long been taken as signs of dynastic collapse, and it seemed that the powers that be had lost their mandate from heaven. Stumbling from one setback to another, with the scent of decay and impending change in the air, Japan, Inc. was struggling to maintain public credibility. The earthquake exposed the government's lack of preparedness for a natural disaster that all Japanese are trained to cope with, while the terrorist attacks in Tokyo's subways heightened a sense of vulnerability that was already present.

The Great Hanshin-Awaji Earthquake struck Kobe on January 17, 1995, devastating the city and raising questions about construction safety standards and the government's disaster relief preparations. The earthquake registered 7.2 on the Richter scale, causing 6,200 deaths, and damages estimated at $100 billion. At the peak of the relief effort, nearly 1,300 shelters had been erected for more than 320,000 evacuees. About one-third of Kobe was partially or completely destroyed, and more than half the central district razed by fires feeding on ruptured gas lines and flimsy wooden housing. While most of the city's modern high-rise buildings fared reasonably well, 20 percent of structures over six stories suffered significant damage. The man-made islands in Kobe's port suffered liquefaction, and container facilities were devastated. Part of an urban expressway keeled over, landmark commercial buildings were badly damaged, and the urban infrastructure was clogged with debris.

The scale of the destruction and the inept response of both the municipal and central governments took the nation by surprise. Some commentators interpreted the earthquake as an omen foreshadowing the end of Japan's heyday. Supposedly high safety standards and well-practiced earthquake drills had failed to mitigate a devastating natural disaster. Incredibly, there were no prearranged emergency relief centers and no contingency disaster plan. Offers of assistance by foreign relief agencies and US military forces stationed in Japan were initially turned down, and the SDF (Self-Defense Forces) remained in nearby barracks while Kobe burned. It became apparent that some of the damage was due to shoddy construction and human error. The slow response of government authorities and the inadequate relief efforts left a lasting impression on a nation accustomed to believing that government officials know best because they are the best and the brightest. On the contrary, their incompetence and inflexibility added to the death toll and damaged the already waning credibility of government institutions. What could be more damning than media coverage focusing on the *yakuza* role in opening the first soup kitchens for displaced survivors?

If the government had failed to act effectively, others were not so slow. The response of young Japanese to the quake was widely praised as reflecting a public-spirited attitude not often evident among their elders. During the weeks and months following the tragedy, over one million student volunteers poured into Kobe from all over the country. Their goodwill and enthusiasm stood in stark contrast to the bureaucrats' sluggish and bungling response. Japanese NPOs played a crucial role in providing relief and working with devastated communities. Their effective and prompt response, along with the massive volunteer effort, generated political pressures to make it easier for NPOs to operate in Japan (see Chapter 3). Their value quickly became apparent to the public, businesses, and the government alike, and in 1998 the government passed supportive legislation aimed at tapping the potential of NPOs. The surge in volunteerism is interpreted as a welcome sign that a sense of community is alive and well in Japan. Such responses run counter to media reportage, which generally paints a bleak portrait of Japan's future by focusing on the decay of community spirit and the rise of individualism.

Two months after the earthquake, the Japanese were shaken by another traumatic event. On March 20, 1995, members of the Aum Shinrikyo (Supreme Truth Sect) released sarin gas in Tokyo's metro, killing 12 people and causing a further 5,500 commuters to fall ill.[26] This act of terrorism was preceded by an attack against court officials in Matsumoto (Nagano Prefecture), although this incident was not linked initially to Aum. The metro attack was followed on May 5 by a failed attempt to spread hydrogen cyanide at Tokyo's busiest commuter station, Shinjuku. On May 16, police arrested the cult's guru, Asahara Shoko, and rounded up as many of his lieutenants and followers as they could find.

The cult had grown alarmingly from modest beginnings. Aum was established in Tokyo in 1984, one of the thousands of new religions that emerged in Japan towards the end of the twentieth century. In 1989 the government extended it recognition as a religion and the half-blind Asahara, whose real name is Matsumoto Chizuo, began to attract attention with his syncretic blend of Buddhism, Hinduism, yoga, and the apocalyptic sixteenth-century predictions of Nostradamus. Aum preached that the end of the world was near and that the USA would ignite the apocalypse in 1997. New recruits signed over their worldly assets and lived communally in the cult's compounds where, according to critics, they were subjected to a stringent training regime, solitary confinement, food and sleep deprivation, beatings, and other techniques of brainwashing including the use of headgear with attached electrodes to synchronize brain waves (or erase memory). Sometime in 1994 Asahara is believed to have changed tack, and rather than merely preparing for Armageddon Aum began planning to initiate it. At this point the cult mobilized its considerable assets and highly educated followers to develop weapons of mass destruction (laser, nuclear, chemical, and biological).

In 1995, Aum became a media phenomenon comparable to the O.J. Simpson case in the USA. Coverage of their activities dominated the airwaves and the printed media. Everyone wanted to know why the worst terrorist attack ever experienced in Japan had been launched by a religious group. More intriguingly, why were many of the cult's top members graduates of Japan's most prestigious universities? It seemed impossible to explain why these talented young men and women had laid aside bright futures to join a marginal cult and participate in planning the destruction of Japan. In addition to establishing a lucrative computer business for the sect, these technologically savvy recruits played a key role in producing an array of chemical weapons and conducting experiments with various biological agents.

It is hard to determine Asahara's motives in planning the destruction of Japan and indeed the world. Although the apocalyptic predictions of Nostradamus played a key role, much remains unknown about the guru's motivations. Commentators ponder why so many gifted graduates were attracted to the cult. It is often argued that they reacted against a straitjacket society, the suffocation of youth and a pressure-cooker educational system; joining Aum was an extreme backlash against the conformity that is often the cost of success in Japan. Others argue that they were cajoled and flattered into joining, given enormous power and influence at an age when they would still have relatively low-level positions in the corporate or bureaucratic sector. Still others pointed to the materialism and spiritual void of modern Japan to explain their alienation and rejection of the status quo. Yet none of these explanations seems compelling, and the mystery of Aum continues to haunt the Japanese. The sense of security and predictability that postwar Japanese had come to view as a birthright, and as an expression of national solidarity, was shattered by this cataclysmic event, forcing an uncomfortable reassessment of the social forces that percolate beneath the surface of modern Japan (Lifton 1999; Reader 1996).

Nuclear mishaps

Japan has suffered a string of nuclear accidents since the 1990s that raise serious concerns about public safety in an earthquake-prone nation and underline the need for improved monitoring by the public of corporate and government activities. Japan is highly dependent on imported energy and has invested billions of dollars since the 1950s in developing its nuclear energy program. In 2000 it had 53 reactors and plans to build a further 20. At the advent of the twenty-first century, Japan derived 37 percent of its electricity from nuclear power facilities and in response to growing power demand the government is proceeding with ambitious expansion plans.

Public concerns about the safety of nuclear power contrast sharply with official insistence that the nation's facilities are both safe and necessary. Polls consistently reveal that 70–75 percent of Japanese people harbor deep misgivings about nuclear power and express anxiety that serious accidents

Figure 1.5 Monju, a fast-breeder reactor where a serious nuclear accident occurred in 1995. Since being shut down, it has become a costly symbol of the overwhelming public distrust of nuclear power. (Photo: Mainichi Newspapers)

will happen. Their fears were realized in September 1999, when the world's most serious nuclear accident since the Chernobyl meltdown in 1986 occurred in Tokaimura. This small village, about 70 miles from Tokyo, is known as 'Nuclear Alley' as it is home to fifteen nuclear processing facilities. In 1999 workers at a uranium reprocessing plant with no containment barriers accidentally triggered a runaway chain reaction as they were preparing fuel for an experimental fast-breeder plutonium reactor. The incident lasted for twenty hours.

A stunned nation learned that the accident occurred while workers were transferring enriched uranium in stainless steel buckets, mixing the uranium by hand and then pouring it into a holding tank. The use of such primitive techniques in a nation that takes justifiable pride in its advanced technology was shocking and revealed troubling flaws in the high-tech safety procedures lauded by nuclear industry proponents. The workers made a serious error in the quantities of the solution they mixed and, in order to save time and money, they failed to use sophisticated processing equipment whose automatic controls were designed to prevent such an accident. Investigators discovered that not only were the workers poorly trained, but they were actually following instructions from a company manual in violating safety protocols. Since there would be no risk of an accident if regulations were followed, there was no contingency plan for such an accident and no form of containment to protect local residents from radiation.

Despite three previous nuclear mishaps at Tokaimura, public authorities were slow to react and the Prime Minister's Office did not learn of the accident for several hours. Lacking a formal request for assistance, nearby SDF troops remained at their base. The town authorities had no contingency plans and poorly informed firefighters arrived without protective clothing. Inexplicably, it took two days to arrange proper medical care for the three workers directly exposed to the nuclear fission. The sole hospital designated for treatment of radiation victims in all the emergency plans prepared by the fifteen prefectures with nuclear facilities was not, in the end, prepared to handle such cases. Two workers died of excessive exposure to radiation while more than 600 local residents suffered from irradiation.[27]

This exposure of official bungling, and the consequences of a business more concerned about profits than safety, left the public deeply skeptical about a nuclear program that has been plagued by safety flaws, radiation leaks, shutdowns, fires, and cover-ups. Prior to the criticality incident at Tokaimura, the most serious accident had occurred at the Monju fast-breeder reactor in 1995. This $6 billion facility relies on the fast-breeder plutonium-producing technology that has been abandoned elsewhere in the world due to safety problems. Of the ten known accidents at fast-breeder plants, the Monju accident is considered the most serious. Whereas an accident at a uranium-fueled reactor results in meltdown of the nuclear core, plutonium-fueled reactors can explode. Since the sodium leak and fire at Monju, the plant has remained shut down.[28] It has never performed up to expectations and has generated very little electricity. The public learned of an attempted cover-up of the extent of the Monju accident when the chief investigator committed suicide in 1995 and left a note implicating his superiors for ordering suppression of evidence.

In the summer of 2002, further evidence was brought to light about the neglect of public safety issues by officials in both the nuclear industry and the public service. Revelations emerged of a widespread cover-up, dating back to the early 1990s, of potentially dangerous problems in a number of the nation's aging nuclear power plants. The public learned that dozens of high-level industry executives knew of the problems and participated in a well-orchestrated cover-up to falsify inspection and repair records and certify the safety of power plants where engineers had found potentially dangerous cracks and fissures. More damning still was the role of the Ministry of Economy, Trade, and Industry (METI) in failing to act on a whistleblower's report about the falsified reports. A foreign subcontractor who participated in the inspections was appalled by the industry cover-up and was ignored when he reported his concerns to METI, the government ministry charged with oversight of the nuclear power industry. Moreover, ministry officials apparently alerted the power companies to the whistleblower's identity and activities.

The media eventually blew the lid on this tawdry tale, forcing the government and power industry to do what they should have done in the first place – put safety first. Ironically, the cover-up was aimed at allaying public concerns about nuclear power and avoiding expensive plant shut-downs to carry out the repairs that have been the financial bane of the industry.[29] Those concerns and costs rose substantially due to this failure to comply with existing regulations. Yet again, the low level of corporate and government ethics that lay at the heart of this scandal underlined the need for better public oversight. It is an index of the changes occurring in contemporary Japan that this story ever came to light at all, and points to the growing openness about issues that were once considered taboo or routinely suppressed.[30]

Soured system

The logic of the economic and political arrangements that characterized Japan, Inc. grew ever less compelling over the years. Katz (1998) details the workings of the development state and how it has been sustained by political machinations since the 1970s, despite ever more evident shortcomings. He shows how the strictly regulated, highly protected, and state-orchestrated economy served Japan well in recovering from war and in making the 'economic miracle' possible. However, this system bred inefficiencies that have undermined its competitiveness and propped up uncompetitive sectors, resulting in high domestic production costs and lowered productivity. The most competitive, export-oriented firms that represent Japan's most advanced sectors have been carrying the less competitive firms in its least advanced sectors. In the context of globalization and intensified competition in the 1990s, the leading firms can no longer afford this handicap. Katz argues that the transition that should have been taking place since the mid-1970s has been delayed for political reasons, a delay that is making economic reform ever more difficult.

Curtis (1999) similarly argues that the shelf life of Japan's political system has expired. One of the nation's greatest problems is a political system more efficient at influence-peddling and distributing the fruits of growth than bold reforms and policymaking. The wrenching economic changes of the 1990s have highlighted the shortcomings of the nation's political elite and led to piecemeal efforts at political reform. Japan's dysfunctional democracy and structural corruption (*kozo oshoku*) have never been more obvious or more widely excoriated.[31]

To understand the depth of change that overtook Japanese politics in the 1990s it is useful to consider the main features of the so-called '1955 system,' which in effect created a one-party state ruled by the LDP. As Curtis argues,

There were four crucial pillars supporting the '55 system. One was a pervasive public consensus in support of policies to achieve the catch-up-with-the-West goal. A second was the presence of large integrative interest groups with close links to political parties. The third was a bureaucracy of immense prestige and power. And the fourth was a system of one-party dominance. Just to list these features of the '55 system is to indicate how profoundly Japan changed in the 1990s. All of these pillars of policy making had either weakened or crumbled.

(Curtis 1999: 39)

By the 1990s Japan had caught up with the West; the major interest groups (such as the unions) were no longer so unified or close to the political parties; the bureaucracy's reputation was in tatters due to a series of widely publicized corruption scandals; and one-party dominance had given way to LDP-led coalition governments. Moreover, the Socialist Party, which had waged political battles with the LDP since 1955, all but disappeared as a political force in the 1990s, marking an end to the ideological disputes that had animated Japanese postwar politics.

The LDP has dominated Japanese politics since its establishment in 1955, losing power only once – and that briefly – in 1993. Although it continues to dominate the Japanese political scene with its coalition partners, its future looks considerably dimmer than its past. Its dominance of Japanese politics links it to a discredited system widely viewed as one of the major impediments to reform. However, the LDP has long demonstrated a Machiavellian capacity for reinventing itself and co-opting its opponents' agendas, and may pull it off again. Until now, paying attention to the theater of politics has never interfered with the business of politics as far as the party is concerned.

The dismal experiences of the 1990s have taught the Japanese that it is well past time for change and that the existing system is part of the problem. Everybody wants change and is waiting for it to happen. But everyone wants change that will be minimally disruptive to their lives. The 1990s was characterized by both a strong popular sentiment for reform and the failure of reformers to achieve substantial results (Mulgan 2002). In the early years of the twenty-first century, the public seems more inclined to support incremental change rather than rapid transformation. The patterns and practices of the past are fading, but in a gradual and measured manner that is at odds with the prevailing sense of anxiety and urgency. In Japan the dynamics of transformation involve an emphasis on minimizing social dislocation at the expense of rapid, far-reaching implementation of the reform agenda.[32] While this inclination may diminish the benefits of reform by delay and dilution, the negative fallout has thus far been more limited. The key challenge in the early twenty-first century will be whether Japan can enjoy the same degree of success in reinventing and reinvigorating the nation as it did during the Meiji era and the US Occupation.

In the early twenty-first century, the political world of Japan appears little changed. The LDP is still in power, corruption is endemic, voters are alienated, the government is spending vast sums on public works projects, and a geriatric elite seems more concerned about propping up a sclerotic system than meaningful reform. The dilatory response to the threat of financial collapse precipitated by non-performing loans is symptomatic of policy gridlock and the inability of the nation's political leadership to tackle a daunting array of economic problems (Katz 2003).[33] And yet, despite such evidence of stagnation and paralysis, during the 1990s the Diet sponsored a number of legislative initiatives that are laying the foundations for a civil society discussed in the following chapters.

This 'quiet transformation' involves a series of reforms that considered on their own seem of little consequence, but taken together are generating the momentum to create more favorable conditions for civil society. These changes would not be happening unless there were powerful forces pushing for a strengthening of civil society. The mere fact that powerful groups in Japan feel a need to invigorate civil society, and are doing something about it, marks a significant break with the past. Even in the short time since the passage of national information disclosure legislation in 1999, rising support for increased levels of transparency in government has had an enormous impact on standards of bureaucratic conduct and public expectations. As discussed in Chapters 2 and 3, these changes have been reinforced by institutional reforms set in motion by NPO legislation passed in 1998 and judicial reforms adopted in 2002. The legislative building blocks of the quiet transformation are being slipped into place and now it is a question of building on this foundation. Much will depend on how elected representatives and government bureaucrats wield their power and implement the reforms. Recent developments suggest a basis for cautious optimism that a broad coalition of interests will continue to support the reforms – if only because they are consistent with a diverse array of agendas, and there is no viable alternative. Whether it is a case of NPOs, information disclosure or judicial reforms, conservative business organizations and politicians find themselves on board the same train as progressive social activists, all seeing hope for their respective goals in a more robust civil society. This constitutes a truly revolutionary break from the 1955 system.

Corruption

In all societies political corruption has been a blot on democratic development and Japan is no exception (Bowen 2003; Samuels 2003). In prewar Japan, militarists cited widespread corruption as justification for their destruction of the political party system and assumption of power. The vast majority of postwar prime ministers have been implicated in corruption scandals and every decade has featured at least one major scandal – beginning with the Showa Denko scandal in the 1940s and continuing with a shipbuilding scandal in the 1950s, a series of scandals in the 1960s known as the 'black mist,' and the Lockheed scandal of the 1970s involving Prime Minister Tanaka Kakuei (1972–74). In the 1980s and 1990s, the scandals grew more blatant and the press played a more aggressive role in exposing the venality of politicians and bureaucrats (Schlesinger 1997). The economic bubble of the late 1980s raised the stakes and led to widespread corruption involving astronomical sums. The Recruit (1988) and Sagawa Kyubin (1992) scandals were a sign of the times, confronting the public with the dirty facts of their political system. While corruption among politicians left few people surprised, the vast extent of money politics (*kinken seiji*) was unexpected. The extensive involvement of bureaucrats in a number of influence-buying scandals also challenged the public's perceptions of their civil servants. The mandarins had always been seen as the best and brightest Japan could offer and therefore beyond the reach of corruption. However, once their indiscretions came to light the public mood turned ugly and the media delighted in revealing the dirty laundry, pettiness and incompetence of government officials. Public disenchantment with this sordid state of affairs became a significant factor in ending one-party rule, however briefly, and creating momentum for political reform.

Corruption is an enduring and powerful theme in Japanese film and fiction. *The Bad Sleep Well* (1960) is a classic movie by Japan's most famous film director, Kurosawa Akira; its focus on the nexus of corruption involving politicians, bureaucrats, big business, and the *yakuza* earned it a revival on television in the late 1980s and 1990s. As press reports detailed the latest corruption scandal in the 1990s, Kurosawa's timeless black-and-white film offered a disturbing portrait of a society that had lost its bearings. In a culture obsessed with the race for growth and material gain, the film reflects wistfully on the hollowness of a society where the line between right and wrong is blurred and ethics sacrificed. It is not lost on viewers that the men on the take go unpunished while those who strive for justice suffer for their efforts.[34] Robert Whiting's non-fiction book, *Tokyo Underworld* (1999), examines similar themes and the Japanese translation became a bestseller. His hardboiled look at the underside of Japan tapped into popular fascination with systemic malfeasance. His readers take scant comfort in the fact that the truth is more sordid than fiction.

The two most notorious scandals of the period were the Recruit and Sagawa Kyubin scandals. The former first came to public attention in June 1988. In the 1980s, Recruit was an up-and-coming company with a range of ventures connected with the information industry. While it was best known for its job-information services, the scandal involved an unlisted real estate affiliate called Recruit Cosmos. In 1986, unlisted shares in the company were offered at low prices to influential government officials and politicians, many of whom bought the shares with money lent by Recruit. Once the stock went public, share prices soared and enormous profits were salted away. Public anger mounted as it became apparent that the beneficiaries included a who's who of Japanese politicians, including leading figures from the opposition parties. In addition, Recruit purchased millions of dollars' worth of tickets to fund-raising parties for LDP leaders, again involving the most prominent political luminaries of the day. In the wake of this scandal Prime Minister Takeshita Noburu was forced to step down in 1989.

The motives for Recruit's shady dealings were readily evident. Ezoe Hiromasu, the founder and head of the company, was seeking to purchase influence, connections, and favorable decisions on projects or regulations connected with his business ventures. His extensive efforts to rig the system also extended to the bureaucrats whose once high reputation rapidly declined over the ensuing years. The endless exposés and scandals made it glaringly apparent that government officials could be bought. The society that had embraced economic growth at all costs in the 1960s was forced to confront the consequences of unabashed materialism in the 1990s. It also witnessed the strange twists of justice; it took fourteen years to convict Ezoe of bribery and he was then handed a suspended sentence. Given that the Recruit affair was the biggest case of bribery since the 1976 Lockheed scandal, the token punishment handed down to Ezoe in 2003 confirms that the bad still sleep well.

A second major exposé proved equally traumatic to the Japanese body politic. The Sagawa Kyubin trucking firm scandal that broke in the summer of 1992 involved quite literal 'deliveries' of astronomical sums of cash. Over a period of twenty years Sagawa Kyubin had donated sums of money to politicians that were well in excess of official limits and that dwarfed the Recruit donations. Even a public inured to venality took notice of press reports of a cart piled high with ¥500 million (about $4 million) in cash being wheeled into the office of the LDP's chief fixer, Kanemaru Shin. Later it emerged that Kanemaru had also used Sagawa Kyubin as an intermediary in enrolling the *yakuza* to silence right-wing political activists who were harassing Takeshita Noburu, faction leader, kingmaker, and former prime minister (1987–89) in the LDP. A dinner hosted by Kanemaru to express his gratitude to a ranking *yakuza*, also arranged by the trucking firm, was played up by the press to illustrate the confluence of power in contemporary Japan. Kanemaru, a gruff old-school politician who had teamed up with Takeshita in 1987 to gain control of the LDP, was later forced to resign from politics as the Sagawa Kyubin scandal triggered a wider investigation into his finances. A raid on his home uncovered a hoard of 100 kg of gold, ¥3 billion in bond certificates, and stacks of cash – the accumulated booty of decades of political deals and back-handers from construction firms, all duly noted in his files. Kanemaru's files served as the basis for investigations into public works contracts around the nation, implicating dozens of construction firms and local government officials who had been on the take. In 1993, five months after Kanemaru's conviction for tax evasion, the public decided to 'vote the bums out of office,' ending the LDP's stranglehold on power.

Revelations of corruption arising from information disclosure requests during the 1990s have further soured the public mood towards those entrusted with governing the nation. Mandated information disclosure has forced governments to yield public documents that show just how prone government officials are to squandering and stealing taxpayers' money, ranging from lavish wining-and-dining escapades to false expense claims. As discussed in the following chapter, the paper trail also reveals that it was standard bureaucratic practice to inflate expense claims in order to accumulate funds for discretionary spending. These seedy and unseemly practices have been unveiled only because the new information disclosure laws have made government offices far more accountable to the people. Nothing has aroused more public support for information disclosure than these betrayals of the public trust, generating a momentum for even greater disclosure and accountability. Moreover, prosecution and penalties based on information disclosure have generated rising expectations for both the rule of law and those who have all too often acted as if they were above it.

Unraveling

As the century drew to a close, concerns about deteriorating public ethics, moral values, and social order were widely felt as the certainties of the past began unraveling. Throughout the postwar era, the younger generation or *shinjinrui* (literally 'the new breed,' but carrying negative connotations) has been the subject of censure by its elders. Although this intergenerational divide is common everywhere, in Japan, where a strong ideology of filial piety persists, the repercussions are powerful for the national psyche (see Chapter 2 for further discussion). A perusal of subway courtesy signs indicates just how much has changed in Japan, a nation rightly known for its high level of politeness. Until the mid-1990s the only signs to be seen were small reminders suggesting that passengers surrender designated seats to the elderly or pregnant women. Since then, train companies have posted signs requesting that passengers refrain from punching train company employees, groping women, smashing ticket machines, and chatting on their mobile phones, indicating the sorts of problems that seem to be occurring with greater frequency.

One problem that pervades Japanese society is *ijime* (bullying), an issue stretching from the classroom up to the office. Bullying encompasses a variety of common social sanctions in Japan, including the tradition of *mura hachibu* (ostracization) at the village or neighborhood level. Those who do not conform to local norms are subject to a form of psychological group harassment. In the educational system and at the office, bullying is intrinsic to a precise and rigid sense of hierarchy and order. It is an effective method of keeping people in their place and as such is tolerated and indeed, to some extent, encouraged. Although this is not a new phenomenon, society has become more open in discussing it. A number of student suicides and killings in the 1980s and 1990s were directly attributed to bullying at school, raising questions about both the high-pressure atmosphere of a school system that

Figure 1.6 A crowded train in the Tokyo rush hour, where average commutes are 90
minutes. (Photo: Andreas Seibert/Lookat)

produces such behavior and a society that sanctions such methods as a means
of social control.

Rising rates of truancy are partially attributed to bullying as targets stay
away from school to avoid mistreatment. Truancy is also seen as a rejection
of the stifling conformity and rigid curriculum in a school system widely criticized in Japan for not serving growing social diversity or stimulating
creativity. In addition, truancy and the breakdown of classroom order are
seen to be symptoms of a wider social problem. Compared to other societies,
Japan's problems may seem almost quaint, but they are nonetheless a cause
for alarm in a nation that places great value on orderly behavior. There is
widespread concern that traditional values such as deference to authority,
willingness to accept discipline and *messhi hoko* (self-sacrifice) – values that
many Japanese believe have been crucial to Japan's economic success and
social cohesion – are on the decline (Miyamoto 1994).

The sexual mores of the young are also under scrutiny. Since the mid-1990s,
enjo kosai (literally 'compensated dates,' referring to prostitution involving high-
school or junior-high-school girls and middle-aged men) has become the focus
of intense public interest. Although reliable information about the extent of
enjo kosai and participation of young women in telephone date clubs is lacking,
most guesstimates suggest that as many as 5 percent of female students are
involved. There appears to be little peer disapprobation, as surveys indicate
that a majority of high-school students think it is acceptable for female students
to sell sex to strangers. Stricter laws governing sexual relations between minors

Figure 1.7 Young people staying connected with their *keitai* (mobile phones). (Photo: Andreas Seibert/Lookat)

and adults have been enacted and teachers, monks, government officials, company executives, and others with high social status have been arrested for their involvement in *enjo kosai.* To judge by media reporting, *enjo kosai* does not seem a rare phenomenon; the 1997 film *Bounce Kogal,* which explores the issue, suggests that it is both common and lucrative. One of the girls in the movie tells a *yakuza* who wants to become her pimp that young girls can make a lot of money from men who are prey to their own childish desires; indulging the fantasies of these middle-aged 'infants' and ripping them off are portrayed as part of the game. Commentators point out that unlike most women who engage in prostitution, the girls involved in *enjo kosai* and date clubs are usually from middle-class backgrounds and not in desperate economic circumstances. Rather, the girls want discretionary income to purchase expensive designer clothes and accessories and pay their *keitai* (cellular phone) bills. While this materialism and exploitation of sex is lamented, such behavior reflects the

Figure 1.8 Japan's massive sex industry caters to all tastes. (Photo: Andreas Seibert/
   Lookat)

mores of the wider society. Japan's sex industry is enormous, very public and
generally tolerated by the authorities. It was not until 1999 that Japan joined
the international community in banning child pornography – not out of moral
concern, but mostly due to the bad publicity associated with being identified as
the primary source of this seedy commodity on the internet.

  The rising levels of truancy, bullying, materialism, moral laxity and delinquency among youth have spurred vigorous national debate. Conservatives
argue that teaching ethics in school, encouraging respect for national
symbols, and a renewed emphasis on traditional Japanese culture will alleviate the anomie and alienation that plague society. However, it will take
more than rhetoric to convince young people to identify with a culture that
seems unattractive, stifling, and demanding of self-sacrifice for unpersuasive
reasons. Progressives tend to focus on recasting society to permit more individuality and self-fulfillment. There is a widely shared perception that today's

Figure 1.9 Some of Japan's unemployed demonstrate against job cuts. (Photo: Stuart
    Issett)

youth are not what Japanese used to be, but whether this is an ill omen, as
many seem to think, is yet to be seen.

This is a fascinating time to witness social and cultural transformations
being hammered out, debated, implemented, diluted, resisted, and asserted,
a time when people are facing up to a Japan at odds with the prevailing
stereotypes of harmony, conformity, passivity, and paralysis. This is an era of
contesting terrain, a time when controversy and debate are defining and
building civil society. Japan's prolonged economic malaise has undermined
the status quo and forced a reconsideration of established practices and rapid
adjustments to new ones. A sense of urgency and of looming catastrophe are
animating public debate and policy initiatives. The interesting story of the
early twenty-first century is that many of these changes would not be
happening without the support of conservative politicians and executives,
who have come to recognize that the reform train is leaving the station and
are jumping on board before it leaves without them.

The traditional face of Japan is fast becoming unrecognizable. The social
relationships, assumptions, and norms characteristic of postwar Japan began
to unravel with stunning speed in the 1990s. The 'three jewels' of Japan's
employment system – lifetime employment, seniority-based wages, and
enterprise unions – are all fading away, with significant consequences for
society. The sharp rise in unemployment during the late 1990s has been a
barometer of Japan's deep economic problems. A nation accustomed to
unemployment levels of around 2 percent has been ill-prepared, both
psychologically and in terms of public policies, to cope with unemployment

(Roger Dahl)

approaching 6 percent, involving nearly 4 million workers, as of 2003. Workers and policymakers are suddenly faced with the stark reality that the social contract and security assumed to be intrinsic to Japan's distinctive employment system have been sundered. The reciprocal arrangement of unstinting loyalty to the firm in exchange for a secure job is unraveling or, perhaps more accurately, the myth of lifetime employment has been exposed.

Labor economists have long pointed out that lifetime employment never applied to more than one-third of the workforce, as workers in small and medium-size enterprises did not enjoy the same employment conditions as their counterparts in larger firms. Nevertheless, lifetime employment was widely regarded as a keystone of Japan's employment paradigm, and the realization that it is no longer sacrosanct has had an enormous impact on employment relationships and policy planning. A social safety net is hastily being put in place – there was little need for such support in the past and the family unit always served as a refuge of last resort. But now that Japan's divorce rates are on a par with those in Germany, fourth highest in the industrialized world, the myth of the stable family is also unraveling, forcing further reconsideration of existing policies.

The fading of lifetime employment has been accompanied by a gradual move away from the *nenko* (seniority wage) system. The *nenko* system is based on paying young workers below their productivity but gradually increasing wages above productivity as they age and come to have more family expenses. This system was aimed at retaining workers so that the firm could continue to benefit from significant investments in their training. It was also helpful in capping total wage outlays on a relatively young workforce in the 1950s when businesses were short of cash. The system demanded worker loyalty in exchange for paternalistic employment practices – 'stick with us and we will take care of you.' Now it appears that increasing numbers of firms are not keeping their side of the bargain. With too many older, less

(Roger Dahl)

productive workers entering their peak earnings years at a time when firms are faced with a prolonged recession and intensified competition, many are being pressured into early retirement, taking hefty pay cuts or being laid off. Firms are now shifting towards a merit-oriented wage system that compensates workers for their achievements rather than years of service. Given the hierarchical relationships and respect for elders that are still widespread in Japan's Confucian culture, this constitutes a wrenching shift in the employment system, affecting relationships among workers, and between workers and employers. The 'betrayal' of older staff is also affecting perceptions among younger workers, making it more difficult for firms to inspire their loyalty and willingness to make personal sacrifices as they have in the past.

Unionization in Japan has declined over recent decades, a trend reinforced by developments in the 1990s. Enterprise unions have long been part of the institutional structure of labor in Japan, eschewing a confrontational, anti-management stance in favor of a cooperative relationship with employers. Unions have been strong advocates of stable, secure jobs and have fought to preserve the perquisites of core workers. However, the trend in the 1990s has been against them as firms have moved away from the rigid, expensive employment policies associated with the prevailing paradigm and sought to introduce more flexibility and lower costs by hiring more non-standard workers on less secure, less well-remunerated terms. This explains the surge in part-time and temporary employment contracts. Unions have had little success in resisting these developments and as a result now represent only about one-fifth of the regular workforce; the non-standard workers who account for the largest source of employment growth have been left out in the cold. Under these conditions, where the unions have failed either to defend their traditional turf or to adapt to the ongoing transformation, their future looks bleak. Ironically, the unions' success in the postwar era has been their undoing, as workers failed to recognize the virtues of collective bargaining when all regular workers received the same benefits regardless of whether or not they belonged to the union. Now that times are tough, the unions are weak and tied to a declining constituency of core workers, which prevents them from reaching out to the more vulnerable, non-standard workers who enjoy no security and very limited fringe benefits. Given this situation, it is hard to be any more optimistic about the prospects for unions in Japan than for the continuation of job security and seniority wages with which their fortunes have traditionally been linked. As discussed in Chapter 10, the emerging employment paradigm is adopting practices associated with the peripheral workforce of part-time and temporary workers, involving diminished security, and lower benefits and wages.

The unraveling of Japan's employment system is a direct consequence of the economic implosion of the 1990s and the widening penetration of global competition within Japan. The consequences of this unraveling are still uncertain, but will be enormous as the domino effect wends its way through this interlocking system. Housing loan officers, for example, who in the past could calculate loans based on stable employment and a predictably rising income trajectory now must assess credit risk and price loans accordingly. When in 2001 a foreign-controlled bank began charging differential loan rates to customers based on their credit rating, this caused a stir in a stodgy banking sector accustomed to charging one flat rate. Now this 'foreign' standard is a common lending policy.

The shape of things to come

Japan is a better place to live in 2003 than it was in 1990 and, aside from those who lost power, prestige, privileges, and stock investments, few Japanese wish to return to an era associated with avarice, excess, and slavish devotion to corporate life. But life is still very tough for many. For those still reeling from the effects of the bursting bubble and corporate retrenchment, conditions are decidedly bleak. Workers in their 40s and 50s who have lost their jobs will have trouble finding new positions, and homeowners who avoid foreclosures still have to deal with negative equity in their homes. Further casualties are those families that have been forced to cope with suicide, divorce and domestic violence stemming from the dislocation of the era.

Yet without disregarding this palpable suffering, it does seem that by many criteria the quality of life is improving for many Japanese. Housing is the biggest purchase that any Japanese family is likely to make and by 2003 prices have fallen 60 percent from the early 1990s. Small comfort for those who bought then, but an enormous boon to those who are buying or will be buying housing in coming years. Given demographic and zoning trends, housing prices will likely remain depressed and far more affordable than they used to be. Aside from more affordable housing, families are benefiting from improved social services. Women's lives have been vastly improved by better access to childcare facilities and nursing assistance for elderly parents. While family-related social policies and programs are far from ideal, initiatives taken in the 1990s are helping women better balance the competing demands on their time and energy. People are also benefiting from medical, environmental, and food safety advances, and are far better informed about the world they live in, enjoying better access to information about hobbies, services, entertainment, and healthy living.

This is a far more diverse and dynamic society and, from an outsider's perspective, one that is more interesting and stimulating than in the past. Whereas in the early 1990s the best students dreamed of careers in domestic securities and life insurance, they are now drawn to the mass media, software, and internet-related careers and the very different atmosphere and practices of multinationals. There has been a revival of interest in Japanese tradition and culture, from tea ceremony to Go, and rising interest in volunteerism. Travel has become an item of mass consumption, and the droves of Japanese who go abroad return with bags bulging with bargains and perspectives influenced, however subtly, by what they have seen and experienced. In 1997, 17 million Japanese traveled abroad, doubling the number in 1988, and many now travel independently and venture off the beaten track. This travel boom, combined with the revolution in communications, has made internationalization a reality in even the most remote hamlets, exposing people to new ways of thinking and the normalcy of diversity.

The economic gloom is not reflected on the streets and in the skies. Japan has not avoided the problems typical of an industrial economy on the ropes, but it seems to have coped with these challenges relatively successfully and with considerably less social fallout. Although homelessness and crime have increased as a consequence of prolonged recession, levels remain relatively modest by Western standards. Despite the stagnant economy, there has been a building boom encompassing skyscrapers and office towers in addition to residential houses. Lamentably, Japanese architecture has sacrificed its distinctive characteristics, but newer buildings are brighter, smarter, more airy, handicap-accessible, energy-efficient, and user-friendly. Automobile makers are producing more ecofriendly cars and, despite the premium price they command, sales have far exceeded expectations. Moreover, there has been a shift away from dirty diesel fuel for trucks and buses, and stricter emission regulations are being enforced.

On the social front, society has made some progress in treating the weak and vulnerable with greater dignity and assumed more responsibility towards them. Although much work remains to be done, considerable progress has been achieved in a very few years. Landmark medical cases in the late 1990s – involving hemophiliacs infected with HIV-tainted blood products, and leprosy patients – are part of a larger pattern of seeking and realizing social justice for those who have been shortchanged for too long (these cases are discussed in Chapters 5 and 6). Issues involving people with disabilities have received sustained and informed media coverage, with positive results for change, and people have been exposed and responded to the need for doing more. It is telling that there has been widespread public interest and support

(Roger Dahl)

for handicapped rights, including a popular TV drama and a number of best-selling books. Handicap access to buildings is improving and there are job placement firms specializing in placing the handicapped. On the domestic scene, the media is providing more extensive coverage of wife and child abuse – not because it has become more common but because it is no longer a taboo subject and ignoring it is no longer acceptable.

In the commercial sector, unprecedented changes are occurring. Foreign investments have increased in Japan since the late 1990s and foreign joint ventures have received prominent and largely positive media coverage.[35] It was once unthinkable that some of Japan's leading companies would be taken over by foreign competitors, yet this is what happened with such prominent institutions as Nissan, Mazda, Mitsubishi Motors, the Long-Term Credit Bank, Yamaicihi Securities and numerous others. Foreign consortiums have bought up distressed properties and businesses, tied up with troubled retailers and insurance firms, and launched ambitious projects in the midst of a plodding economy. These changes have been grudgingly accepted only because there seems no alternative, but anxieties and resistance persist.

At the end of 1999, 'News Station,' the popular evening program on Asahi television, aired a skit about how Japanese managers in a bank were coping with a foreign takeover. Not very well it seems. Their worst nightmare was realized when the new boss, a brassy American woman, made it clear to the staff that things would be done her way or they would be out of a job. She managed to trample over both male pride and an assortment of cultural taboos in short order. The show presented an entirely negative view of foreign management styles – obsessed with profits and performance and showing little consideration for clients and long-term relationships. In changing the rules of the game, foreigners are depicted as taking the soul out of Japanese-style capitalism. Yet more recently, the media has been glowing in its praise of foreign managers, praising their success in rescuing ailing businesses and applauding their tactics. Carlos Ghosn, a Renault manager assigned to lead Nissan out of the doldrums, has become a media star and is widely admired.[36] Although the corporate scandals in the USA in 2002, together with the meltdown of the US stock market, have taken some of the gloss off the new reverence for foreign business practices, there is little enthusiasm for a return to the old ways. In an era of intensified global competition, businesspeople are keen to learn the strategies and technologies that spell success. It is not lost on Japanese leaders that, according to the Organization for Economic Cooperation and Development (OECD), Japan's overall productivity ranks alongside Spain. Given the Japanese attachment to the work ethic, it is unsettling that a nation associated more with siestas somehow manages to hold its own.

The influx of foreign businesses is one of many factors contributing to the rapid spread of information technology in business. It is no secret that Japan, despite being a world leader in various sectors of information technology, lags behind its rivals in tapping the benefits of information technologies. Nevertheless, the gap is rapidly closing. Whereas in 1989 the internet was virtually unknown in Japan, now it is ubiquitous. The technologically challenged, middle-aged managers who struggle with the office copier and fax are giving way to a new generation of managers who are speeding the computer-driven revolution in business practices and communications. The fact that Japan has yet to reap many of the benefits of this impending revolution suggests that the economy of the future will be more dynamic than most forecasters are predicting.

All these developments reflect major and abrupt shifts in national ideology – many of the myths and taboos that up till now have stymied critical analysis of society have been shattered, trampled upon and superceded by events. Only those who have lived through it can truly appreciate what a dynamic and tumultuous period this has been. While some taboos and myths persist, few other societies have stripped them away and moved beyond so many so rapidly. Traditional stereotypes of family, work, government, foreigners, and women have been challenged and many swept away. It is no longer possible to deny fading job security, married women in the workforce, declining respect for the elderly or rising rates of divorce and child abuse – developments that were barely acknowledged until recent years. Even the most cherished myths have not been spared. It has become public knowledge, thanks to the Emperor's end-of-year speech in 2001, that the Imperial family's ancestors are from Korea – a dramatic admission given longstanding anti-Korean prejudices in Japan. The slaughtering of such sacred cows has been liberating in many respects, but life in the abattoir has also been unsettling and divisive. This process is fraught with conflict and is another area of contested terrain that is transforming the sociocultural landscape.

Perhaps the most encouraging development in the Lost Decade has been the rise in volunteerism. This began with Japan's involvement with UNTAC

(UN Transitional Authority for Cambodia), the UN body charged with over-seeing the1994 Cambodian elections, and surged in response to the Kobe earthquake in 1995. More than ever, people want to improve society and are seeking involvement beyond the bounds of state- and corporate-organized activities. Thanks to the 1998 legislation facilitating legal recognition for NPOs, it is now easier for people to act on their good impulses.[37] This is an important part of the story of how Japan began building a more robust civil society during the 1990s, perhaps one of the most valuable legacies inherited by the Japanese in the twenty-first century. The potential of volunteerism is substantial and promises to rekindle community spirit and civic-mindedness while helping people better shape the society they live in. However, the social malaise of youth, rising disaffection with work and education, and growing problems in the family challenge optimistic assumptions about a citizen-driven society. Realizing the potential for a robust civil society will depend on the quality and staying power of citizens' participation, making clear that the quiet transformation is far from over.

NPOs armed with legal rights to demand information disclosure can play a key role in enhancing citizen participation in government policymaking and exercising oversight. NPOs are encouraging and sustaining the trend towards greater openness in Japan. This in turn is a catalyst for the quiet transformation; greater transparency and accountability are removing the cloak of secrecy and impunity that are the root cause of the endemic negligence, corruption and mismanagement that is now gaining so much publicity. People have become more skeptical and less trusting of those who govern and thus support moni-toring their activities more carefully. As discussed in Chapter 2, the massive popular opposition to Juki Net, the centralized registration of citizens' informa-tion, involves large-scale, careful acts of civil disobedience. The declining legit-imacy of the political establishment is not only spurring greater citizens' participation but also stimulating long-neglected civic virtues. The promise of judicial reform and the impending proliferation of legal professionals will rein-force this trend towards building civil society. The need of government to rely more extensively on NPOs to deliver a range of social services in the future means that significant resources will be channeled through them and will strengthen them still further. As a result, they will be better able to influence government policy and involve citizens in setting and implementing the national agenda. These various legal and administrative changes are enabling people to have an enormous impact on shaping outcomes in ways that more closely reflect popular aspirations and expectations.

In 1992 Prime Minister Miyazawa raised eyebrows – and smiles – when he expressed his desire to transform Japan into a 'lifestyle superpower.' Although this remains an elusive goal, since that time Japan has become a vastly improved place to live, work, eat, relax, exercise, shop, and raise a family. And it remains relatively safe, with little violent crime. The bursting of the economic bubble ushered in improved living conditions – it led to lower prices, shortened working hours, and forced people to reconsider their

(Roger Dahl)

priorities in favor of private time and family life. (Obviously, for those on the employment scrapheap, such improvements are small consolation.) Life is more convenient in both trivial and important ways, ranging from longer shopping and banking hours, more escalators at train stations, and cheaper air travel to improved social services for mothers and the elderly, better housing, and easier access to useful information on the internet. Communicating with friends or relatives is also far easier than it used to be as nearly half of Japan's 126 million citizens are logging onto the internet, and more than a third of them do so on their cellphones.

The Lost Decade saw the barriers to information tumble, a process with dramatic consequences for a society where information has always been closely guarded. By 1996 every prefecture had an information disclosure ordinance, and in 1999 the Diet finally passed a national law promoting freedom of information. The quiet transformation has given citizens the means to hold elected representatives and government officials accountable, exposing their decisions and policies to far greater scrutiny than ever before. And, taking skeptics by surprise, the courts have been extraordinarily supportive of *joho kokai* (information disclosure), rendering it much more effective than people initially hoped.

The free flow of information about the quality of living and prices of goods in other countries has also contributed to raising Japan's standard of living. The 1990s was a time of price destruction (*kakaku hakkai*) and discount retailers proliferated. Now consumers have a much wider range of choices at lower prices than in 1990, and a product liability law introduced in 1994 offers consumer protection against defective merchandise. The 'malling' of suburban Japan may not be aesthetically pleasing, but malls have made shopping more convenient and less time-consuming. As a result, time is running out on the 'mom and pop' stores sprinkled over the countryside as thrifty customers choose bargains over the personal service, neighborhood gossip and cup of tea offered at local shops.

If one can judge a country by what is served at its tables and restaurants, one can only be heartened by recent trends. Local supermarkets are stocked with a vast range of specialty items and even in rural areas one can find balsamic vinegars, olive oils, cheeses, Thai curry mixes, tandoori spices, rucola, sun-dried tomatoes, a full range of pastas and many other items that used to be the preserve of gourmet shops in urban areas. Even in inland areas one can find excellent fresh raw fish (*sashimi*) in a dazzling array of varieties, while the selection of tofu and other soybean products has rapidly expanded. Shopping for *soba*, *udon*, and *ramen* involves a selection of fresh noodles of differing quality from various prefectures and a bewildering array of sauces and soups. Organic produce has now spread from small specialty stores to mainstream hypermarkets and the internet so that consumers can buy direct. Things have changed a good deal since the early 1980s, when tense trade talks with the USA led one Japanese minister to explain to foreign journalists that the reason beef was not selling well in Japan was that Japanese were unable to digest it with their longer intestines! Apparently intestines shrank rapidly and beef imports surged in the 1990s, while *yakiniku* and *gyudon* shops did good business serving up dishes with cheap foreign beef – at least until the 'mad cow' scare and the false labeling scandals (discussed in Chapter 8) drove them to despair.

Food prices have fallen, even if they remain high by world standards. Increasing numbers of young Japanese have trained overseas and are returning as sommeliers and inventive chefs, running Asian-fusion, French, and Italian restaurants that would make New Yorkers envious. Refined Kyoto-style *kaiseki* cuisine, once limited to those with cash to burn, is now served up more informally at low-key, jazzy bars at reasonable prices. While in 1990 ¥2,000 would only buy a bottle of plonk, it now buys a fine estate-bottled wine. In 2002, I stopped by a liquor shop in a rural hamlet to buy a can of soda and left with a number of superb imported wines from around the globe, helpfully selected by the owner and a fellow shopper who happened to be a certified sommelier from an Italian restaurant in a nearby town. Knowing this farming area to be beer, *shochu*, and *sake* territory, I asked how such a specialty wine shop could survive. 'Internet sales,' came the answer from the proprietor who cheerfully admitted not having known his RAM from his ISDN line when he started out.[38]

The breadth and pace of change in turn-of-the-century Japan has produced a lifestyle revolution and made Japan a much more livable country. The hectic go-go attitudes of the bubble era when time was money and people had cash to burn has given way to a reflective, enjoyable lifestyle evident in quirky advertising slogans such as 'Slow Down, Relax Up.'[39] Lifestyle and career choices for Japanese have dramatically expanded and there is more space and tolerance for those who do not fit the mold. It seems almost quaint to recall that in 1990 a high-school senior with dyed hair would have been refused a picture in the class yearbook. And while Japanese athletes were once stoic and self-contained, exuberant displays of hip-jiggling and high fives are now commonplace. People seem more animated and less dour. Many things that used to be frowned on no longer raise an eyebrow and in this sense pressures to conform are abating. In the new Japan there are more niches, more respect for individuality and greater appreciation of special talents and interests.

Unfortunately these improvements have not been fully enjoyed by the foreign community, which constitutes just over 1 percent of the population. In Japan, not all foreigners are equal. Whites are relatively privileged and experience little more than petty discrimination. Non-whites, on the other hand, face more systematic discrimination in areas such as employment, education, housing, marriage, and eligibility for visas. Most of those registered as foreigners in Japan are ethnic Koreans who still encounter discrimination despite the fact that their families have been resident in Japan since before World War II. In general, these ethnic Koreans are indistinguishable from Japanese, are fluent in the language and have assimilated to varying degrees (Lie 2001). During the 1990s it has become easier for them to become citizens and some forms of official harassment, such as routine fingerprinting, have been terminated.[40] Lie characterizes Japan as a multi-ethnic society in denial, maintaining a myth of homogeneity despite the presence of various ethnic groups (Ainu, Okinawan, Korean, Chinese) and a large underclass of *burakumin* (hamlet people) who still struggle with a legacy of caste discrimination dating back to the seventeenth century.[41]

Even more serious problems face foreign workers who come to Japan to take up low-paid jobs eschewed by the Japanese, many without proper working visas. Those working in the sex industry are often recruited under false pretenses and become involved through a combination of deception and coercion. For these people, the promise of a more vibrant civil society remains remote (Douglass and Roberts 2000). Their presence underlines the critical issue for Japan of the demographic time-bomb (described in Chapter 10). Policymakers predict a serious shortfall of workers as a result of the sharp drop in the birthrate, meaning lower economic growth and less tax revenues to pay for medical and pension insurance programs for the aging baby-boomer generation. While increasing the number of foreign workers and allowing them to settle and raise families in Japan has been touted as a solution, opposition to this option is strong and is fed by discriminatory attitudes and practices.

Despite the objective trends and figures presented in the following chapters, the thesis proposed in this book reflects a personal view – albeit one based on a wide experience of contemporary Japan. Talking with cab drivers, neighbors, colleagues, carpenters, clairvoyants, musicians, reporters, potters, activists, farmers, businesspeople, illegal immigrants, foreign brides, landscapers, restructured corporate warriors, video artists, writers, students, and others over the years, I perceive no consensus about whether life is improving or getting worse, although the edge probably goes to the pessimists. Although few of the topics discussed below seem foremost in their minds, in many ways this book is animated by their perspectives and observations.

Almost everyone I know acknowledges that Japan's economic glory days are history and there is little expectation, or expressed desire, for a comeback. The notion of Japan as #1 has lost its appeal. People are no longer obsessed with economic growth and express more interest in diversifying cultural values and improving the quality of life. Both in the press and in casual conversations people's aspirations for a 'mature society' (*seijukushakai*) are frequently expressed – a concept consistent with movement towards a civil society and one that, significantly, constitutes a repudiation of many aspects of contemporary society. If there is any common thread to the *seijukushakai* it is the desire for a more people-friendly, less stifling society no longer obsessed by materialistic goals and more in tune with nature and spiritual needs. Perhaps, in some ways, Prime Minister Miyazawa's vision is taking root.

The Japanese and others will no doubt become impatient for their civil society to grow more robust. They will become frustrated when solutions to the nation's problems prove elusive and incomplete. However, there is no deadline in creating a society that will better serve and accommodate the interests of its people. In future years the Lost Decade will be looked upon as the great turning point, the finale for the postwar system and the beginning of the untidy and illuminating transition to whatever Japan is becoming. This book charts some of those transformations as they are happening and in doing so challenges stereotypes and projections of listless decline. In elucidating how the Japanese are contesting the terrain of their economy, society and culture, the following chapters raise important questions about how we understand Japan and what matters to its citizens. This is a story about dynamic transformations that challenge what many readers think they know about this oft-misconstrued nation.

Quiet transformation

The political scandals, bureaucratic bungling, economic crisis, and social fallout outlined above are resonating throughout Japanese society and placing enormous pressure on those who govern. The loss of credibility and trust during the 1990s marks an important change in Japan, eroding the façade of legitimacy and the basis of power in the nation. The scandals and crises of the 1990s exposed the shortcomings of the postwar system and created an atmosphere favorable to reform. Recalling how Japan was on top of the world in 1989, it is stunning how fast and far it has fallen. The system is so bankrupt and the rot has spread so far that even conservative forces are abandoning many of the old ways and embracing reform. The story of change in the 1990s is the widespread support for it among unlikely supporters. Many of those who benefited most from the status quo are those now most eager to jettison the old ways and advocate reform. Japan's quiet transformation is happening because many of those who wield power know that it must happen. The logic of economic and political change is transforming existing patterns of governance, institutions, and relations between people and the state. It is also creating common ground for diverse groups who are seeking to channel change in desirable directions.

The trend towards a more open society, more transparent government and the policy imperatives of the demographic time-bomb are driving the reinvention of Japan.[42] This quiet transformation is not on media radar screens for a variety of reasons, perhaps mostly because these myriad small changes will not suddenly boost Japan's economy, rescue its banks, reduce unemployment or solve any of the nation's pressing problems within a year or two. The flow of regulatory changes, administrative reforms, legislative initiatives, judicial decisions, and new alliances is often ignored or dismissed by the media as creating the image of reform without delivering the substance. It is only when these individual initiatives are considered cumulatively and collectively as mutually reinforcing pieces of a larger mosaic that one can appreciate the potential for substantive change in the coming decades.

2   Information disclosure

Popular Government without popular information, or the means of acquiring it, is but a Prologue to a Farce or a Tragedy; or perhaps both.

James Madison, 1822

Information is the currency of democracy.

Ralph Nader, 1989 Japan lecture tour

There is no single change that would do more to weaken the [Japanese] bureaucracy and protect consumers than a national freedom of information law.

Miyake Hiroshi, Attorney

If information is indeed the currency of democracy, Japanese citizens have been grievously shortchanged. However, recent developments suggest they are on the road to getting more of their money's worth. Since the 1970s there has been a sustained effort by a handful of citizens' groups to promote greater information disclosure at the local and national levels of government. This effort to broaden access to official information has been animated by public outrage over a number of bureaucratic and political scandals and inspired by the evident costs of opacity. Public officials free from scrutiny and accountability have too often betrayed the public trust and conspired against the public interest, leaving behind an onerous tab for ordinary taxpayers and citizens. As the profligate ways of Japan's governing elite have been unveiled in a long-running series of scandals, heightened public awareness of the benefits of transparency has gradually eroded their cocoon of privilege and privacy. As a result, there has been a diminution of their immunity from accountability, albeit a gradual and limited one.

This is not to argue that transparency has become the norm; it is certain that there will be sustained resistance to the principle of open government. However, the rising tide of public expectations, greater awareness about the benefits of transparency, the growing sophistication of pressure groups and the proliferation of NPOs are all exerting pressure for greater accountability and public participation in government policymaking. The fundamental crisis in the legitimacy of government is both sustaining demands for greater citizen participation and trimming the wings of the mandarins.

The US Freedom of Information Act, enacted in 1966 and amended in 1974 in the aftermath of the Watergate scandal (over the veto of President Gerald Ford), has been a model for advocates in Japan. Disclosure laws are designed to set the ground rules for relations between private citizens and public servants, obligating the latter to release public documents on demand subject to the rules and procedures stipulated in the legislation. Approximately 55 democracies around the world have such legislation in place.[1]

In Japan, citizens' groups began to request information about pesticide use, food additives, and drug side effects in the 1960s; they aimed to prevent public health tragedies by pressuring bureaucrats to disclose information and act with greater concern for public safety. While advocates suspected the government of negligence in these areas, they had no way of lifting the veil of secrecy that shrouded government deliberations and policymaking. In the end, their efforts proved in vain.

In the 1970s, growing support for a freedom of information policy was fueled by the Lockheed bribery scandal involving Prime Minister Tanaka Kakuei. It was information made public in the USA that proved decisive in breaking open the case and highlighting the merits of greater transparency to Japanese citizens. In 1976 growing interest in the ethics of disclosure led to a public demand for a freedom of information law by the Japan Consumers Federation. This was followed in 1979 by a proposal from the Japan Civil Liberties Union (Jiyu Jinken Kyokai) that set out guidelines for a national disclosure law and, in 1981, by a Declaration of Rights to Information Disclosure by the newly formed Citizens' Movement, an umbrella group for organizations involved with consumer rights and civil liberties.

Throughout the 1980s there was a lively debate about the need for transparency (*joho kokai* – literally 'information disclosure') and the principle of *shiru kenri* (the right to know). Transparency and disclosure were actively promoted as ways of improving democracy and government while facilitating public participation in creating the nation's social and political agenda. Poor access to information was depicted as a significant national defect with great potential for harm to the people and an obstacle to the assertion of their constitutional rights.

In 1985, families of victims involved in Japan's largest air crash were driven to use the US Freedom of Information Act to acquire information related to their litigation. The media focused on the irony that information about events in Japan was more readily available overseas, generating a feeling that Japan was out of step with international standards. Citizens' groups such as the Japan Civil Liberties Union capitalized on this sense of embarrassment by lobbying to have information disclosure placed on the national agenda.

The first opportunity to translate this increasing pressure from citizens' groups into legislation came in the late 1970s. As with environmental issues, the LDP found itself on the defensive and sought to undermine its opponents by co-opting elements of their political agenda. By embracing the rhetoric of information disclosure the LDP was able to blunt some of the criticism directed against it and recast itself as reform-minded. This tactic proved especially critical towards the end of the 1970s when the LDP's political fortunes seemed to be waning under PM Ohira. The ruling coalition partner, New Liberal Club (NLC), was also an advocate of information disclosure so taking on this issue was politically convenient. Over the next few years the issue was debated in the Diet while several study committees and panels generated a sense of movement without actually making any progress. In 1980 the Cabinet affirmed information disclosure as national policy and ministries subsequently set up 'information windows' and created guidelines for requests.

However, in the absence of legal sanction, the spirit of disclosure languished amidst official inertia and resistance. In Japan, government is to a large extent at the mercy of the bureaucracy. Many LDP members are themselves former civil servants, and politicians are heavily dependent on bureaucrats for information and drafting legislation. In addition, many politicians play a brokering role between business and the bureaucracy and would prefer to shield such activities from public scrutiny. This helps explain why LDP politicians have been such reluctant supporters of information disclosure. Thus, while the theater of reform inched along at the national level, the substance of reform was left to citizen advocates at the local level.

Modest origins, growing expectations

While politicians postured on the national stage, a handful of activists and grassroots citizens' groups were working effectively to advocate transparency as a basic principle of democracy.[2] Although demands for disclosure started modestly, a wildfire of expectations rapidly engulfed Japan, overcoming the best efforts of bureaucratic firefighters to bring it under control. At the beginning of the 1980s, few could have anticipated the developments that in the 1990s popularized the concept of public access to government files and made it a yardstick by which Japanese governments are judged. In a short span of two decades, what was once anathema to the ruling elite has now become a common and judicially sanctioned practice that officials are trained to implement. As elsewhere in the world, freedom of information is now regarded as a threshold requirement for democratic government.[3]

After the first hesitant steps in the 1970s, the pace of activism quickened. The Japan Federation of Housewives' Associations (Shufuren) took the government to task for its lack of transparency, while the Consumers' Union of Japan (Nihon Shohisha Renmei) and the Japan Civil Liberties Union lobbied for an information disclosure law on the US model. In 1981 the latter group published a model ordinance that has been used extensively by local government bodies in crafting their own laws. In tandem with local citizens' groups, lawyers' associations, and opposition party politicians, and drawing on favorable media coverage, advocates campaigned for information disclosure ordinances at the local and prefectural levels.

In response to this grassroots campaign, localities acceded to demands for greater citizen input, probably never imagining that it would become such a 'nuisance.' In 1982 the first town and prefectural information disclosure ordinances were enacted, initiating a trend that swept through Japan involving 36 prefectures and 136 towns and cities by the end of the decade. By 1996 all 47 prefectures had passed information disclosure legislation and by the end of the century more than 500 towns, including all major population centers, had adopted similar ordinances – a bewilderingly rapid transformation only made possible by the efforts of citizen groups. Conservative politicians joined their progressive colleagues and climbed on board the transparency train, recognizing the electoral advantages in an era of growing public skepticism about politicians and bureaucrats. Their support was crucial in transforming it into a mainstream issue and encouraging local and prefectural governments to adopt such ground-breaking legislation. They may have underestimated the implications of their actions and probably did not expect that the new rules would have such a strong impact in the years to come.

However, the adoption of new legislation did not mean that all the barriers to transparency were removed overnight. Patricia Maclachlan (2000: 17) notes that the disparate ordinances share a core of principles based on 'the promotion of citizen participation in local government; the enhancement of citizen trust in and understanding of local administration; the promotion of the impartial implementation of government policy; and the realization of governmental openness.' However, the achievement of such grand ideals has been a great challenge. At the outset, citizens who asserted their rights under these ordinances found that the spirit of transparency had not permeated among the officials responsible for implementing them. Many of the statutes are couched in vague language that allows bureaucrats considerable latitude in deciding what documents should be open to public perusal. On the other hand, the categories of documents exempted from public access are very strictly defined, while the legislative activities of local assemblies generally lie beyond the bounds of the new ordinances. The opportunities for stonewalling, manipulation and obfuscation are rife and draw considerable public ire. Maclachlan (2000: 20) concludes: 'Ironically, local government procedures to guarantee transparency had created public expectations that the procedures themselves proved incapable of fulfilling.'

Where citizens wish to challenge the authorities, there are various routes for appeal. In cases where requests for information are denied (*hikokai*), people can appeal to a local government review committee established to deal with disclosure cases. Generally, the local executive appoints these committees subject to legislative approval. While these review boards make recommendations, they cannot force disclosure. Citizens also have resort to legal action and can appeal to the courts for a legally binding ruling forcing disclosure. There have been a number of such lawsuits in the 1990s, heavily covered in the media, leading to revelations of lavish entertainment and faked travel expense claims. In exposing the profligate spending of local officials, citizen groups have reinforced public skepticism towards bureaucrats and provided impetus for a national information disclosure law. The sensationalizing of these cases by the media has also ensured maximum publicity for their efforts and public sympathy for their goals.

Local efforts, national consequences

The local information disclosure ordinances and their role in instituting greater levels of accountability have been examined by Lawrence Repeta (1999: 19) who regards them as creating a 'revolution in the nature of the relationship between citizen and government.' He focuses on the role of lawyers affiliated with the Zenkoku Shimin Ombudsmen (National Citizen Ombudsmen group) who have run several well-organized disclosure campaigns and devised a system of rating prefectures in terms of their openness. Repeta tells a fascinating story of how the legal system has been used by activists to promote open government and democracy. It is an object lesson in the unforeseen consequences of legal change and the degree to which seemingly inadequate reforms can be made to alter traditional forms of governance and the relationship between officialdom and the public. The bureaucrats, once referred to as *okami* (gods) with a mixture of fear and reverence, have been transformed into objects of recrimination, scorn and ridicule. The revolution referred to by Repeta is nothing less than the broad (and novel) expectation that officials are accountable for their actions to the people.

As a result of the new laws and heightened public awareness of transparency issues, official prodigality has come under increasing scrutiny. During the 1990s the Japanese lexicon was enriched by three new terms – *kan-kan settai*, *enkai gyosei*, and *karashutcho* – describing some of the seamy realities of public life. *Kan-kan settai* (official-to-official entertainment) refers to the widespread practice of local government officials entertaining national government bureaucrats to curry favor and hopefully tap into central government funding. *Enkai gyosei* (partying bureaucrats) is the derisive appellation for officials who enjoy high living on the public purse. *Karashutcho* (empty business trip) refers to the claiming of travel expenses for non-existent business trips. Since 1994, media exposés of such practices have molded perceptions of public officials, highlighting the need for greater oversight and generating widespread public enthusiasm for still greater levels of information disclosure.

Abuse of entertainment allowances is a common practice in Japan. When activist lawyers and citizens have used local ordinances to request information on the entertainment expenses of local government officials, they have all too often uncovered evidence of lavish wining and dining at posh restaurants. These outings are usually hidden in innocuous-sounding accounts such as *shokuryohi* (food and beverage expenses), intended to provide meals for staff working after hours and to cover the cost of snacks and coffee at staff meetings. Thus, discovery of millions of yen of spending under this account category in Miyagi Prefecture seemed odd. Further investigation revealed that large sums of money were spent on dubiously large amounts of alcohol and expensive meals for relatively small groups of officials, leading to speculation that inflated wining and dining expenses were designed to cover other more salacious entertainment expenses or the outright theft of public funds.

Similar practices have been uncovered in virtually all of the nation's 47 prefectures, although some governments proved to be less forthcoming than others. The Citizen Ombudsmen, a national network of activist lawyers, has focused on these variations by simultaneously filing similar information requests to all prefectural governments. In comparing the responses and then rating the openness of the various governments, the Ombudsmen generated considerable media interest and sent two clear messages to government officials: insufficient transparency would produce a lower rating that would reflect badly on both the prefecture and its public officials; and lavish wining and dining and falsifying expense claims would no longer be tolerated.

The size of local government entertainment budgets has been another key issue. The cost of entertaining central government officials, usually undertaken by prefectural government representatives dispatched to Tokyo solely for this purpose, amounted until recently to tens of millions of dollars and was hardly the nation's best-kept secret. However, the media had ignored this practice until citizens exercised their new rights to access government information and uncovered the extent of the spending and how it was systematically covered up. The public was shocked to learn that the 47 prefectural offices spent some $250 million a year on entertaining central government bureaucrats, a revelation that provoked considerable anger given the prolonged economic slump and declining tolerance of extravagant spending of taxpayer money. Once the story broke, the media played a key role in keeping such practices at the center of public attention for many months. During the latter half of 1995 alone, fifteen editorials appeared in national newspapers condemning excessive entertainment by civil servants.

These investigations showed that filing false or inflated expense claims had become routine and that preparing an obscuring paper trail was part of the clerical norm. It became clear that false documentation, padding expenses, and the sequestering of fraudulently claimed funds in unofficial accounts was standard practice throughout the nation, a clever shell game that had gone unquestioned until citizens blew the whistle. Even government auditors were caught padding expenses. One of the more eye-opening exposés involved counting the number of trips (37) ostensibly taken by Fukuoka officials on the bullet train at a total cost of ¥3.7 million – at a time when the tracks were so badly damaged by the 1995 Kobe earthquake that the train in question was out of service!

The media coverage and public outrage over this squandering of public funds reveals how in a very short span of time the local disclosure ordinances have transformed the relations between the people and government. These revelations also changed the conduct and habits of government. Moreover, prosecutors also began taking a dim view of such practices, arguing that entertainment at such lavish levels can constitute a bribe. Suddenly, prefecture after prefecture began to clamp down on such entertainment. More than 20,000 officials around the country were reprimanded for filing false expense claims. What had been 'business as usual' was now forbidden and subject to punishment – demonstrating the effectiveness of the legal system in promoting and applying standards of conduct in the public service, and the costs to those who do not comply.

As prefectural and local government officials came to terms with the new rules, they learned to their regret and embarrassment the costs of trying to obstruct the trend towards transparency. Clearly, monopolizing information was seen as one of the bureaucrat's sources of power and sharing it was viewed as infringing on their established prerogatives and authority. Of course, this was the intent of the new information disclosure ordinances, but old habits cannot be abruptly reversed by legal fiat. Thus, information-seekers have been often frustrated by refusals, arbitrary exclusions, and classifications specifically designed to thwart requests, while excessive censoring of documents frequently renders them virtually useless as sources of information.

The public has responded to these efforts to derail information disclosure and obstruct access to public documents in a variety of ways. Some requestors lodge appeals with local review boards or sue local authorities that attempt to obstruct access to information in contravention of the disclosure ordinances. Although local review panels frequently rule in favor of disclosure, they have become clogged with requests. To the extent that they are working, however, they are promoting transparency. The Citizen Ombudsmen reported that of 3,517 appeals heard at the prefectural level as of 1998, review boards made 1,234 recommendations of which 52 percent recommended expanded disclosure and an additional 9 percent supported full disclosure – an overall reversal ratio of 61 percent.

The courts also have been surprisingly supportive of transparency, or at least far less obstructive than disclosure advocates feared. Certainly the Supreme Court has been less supportive than lower courts, and there have been many controversial decisions against transparency. However, some judges have intervened to compel disclosure as mandated by law and have taken a dim view of bureaucratic evasiveness: they have placed the burden of proof on the government to demonstrate how their denial of access to information is consistent with the law. While it would be misleading to suggest that this has become the general rule, there have certainly been more victories in the courts than many disclosure advocates anticipated, given the conservative training and selection process that shapes judges and influences their career prospects. Legal exemptions to information access have in many instances been strictly interpreted and attempts to apply them more widely struck down. The courts have also tackled the privacy issue by rejecting government claims that revealing the names of people involved in government-sponsored activities constitutes an infringement on their privacy and grounds for denying disclosure of requested documents (Repeta 1999: 39). In 1996, the Sendai Court ruled that public officials engaged in public business have no recourse to claims of infringement on privacy. It further ruled that the privacy of non-government participants at publicly sponsored events or meetings could not be used to obstruct 'the maximum disclosure of information concerning those charged with prefectural administration as well as those they deal with' (Repeta 1999: 39). This ruling has set a high burden of proof for government exceptions to the principle of open disclosure.

The Sendai Court decision has been hailed as a landmark in the battle to promote information disclosure. It compelled the prefectural government to release information that it had not wanted to release. However, the court's decision prevailed only as a result of political intervention by Governor Asano, who rejected the possibility of an appeal by the Miyagi prefectural government, in effect rescuing the case from the jurisdiction of the higher courts. Asano instructed his subordinates to comply with the decision in a written directive:

> We must choose one of two avenues. Either we will sincerely devote our-
> selves to … explication of the real truth, or we will direct all of our efforts
> to protection of prefectural officials, even if it means concealing the truth.
> In all ways we will seek to show the truth. This statement is not merely for
> discussion; this is an order. For those of you who cannot follow this guide-
> line, resignation is the only course.
>
> (Repeta 1999: 33)

This former Ministry of Health and Welfare bureaucrat has demonstrated what a progressive administrator is capable of and, in the process, made information disclosure a litmus test of good governance.

Asano's decision was a critical one, as senior judges in the upper courts tend to be more conservative and more inclined to support the government than their colleagues in the lower courts – reflecting the promotion process in the judiciary discussed in Chapter 3. The path to the top is not easy for judges who offend those in the Supreme Court who control promotions. It is worth recalling that judges in Japan are not political appointees or elected officials, but are elite civil servants. This helps explain why a number of prodisclosure decisions by lower courts have been reversed by the high courts and the Supreme Court where judges more readily accept government interpreta-tions of disclosure statutes.

Governor Asano's intervention in the Sendai Court decision highlights the critical role of directly elected local and prefectural politicians in promoting greater transparency. Without the support of these politicians, disclosure ordinances either would not have been passed or would have languished as little more than legislative ornaments. What is interesting is that these politi-cians range from outspoken defenders of freedom of information to

Figure 2.1 Governor Asano of Miyagi Prefecture played a key role in promoting information disclosure. (Photo: Mainichi Newspapers)

opportunists, and include conservatives, liberals, mavericks, and main-streamers. Because they are accountable to their constituents rather than to the government, they have pushed transparency more forcefully and effectively than the courts. The emergence of such politicians across the political spectrum reflects popular support for disclosure and a desire for information on how taxes are being spent or squandered.

Despite the vagaries of the judiciary, the prodisclosure posture of the courts has far exceeded expectations and has influenced bureaucratic practices and attitudes. Prefectures now run annual training seminars aimed at weaning officials responsible for documents from established anti-disclosure attitudes. Officials are trained in how to handle requests and, in some prefectures, information specialists are employed to ensure proper interpretation of disclosure guidelines. In many cases, but certainly not all, local legislatures have revised ordinances in tune with user complaints and in line with court rulings, effectively expanding the scope of transparency and limiting exemptions and discretionary denials. Limits on who may request documents have been liberalized and reforms instituted to facilitate information requests. And disgruntled citizens know they have recourse to the courts, something that may come as a surprise to many observers who have assumed, with considerable justification, that the court system is biased in favor of the government. A reversal ratio of 65.2 percent as of March 1999, in which the courts overturned information disclosure denials by local and prefectural governments in two-thirds of cases heard, is surprisingly high. As Repeta (1999: 19) asserts, 'The courts' adoption of such an aggressive role in correcting administrative behavior is without precedent in Japan's modern legal history.'

More recently, Jonathan Marshall (2002) has confirmed the prodisclosure inclinations of the courts, finding that in more than 50 percent of cases plaintiffs were successful in gaining greater disclosure than local authorities had decided to grant. It is worth bearing in mind that expanded disclosure does not mean full disclosure and may very well be trivial in its effects. Nevertheless, this is still an astounding figure given the courts' usual reluctance to second-guess administrative decisions; plaintiffs typically win in less than 10 percent of all administrative lawsuits. It is also encouraging that, even with a larger number of cases, inevitably including more frivolous or nuisance appeals, the reversal ratio remains so high. The courts have been thrust into the role of administrative overseer and are helping to shape the ongoing transformation in state–society relations sparked by information disclosure laws. Given the prospects for significant judicial reform discussed in the following chapter, aimed at creating a more activist judiciary, the implications of this trend are vast.

Information disclosure ordinances have also led to a surge in lawsuits involving taxpayers suing government officials to repay illegally spent public monies. Although a law to this effect has been on the books since 1948, it was seldom used because of the difficulty in gathering incriminating information. However, armed with the new powers at their disposal, litigants can now compel release of relevant information and appeal denials. This development led to a doubling of taxpayer lawsuits in the latter half of the 1990s, a sign that information disclosure was working in the public interest and enabling citizens to hold officials accountable for their misdeeds. The surge in information disclosure and taxpayer lawsuits is reflected in the sharp rise in district court cases dealing with appeals against administrative actions – from 12 percent of all such cases in 1990 to 25 percent by 2000. Marshall (2002: 13) concludes: 'Court intervention in these two areas has eroded the bureaucracy's control over statutory interpretation and indeed its own oversight. It will be difficult for courts to ignore plaintiff victories in disclosure disputes with local governments when they decide similar cases brought under the national Information Disclosure Act.'

However, the new gains are under constant threat. In 2002, the Diet responded to the threat of these taxpayer lawsuits and passed legislation to curtail access to this effective tool for monitoring the spending of public monies. This response of the political establishment is a significant setback to the struggle for effective citizens' oversight of government and reveals how difficult the struggle for transparency and accountability remains. It is a sobering reminder of the long road ahead to overcome established practices and vested interests. Developments in the United States, where there is growing government resistance to the Freedom of Information Act, offer a further reminder of the need for public vigilance in protecting and enforcing rights of oversight.[4]

Fifteen years of information disclosure at the local and prefectural levels between 1982 and 1997 generated strong popular demand for a national information disclosure system. The prodisclosure stance of the media, echoed to some degree in the courts, created an extraordinarily favorable environment for its implementation. Successful application of information disclosure has altered citizen–state relations and generated higher expectations inimical to the closed file approach to information access that has been the bureaucratic norm. This revolutionary development cannot easily be squelched: too many positive precedents favoring greater transparency have been established while bureaucratic efforts at defending institutional turf have lost credibility and raised the public ire. As a result of *kanson mimpi* (literally 'revere the official, despise the people,' shorthand for bureaucratic arrogance), public officials in Japan have lost their privileged status and freedom from scrutiny for good. Self-inflicted wounds have irreparably undermined the façade of power and cocoon of privilege that in the past have permitted excesses, facilitated systematic defrauding of the public purse and stymied public oversight. The bureaucrats have lost their unbridled autonomy and more than ever are subject to popular sovereignty, a trend that is gaining momentum.

National information disclosure

It was an idea whose time had finally arrived. In 1993 advocates for freedom of information were presented with an unprecedented opportunity with the collapse of the LDP's stranglehold on political power. The emergence of coalition politics, led by reformers who had run for election on an anticorruption ticket, was a sign of the times. The public mood was ugly and voters delighted in 'throwing the bums out of office.' In the early 1990s, four major scandals had created an atmosphere where even the most hardened backroom politicians felt the need to reinvent themselves as reformers (Inoguchi 1997). Money politics was evident on an unprecedented scale in the Recruit and Sagawa Kyubin scandals, while bureaucratic incompetence was glaringly revealed in the Ministry of Finance's mishandling of the *jusen* (firms specializing in real estate loans) crisis. Finally, negligence in the Ministry of Health and Welfare (MHW) led to an epidemic of HIV infection in hemophiliacs. Opponents of reform were in danger of jeopardizing their political future, and thus conservatives and progressives found themselves working together on measures such as electoral reform and information disclosure on which they were not natural allies. Under the relatively progressive, non-LDP Hosokawa and Hata administrations in 1993 and 1994, momentum developed for enacting some form of information disclosure law; only the timing of enabling legislation seemed in doubt.

The passage of the Act was the result of an unlikely alliance of political forces. In 1994 the LDP regained power by forming a coalition government with the Socialists, longtime advocates of information disclosure. As a price of coalition, Murayama Tomiichi became prime minister. While critics have castigated him for selling out core political principles, he played a crucial role in ensuring the passage of information disclosure legislation. Murayama oversaw the establishment of the Administrative Reform Council in 1994, which included a committee on information disclosure. The final report of this committee was submitted to Prime Minister Hashimoto Ryutaro in December 1996, when the LDP was again in coalition government with more progressive parties and desperate to expand its electoral base. The Cabinet endorsed the report, setting the stage for a freedom of information law that finally took effect in 2001. Hashimoto appointed Kan Naoto, an outspoken liberal, as his Minister of Health and Welfare and agreed to include some progressive issues in the coalition's electoral platform (see further Chapter 6). The alignment of political forces and public sentiment forced Hashimoto and the LDP old guard to grudgingly support measures they normally would find anathema, and an information disclosure bill was submitted to the Diet in 1998. The following year, an amended bill was passed by the Diet. Although the legislation was approved in 1999, its promulgation was delayed until 2001 to allow public officials time to prepare for this dramatic innovation at the same time they faced other administrative reforms including a reduction in the number of national ministries. The task of establishing a unified filing system was another major reason for the delayed implementation. In addition, critics have pointed to the time-consuming process of weeding out 'inconvenient' documents.

The favorable political environment of the mid-1990s facilitated passage of a law that was unexpectedly progressive given its conservative sponsors. With reform in the air and the creation of an administrative reform council, support for freedom of information gained momentum. Politicians and the media raised public expectations that improved governance would be the major benefit of increased transparency in government proceedings and policy deliberations. The logic of reform rested on open government and those opposing it were easily depicted as defenders of vested interests and part of the problem; transparency was the solution. The public's right to know and ability to access pertinent information also fit with the spirit of deregulation. With Thatcherian enthusiasm, the Hashimoto administration advocated a reduced role for government and saw deregulation as a means to revive the economy and improve efficiency. The mantra of deregulation and restructuring – the oversold solution to what ails contemporary Japan – proved popular at this time and had consequences for information disclosure. In a changed environment where the government's refereeing role would decline, consumer citizens were encouraged to become more involved and knowledgeable. Thus, the government was trapped by its own logic – it could not advocate deregulation and at the same time restrict the flow of information citizens would need to participate more effectively in society and better protect their own interests.

The final legislation reflects a compromise. Bureaucratic hostility and political wrangling led to the insertion of provisions that weakened the law as a tool of transparency. Exemptions to disclosure were expanded and the scope of non-disclosure was kept vague, while special public corporations (*tokushu hojin*) were not subjected to the law. Despite these deficiencies, the new legislation provides the legal basis for expanding public oversight of, and participation in, the affairs of government. It includes some significant improvements over local disclosure ordinances. For example, the national government is bound to respond to requests from any person and there is no residency requirement as is common in the local ordinances. In another major step forward, the national law applies to any document in the possession of an administrative agency and available to officials in the performance of their duties; local regulations typically applied only to documents reflecting some formal action by a government official.

Thus, at the advent of the twenty-first century, an era of transparency was dawning for the Japanese. Finally, after decades of campaigning, advocates have earned a means to slowly and incrementally bring about an end to unaccountable government and official impunity. However, despite grassroots support for open government and the new legislation, successful implementation will require well-organized and independent citizen groups that are able to sustain pressure, focus on critical issues and effectively marshal the information they gather. The legislation will have little impact unless there is a significant community of requestors able to demand specific kinds of information and put it to effective use in the policymaking process. In this sense, the 1998 NPO legislation (discussed at greater length in the following chapter) is partially encouraging in that independent policy organizations can now obtain independent legal status. However, this legislation is also problematic and reflects the government's inclination to monopolize the policymaking process and to keep NGOs dependent and subject to bureaucratic oversight. Nonetheless, Repeta (1999: 42) draws a more optimistic conclusion: 'The NPO law may be a harbinger to the appearance of better organized and informed citizen groups articulating alternative visions of the public interest and more effectively participating in policy debates of the future.'

Electoral implications

The mayor of Yokohama, Nakada Hiroshi, was elected in 2002 promising to make government more open to public scrutiny. Upon assuming office, the 37-year-old Nakada encountered the expected bureaucratic resistance to open disclosure. City officials complained that publishing lists of people attending public functions would infringe on their privacy – an example of how selective concerns about privacy are often invoked to inhibit transparency. The mayor responded with the clear message that public money should not be spent on anything that cannot pass public scrutiny. Details of his own social expenses are accessible on the city's homepage and he has set other disclosure precedents by divulging the balance of municipal debt and the market price of real estate owned by the city.

Supporting transparency has become good politics. Around the country, advocates have generated a groundswell of popular concern about dysfunctional government practices and put information disclosure on the nation's political agenda. These concerns are having a pay-off at the ballot box: in several prefectures, candidates in gubernatorial elections backed by mainstream political parties have been defeated, often by political neophytes with no organization and limited campaign funds. In recent years voters have elected governors eschewing party affiliation in the prefectures of Akita, Chiba, Miyagi, Nagano, Tokushima, and Tochigi. These newcomers have run against the establishment, embracing open government as a keystone of their campaigns. They have effectively tapped public anger against a rigged system that is widely viewed as a major obstacle to Japan's recovery from a prolonged economic slump.

Until the economic implosion of the 1990s, voters tolerated the peccadilloes of their politicians as long as they delivered the goods. In Japanese politics, pork-barrel projects are the basis of the *doken kokka* (the construction state). As detailed by Gavan McCormack (1996) and Alex Kerr (2001), and discussed at greater length in Chapter 5, the vast amounts of money channeled into Japan's largest industry literally cement the political ties between central government politicians and their local support base. They also provide ample opportunity for siphoning off campaign funds and give politicians at all levels the wherewithal to maintain and expand their influence. The system of bid rigging (*dango*) revealed in a series of scandals in the 1990s exposed the systematic plundering of the public purse by unscrupulous businessmen and their political sponsors. Information disclosure laws were essential to gathering evidence on bid rigging on sewer systems in particular. Armed with this experience, activists are expanding their investigations into other misappropriations of taxpayer monies, estimated at 15–30 percent of the value of typical public works contracts.

The early years of the twenty-first century thus provide a basis for limited optimism about the trend favoring open government and a significant diminution of the immunity from scrutiny and accountability that enables corruption to flourish. Just as exposés of lavish entertainment spending and falsification of expense claims drew public ire, the squandering of the far larger sums involved in the *doken kokka* has shaped public perceptions of Japan's elected and non-elected government officials. They have emerged as co-conspirators in a massive fraud at a time when people were feeling the economic pinch and growing anxious about possible loss of jobs and security.

Japan's *glasnost*

Developments at the local level have nurtured new attitudes, raised public expectations and generated new norms in the practices of government and in the relations between citizens and government officials. In the nearly two decades between the enactment of the first local information disclosure statute (1982) and the implementation of the national information disclosure law (2001), the political landscape has changed dramatically in favor of open government, as revelations of abuses have generated a momentum in support of transparency. Central government officials have been presented with a fait accompli, an insurrection that began at the fringe and has relentlessly bored into the political mainstream. Adapting rapidly to the new rules and their perceived benefits, the public has effectively tied the hands of even the most ardent defenders of the status quo. The battles won in the legislatures, courts, local assemblies, and media have created a more favorable context for fuller information disclosure. Transparency advocates have won the hearts and minds of the people, generating a climate of *glasnost* aimed against the bureaucrats and their grudging concession of power. Their ability to control the information that has enabled them to monopolize and direct policymaking is slowly, incrementally eroding. It is becoming ever more difficult to shield policymaking from public view. The verities and assumptions of governance are fading and the relations between civil servants and the public are being altered by Japan's quiet transformation.

Naturally it is too soon to proclaim victory and exult in unconditional surrender. So much change has happened so rapidly that the implications are still being digested and defenders of the status quo remain well entrenched. Furthermore, the institutions in place to support transparency remain very weak. Clearly the system has some serious teething problems. In the first nine months of the information disclosure law's operation (April–December 2001), about three-quarters of the more than 1,000 appeals filed against the central government for rejecting information requests were not processed according to the law's appeal provisions. Requestors must first file a request for information and, if it is turned down, can petition the ministry involved for reconsideration. If the ministry declines to reverse its decision, it is obliged to turn the case over to the review panel based in the Cabinet Office along with an explanation about why the disclosure was denied. Requestors have the right to present their case before the panel and state their opinions. They also have the right to bring a lawsuit in the courts to compel disclosure, a more expensive option.

It appears that the logjam in processing citizens' complaints is caused by the ministries' tardiness in turning appeals over to the review panel. Thus, rather than a quick and timely remedy for appeals, the review panel's work is being impaired by bureaucratic stonewalling. Some ministries have been better than others in responding to appeals and transmitting them to the review panel, notably the Justice Ministry. Others such as the Financial Services Agency, Ministry of Foreign Affairs, and Ministry of Health and Welfare, all bogged down in scandals that have attracted a large volume of requests, have a relatively poor record of compliance. For example, the Ministry of Foreign Affairs completed the processing of appeals and transferring of documents to the review panel in only 22 of 193 cases – and in none of the requests concerning a notorious embezzlement scandal. This is a sorry state of affairs for a ministry that has demonstrated a flair for self-inflicted wounds in the early years of the twenty-first century. This poor initial report card may reflect inadequate preparation and staffing levels as the system gets into gear. Clearly, the longer this situation persists, non-complying ministries can anticipate negative media coverage and rising pressure from the public, lawmakers and the courts to play by the new rules.

From freedom of information to freedom of surveillance

Despite the very real signs of change vestiges of the old ways are evident, perhaps most alarmingly in the Defense Agency. In May 2002, barely a year after the Freedom of Information law took effect, the Defense Agency was caught transforming it into an excuse to compile dossiers on 142 requestors. The *Asahi* warned: 'There is something ominously anachronistic about the fact that the Defense Agency abused the very system of information disclosure intended to encourage "administrative openness".'[5] Temple University Japan's Lawrence Repeta added: 'A freedom of information law is intended to promote citizen knowledge of government, not government surveillance of citizens.'[6]

All government agencies are subject to the disclosure law and must provide requested documents unless they can demonstrate that any of six exemptions applies. Both Japanese and foreign nationals may request documents and need not state a reason for the request or provide personal details. In violation of a 1988 privacy law and clearly trampling over the spirit and intent of the Freedom of Information law, Defense Agency officials compiled lists of requestors, conducted investigations on their backgrounds and classified them so as to identify likely 'troublemakers.' Staff at the Agency then tried to cover up these extracurricular activities once reporters had gotten wind of them.

A reporter was tipped off about the illicit background investigations and the storage of requestors' dossiers on the Agency's computer system where they would be widely accessible to staff. The media pounced on the story, raising questions about why the Agency would mount unauthorized investigations against Japanese nationals trying to find out what the armed forces are up to. The resulting brouhaha killed debate on proposed legislation on information protection that had drawn sharp criticism from advocates of transparency. The new legislation would have effectively become the media muzzling law in that reporters who uncovered evidence of corruption among public officials would not have been allowed to name the people involved without receiving their permission first. The government tried to portray the proposed law as an attempt to protect the privacy of individuals from a predatory press, citing cases of an insensitive media intruding on the grief of bereaved relatives and otherwise offending public sensibilities. There is no shortage of such cases. In their coverage of a Wakayama curry-poisoning incident ('the crime of the century') and a sarin gas attack in Nagano in the 1990s, the press acted as both prosecutor and judge, convicting the accused with sensational, obsessive coverage akin to that accorded to the O.J. Simpson case in the USA. In response, media organizations have adopted tougher rules of conduct and self-imposed restraints aimed at placating critics and warding off legislation they regard as placing unconstitutional and unwarranted restrictions on their activities. Media advocates argue that it is their very success in keeping the public informed, and digging out information damaging to politicians and government officials, that has motivated the government's push for new controls, using evident media abuses of private individuals to draw a curtain around the activities of public officials.

The Defense Agency scandal has effectively worked against these attempts to muzzle the media. Even before the story broke, the new legislation faced substantial revisions; but in the wake of the scandal further attempts to place restrictions on the press face an uphill battle in the court of public opinion.[7] Yet again, government officials were caught breaking the rules thanks to media oversight. In this climate, those seeking to curb the media are suspected of having something to hide.

While the proposed bills on information protection and human rights started out as vehicles to protect people from government abuses, they were deftly transformed into measures to regulate the media and clamp down on whistleblowers and negative coverage about politicians and bureaucrats. Such seems to be the logic behind the Defense Agency's own efforts to reinterpret freedom of information as an excuse for prying.

Why would the Agency gather such information? Presumably requestors were viewed as potential enemies and exercising their legal rights was the basis for suspecting them. Gregory Clark suspects that the SDF 'have been creating and distributing dossiers on the ideological beliefs of those who exercise their right to inquire into SDF affairs ... [because] Japan's security agencies have long provided similar dossiers to firms keen to deny employment to pro-communists and other leftwing elements.'[8] Ironically, a statute designed to facilitate public oversight has been interpreted as a license to investigate anyone exercising this right. This is a significant threat to information disclosure and sends a chilling message to other citizens inclined to exercise their legal rights: Big Brother really is watching.

After being caught violating the 1988 privacy statute and subverting the information disclosure law, the Agency managed to inflict additional wounds on itself. First, it denied compiling lists and posting them on its internal computer network; it then admitted it had done so, but denied any wrong-doing. The bungled handling of a report generated by an inhouse investigation into the case made matters worse. Initially the Agency released a four-page, sanitized summary of a longer report, but leaks about the longer version and reference to an aborted cover-up forced its subsequent release. This episode demonstrated a flair for disastrous public relations and reinforced perceptions that the Agency had something to hide. Moreover, the involvement of party bosses in deciding which version of the report to release implicated Prime Minister Koizumi's ruling coalition and further tarnished his claims to be a committed reformer. The desperate attempts by party bosses to evade responsibility for suppressing the longer, damning version of the report only added to the debacle.

Although political embarrassment over the affair has been acute, it has made it even more difficult to obstruct transparency. On a larger and more humiliating scale, central government officials have learned the hard way the lesson already learned by their local government counterparts: thwarting public sentiments on open government is a recipe for disaster. The collateral damage to the government has also been substantial as opposition parties took the opportunity to shelve debate on crucial legislation aimed at transforming Japan's military posture and ability to act in emergency situations. The attempt to neutralize the Freedom of Information law has only served to highlight the dysfunctional character of the government and reinforce the perceived need for the law. The disingenuous and clumsy handling of the affair made a mockery of the public trust and underlined the need for civilian oversight.

The damage that the Defense Agency has inflicted on itself is incalculable. After World War II, at the insistence of the USA the armed forces were disbanded and then resurrected under a constitutional subterfuge. The constitutional legitimacy of the SDF has been questioned from the outset and the Defense Agency has taken pains to cultivate an image distanced from the military abuses of the past and memories of political suppression under military-controlled governments in the 1930s and 1940s. This affair has undone those efforts and revived invidious comparisons. The SDF operates under a bitter legacy that places it under special scrutiny and is expected to meet the highest standards of conduct. Even its advocates would be hard pressed to defend this blatant attempt to derail the spirit of transparency in a way that can only arouse suspicion about its motives and routine practices.

Prominent among the Agency's critics is Umebayashi Hiromichi, president of the NPO Peace Depot. In his view,

> the Defense Agency failed to honor even the most basic of human rights, which is that no administrative entity may discriminate against citizens for their thoughts or beliefs. The Agency's failure goes to show there are administrative authorities who think nothing of arbitrarily deciding what constitutes human rights ... It is now clear that these individuals

understood squat about the spirit of the law ... Was this Defense Agency scandal just an aberration? I don't think so. On the contrary, it simply embodied what is totally 'normal' among central government bureaucrats who believe their job is to keep the citizenry in line.[9]

Umebayashi expresses pessimism about the prospects for freedom of information in the absence of a fundamental 'cultural revolution' among bureaucrats.

The public furor over the affair, however, reveals an encouraging vibrancy and resilience in Japanese society. Not too many years ago a scandal like this might never have seen the light of day. Now, the media is shining a harsher light on the government, ferreting out stories that keep the public informed about what the government is up to. The scandal has produced a consensus that personal 'background checks' are inimical to the spirit and practice of information disclosure. In addition, the public has been alerted to the need for increased vigilance and oversight of the government. In this sense, the Defense Agency has unwittingly buttressed support for transparency and undermined government resistance to information disclosure and the media's watchdog role.

Juki Net

The Defense Agency scandal has stoked misgivings about Juki Net, or the Basic Residential Register Network System, a massive computerized database of citizen information. Juki Net is a controversial result of amendments to the Basic Resident Registration Law approved in 1999 that came into effect in August 2002. With the introduction of this system, personal information about citizens is stored on a nationwide database and is accessible to government officials. Each resident can be identified by a *sebango* (a term normally used for the number on the back of a sports-player's uniform), an eleven-digit number similar to the social security number in the USA, which provides full access to their files. Advocates tout the efficiency of computerizing records for government processing of paperwork requested by citizens, a logical extension of 'E-government.' For example, citizens who need a copy of their resident registration certificate, something required in a variety of transactions, will be able to get one at any local government office nationwide rather than travel to the office where their registration is kept. The government also hopes to use the identification numbers to process pension payments, payment of unemployment and workers' compensation insurance, issuance of construction permits, and to correct identity information on passports. In 2003, agencies plan to share individual data on 93 kinds of administrative matters, but legislation is pending to expand this to cover 264 varieties. Beginning in August 2003, local municipalities will issue citizens with Juki cards embedded with integrated-circuit (IC) chips that hold various forms of information on the bearer. These cards can be used for various administrative

(Roger Dahl)

tasks such as registering marriages and divorces and filing internet tax returns.

Critics warn about creeping, or in this case leaping, expansion of the system, citing the establishment in 1936 of the US social security numbering system that has grown to encompass almost all interactions between individuals and the government. Although the Japanese government has stated that it 'will never, ever' expand use of the ID system to monitor income, savings and investments for purposes of taxation, with public trust in the government running on empty these assurances ring hollow. The biggest complaint against Juki Net has been the government's failure to follow through on the promise of the late Prime Minister Obuchi who declared in 1999, when the enabling legislation was introduced, that privacy protection legislation would be enacted *before* implementing Juki Net.

The government has paid the price for this broken promise in high levels of public skepticism and opposition. Rather than pass legislation to safeguard data gathered under Juki Net, the government chose to include controversial provisions that would have effectively muzzled the press, inhibited reporting on government scandals and exposed whistleblowers. This doomed the legislation and placed citizens in a vulnerable position. In an atmosphere of distrust and legitimate fears about the potential for abuse, the absence of reassuring privacy legislation ensured Juki Net a hostile public reception. The Orwellian specter of government snooping and unauthorized sharing of information has been raised. It is exactly the type of abuse committed by the Defense Agency earlier in 2002 that is cited by critics as the reason for resisting computerization of resident information; the government has earned the public's distrust. In addition, there are concerns that there are inadequate safeguards to prevent unauthorized access. It is feared that consumer loan companies and other commercial enterprises will now find it easier to acquire valuable personal information. In an editorial run on June 14, 2002, the *Asahi* took the government to task over inadequate safeguards

Figure 2.2 Mayor Yamada of Suginami Ward, Tokyo, led a campaign of civil disobedience against Juki Net. (Photo: Mainichi Newspapers)

for personal data: 'People have come to realize the dangers inherent in huge
data networks. As we have seen in the controversial compilation of ... lists of
background information on people seeking information from the Defense
Agency by agency officials, there are many instances in which administrative
agencies put their own interests ahead of those of the people.'

In response, the government passed privacy protection legislation in 2003
and has announced that it will monitor local government use of Juki Net
information through a computer watchdog program able to detect suspicious
patterns of data searches. The program will also maintain a log of searches by
authorized users so that officials involved in accessing Juki Net will know that
their activities are being monitored. The system is designed to ensure that
incidents of improper access or misuse of the system at any municipal
government office can be properly dealt with, including denying access.
These initiatives have done little to mollify opponents of Juki Net who assert
that hackers can bypass the watchdog system and other safeguards. While the
new privacy protection legislation does enable citizens to check what kind of
information the government maintains about them and they can demand

removal of information obtained illegitimately, there are no provisions for people to legally pursue entities that divulge information about them. The Japan Federation of Bar Associations greeted the full implementation of Juki Net on August 25, 2003 by calling for its immediate suspension, stating that 'Legislation to protect personal information is insufficient.' The crash of the network's national server within minutes of going into full operation left skeptics confirmed in their doubts about the government's reassurances concerning failsafe information protection.

One of the surprising outcomes of this saga is the emergence of widespread civil disobedience in a country not well known for acts of open defiance of authority. Often depicted as conformist and submissive, the Japanese are shredding such stereotypes, demanding their rights, and reining in government. In fact, Japan has a long and rich tradition of defiance towards authority and well-organized citizen movements, but this reality does not jibe with prevailing portrayals and has thus not become part of Japan's overseas image. Resistance took the form of six municipalities (with a population of four million) opting out of the Juki Net system in protest against inadequate safeguards. Their non-compliance has drawn considerable interest from other municipalities. The media has been supportive of this careful campaign of civil disobedience, noting that such actions are at the heart of democracy and civil society. It is significant that the campaign is being led not by radicals or anti-establishment figures but by municipal officials and politicians acting in the public interest and in pursuit of their duties. It is an inspiring tale of David-and-Goliath proportions, local government versus the central government, showing the lengths to which people and their representatives are willing to go to make civil society a reality. Four million people represent more than a gesture of protest: their action is an indictment of a poorly prepared system hatched without proper precautions, in short a perfectly rational response to a half-baked, potentially harmful government policy. It is exactly initiatives such as these that are galvanizing support for more transparency, more rigorous monitoring of the government, civil society, and Japan's quiet transformation.

More astonishing still is the initiative taken by 840,000 residents of Yokohama, who withdrew from the Juki Net after their mayor gave them the option to do so. This means that 24 percent of Yokohama's citizens already registered with Juki Net chose to opt out of the system. This number exceeded all expectations and confounded the image of apathy based on media representations. In the other municipalities, citizens were not called upon to deregister as this was a political decision taken by the mayors. The Yokohama experience demonstrates people's lack of trust in the government and the lengths to which contemporary Japanese will go to exercise their rights as citizens. Again, the media has commented favorably on these actions and residents feel pride in the signal they have sent to the national government and to other localities considering withdrawal.

Mayor Yamada Hiroshi of Suginami Ward, one of the municipalities that opted out of Juki Net, reported that 70 percent of residents surveyed in 2002 did not want to participate in the system.[10] He claims that pulling out of the system has been his most popular decision, and that now when he visits local festivals he is mobbed by well-wishers applauding his stance. As a resident of Suginami, my own observation since August 2002 is that locals feel great pride in the stance their ward has taken – even though three months earlier I had not encountered anyone who knew that Juki Net was about to be implemented, or even what it was. National opinion polls taken in October 2002 indicate that fewer than 10 percent of the population feel positive about the centralized registry system, while nearly half are opposed to it.

Mayor Yamada questions the whole rationale of Juki Net. While the government justifies the new system by touting the convenience of accessing personal information from anywhere in Japan, Yamada points out that there is no demand for such a service. In his view, 'Government agencies have an inherent desire to check up on individuals who resist government policies or who have unique opinions. With a unified code, it would be so easy for the government to collect a vast amount of data on citizens, which could be used against their interest.' He argues that the loss of freedom entailed is not worth the questionable convenience.[11] It is worth bearing in mind that these comments are from a mainstream politician.

The system continues to reveal shortcomings even on a practical level. On one of Japan's most popular evening television programs, Asahi TV's 'Newstation' (August 14, 2002), the presenter, Kume Hiroshi, made a graphic demonstration of why Juki Net is insecure. He took a typical unopened letter sent out by the government to citizens informing them of their registration number, and shined a special light on it that allowed him to read the contents through the envelope, including the name and identification number of the recipient. It is just this sort of lax approach to security that has provoked such a negative reaction and made people anxious about unauthorized access to their personal information.

Sakurai Yoshiko, a pundit famous for her acerbic critiques of the government, links criticism of Juki Net with the government's grudging compliance with information disclosure legislation: 'The bureaucrats have taken information in a one-sided manner from the people but have been reluctant to disclose information, but this is against the trend of democracy. Controlled and tamed people cannot produce culture and art.'[12] Indeed, widespread doubts about privacy protection are closely linked in the media with the government's poor record on information disclosure. Officials are frequently criticized for not accepting the principle that all information held by the government is the property of the people who have paid for it through their taxes and who should therefore, except in exceptional circumstances, have unhindered access to it. However, others point to the natural lag between new policies being introduced and shifts in official attitudes; it will take time for the potential of information disclosure to blossom. Similar legislation in

(Roger Dahl)

the USA also offered initially disappointing results, but has since evolved into a powerful weapon to ensure transparency and promote accountability.

The furor surrounding the introduction of Juki Net, like the Defense Agency scandal, has revealed a surprisingly feisty civil society beneath the conformist surface. The large-scale boycott, massive withdrawals from the system and the ensuing public debate about the government's role in information management reveals a changing nation where people are increasingly prepared to question and challenge the government. This is all part of Japan's quiet transformation, and jars disconcertingly with prevailing images in the overseas media of a nation of stolidly conformist citizens uniformly bowing to commands from above. For all its advantages to the bureaucracy, Juki Net has aroused a healthy skepticism about the actions and motives of government. In this sense it will stoke support for transparency and accountability if only to reassure people that Big Brother is kept on a short leash.

Wiretapping

In 1999, the same year that the information disclosure law was passed, the government approved wiretapping for use in investigations of organized crime beginning in 2000. At the same session, the Diet approved the allocation of identification numbers to citizens in conjunction with Juki Net. The wiretapping is confined to investigations into organized crime cases involving drugs, guns, premeditated murder and people-smuggling. The legislation also includes stiffer penalties for money laundering. Advocates claim that these measures will bolster efforts to curb organized crime and cooperate with other countries. Critics link the eavesdropping law with the Juki Net, arguing that the power of the government to invade the privacy of individuals is increasing, especially in the absence of adequate safeguards. These concerns have been heightened by recent police scandals, including mob ties and corruption, that have eroded public trust in law-enforcement authorities. It is also a matter for concern that the new law permits the tapping of media communications, potentially interfering with press freedoms and discouraging informants. While surveys suggest that the Japanese public is almost evenly divided over the issue, information about the actual use of these powers is not in the public domain.

Overseas experience is far from reassuring. The Japanese media has reported the fact that, of the 12 million cases of wiretapping recorded in the USA between 1985 and 1995, most had nothing to do with crime.[13] In 1995 alone, 2 million conversations unrelated to crime were monitored in the USA, raising questions of how carefully such powers are policed. It is telling that between 1991 and 2000, reportedly only one wiretapping warrant request in the USA was turned down, indicating that judges are inclined to give law enforcement authorities the benefit of the doubt. This phenomenon raises serious questions about the efficacy of checks on surveillance powers incorporated into the legislation. In light of the Defense Agency scandal, the new wiretapping powers raise the basic issue of civil liberties and how to balance the government's duty to protect the public against intrusions on the privacy and rights of those it is protecting.

Conclusion

Information disclosure is changing the way governments and officials conduct their business. Open government is viewed as intrinsic to democratic governance. Citizens are propelling Japan's quiet transformation by exercising their new power to monitor government officials and hold them accountable. This surprisingly successful experience has fundamentally changed citizens' assumptions about the nature of political power and raised their expectations, forcing bureaucrats and politicians to scramble to keep pace. Bureaucratic foot-dragging and stonewalling have served only to galvanize public support for more transparency, cheered on by a generally supportive media. In order to win votes and address the concerns of their constituents, politicians have jumped on board the disclosure bandwagon, lending power and legitimacy to the popular quest for enhanced oversight of government activities. One unanticipated development in this story is the support shown for disclosure by some of the courts and their emergence as administrative overseers in a manner that has eroded the bureaucracy's power, autonomy, and practice of self-oversight. In this sense the 1990s was a lost decade for the bureaucracy, as the emergence of a more vibrant civil society has been achieved at the expense of its cherished prerogatives. This quiet transformation is proceeding case by case, incrementally and cumulatively as citizens learn how to use their new-found powers and wield them more effectively. This process is gradually leading to more informed and responsible citizen participation in the affairs of government and society.

A review of the national freedom of information law is slated for 2005, providing an opportunity to fine-tune the law in the light of experience.

Clearly, transparency advocates have their sights on narrowing the rather broad exemptions to disclosure in the current law. There is considerable curiosity about the workings of the public corporations and other bodies that spend public money and make policies that impact on society. As the doors to information disclosure creak open, and as the habits and assumptions of disclosure become ingrained, it will become harder to justify such broad exemptions.

The success of information disclosure in Japan depends on a number of interrelated factors. Clearly, there have to be individuals and organizations willing to submit requests and deal with the time- and energy-consuming obstacles to accessing government information. It is also crucial that there are organizations enjoying a degree of autonomy insulating them from government pressures that know how to effectively use requested information to exercise oversight and participate in policymaking. Voters also need to elect politicians who will support disclosure. Intervention by politicians has proved decisive in many cases, for better and worse, highlighting the importance of electing political leaders who will establish and interpret rules favorable to transparency. Since the Diet will in coming years play a key role in determining the extent and evolution of information disclosure, representatives' stance on the issue will be a decisive factor. In addition, proposed judicial reforms that would reduce the influence of the government in the training of judges, and shift promotion decisions out of the Supreme Court, offer the opportunity to build a more independent judiciary. Thus, the future of information disclosure will be determined by media support, the strength and autonomy of NPOs, elected officials, and implementation of judicial reform. The trend towards improved information disclosure is vulnerable and can be derailed precisely because the institutional support for transparency remains weak while the vested interests opposed to open government remain powerful.

Although the new legislation grew out of the perceived need for greater public participation in government policymaking and exercising oversight, the most frequent requestors have been the media and commercial firms. It is taking time for people to learn to take advantage of their new rights and become more active participants in the democratic process. The Defense Agency's surveillance activities sent a chilling message to potential requestors and will make many people think twice about whether they wish to risk the overzealous actions of rogue bureaucrats. However, based on this author's experience at the Ministry of Health and Welfare in 2002, where I was seeking information on the infamous HIV-hemophiliacs' case, it can be an innocuous and surprisingly easy process. Even as a foreigner I was not asked for any personal information and was not required to submit anything in writing; I was shown a computer terminal and was assisted in calling up even the most sensitive documents from the ministry's 'missing' files on the case. These were the controversial files released in 1996 by then minister Kan Naoto (discussed in Chapter 6) that revealed how officials had systematically lied to the victims to avoid divulging evidence of their own liability. Now any citizen (or foreigner!) in Japan can access these files with keyword searches and print them out at nominal cost. For difficult requests, there are information disclosure specialists assigned in each section of the Ministry who are trained to assist in searches. Whether this is now standard practice throughout the bureaucracy is uncertain but, only one year after the legislation came into effect, it is an encouraging sign. It is worth recalling that, for many years in the USA, the Freedom of Information Act was considered ineffective and it was only after the Nixon Administration had demonstrated the perils of lax oversight that Congress amended the legislation and created a tool that has become increasingly effective over time. The quiet transformation will take time, but important weapons are at hand and momentum is building.

Certainly the public's expectations for information disclosure are high, fanned by bureaucratic scandals and cover-ups. If the litigants in the HIV-hemophiliac case had had recourse to such legislation in their battles with the MHW, their tragic search for justice would not have taken so long. Moreover, if the officials in the blood products division had known that their actions would be subject to public oversight, they might well have placed the interests of patients before those of the pharmaceutical companies. After all, bureaucrats are unlikely to engage in actions that run the risk of public humiliation and possible prosecution.

The kinks in the system are being worked out and bureaucrats are grudgingly getting used to sharing information. The courts have sent mixed but surprisingly encouraging signals about their support for transparency, while party competition for votes is creating a favorable environment for more citizen oversight and greater transparency. Meanwhile, NPOs, citizens, the media, and business all have far more access to public information than ever before and are constantly 'pushing the envelope.' The media is playing a critical role by making the information widely accessible and benefiting from the public's growing appetite for transparency as a threshold requirement for democracy. Officials now feel obliged – if only to cover their backs – to involve a wider range of people and interests in their deliberations and thus government is becoming more inclusive and subject to increasing scrutiny. The process of setting agendas and making policies must now pass more intrusive public inspection and, as a result, outcomes are being influenced by a broader range of opinions and interests than in the past.

A weary and wary public has come to know the value of oversight in curbing waste and corruption. This has whetted their appetite for better and more extensive access. One of a cluster of reforms aimed at promoting transparency and citizen participation in government affairs, freedom of information is being implemented in a social and political context far more favorable than could have been imagined in the late 1980s. Just as the Watergate scandal gave impetus to political reform in the USA after 1974, the fading legitimacy of government in the scandal-plagued 1990s and beyond is boosting support for information disclosure in Japan. Justifiably suspicious of politicians and bureaucrats, citizens are coming to understand the benefits of setting the political agenda, establishing priorities, and shaping a society based on popular sovereignty. The evident benefits of open government and democracy, and the high costs of the alternative, suggest that time is ripening the situation for even greater transparency and a more robust civil society. This process, however, will unfold over a matter of decades rather than years – precisely because those who have so much to lose are still in a strong position to hamper these developments.

3 Building civil society
NPOs and judicial reform

Historically, the Japanese legal system has largely been an instrument of the government to govern citizens.

Miyazawa Setsuo (2001: 32)

... the NPO Law is in itself an important legislative change in state–civil society relations, and that law is part of a broader series of changes rippling through Japanese politics.

Robert Pekkanen (2000: 113)

... the legal profession has played a leading role in many dimensions of the human rights movement acting as advocates for a view of law as a device to regulate state power as opposed to being an instrument at the state's disposal.

Ian Neary (2002: 265)

There is a disconcerting disconnect between the rapidly changing and relatively dynamic Japan I see around me and the 'incredible shrinking' Japan portrayed by the mass media.[1] The chimera of Pax Nipponica and Japan as Number 1 cultivated overseas during the booming days of the 1980s has given way to a more dismissive and denigrating tone in the 1990s. While a more critical analysis of Japan was overdue, in some important ways it is being overstated. At the advent of the twenty-first century, the question of Japan's future is an important one and the answers given will vary greatly depending on one's focus and assumptions. This chapter is an attempt to restore some balance to the debate. I do not argue that Japan's immense economic problems and apparent policy inertia are unimportant, but that the popular obsession with the looming train wreck has obscured significant alterations in the political, administrative, judicial, institutional, and economic landscape. I argue that the growth of NPOs, greater transparency in government, and ongoing judicial reforms reflect a surprising vibrancy in civil society that carries the potential for further significant change in coming decades.

Stagnant images of Japan prevail in the international media. Japan's descent into the economic abyss, policy paralysis, dysfunctional politics, and bureaucratic inertia are all part of the media's focus on the Lost Decade of the 1990s. While these are all important aspects of the nation's decade-long economic implosion and deserve careful analysis, in focusing on such stories there is a risk of missing some of the important developments both in the 1990s and since then that reveal another Japan. Rather than a Lost Decade, the 1990s can be seen as a time of dynamic transformation and reform. The economic crisis that undermined and discredited the postwar system has sent ripples of change throughout society and has spurred a vigorous debate about the need for reform. The 1990s was a decade of intense questioning about the merits and flaws of Japan's government, business practices and principles. It is a time when growing numbers of people realize that the system has soured and is no longer up to the challenges of the twenty-first century. As elsewhere, change is embraced reluctantly and with a degree of resignation by those who are comfortable with, or benefit from, the status quo. But, change is in the air and the building blocks of transformation are being laid with astonishing speed.

It is too soon to appreciate the implications of all the changes that are being implemented and to understand their cumulative impact. Japan is a society in tumult, a society that knows it has gone terribly wrong and is groping for new solutions and paradigms. Unlike the two previous epochs of upheaval and reform – the Meiji Restoration and the American Occupation following World War II – policy reforms are not merely being imposed from above.[2] The trauma of the 1990s has spurred vigorous public debate about what ails society and what can be done to turn things around. Japan has become a hothouse for experimentation and tinkering. The sense of impending national doom has provided unprecedented opportunities for broader public input on setting the agenda of change and policy reforms. The implications of Japan's massive problems are not lost on its people and they are playing a more influential role in recasting society than in the previous two periods of transformation.

Amidst the upheaval of contemporary Japan, the ruling elite in government and business have lost their way. Mounting pressures for change and the failure of traditional remedies have opened up divisions among Japan's leadership and made them receptive to new ideas. There is a not-so-quiet desperation in the air and, while the impetus for reform has built up over recent decades, the time has never been so ripe for change. Groping in the dark, the architects of contemporary Japan are promoting solutions that would have been anathema before the Lost Decade. What until recently were radical critiques and revolutionary proposals for change have now become common sense. A sense of how far Japan has come in just the last five years of the twentieth century is reflected in the reception of Gavan McCormack's excellent analysis of Japan's contemporary problems, *The Emptiness of Japanese Affluence* (1996). While his critical views trampled over still-cherished myths and taboos, by the time the book was reissued in 2001 the core of his arguments had become almost mainstream.[3] Improbably and swiftly, important elements in the establishment have come to echo his once radical views. Naturally, others have circled the wagons, determined to protect their vested interests against the wave of reforms, ensuring that the process of change will be fraught with conflict, setbacks and fitful progress. This kind of friction and debate is intrinsic to civil society and certainly does not indicate that reform is doomed.

The credibility of Japan's bureaucratically orchestrated, corporate-centered society has been shattered by economic crisis. These problems are generating new opportunities and responses. In the 1990s, Japan has put in place a number of key building blocks for cultivating a more vibrant civil society. These initiatives are changing practices, attitudes, and patterns of interaction, undermining the edifice of Japan, Inc., and altering how citizens view the state and their role in the polity. The emergence of NPOs, the growing transparency of government resulting from information disclosure legislation, and judicial reform are three key developments that are shaping the emergence of civil society in Japan. They are mutually reinforcing and sending out ripples of change throughout the archipelago. The Lost Decade has been a decade of reforms; a time when change is happening and is being anticipated. While the status quo is still a formidable edifice, its foundations are eroding as the currents of reform swirl all around it.

Nonprofit organizations

The passage of the NPO law in 1998 was one of the most promising developments in efforts to build civil society in Japan during the Lost Decade. It reflects the struggle by citizens' groups to reform Japanese society and provide a channel for more effective citizen participation in setting the nation's agenda and implementing it.[4] The success of the legislation should be seen against the backdrop of the struggle of ordinary Japanese to contribute to society, fight injustice, and promote change throughout the postwar era, always in the face of resistance from the ruling elite. The NPO law is the fruit of their sacrifices and struggles to make civil society a reality. In conjunction with expanded information disclosure and judicial reform, the growth of NPOs is diluting the concentration of power that has stifled Japan and its people.

Impetus for the NPO law

In the 1990s, widespread popular perception of the government's failure to meet the challenges facing Japan meant that the time was ripe for change. The disastrous mismanagement of the economy, a series of high-profile bureaucratic and political corruption scandals, and bungled efforts to cope with the Kobe earthquake in 1995 all exposed the failings of the government. The army of volunteers that descended on quake-devastated Kobe from all corners of Japan demonstrated how much citizens can contribute if permitted to do so. Nowhere were the bureaucrats more compellingly revealed as 'part of the problem' than in Kobe, where officials were paralyzed by their own red tape. It was a sad commentary on the government's effectiveness that it was the *yakuza* who established the first food kitchens while the SDF remained in their barracks, waiting for a summons. This came belatedly from a government singularly unprepared for the one natural disaster all Japanese are taught to expect and prepare for. The aftershocks of Kobe were felt throughout the polity, weakening the foundations of the bureaucracy and shaking people's confidence in those who govern.[5]

The background to the NPO law (or more correctly, the Special Nonprofit Activities Law) has been described in detail by Pekkanen (2000). Aside from the impetus provided by the popular response to the Kobe earthquake, the legislation made political sense in the context of waning support for the LDP and the need to satisfy coalition parties. As has happened frequently in the past, the LDP co-opted an opposition issue that might prove threatening at the polls and used it to broaden its own base of political support. By making it happen, the LDP could claim the political glory even if the impetus for the new law came from sectors of society that viewed the LDP as a major obstacle to reform. The breadth of support for the NPO legislation was reflected in the fact that five political parties produced their own draft legislation. It is symbolically significant that this law was not drafted by bureaucrats, as is usually the case with legislation, and thus came closer to reflecting the views of citizen advocates.

The new legislation was aimed at simplifying the paperwork involved in applying for legal recognition for nonprofit organizations. Previously, Japan boasted one of the most difficult regulatory environments for NPOs, involving strong bureaucratic screening, supervisory, and sanction powers. Japanese law required that such organizations obtain the explicit permission of the competent bureaucratic authority, meaning that applicants had to meet criteria and accept continual monitoring from government officials, undermining their independence and making them vulnerable to pressure. Under these conditions it was not surprising that NPOs were somewhat muted voices in society and, in the absence of official recognition as legal entities (*koeki hojin* – literally, 'public interest legal persons'), suffered both stigma and inconvenience. Lacking such status meant that mundane matters such as signing a lease or obtaining a phone number required individuals in the organization to assume full responsibility. Tax benefits were very limited compared to other industrialized nations, while the large amounts of capital required to incorporate created an extraordinarily high barrier to entry. Onerous reporting requirements and bureaucratic interference discouraged many NPOs from seeking official recognition.

This unfriendly legal landscape prompted advocates to lobby for the new legislation, arguing that the potential of these groups to revitalize society was being squandered. In the 1990s, desperate for new solutions to mounting problems and driven by effective lobbying by citizen groups, the governing elite decided to give NPOs a longer leash. The media played a crucial role in pressuring the government to act and ensuring that the debacle surrounding the Kobe earthquake was not forgotten. This raised the political stakes involved in both supporting and being seen to oppose the legislation: a reluctant bureaucracy was forced to soft-pedal its efforts to thwart the granting of real autonomy to NPOs. For politicians there was little incentive to back the bureaucrats and antagonize an aroused public. However, efforts to liberalize tax benefits came under the purview of the Ministry of Finance, which wields considerable clout among legislators owing to its control over the budget.

The tide began to turn when the forces of the Japanese establishment indicated their support for change. Keidanren, Japan's conservative business association, emerged as a forceful and influential advocate for far more progressive legislation than the LDP initially favored. The Keidanren's Social Contribution Group had played a key role in coordinating the Kobe earthquake relief efforts and thus had first-hand experience and expertise in mobilizing the potential of NPOs. In addition, member companies with overseas operations had learned the benefits of cultivating good corporate citizenship and had seen the positive impact of NPO participation on their employees and local communities. Given the importance of Keidanren to the LDP, not least because of campaign contributions, its views could not be ignored.

The coalition of conservative forces rallying on behalf of a relatively progressive NPO law included the *Nikkei*, Japan's leading newspaper with extensive influence in the corridors of power. Between 1995 and 1997 Japan's counterpart of the *Wall Street Journal* ran a series of articles asserting that opposing enabling legislation for NPOs would run counter to administrative reform efforts. The *Nikkei* was an outspoken advocate of administrative reform to streamline government and make it more cost-effective. For the *Nikkei*, the NPOs were part of a larger trend towards smaller government and a political environment where individuals would take greater responsibility in areas where the government's role would be reduced or eliminated. By invoking these New Right policies, the newspaper created a climate where the NPO law became a litmus test of the LDP's commitment to reform at a time when openly opposing reform was politically hazardous. Other national newspapers such as the more progressive *Asahi* emphasized the role of NPOs in empowering citizens and strengthening democracy. The progressive media thus stressed the benefits to society from a strong NPO movement free from bureaucratic interference. In addition to widespread pressure from politicians of all stripes keen to air their new-found reform credentials, the LDP faced well-orchestrated lobbying by citizen groups whose grassroots ties and media connections enabled them to pressure the party to adopt a more progressive law than anyone had anticipated.

In its eventual support for the legislation, the LDP was also motivated by more pragmatic reasons. The NPO Law must be viewed in the larger context of integrated policy reforms in the area of social services. The rapid graying of Japan's population and its fiscal implications in terms of healthcare costs and pensions has had an enormous impact throughout the policy process. Here, NPOs are seen as a significant source for mobilizing relatively cheap volunteer participation in providing care services for the elderly. The government regards this public-interest role as crucial in preparing for the social and economic challenges Japan will face in the twenty-first century.

Despite the constellation of both conservative and progressive forces endorsing NPOs, legislative wrangling and a foot-dragging bureaucracy delayed passage of the legislation until the end of 1998. The enabling legislation was a rare Diet member's bill and, although it reflected the concerns of citizens' advocates in general terms, it failed to grant the tax advantages enjoyed by NPOs in other OECD nations. In short, although the new law made it far easier for NPOs to get the legal status crucial to operate in Japan, it did little to improve their financial prospects. The new law was also designed to limit bureaucratic screening of applicants and placed strict limits on administrative oversight. These fairly significant changes were amended in 2000 to permit tax benefits for donors and lower tax rates on NPO operations.

Perhaps the most significant benefit of the NPO law has been the conferring of legal status on organizations that seek it. However, many NPOs and NGOs have not sought to gain official recognition due to a reluctance to submit to government oversight and the burden of meeting established criteria. Ironically, in view of what the legislation set out to achieve, they have criticized the legislative reforms for conferring monitoring powers on the government that might allow it to tame activist organizations. However, for the nearly 16,000 NPOs that have received recognition as of 2003, official status confers major advantages and removes impediments to their operations in Japan.

Unfulfilled expectations

Will the NPO law have a positive impact on the development of civil society? Much depends on how the law is implemented and revised in coming years. The response of the NPO community has been ambivalent, with many seeking legal status while criticizing aspects of the law and its implementation. Much dissatisfaction focuses on the degree of autonomy conferred by the legislation. Although 16,000 NPOs had received recognition as of early 2004, there is still considerable scope for expansion given the estimated 80,000 volunteer groups in Japan. Screening and guidance are still exercised by bureaucrats, and access to policymaking bodies is vetted by officials who are also in a position to select which NPOs receive government funding. NPOs need a steady, reliable source of funds to exercise the autonomy they need to have a significant impact on policymaking and to monitor policy outcomes. However, reliance on government funding undermines this autonomy and raises concerns that the government aims to co-opt NPOs to carry out its agenda and thus divert rather than respond to the concerns of citizens, and the desire for their greater participation.[6] In addition, restrictions on use of government funds make it difficult for cash-starved NPOs to cover everyday operating expenses, and alternative funding is hard to come by in a nation with an underdeveloped foundation sector and low priority for substantial grants from overseas.

The tax exemption provisions highlight the problems of implementation.[7] Although the original NPO law did not include tax exemptions, these were approved by the Diet in 2000. However, between 2000 and mid-2002, only five NPOs were awarded the tax exemption status. The exemptions allow companies to treat as expenses NPO donations of up to 2.5 percent of their revenues, while individuals can deduct up to 12.5 percent of their income as donations. NPOs are also granted slightly reduced corporate tax rates. It is problematic that the National Tax Agency plays the gate-keeping role for determining tax exemption status since it takes a dim view of exemptions. Instead of making conferral of NPO status the sole grounds for tax advantages, as advocates suggested, the government retains significant power to interfere in the business of NPOs, limit their autonomy, screen applications, and monitor their finances. This is exactly the situation proponents lobbied against and remains the target of complaints.

It is also problematic that many would-be volunteers do not enjoy a supportive work environment that would allow them scope for their activities. Whereas community service is often encouraged by larger companies in OECD nations, this remains rare in Japan where a survey conducted by the Ministry of Labor in 1997 found that only 2 percent of firms permitted time off for volunteer activities. As Matsubara Akira of the nonprofit Coalition for Legislation to Support Citizens' Organizations, known as Cs, remarked: 'US companies tend to encourage their workers to volunteer, but Japanese employers don't and that makes a big difference.'[8] Indeed, corporate philanthropy has yet to blossom in Japan – only about one-third of Keidanren's membership has enrolled in the One Percent Club, an arm of the business association aimed at encouraging charitable donations and good corporate citizenship.[9] Again, while it is too soon to draw conclusions about likely developments in this area, at least there has been a start. There is growing interest in volunteer activities, and media support may again prove crucial in encouraging expanded corporate sponsorship and more flexible work policies. There are popular internet job sites for *borabaito* (volunteer work) run by NHK (Japan Broadcasting Corporation) and Sanka Network, among others, that are geared towards young workers looking for jobs in NPOs, community service or caring for those with disabilities.

More significantly, the Ministry of Education, Sports, Science, Technology, and Culture (Monkasho) is recommending curriculum reforms that would make voluntary activities mandatory for high-school students.[10] While Monkasho's proposals for compulsory volunteerism may seem a contradiction in terms, like it or not, young Japanese will gain experience as volunteers and many may come to see such activities as normal. The planned reforms will be a powerful vehicle for channeling the good intentions of young people and preparing a new generation of Japanese who understand the importance of such participation and will lobby employers and the government accordingly. The rising demand for social services in an aging society and increasing pressure for environmental restoration are two important areas where student volunteers can make a contribution. To the extent that they feel what they are doing is worthwhile, they will carry into their adult lives a perception about volunteerism that most Japanese adults today have never had. This augurs a revival of a community spirit that many observers have written off as a casualty of modernization. In stimulating volunteerism and the institutions that support it the government is meeting some pressing social needs and filling a void. In so doing, it is adding to Japan's social capital and nurturing citizen participation in civil society.

While the volunteer movement in Japan may not have reached the levels seen in some other countries, it has nonetheless grown significantly in recent years. The Economic Planning Agency (EPA) estimates that in 2000 as many as one in three Japanese were engaged at some level in volunteer work or community service, up from about 10 percent in 1983. The Japanese Council of Social Welfare estimates that by the end of the twentieth century nearly 7 million Japanese were engaged in some form of volunteer work, with homemakers accounting for 42 percent of this number and retirees an additional 16 percent. Although this participation rate is lower than in the UK and USA, it is on a par with France and the Netherlands. The EPA's recent white papers stress the growing importance of NPOs and volunteerism as ways of enhancing social services and lifestyles, and encourage firms to introduce leave systems to enable employees to participate more fully in such activities. In sentiments echoed by Keidanren, the EPA argues that, as a human resource development policy, volunteerism will expose workers to a range of experiences that will help them contribute to their companies. Its survey from 2000 indicates that 20 percent of firms have already introduced such policies. (While this figure is ten times higher than the 1997 Ministry of Labor survey noted above, the sample differs and one should not read too much into this apparent surge.) This reported increase in flexible corporate policies aimed at facilitating volunteer activities by employees is consistent with the overall boom in volunteerism depicted by the media in turn-of-the-century Japan.[11]

A number of commentators have expressed optimism about the implications of the NPO law. As Pekkanen concludes, in his discussion of the law:

> First, it is in itself an important reworking of relations between the state and civil society. The long-term implications will be crucial for Japan. Second, the process itself will lead to further changes in Japanese politics. Three parts of the process could erode central bureaucratic decision-making: successful lobbying of citizen groups, the legislative experience of local governments, and Diet member bills. Third, the making of the law offers a revealing glimpse of the altered political landscape of post-1993 Japan. Much has been discussed about how Japan will change, but in the

case of the NPO Law we can see specifically a legislative difference – in result and process.

(Pekkanen 2000: 143)

As Yamamoto Tadashi, a prominent member of several official foundations and government advisory committees, commented to the *Japan Times* (September 28, 2000) the new law reflects 'a growing movement in Japan to reduce the influence of government bureaucrats and have citizens take the public interest into their own hands.'

However, the experience of NPOs since 1998 suggests caution about any millenarian expectations aroused by jumping the first legislative hurdle. The new law has satisfied few of those affected by it and there have been mixed reactions to the potential of NPOs as agents of social change and participants in policymaking and monitoring outcomes. Some have already been severely disappointed. A graduate student conducting research as a participant-observer in a Tokyo-based NPO told me in 2002 that 'Japanese NPOs are hopeless' and went on to lament the parochial vision of fellow volunteers and detail their failings. His comments were in marked contrast to his enthusiasm nine months earlier when he had praised the potential of NGOs to transform Japan and build civil society. By contrast, another former student, working as an executive director at a leading NPO in 2003, is far more enthusiastic and optimistic: while admitting it has been very grueling she also felt great satisfaction in looking back at the dramatic results achieved in a relatively short time. She could see that her efforts had made a significant difference in improving conditions for NPO activities, the avowed aim of her organization. By lobbying legislators, running symposia, educating people, training volunteers, publishing newsletters, raising funds, recruiting members, and cultivating the media, her NPO had participated in promoting the NPO legislation, advocating crucial revisions, and altering both the rules of the game and the playing field. Her organization nurtured and channeled citizen participation and social activism, carving out an autonomous role and contributing to Japan's quiet transformation. While the graduate student seemed to judge the NPO movement by external criteria and could not see beyond the day-to-day disappointments, the veteran NPO activist expressed more tempered expectations and accepted the challenges and frustrations of nurturing civil society. His experience underscores the reality that there is a wide variety of NPOs, ranging from those that are dynamic and effective to those that are not; hers the pay-off in hanging in there to see the fruits of one's toil. Clearly, some NPOs are able to find space for their activism free from government control. Frustrated activists may well become more alienated, but those that do see they have made a difference are likely to become more enthusiastic advocates of greater civic participation. The lessons of their divergent experiences suggest that strengthening NPOs is a crucial and a long-term process.

Multitasking

Perhaps it is not surprising that NPOs have failed to live up to expectations when so much is expected of them by a diverse array of interest groups. NPOs are expected to serve as a channel for volunteerism; run hotlines and domestic abuse shelters; promote small government, local autonomy, and administrative reform; facilitate deregulation; provide expanded social services for the disabled, children and the elderly; develop environmentally sound policies; engage in oversight of government; expand information disclosure; and participate in educational activities, consumer protection, and civil society – and do all of this cheaply and efficiently. In short, NPOs have become a 'garbage can' where a large assortment of ambitious hopes, expectations, and policy initiatives have all been dumped together.

Although NPO activists assert that they could achieve much more in a more favorable regulatory environment, it is doubtful that NPOs could meet all the demands and expectations heaped upon them even if conditions were as favorable as in the NPO-friendly Netherlands. It is this very enthusiasm for their role that suggests that NPOs have found their niche and will eventually succeed in carving out a more favorable environment in which to encourage the growth of civil society and promote self-responsibility. This will take time, however, and early disappointments should not obscure their substantial potential. As everywhere else in the world, NPOs have developed with difficulty and face a variety of obstacles that divert energy from their work. In addition, most NPOs are small and understaffed; around 70 percent have budgets of less than ¥50 million (US$400,000) and of this number half operate on less than US$40,000. Limited resources often translate into limited impact while intrusive screening, regulations, and supervision involve much time-consuming paperwork. NPOs suffer from trying to meet overly optimistic expectations and success is a long haul marked by incremental progress, setbacks, and compromises rather than a smooth upward trajectory. Solutions to their problems will depend on the right confluence of political forces.

What is expected of NPOs in the new millennium? With nearly 4 million Japanese out of work and unemployment edging towards 6 percent of the workforce, NPOs have suddenly found themselves designated 'job-generators.' Trade unions, political parties, business organizations, pundits, study groups, and government bureaucrats all view NPOs as an employment panacea, serving as a dynamic force in the economy and offering significant job opportunities, especially for the retired, restructured, women, and young job-seekers. Comparing conditions in Japan to the USA, where millions of workers are employed at NPOs, it is understandable that economic circumstances have placed a greater premium on the potential economic contributions of NPOs. However, it does not seem that equal attention has been focused on the conditions that have made this situation possible in the USA, nor an appreciation for the length of time it has taken to spawn the vast not-for-profit sector there.

US model

In the USA, the relationships formed between the government and NPOs are extensive. There is a remarkable degree of reliance by the government on NPOs in the areas of health, education, and welfare services, and independent think tanks play an important role in shaping government policies. While there is always potential for adversarial relations to develop, the dominant model is based on partnership; similar cooperative relationships are evident in the EU.

While the US situation is scarcely comparable to Japan given their vastly different historical experiences and context, the US case is often presented as a model for Japanese NPOs and is worth a brief discussion. In the USA there are 1.4 million tax-exempt NPOs registered with the Internal Revenue Service (IRS) and an additional 350,000 tax-exempt religious organizations that are not required to register. These NPOs run 51 percent of all hospitals, 46 percent of all colleges and universities, 87 percent of all libraries, 86 percent of all museums, 90 percent of all orchestral, dance, and art organizations, and 58 percent of all social service providers.[12] Donations to support this vast network of NPOs exceeded $200 billion in 2002, 83 percent of which came from individuals, 12 percent from foundations, and 5 percent from corporations – a pattern that has persisted since data were first collected in 1964. However, donations account for only 20 percent of the income of nonprofit organizations in the USA. An additional 31 percent comes from government grants and contracts, while 49 percent is generated from dues, fees, investments, and other earned income.

In a speech given in Tokyo at the Symposium on State–NGO Relations in Japan, the USA, and Europe (May 27, 2002), the Asia Foundation's Barnett Baron drew some important links with the US experience. Drawing on the US model, he called for the development of a stronger partnership between the government and Japanese NPOs. Baron points out that in the USA the boom of NPOs in the 1960s and 1970s grew out of the 'Great Society' vision of President Lyndon Johnson and the consequent expansion of programs of poverty alleviation and social services. By channeling funding through NPOs and community-based organizations the government supported their growth and benefited from their participation. Thus, the growth of NPOs did not result from a surge of volunteerism or charity, but rather from supportive government policies.

The US comparison suggests that the state has a key role to play in Japan to expand civil society by fostering a healthier NGO sector. Baron identified seven key areas where the government can improve its contribution to NPOs. First, the government could make it easier for NPOs to incorporate and gain official recognition, and also reduce the scope of bureaucratic discretion in the granting of NPO status. Second, the state should demonstrate that it trusts NPOs by simplifying complex laws affecting them, and reducing the level of administrative oversight. Third, it should foster self-governance by reducing government supervision and encouraging the autonomy of NPO boards of directors in overseeing their own operations. Fourth, there is a need to simplify and clarify government procurement policies and encourage NPOs to compete for government grants and contracts for the provision of social services, including payment for staff salaries and administrative costs. Fifth, tax codes should be simplified to make it easier and more worthwhile for individuals to make contributions to NPOs. Sixth, the government should enhance public appreciation of the role of NPOs in civil society by introducing relevant subject matter into the elementary- and middle-school curriculum. Finally, the government should encourage professionalization by financially supporting more university-based programs that offer courses and fieldwork research opportunities related to NPOs, and so make this an attractive career choice for young people. Unfortunately, Japan has so far made little progress in implementing Baron's action plan.

Government partners or subcontractors?

While the government wants NPOs to play a larger role in society, it is not clear that it knows how to achieve this goal. Prime Minister Koizumi, in his first major policy speech in May 2001, expressed his desire to create a society that provides more channels for popular participation in politics and other areas traditionally dominated by government. In order to support the social welfare system, he said, 'I intend to reach out widely to local community residents, volunteers, and nonprofit organizations (NPOs) to create a society sustained through mutual assistance in taking care of the sick, elderly, and children.' At a town hall meeting on July 20, 2002, Foreign Minister Kawaguchi Yoriko called for a stronger partnership with NPOs, making this a key to ongoing efforts to promote ODA (Official Development Assistance) reform. She expressed a clear commitment to involving NPOs in ODA policymaking and implementation, arguing that this would make development efforts more effective and in tune with local needs. Shortly before this meeting, her ministry had pledged significant funding for Japan NPO Platform, an umbrella organization of NPOs with an international orientation. Clearly, in getting its troubled house in order, the scandal-plagued Foreign Ministry sees NPOs as an important vehicle for restoring its credibility, winning back public trust, and instituting overdue reforms in the dispersal of economic assistance.

Such pragmatic pretexts for reform are being taken up throughout the government. From the bureaucrat's point of view, the most logical reason to sponsor NPOs is to ensure a larger budget, or at least to stem budget cuts in an era when the government is strapped for cash. NPOs are about marking out turf, about popular justification for budget allocations and ministries are waking up to the possibilities inherent in closer links. Many ministries sponsor *shingikai* (advisory councils) that focus on the role of NPOs in preparation for the creation of more extensive ties. Given the battering that the bureaucratic image has taken over recent years – as a result of bungling the banking crisis, earthquake relief, HIV infections of hemophiliacs, mad cow disease, and pilfering taxpayers' money – winning back the public trust is a priority. Working with NPOs and accommodating demands for greater transparency and more involvement by people in policies affecting their lives are the radical measures needed to restore the government's shattered credibility.

NPOs are also expected to serve the cause of administrative reform by providing services more efficiently and cheaply than the government could and replacing the 'nanny state' with self-responsibility. As Andrew Horvat, Director of the Asia Foundation's Japan office argued: 'Japan's fiscal situation is so bad that getting NPOs to do the work of government is now a legitimate way to think. Fostering nonprofits is a lot cheaper than raising taxes and hiring government officials who are likely to be far less efficient' (quoted in *Japan Times* September 28, 2000). The government expects NPOs to step in and provide a range of social services, from drug rehabilitation to childcare and elderly care. There are some services that private business will not find attractive and some specialized programs that seem well suited to NPO initiatives. However, regulations continue to hamper entry into various social services. For example, childcare facilities are heavily regulated and impose strict licensing requirements to guarantee safety and professionalism. Given unfilled demand in major urban areas, this might be a promising area for NPO expansion. However, running a daycare center under existing regulations is too expensive without government subsidies and there is considerable resistance to a relaxation of standards.

Of course, it is this very notion of NPOs as cheap outsourcing for government services that is decried by advocates. It reflects a mindset among officials that undermines the development of NPOs as a professionalized force in society to be taken seriously and valued for its special contributions and potential. For NPOs to flourish in Japan they need to attract financial resources, develop international networks, and recruit and retain skilled professionals. Educating citizens, participating in policymaking, and monitoring policy outcomes – essential roles for building civil society – become especially difficult projects in an environment where NPOs are chiefly valued for their ability to carry out tasks set by the government as costcutting measures.

Along with the information disclosure legislation discussed in the previous chapter, the NPO law marks a turning point in relations between the state and citizens and provides a platform for citizens to have their say on the critical issues facing society in the twenty-first century. In addition, NPOs can exercise oversight on the conduct of government agencies, provide input on policymaking and monitor policy outcomes. Citizen advocates of NPOs see these organizations as supplementing government efforts and filling in where the government has come up short or has not delivered at all. These advocates also desire a role for NPOs in setting the agenda of government and influencing the policymaking process. NPOs are seen as active instruments, participating in, shaping, and carrying out crucial activities.

The government's perspective is rather different. While officials who support the proliferation of NGOs do so for a range of reasons, many regard them as subcontractors, convenient organizations that will carry out assigned tasks on small budgets. The beauty of NPOs for officialdom is that the costs are relatively cheap, responsibility can be shifted onto others, and unattractive tasks can be outsourced. Government officials evince less enthusiasm for the roles that NPOs most covet: setting the agenda and shaping policies.

As a result of these divergent aims and interests, the relationship between NPOs and government in Japan is based on mutual suspicion. NPOs see the government as an adversary unwilling to empower them to play the role they believe they are capable of – builders of civil society. The NPO law has placed restraints on NPOs, retaining monitoring and oversight rights for relevant government agencies while ensuring that the NPOs will have considerable difficulty in achieving financial independence. The law seems designed to prevent NPOs from becoming autonomous actors and evolving as threats to the power and prerogatives of the government. By keeping NGOs on a short leash, officials hope to have the best of both worlds – submissive, dependent organizations that will do the government's bidding while cultivating the image of a vibrant civil society minus the threatening substance of vigorous citizen input. In short, the law seeks to nurture a compliant NPO sector able to provide health and welfare services at reasonable rates.

In contrast, the NPO movement nurtures a suspicion of government motives and a belief that the government opposes the prospect of an active and informed citizenry holding it accountable and making use of state resources to serve civil society. At the same time, advocates of a larger role for NPOs recognize the importance of cooperating with government authorities to secure the status and funding needed to operate effectively. Walking this tightrope is a formidable challenge. Keeping the government at a respectable distance while taking its money and lobbying it on policy issues generates conflicts of interest. NPOs that are harshly critical of the government or that use the media to pressure the government are vulnerable to retaliation in the form of funding cuts and denial of access to information and key policymakers. Those that are overly dependent on government financing or project funding will not be in a strong position to resist pressures to modify their views and actions.

The 2002 Symposium on State and NGO Relations held in Tokyo focused on the problems of this relationship in Japan and how the constraints imposed by government are hampering the movement. Conference participants enumerated the shortcomings of the legislation, the difficulties in dealing with government officials, and the need to modify the operating environment for NGOs to ensure their autonomy. Foreign participants shared lessons from their countries, and highlighted the need for autonomy from government monitoring and influence. They emphasized that for Japan to reap the rewards of NPOs the government had to demonstrate the courage to liberate them. More liberal tax exemption status and 'no-strings attached' government funding were cited as crucial to tapping the potential of NPOs.

The problems implicit in the dependent relationship favored by the Japanese government were evident in the haughty demeanor of the MOFA (Ministry of Foreign Affairs) official who attended the conference and the deference accorded him by some of the NPO representatives who shared a panel with him. Since this official exercises influence over funding and participation in government policymaking advisory bodies, NPO representatives heaped praise on him while castigating the system that compelled them to act in this way. Although they were playing the game by the established 'rules,' it was uncomfortable to watch at first hand.

One of the more humorous moments of the conference came when the MOFA official claimed that while it was fine for Americans and Europeans to talk about no-strings government funding and encouraging large flows of funding to NPOs, such sentiments were not applicable in Japan. He argued that Japanese NPOs are too small, unsophisticated, and inexperienced to handle large sums of money without oversight and assistance. Given that his own ministry had been prominently featured in the media over the preceding year for a series of corruption scandals and systematic misuse and pilfering of public funds (see Chapter 4), his unctuous remarks were especially ironic and grating. Moreover, his comments betrayed the fundamental mistrust of citizens among Japan's mandarins, who regard any concession of responsibility to citizens' groups or NPOs as an abnegation of duty. So in justifying the government's lukewarm attitude and strict policies towards NPOs in terms of their shortcomings, the official was making a case for keeping them on a short leash. This tautological reasoning has a seductive simplicity: since NPOs are small and underfunded and lack skilled people we must continue to pursue policies that limit their financial autonomy, hamper their growth, and prevent them from developing the scale and expertise needed to pursue their agendas effectively.

The official's remarks indicated some of the ways in which the government uses its power to constrain the potential of NPOs. Hostility towards civil society among the governing elite is marked, and the fundamental distrust of NPOs evident among bureaucrats and many politicians is not surprising. NPOs are viewed as issue-oriented advocacy groups that openly criticize the government and are thus unwelcome adversaries. There is little real appreciation of the role of citizen watchdog groups or organizations that see their primary role as challenging government policies that fail to meet the needs and expectations of ordinary people. Officials see an engaged and questioning citizenry as an erosion of their power and prerogatives, and oppose the rise of a vital third force that will subject bureaucrats to the supervision of the people they are supposed to serve, but prefer to govern.

However, this scenario is likely to change: the logic of the government's troubled finances, the push for deregulation, and the need to expand social services suggest that a more extensive partnership with NPOs can be anticipated. Ministries are getting used to tapping into the NPO movement for justifying part of their budget allocations and, as tighter budgets loom, are likely to become ever more ardent, if not inspired, sponsors of NPOs. Although the nature of this partnership will probably fall short of NPO desires, to the extent that the government moves to rely more on NPOs and involve them in the work of government, they stand to gain from stable funding and significant growth. Over time this will compel a higher degree of professionalization that in turn will lead to NPOs having a growing impact on the wider community. Their role will become assumed, their niche ensured as they provide services and take on tasks that people rely on and appreciate. In coming decades, many NPOs will slowly move from the fringe they now occupy to more mainstream roles, conferring legitimacy on the entire movement and making it easier for all to operate. Reluctantly embracing NPOs, begrudgingly conceding them a greater role, using them to procure slices of the budget pie, the government is nurturing a more robust NPO movement despite itself and, in the process, may well create a powerful force of transformation. By 2050, one can imagine Japan's NPOs emulating the success of their counterparts in Europe and the USA, making public participation in support of a people-centered polity the norm.

Judicial reform

If the Judicial Reform Council (JRC) has its way, Japan will rapidly move towards the rule of law and the numbers of legal professionals will rapidly increase. The JRC's proposal, submitted in June 2001 to Prime Minister Koizumi, seeks to lead Japan away from the informal and personalistic modes of arbitration, compromise, and dispute settlement that have long been intrinsic to Japan's legal culture and which have helped keep it free from the litigation excesses deplored in the USA. Oddly, the proposal to promote the rule of law in Japan, and massively increase the number of lawyers, is supported by a diverse array of progressive and conservative political forces, including some especially unlikely allies. Significantly, the most serious opposition to the proposed reforms comes from within the judiciary, notably the Supreme Court.

What other government in the world thinks that doubling the number of lawyers is such a good idea?[13] Why does such an assortment of political allies think that having more lawyers is a solution to Japan's problems? Economic globalization is one important answer. Intensified global competition, the need to mesh with global standards and the belief that Japan needs to develop a more market-oriented economy to cope with these challenges, has led business leaders to become advocates of judicial reform. Their powerful voice is reflected in LDP support for sweeping changes to the legal system.

Both big business leaders and the LDP view legal reform as a logical consequence of ongoing initiatives in administrative reform and deregulation that
began in the 1980s and have intensified in response to the economic troubles
of the 1990s. Thus the two groups that have benefited most from a passive
judicial system, where courts have been extremely reluctant to review the
constitutionality of legislation and consumers/individuals seldom have the
money and time needed to sue companies, have come out in favor of invigorating the judiciary. They have come around to the belief that the merits of
the *rule of law* outweigh the benefits of *rule by law*. Transparent, impartial, and
accessible courts are seen to be crucial to managing the transition to deregulation and coping with a greater reliance on free-market mechanisms. Judicial
reform is also a consequence of globalization and a need to placate, and
protect against, international trading partners and competitors.

Administrative reform measures began in earnest under Prime Minister
Nakasone in the early 1980s in a bid to cut public deficits and energize the
economy by shrinking government. This meant, inter alia, promoting deregulation and privatization. The impetus for reform intensified towards the end
of the twentieth century and persists in the early twenty-first century. Ratio-
nalizing and downsizing the bureaucracy implies a reduced role for the
government in regulating the economy, a trend reinforced by the embrace of
market-oriented principles by Prime Minister Hashimoto in the mid-1990s.
During this decade there were a number of initiatives aimed at promoting the
rule of law and thus also encouraging judicial expansion. In 1993 the government strengthened shareholder rights and facilitated legal action by shareholders. In 1994 it placed constraints on *gyosei shido* (administrative
guidance), an informal and often arbitrary exercise of power by officials over
firms under their purview. In 1994 the Diet passed a Products Liability Act
helping consumers seek legal redress, and then in 1999 approved the
Freedom of Information Act. As part of a larger tapestry of social change,
these reforms carried significant implications for judicial reform by paving
the way for legal expansion and activism.

Whereas bureaucrats played a crucial and informal role in resolving
disputes and conflicts in postwar Japan, by the twenty-first century the resort
to *gyosei shido* seems outmoded and counterproductive. It is inconsistent to
attempt to invigorate economic growth by unshackling business from excessive regulations and endorsing market principles while at the same time
maintaining a referee role for bureaucrats. This is also a source of friction
with trading partners who have sometimes interpreted such oversight as
evidence that the market was fixed (Structural Impediments Initiative – First
Bush Administration) and at other times enjoined the government to exercise
this role in order to ensure desired outcomes (numerical targets – Clinton
Administration).

Support for judicial reform also reflects concerns in the bureaucracy and
business world about the risks of informal ties and dealings that have been at
the heart of recent scandals. With information disclosure promoting more

transparent governance, and providing the basis for prosecutions, the risks of bending the rules and favoritism are increasing. Reliance on the rule of law is a means to restore credibility, reduce improprieties, and render decisions based on what are seen to be fair and objective criteria.

Less government, market-oriented capitalism, and globalization facilitated by the World Trade Organization means that the rules of the game are changing and there is a need for new mechanisms of resolving conflicts in a fair and transparent manner that will pass international muster and enjoy the confidence of those involved in disputes. Hence the leadership of business groups in advocating judicial reform and pressuring the LDP to exercise its political influence to place this issue high on the government's agenda. As the Japan Association of Corporate Executives (Keizai Doyukai) argued, in cases where 'the market does not function successfully, the role of the judiciary in resolving the dispute ex post facto becomes important. We do not hope for a litigious society, but we consider it necessary to reform the judicial system in order that the judiciary can play its expected role more fairly and rapidly.'[14]

Significantly, the legislature regarded this issue as weighty enough to bypass the bureaucracy, passing legislation in 1999 to establish a Judicial Reform Council reporting directly to the Prime Minister's Office. In June 2001 the JRC submitted recommendations to Prime Minister Koizumi, and laid out a relatively tight timetable for implementation that received his endorsement. The reforms also enjoy the public support of Rengo, the nation's largest umbrella trade union organization, and the Japan Federation of Bar Associations, both of which see judicial reform as key to protecting people from the risks of a market economy. As Miyazawa (2001: 11) argues, 'legal protection of people must be expanded if administrative regulation is to be reduced.'

Selling judicial reform also means convincing the public that the reforms are not just a way of rigging the system for the vested interests that are its most vocal advocates. In an environment where the government will have considerably less leeway to protect public interests and is introducing the uncertainties and insecurities of market-oriented reforms, expanding public access to legal services is a logical safeguard. So is breaking the logjam of court proceedings that slows litigation and postpones resolution of disputes, at least through formal channels.[15]

Demand for legal services is being driven by legislative reforms ranging from improved shareholder and consumer rights establishment of NPOs and information disclosure legislation. In addition, expansion of legal assistance to defendants as part of the current judicial reform initiative will further fuel demand for legal services. Logically, the rule of law cannot happen without more lawyers to make it a reality.

Imagining the legal revolution

Will the potential of judicial reform be realized? Judging from the strong and wide base of support that it already enjoys, significant reform will occur: one of its chief features is likely to be an epochal change in the role of the judiciary in twenty-first century Japan. The strengthening of the rule of law and the massive expansion in the numbers of legal professionals will permit greater access to legal services, promote generalized, formal rules of conduct in the legal arena, and substantially encroach on the informal, opaque practices, and reliance on personal networks, that have been the hallmark of Japan, Inc. A more accessible legal system is expected to play a much more important role in the polity and facilitate the deregulation initiatives that the government is keen to implement.

The reasons why Japan has developed a relatively limited and passive judicial system have been the subject of a longstanding debate (Feldman 2000b; Haley 1978). The response of the JRC seems to be that the rule of law depends on rapidly expanding the numbers of legal professionals. The paucity of lawyers in Japan certainly limits access to legal services and places the costs of such services out of the range of many potential litigants. As of 1999, Japan had 22,417 legal professionals (17,268 lawyers, 2,926 judges, and 2,223 prosecutors) for a per capita ratio of 16.5 legal professionals per 100,000 people, compared to 61.3 in France, 151.1 in Germany, 164.5 in England and Wales, and 350.4 in the USA (Sato 2002: 74). One of the chief obstacles to a larger legal profession is the national bar examination, which has been used to limit the entry of new lawyers. Since the mid-1960s about 500 applicants passed the exam every year. During the 1990s this policy was relaxed and 1,000 applicants passed in 1999. This figure is slated to rise to 1,500 by 2004, prompting a significant increase in bar exam applications, up 17 percent in 2002 alone.[16]

The JRC report submitted to Prime Minister Koizumi advocates vast increases in the numbers of practicing lawyers and significant changes in their training. In order to increase the number of legal professionals to around 50,000 by 2018, the report calls for a minimum target of 3,000 candidates passing the bar exam every year, beginning in 2010. This would place Japan on a par with France in terms of legal professionals per capita. The JRC also advocates establishment of professional law schools as a way of improving legal education and diluting the influence of the sole government-run training institute on legal ideology and philosophy. The JRC also recommends speedier legal proceedings and a concomitant expansion in the number of judges to lessen caseloads. In order to reduce the barriers to legal services, the report also suggests lowering court fees, providing for payment of legal fees by losing parties (key to litigation against the government or businesses who can use their superior resources to successfully bankrupt hostile proceedings), and expansion of legal aid. It also seeks an overhaul of the selection system for judges, making it more open and including some form of popular participation in nominations. In addition, reflecting concerns that judges are too narrowly trained and cast from the same mold, the JRC recommends recruiting experienced legal professionals from outside the judiciary to serve as judges. These reforms are seen as necessary to promote the independence of lower courts by diminishing the influence of the Supreme Court and its General Secretariat over recruitment and promotions.

In addition to these sweeping measures, the JRC also seeks to restore, after a six-decade hiatus, popular participation in trials, initially introduced in 1928 but suspended in 1943. Reviving a modified jury system would lessen the insulation of the judiciary from popular influences and deepen its roots in society. The remoteness of the judicial system from society is seen as a significant weakness and popular participation as a means of bridging this gap, conferring credibility and encouraging greater trust.

In short, the JRC has set out a blueprint for a revolution in Japan's judicial system. The current system of rationed legal services, establishment-oriented judges and a heavy conservative bias to judicial review is destined to change. Because the nation's ruling elite has agreed to these changes, the legal foundations of contemporary Japan are being transformed – various stalling measures and modifications notwithstanding. By pushing the legal system to accommodate greater public participation, the architects of reform are forcing it to shed its cocoon of privilege and gradually become attuned to popular norms and values. In doing so, one of the largest barriers to Japan's social transformation now has the potential to become a key engine of change. While this will take time and there is certain to be a degree of backsliding, the process has started, fraught with unpredictable results and unintended consequences.

At the end of 2002, the Diet acted on the JRC recommendations by passing legislation that will transform legal education by linking law schools, bar exams and legal apprenticeships. The new system will lessen the importance of the bar exam, until now the sole gateway to a legal career, and emphasize education at law schools. There will be a transition period extending until 2010, by which time the bar exam system will be comprehensively overhauled. Until 2010, it will still be possible for candidates to enter the law profession without attending law school by passing two rounds of exams, a compromise that some critics worry may vitiate the impact of professionalizing legal education. However, the establishment of professional law schools beginning in 2004 does mark a major step forward for reformers eager to promote a more independent judiciary by removing training in the theory and practice of law from direct government control.

Passage of the 'speedy trial bill' in 2003 is another key element of judicial reform that places a two-year limit on all first-instance trials for criminal and civil cases at the district, summary, and family court level. The new legislation amends the Civil Code of Procedure and among other provisions requires specific schedules for trial proceedings even for complex litigation like medical malpractice. The bill also standardizes procedures for evidence findings prior to trial proceedings and paves the way for appointment of experts to assist trial judges. This marks a significant innovation and demonstrates just how rapidly change is happening. Swifter resolution of legal disputes will lower the costs of litigation and limit the scope for delaying tactics that favor compromise settlements and those with greater financial resources. By establishing a specialized court for adjudicating intellectual property rights (IPR), the government is also supporting more timely resolution of IPR disputes in which prolonged legal battles can prove extremely damaging to effective protection of such rights.[17]

Changes are also afoot for enhanced public participation in trial proceedings. Legislation is still being debated as of 2003, but it appears that by 2009 the government will establish a system of 'citizen judges' who will collaborate with professional judges to reach a verdict through consultation.[18] The biggest controversy surrounding the anticipated legislation focuses on the extent of restrictions to be imposed on the media in order to ensure unbiased verdicts and insulate citizen judges from external pressures and intrusion on their private lives. There is also concern about undue confidentiality requirements being imposed on citizen judges that would impede them from sharing their experiences after the trial. In cases where verdicts are questioned or controversial, a more open system provides a reassuring ability to monitor outcomes. Welcoming this innovation, one newspaper editorial noted that: 'The citizen judge system is expected to enhance the public sense of participation in the trial process and improve the nation's justice system along more democratic lines. It is a move long overdue.'[19]

Twice as many lawyers? Professional law schools free of government influence? Judges selected mid-career from among practicing lawyers? Citizen judges? Speedy trials? Merely contemplating the potential for change raised by these questions alone suggests an array of plausible outcomes that defy confident projections. It is as if the establishment has let loose a subversive dynamic within its own ranks. No single reform has a greater potential for reinventing Japan than this wholesale reworking of the judiciary and its role in society. One does not have to raise the doubtful possibility of Japan's legal system coming to resemble the USA to appreciate the potentials and risks associated with this venture. The currents of changes unleashed by the advocates of reform will almost certainly spill over their banks and sweep over parts of the landscape that nobody ever imagined would be affected.

The reforms proposed by the JRC are set to accelerate the speed of Japan's transformation. We have already seen that the freedom of information law owed its existence to the efforts of a handful of lawyers passionate about invigorating civil society. Litigation became a tool of progressive activists, and conflicts were brought into the realm of the courts. The prospect of many more lawyers, independently educated and socially diverse – perhaps including a higher proportion of women and more graduates from outside the elite universities – vastly enlarges the pool of autonomous actors who have the skills and resources to make change happen. And the courts will be presided over by a more diverse group of judges less beholden to their supe-riors for promotion and less committed to upholding a state ideology. In addition, it is likely that some of these new lawyers will run for public office and play an influential role in drafting policies and legislation that has until recently been the preserve of bureaucrats. One only has to look at recent policy proposals and legislation drafted by non-bureaucrats – the NPO Law of 1998, the Freedom of Information Act of 1999, and the JRC report of 2001 – to anticipate the way ahead. Whereas up till now Japan has been guided by its bureaucratic mandarins by default, the potential of the legislature and judi-ciary to more fully exercise their constitutional powers will introduce a new vitality and energy to the polity.

Judicial reform along the lines endorsed by the key players in Japan will irretrievably alter the relationship between the people and the law and thus their relationship with the state. The law's substantially untapped potential as a weapon of the weak and agent of social change is now on the verge of becoming reality. The strengthening of the rule of law will also reduce the potential for arbitrary intrusions by officials and politicians, creating a more predictable and level playing field predicated on generalized rules rather than preferential treatment and networks of informal influence. The rule of law also promises to reduce the venality of those in a position to manipulate the regulatory environment. Plainly, deregulation, transparency, and the rule of law will reduce the opportunities for corruption, the benefits of which will diminish and carry greater risk to those involved.

Perhaps the most likely outcome of Japan's impending legal revolution is an enrichment of civil society. Although it will inevitably be a slow and subtle process, over time it will forge a deeper, broader, and stronger civil society. The law will become a more accurate mirror of contemporary society – rather than a rear-view mirror. It will no longer serve as a force to protect the status quo, but will ideally become a platform for activism and a force for fair and (relatively) objective adjudication of disputes. Businesses will have recourse to the law to assert and protect their interests and resolve conflicts based on transparent criteria. Trading partners, investors, and executives will gain greater confidence in the business environment because the rules affecting them will no longer be so vague and subject to arbitrary manipula-tion. Citizens and NPOs will also benefit from an expanded and more vigorous judiciary where barriers to litigation are reduced and practitioners are more diverse and less insulated from social influences. Expanded legal aid and a 'loser pays court costs' system will level the playing field and lessen advantages currently enjoyed by those with deeper pockets.[20] Enhanced citizen participation will tie the legal system closer to community norms and expectations. In short, the public stake in the judicial system – a role removed by military-dominated government and withheld ever since – looks set to be regained and public confidence in their judiciary restored.

Conclusion

Judicial reform and the NPO legislation are part of a larger and longer process of change that will become clearer in retrospect. They are happening in the context of wider political, administrative, and economic reforms that have made it possible to realize aspirations that have been germinating for some time. Circumstances have produced unlikely bedfellows and it is safe to say that supporters of these two reforms do not share identical aims. Both initiatives have created opportunities for strengthening civil society and transforming the relations between citizens and their government. Time will tell whether this potential will be realized or squandered.

Not everyone is so sanguine about the prospects for a Japanese revolution, legal or otherwise. Skeptics have marshaled evidence to make a compelling case that for all of the rhetoric and appearances of change, things have pretty much stayed the same, perhaps with minor modifications. Japan-watchers groan every time someone proclaims the new, new revolution. Lawyer Nakabo Kohei adds to the catalogue of doubts, pointing out that the proposals of the Judicial Reform Council (JRC) enacted as law in November 2001 are being hijacked and diluted by vested interests in the Judicial Reform Headquarters (JRH) responsible for implementing judicial reform.[21] Nakabo participated in drafting the JRC reforms and has a voice in the JRH deliberations. He is concerned that the government is trying to retain control over legal education and thereby stall professionalization of legal training based in universities. And while the JRC is concerned to reduce the importance of the bar exam for entrance into the profession, the JRH appears to be trying to maintain vestiges of the old system. The government wants to retain a right to influence the content of the bar exam and the curriculum of law schools. Seeing a golden opportunity slipping away, Nakabo asks rhetorically in the *Asahi Shimbun*, June 28, 2002: 'Does the government seriously believe this sort of judicial "reform" will produce internationally competitive lawyers who can be relied upon to defend human rights and justice?' (Of course, it is a moot point whether the government sees these as desirable goals.) He also argues that the JRH aims to minimize participation by citizens and avoid anything resembling the jury system where citizens are on a par with legal professionals.

Those who stand to lose influence and power, or are otherwise threatened by an expanded judiciary, more and better educated legal professionals, and courts more attuned to public expectations, will cling tenaciously to the old system. However, it seems likely that, just as the conservatives failed to stop the establishment of a JRC, they will not be able to derail judicial reform. Although they may be able to extract some concessions, the array of powerful interests pressing for change will not permit them to filibuster reform off the agenda. Judicial reform is the key to the matrix of ongoing changes. By transforming the judiciary along the lines recommended by the JRC, the law is being made into a more accessible tool, one that will transform relations between the people and their government. Ongoing judicial reforms are thus rendering the law into a powerful force for social change.

Despite strong opposition from within, judicial reform is benefiting from an unlikely coalition of supporters. As we have seen, members of the LDP and their powerful patrons in the business community support an expanded role for the judiciary. They along with union activists, journalists, civil libertarians, and progressive legal scholars have formed a loose consensus on the need for far-reaching judicial reforms and a more activist role for the judiciary. This process is taking shape remarkably rapidly: an issue that was not on anyone's radar screens until 1999 had resulted in major changes by 2002. In November 2002, the LDP-dominated Diet passed enabling legislation that is making significant judicial reform a reality. According to Dan Foote, a University of Tokyo professor who serves on the government's legal reform committees, this legislation is the culmination of a debate that began as far back as 1964 when Sakai Wakamatsu, a distinguished legal scholar, first proposed a package of reforms strikingly similar to those now adopted. There will be independent law schools from 2004, mostly based in universities, and the pass rate for the bar exam is being set at 70–80 percent so that the target of 3,000 new lawyers every year can be reached by 2010. Reformers have thus largely succeeded in reducing the importance of the exam and the distortions it created. In the past, the bar exam was used as a tool for limiting the number of lawyers and, even in recent years when the target quota for successful candidates was raised, less than 3 percent of applicants passed. This system produced candidates blinkered by the need to acquire the skills to pass the test, rather than lawyers well-versed in jurisprudence. The new bar exam will ensure that those who pass meet established standards and have the requisite knowledge and skills to practice as lawyers.

The process of reforming the education system for lawyers has been fraught with distrust among all the players. Practicing lawyers, legal scholars, judges, bureaucrats, and politicians all fear that the reforms will lead to a decline in standards and disagree about teaching methods, curriculum, graduation requirements, and the role of the government in accreditation and establishing standards. The politics of legal reform have suggested some important lessons about the realities and limits of reform in general.

One such lesson is the reality of compromise. LDP opponents of the new law schools have long argued that the emphasis on the bar exam made it possible for anyone to become a lawyer, even those who could not afford high tuition bills, as long as they studied hard enough. This 'populist' stance ignores the reality that virtually all successful bar exam candidates spent enormous amounts of money and time on legal cram schools. In a nod to these politicians, and those who have lobbied for their support, a two-track qualification system will be introduced. Until 2010, the government will administer a pre-bar exam for those who do not attend law school; those who pass, and law school graduates, will be eligible for the bar exam. The new system will also retain a role for the government's Legal Training and Research Institute, where aspiring lawyers will spend one year as unpaid law clerks.[22] Reformers have thus won a partial victory with the establishment of professional law schools, but have had to concede a continued role for the government's training center. Thus is reform negotiated.

To appreciate the overall prospects of reform it is important to understand how recent reforms are mutually reinforcing. NPOs will benefit considerably from information disclosure and greater transparency in government, making it far easier for them to play an oversight role and claim a bigger role in policymaking. The new legislation also gives them recourse to judicial remedies that will curtail the arbitrary powers of government. The expected expansion in the number of legal professionals will also benefit NPOs, giving them better access to legal advice and tactics to help them challenge existing constraints. A more vigorous judiciary less beholden to the government with greater citizen input is good news for NPOs. Adoption of the 'loser pays court costs' principle, and speedier trials, will embolden NPOs and other activists to pursue legal remedies. The NPOs can become venues for asserting greater public participation in government and work to maximize the legal powers of citizens in redefining and shaping the public interest. Armed with information disclosure powers and access to professional legal advice, NPOs can become highly effective champions of citizens' rights and make the costs of ignoring such rights unacceptably high. Stronger NPOs will in turn be in a better position to advocate changes in the laws governing their own operations that, in the long term, will enhance their role in building civil society. Certainly this will take time, but the government's need to develop partnerships with NPOs renders this a viable scenario.

4 Rogues and riches
The bureaucrats' fall from grace

Among all the categories of powerholders, bureaucrats must be regarded with the greatest suspicion always and everywhere, because much of what they do is not easily visible. And the position of Japanese bureaucrats is extraordinary; they have more power than their counterparts in other advanced industrialized countries, and Japan falls far short in institutional provisions to limit such power.

Karel van Wolferen (1992: 46–7)

In recent years, as Japan's bureaucrats have lurched from one crisis to another and one scandal to the next, exposing unimagined levels of incompetence, negligence, and cupidity, public resentment of their privileged position has reached fever pitch, egged on by a media that loves a story with legs. Bureaucrat-bashing sells and has become something of a national hobby, an outlet for feelings of anger and the need to identify scapegoats. With their arrogant attitude and taste for the high life at public expense, the bureaucrats have only themselves to thank for this sordid state of affairs. Revelations of systemic malfeasance and cozy, lucrative ties with the industries they monitor have further fueled the public backlash.

Before Japan's bubble burst in the early 1990s it would have been hard to imagine bureaucrats as the national punching bag. They are, after all, the best and the brightest, the graduates of the best universities, most notably the University of Tokyo. They were given (and happily claimed) the credit for masterminding Japan's postwar recovery and economic miracle. These were the men who had perfected industrial policy and knew how to make *dirigisme* work. They had fostered social stability and economic security and as a result contributed to Japan's high level of social capital. Their presumed commitment to the national interest was valued as a counterweight to the dubious dealings of politicians. They were relied on to place principle above personal interest and provide the continuity, competence, and vision that would ensure a bright future for the nation. These were powerful men who, with a single phone call, could make 'suggestions' to major companies that they knew would be implemented; businessmen knew better than to cross the powers that be.

(Roger Dahl)

At least this was the myth of the mandarins. The myth also rested on the belief that, although they were relatively underpaid, they were motivated by a sense of duty and willingness to sacrifice personal gain for the good of the nation. These selfless guardians of the national interest were known to be above venality, living the austere lives of high-minded, well-educated individuals like the good mandarins of Chinese lore. But, as Chinese people have learned over the centuries, noble mandarins are in the minority; stories about them are repeated less to celebrate their virtues and more to castigate their numerous rogue colleagues who enrich themselves at public expense. The tales of noble mandarins serve as reminders of duty and morality precisely because such reminders are so often needed.

The fall from grace of Japan's bureaucrats can be traced to the economic collapse of the early 1990s. They have been held responsible for the ill-advised policies that first inflated the bubble and then abruptly deflated it, sparking a prolonged recession from which Japan has not yet emerged. As the nation's economic woes have increased and as the costs of the bureaucrats' mismanagement of the economy have emerged, the public mood has turned angry. The reputation of the Ministry of Finance (MOF) has suffered particularly badly, as the nation's banking system remains crippled by mountains of bad debt that accumulated as the economy collapsed. Revelations about lavish entertainment offered to MOF mandarins by bankers, and well-paid sinecures extended to officials upon retirement, have done nothing to allay suspicions about lax oversight and corrupt practices.

MOF officials also colluded in the shady dealings that came to light over the *jusen* (real estate lending affiliates of banks) affair, involving bankers lending vast sums of money to mob-related real estate developers and speculators with the knowledge of ministry mandarins. When the *jusen* went belly-up, the dirty laundry was exposed for all to see – a rare glimpse of the extent of organized crime in Japan. Taxpayers watched with anger and incredulity as the government mounted a massive bailout for the zombie banks. The bill

Figure 4.1 Political campaigns in 2003 that promise to 'restructure' (fire) bureaucrats. (Photo: Jeff Kingston)

for profligate lending, inadequate risk assessment, and speculation – all done in connivance with the mob – was handed to taxpayers. It all appeared to be a massive confidence trick – official explanations of the bad loan problem never added up, only a few bankers were prosecuted, officials faced no significant penalties and many of the 'bad loans' were invested overseas by lenders nobody wanted to collect from. In Japan, this is a working definition of what economists refer to as 'moral hazard.'

The stench emanating from Kasumigaseki, the geographical center of bureaucratic power in Japan, became more and more fetid during the 1990s as virtually every ministry and agency found itself in the unwelcome spotlight of media scrutiny. Time and again, it emerged that officials had been pilfering taxpayers' money and exchanging favors for bribes with little fear and even less shame. Month after month, new waves of scandal cascaded into public view, each one further undermining the credibility of the government. The myth of clean government took a severe pummeling as details of payoffs, fraud, collusion, lavish entertainment, and embarrassing excess engulfed the bureaucratic community. It became clear that unscrupulous operators had been taking the nation to the cleaners in this cash-and-carry government.

The Lost Decade was a time when the bureaucrats surrendered the public trust, lost their reputations, and shredded the myth of their competence and reliability. Kobe exposed the bureaucracy at its red-tape worst while the banking crisis and episodes such as the HIV-hemophiliac infection scandal and the 'mad cow' outbreak revealed a depressing pattern of negligence and moral laxity. From out of this miasma of miscues it is no surprise that the bureaucrats are seen to be either asleep at the wheel or driving the getaway car. The term *yaku-gai* (harm caused by government officials) gained currency from 1996, reflecting the shock, anger, and disbelief prompted by these revelations.[1] The mere existence of such a term speaks volumes in itself.

This change in public perceptions of the nation's mandarins is contributing to change in the relations between the state and its citizens. The public has learned the hard way the costs of opaque governance and the need for transparency and political oversight. They want to clip the wings of the bureaucracy and hold it to standards of conduct that will meet the expectations of society. While it is hardly fair to tar all bureaucrats with the same brush, as a consequence of their smug *kanson mimpi* (bureaucratic arrogance), their comeuppance is being enjoyed in Japan's theater of the state. This is a show destined for a long run, playing to a full house.

Fat cats

'Bureaucrats are underpaid' – that is what people used to think until Japan's weeklies laid another myth to rest. While people have always known that civil servants enjoy job security and good retirement benefits, these perks were seen as fair because of their low salaries. However, when the national weekly *Shukan Gendai* (June 22, 2002) looked into the issue of pay, it found that over 500 bureaucrats were earning in excess of ¥20 million ($160,000) a year. Information collected by the National Personnel Authority shows that the average bureaucrat is 41 years old and makes ¥6.4 million ($51,000) a year, about 20 percent more than the ¥5.1 million earned by their private-sector counterparts in the 40–44 age cohort. All 122 of Japan's ambassadors earn more than ¥20 million a year while living luxurious and subsidized lives at their overseas postings. The ambassadors to the UK and USA make a staggering ¥36.4 million, edging out the prime minister at ¥35.9 million (approximately $287,000) a year. Sitting on top of the national pay scale is the chief justice of the Supreme Court, who pulls in ¥39.7 million. Other judges, prosecutors, and university presidents fill out the ranks of the crew earning more than ¥20 million.

In addition to high pay, bureaucrats enjoy pensions calculated according to a formula that grants them far more generous retirement benefits than their counterparts in the private sector. On top of this inequity in basic pensions, many civil servants rack up several pensions through post-retirement work in a succession of lucrative sinecures. Retirement allowances, the lump sum that employees receive at the end of their careers, are also surprisingly high in the bureaucracy. Between 1999 and 2002, thirteen bureaucrats received more than ¥90 million ($720,000) as a retirement allowance. Further down the line, 44 officials received approximately ¥80 million, 85 received about ¥70 million and 230 about ¥60 million. These payments are in addition to their basic pensions. And officials who retire before the mandatory retirement age of 60 are eligible for a ¥12 million bonus.

Some public servants also enjoy subsidized housing in centrally located apartments that would usually rent for at least five times what they pay. In addition, bureaucrats who have served in a relevant government agency qualify for automatic certification for some professions that require others to pass difficult exams, such as accountant and legal scrivener certification. Others are given government license plates for traveling on Japan's pricey highways.

All in all, careers in the civil service are the most lucrative option for university graduates, and jobholders do not have to put up with the stress of potential downsizing or meaningful performance reviews. Pay is based on seniority, not merit. And the rising number of second-generation bureaucrats following in the footsteps of their fathers generates suspicions that the prestigious career-track system is not based solely on merit.

Amakudari

Amakudari (literally, 'descent from heaven') is the euphemism used to describe life after retirement for bureaucrats, when many assume well-paid sinecures in firms that they had previously supervised. This arrangement has long been castigated as a recipe for collusion, corruption, and lax oversight. Bureaucrats who anticipate cashing in on their connections after retiring have a strong incentive not to alienate future employers and thus tend to be accommodating and supportive of those they are meant to monitor. Given the discretionary powers of bureaucrats under the system of *gyosei shido* (administrative guidance), regulatory interpretation and enforcement becomes a subjective matter and opportunities to grant favors and dispensations occur frequently. Since the courts have rarely intervened in administrative decisions, interpreting the relevant laws and regulations has been the prerogative of the bureaucrats, thus granting them enormous power and influence.

This power and influence lies at the heart of *amakudari* and explains why it has remained a robust feature of governance in Japan, despite being the subject of such severe criticism for so long. Retirement need not mean cessation of influence: firms hire former high- and even middle-ranking bureaucrats because of their established networks and connections with former colleagues who can exercise their discretionary powers to benefit the retired official's new employer. Banks and stock brokerages favor former Ministry of

Finance men and pay them handsomely – but not because of their business acumen or savvy about hedging strategies; it is all about channels of communication, contacts, and a chance to influence critical decisions via the 'old boy' network. *Amakudari* endow firms with personal networks that are an effective conduit to privileged knowledge and access to those who count in the government. Civil servants contacted by their former *sempai* (one with organizational seniority) to provide information, grant access, and accommodate input on policies, do so because it is established practice and also because it generates favors that can be called in when seeking a cushy post-retirement position for oneself. Those who aspire to *amakudari* have strong incentives to perpetuate the system, and exercise their powers and influence accordingly.

The private sector spends lavishly on *amakudari* because it is logical to do so in a society where governance is subjective and arbitrary, and personal contacts make all the difference in the world. The *amakudari* also provide a two-way street for exchange of information and views, and are part of the reason why *gyosei shido* worked so effectively over the years. Government officials could call on ex-ministry men placed in the private sector for intelligence and to ensure that compliance with their directives and advice was forthcoming. In this sense, *amakudari* has served both the public and private sectors and explains why it has survived prolonged criticism. Although there has been no shortage of efforts to restrict the practice, as Chalmers Johnson noted in the mid-1970s, 'The legal restrictions on *amakudari* are dominated by one huge loophole: very lax enforcement' (Johnson 1995: 143).

Although the practice of *amakudari* will persist in twenty-first century Japan, it is coming under closer scrutiny and is becoming more regulated and transparent. The issue is not so much that close government and business ties are inherently bad, or unique to Japan, but rather that the system has developed in ways that facilitate collusion, favoritism and corruption. As in the USA and Europe, the revolving door is a common and accepted practice. Bureaucrats everywhere end up working for industries they previously supervised and, in some cases, bureaucracies hire from the industries they regulate, a practice known as *amaagari* (ascent to heaven) in Japan.

The revolving door remains open because it channels experts into positions where their expertise – maybe in the form of contacts alone – is valuable. It fails when those who engage in *amakudari* fail to meet rising expectations for proper conduct and good governance. As long as the practices associated with the phenomenon are not scrutinized and those involved not held accountable for their actions, there are legitimate concerns that the public interest may suffer. In Japan, as a consequence of the information disclosure law, recent regulatory reforms governing *amakudari*, and the trend towards greater transparency, the conduct of retired central government bureaucrats has become the public's business. The emergence of a more robust civil society, a more skeptical public, the economic malaise, and concerns about government deficits have created an atmosphere far less tolerant of dubious practices that have, until recently, been the norm. This changing context is slowly transforming *amakudari* and raising the costs of continuing with practices that abuse the public trust. Such abuses will undoubtedly persist, but no longer with impunity.

The Bureaucratic People's Republic of Japan

In Japan the revolving door has gone awry not only because the system breeds collusion and favoritism, but because *amakudari* has become an industry in itself. (The practice of officials transferring to public corporations upon retirement is referred to as *yoko-suberi* – sideslip, or lateral transfer – but is substantially identical to *amakudari* and is referred to here as such.) The bureaucracies have proved adept at establishing special public corporations (*tokushu hojin*) that draw on public monies and also generate sinecures with handsome salaries and perquisites. The number of these state corporations has mushroomed in the past few decades and their close ties with the ministries or agencies that supervise their activities ensures a steady supply of *amakudari* positions. They were first established in the 1960s, partly as a way to create more parity between the salaries of civil servants and private-sector employees and provide a nest egg for men who were at that time retiring in their early 50s. In 2003 there are 77 *tokushu hojin* with 3,000 related companies, 26,000 public corporations and 450,000 employees, including *amakudari* bureaucrats occupying the most coveted positions. If families are included, some 1–2 million Japanese are sipping at this golden trough.

These state organizations are a hotbed of special privileges and waste, and have attracted severe criticism for losing vast sums of public money, generating massive debts that become the responsibility of taxpayers. For example, the Japan Highway Public Corporation has racked up total debts of some ¥25 trillion, an amount equivalent to nearly one-third of the government's annual budget (see Chapter 5). *Shukan Shincho* (May 3–10, 2002) reports that the 77 *tokushu hojin* gobble up ¥40 trillion of taxpayers' money a year and, despite this, still run some ¥3 trillion in the red. These entities are also collectively responsible for some ¥360 trillion in accumulated debts, the equivalent of more than four times the official national budget. The Ministry of Land, Infrastructure, and Transportation has 24 of these entities followed by the Ministry of Education, Culture, Sports, Science, and Technology with 12. They tend to be engaged in activities that could be handled more efficiently and less expensively by private-sector companies; however, they are reluctant to enter the rigged market since they have to pay their own way while the special state corporations do not.

The bulk of the funding for these corporations is not channeled through the official national budget. They are funded in large part through the Fiscal Investment and Loan Program (FILP), commonly referred to as Japan's second budget (*zaito*), which is nearly five times larger than the official budget passed in the Diet. Budgets disbursed under this auxiliary funding are subject

(Roger Dahl)

to only cursory review by the Diet. In 2001 these special funds amounted to ¥391 trillion, compared to an official budget of ¥83 trillion. Overall, some 60 percent of actual government spending is divided among 37 special budget accounts that draw on various sources of funds ranging from postal savings to road maintenance taxes. This complexity makes it very difficult to get a clear grasp of where the money comes from and where it goes. Some funds are channeled through the national budget while others are funneled to local governments and some to the *tokushu hojin.*

In 2001 it was reported that about ¥4 trillion of regular budget funds and about ¥3.5 trillion from the special auxiliary budgets went to the *tokushu hojin.* However, research by the Democratic Party of Japan reported by *Shukan Shincho* suggests the actual figure is closer to ¥40 trillion per annum if one includes all forms of government assistance and investment.

The government is considering privatizing these special state corporations because of its deep fiscal problems. The accumulating debts of these *amakudari*-spinning institutions pose a significant burden and they would certainly not survive if they were run along the lines of the private sector: they are staffed and run by bureaucrats who lack significant business experience and the leadership skills to manage them effectively. Pay for top executives and directors is not linked to merit or performance and is set at levels to ensure that the golden years are well provided for. Moreover, since top positions go to retired bureaucrats who tend to stay for only two to three years, and regard these plums as rewards for service already rendered, there is little incentive for them to control costs and boost efficiency. Since everyone assumes that the government will never allow these firms to go bankrupt, they are run accordingly.

This covey of special state corporations is derisively referred to by the media as the Bureaucratic People's Republic of Japan. The media has been frustrated in ferreting out information about these corporations because they are exempted from the national information disclosure law discussed in

Chapter 2. Despite the law's loopholes and exemptions, government agencies and ministries are required to divulge requested documents that do not fit any of the six broad categories of exemptions. The state corporations, however, are not subject to information disclosure and are not required to meet the standards of transparency required of the government. This blanket exemption has drawn the ire of transparency advocates who point out that since these corporations are funded with taxpayers' money, and are mortgaging the future for tomorrow's taxpayers, they should be subject to the same standards of transparency.

The loose and disparate coalition of forces ranged against the public corporations runs from conservatives favoring deregulation and less state involvement in the economy, to fiscal conservatives who want to cut state losses and debts, and on to progressive advocates of open government who assert that organizations that rely on public monies should be open to public scrutiny and made accountable to the taxpayers who pay the bills. Facing off against them are the seasoned turf fighters of the bureaucracy who see this attack on special corporations as a serious threat to the practice of *amakudari* and the benefits it confers. Despite the public mood favoring reform of these corporations, inroads have been slight.

Golden parachutes

Information about *amakudari* can be gathered from the National Personnel Authority (NPA), which is legally required to maintain records about this practice and make them available to the public. However, under the terms of the law, the reported cases of *amakudari* vastly understate the extent of this practice because many categories of re-employment are not covered and the reporting requirement for ex-officials lapses after a specified period of time, usually two years. The National Public Service Law bans central-government employees from accepting jobs at private firms for two years after their retirement if the firms have close ties to the ministries and agencies where the employees worked during the last five years prior to retirement.

The figures published by the NPA bear little resemblance to reality. In 2000, for example, it reported that the number of *amakudari* was a mere 40, down from 62 in 1999, and the lowest total since 1963 when statistics were first collected. According to the NPA, this practice peaked in 1985 when 318 central government bureaucrats accepted jobs in private firms. However, since this figure does not include officials who were hired by charitable institutions or by state-backed corporations such as the Japan Highway Public Corporation, the NPA report reveals only the tip of the *amakudari* iceberg. In an effort to present a more complete picture, for the first time in 2002 the NPA released statistics that included younger bureaucrats in their 20s and 30s who had 'retired' into private-sector jobs; these numbered 827 in 2001 compared to 69 older (average age 56.5 years) and higher-ranking bureaucrats who took up sinecures. This latter figure is the one usually reported by the NPA and cited by those who argue that *amakudari* is not a widespread practice. Again, it is important to note that this figure only covers private-sector firms related to the retirees' former ministry and does not include *amakudari* sinecures in the *tokushu hojin.*

In an effort to restore flagging confidence in government and regain the public trust, the government has in recent years become more forthcoming about *amakudari* and the less well-known practice of *amaagari*. In 2000 the government released a survey for the first time that covered the practice of *amakudari* at *tokushu hojin.* It reported that 90 percent of the central government's retiring senior bureaucrats had secured *amakudari* positions at state affiliates or government-related organizations. This figure of 538 officials also included disgraced officials who had been forced to resign. A vast majority were hired within three months of retiring. Also for the first time in 2000, the Management and Coordination Agency reported statistics on *amaagari*, indicating that central government offices hired 329 personnel from private-sector firms in 1999. A new law regulating *amaagari* personnel exchanges came into effect in 2000, requiring the government to report relevant data once a year.

Revealing as they are, these measures still fall short of full disclosure and tighter regulations are not proving too cumbersome for officials bent on feathering their retirement nests. Documents released in March 2000 by government agencies and ministries at the request of the Japan Communist Party reveal that two-thirds of the 375 high-ranking officials who retired in 1998 moved into public corporations (158), special corporations (84), or private-sector firms with close ties to these entities (82) that were linked to their former government posts. This suggests that the attempts to break the collusive ties intrinsic to *amakudari* targeted by recent reform initiatives are falling short of the mark. For example, MOF officials moved to the government-affiliated Japan Development Bank or Small Business Finance Corporation, while ranking officials in the Defense Agency found posts at top contracting companies such as Mitsubishi Heavy Industries and Fuji Heavy Industries.

In 2001, the *Asahi Shimbun* ran a story on *amakudari* based on the results of an information disclosure request filed with the National Personnel Authority. The newspaper (July 18, 2001) reported that about 40 percent of officers at the 77 special public corporations in Japan are retired bureaucrats from central government ministries. Out of the 705 officers at these 77 corporations, 292 were retirees from the central government. The costs of this practice ran to ¥5.3 billion in salaries and bonuses for an average annual salary of ¥18.34 million ($147,000) for each official. As of October 2000, of the 26,264 corporations controlled by the central or prefectural governments, including legally incorporated foundations, about 8,000 have trustees who were former bureaucrats. These trustees pull in more than ¥20 million at 128 of these corporations and foundations, and nearly ¥8 million at 70 percent of them.

The information disclosure law has also been used to reveal that the special public corporations are not strictly abiding by existing personnel rules. In 1979 the Cabinet ruled that retired bureaucrats should not constitute more than one half of all officers at special corporations, a rule that was revised in 1997 to apply this limitation to bureaucrats retired from the particular ministry having jurisdiction over the special corporation. Although this latter rule is adhered to, at 34 of the special corporations more than half of officers are former bureaucrats. There were also 19 cases of *watari*, the practice whereby an executive retiring from one special corporation assumes a similar position at another. *Watari* is a means for former officials to accumulate multiple retirement allowances and pensions. This practice was supposedly banned, except under special circumstances, by a Cabinet resolution in 1997. In many cases however, it means that numerous wagons can be hitched to the gravy train.

At most public corporations, the monthly salary is approximately ¥1 million, with bonuses ranging from ¥6–8 million per annum. In two or three years the retirement allowance quickly reaches ¥10 million. By moving on through a series of *amakudari*, bureaucrats can ensure that their parachutes are very golden indeed. In some cases, a senior-level retiree can make some ¥60 million ($480,000) in two years as an *amakudari*. One example cited by *Asahi* involved an ex-Ministry of Finance official who worked at two different government-backed financial institutions for five years at the usual high rates and accumulated retirement allowances totaling ¥30 million. His final post-retirement post was projected to net him an additional ¥38 million in retire-ment pay, in addition to a monthly salary of ¥1.2 million and a lucrative pension from his original MOF job combined with those from other post-retirement jobs. In terms of salaries, bonuses, and retirement allowances alone, twelve years of post-retirement *amakudari* netted him more than ¥280 million ($2.2 million), certainly a golden finale to a mandarin's career.

The practice of *amakudari* also extends to lower-ranked bureaucrats. The figure reported by the NPA is misleadingly small and does not include civil servants ranked assistant division head or lower. This group of bureaucrats are in what is termed the non-career path, meaning that they are not in the fast track to top positions, can only rise so far and are often charged with cler-ical and other non-leadership posts. Despite their lesser status, information compiled in 2001 by the *Asahi Shimbun* (June 4, 2001) indicates that over 2,500 civil servants in this group found jobs in companies with close ties with their former government agency.

News stories touting declines in *amakudari* – citing numbers of between 60 and 70 bureaucrats a year – grossly underestimate the extent of the practice. The reporting discrepancy arises from the requirement that the National Personnel Authority maintain records only on central government bureau-crats who reach division head or higher (i.e. career bureaucrats) who are re-employed within three years of retirement. For those ranked below division head, approval is granted by their own ministry, which is also responsible for maintaining relevant records. The *Asahi* report marks the first time that ministries and agencies have released information on the private-sector jobs obtained by these lower-ranking *amakudari*, an indication that the drive towards transparency is having some impact on correcting exaggerated claims of a decline in *amakudari*. However, the failure to disclose salaries, contractual relationships between the former ministry and the new employer, and orders for products and services by the ministry from the firms involved, indicates that there is still room for improved disclosure. For example, if a government clerk in charge of handling stationery products is subsequently employed by a stationery distributor, records of contracts and orders would be useful information to ensure transparency and discourage illicit practices.

The *Asahi* report drawing on files released under the new information disclosure law covers the period between 1998 and 2000, involving 2,515 bureaucrats at 25 ministries and agencies. The Ministry of Foreign Affairs declined to cooperate in the investigation. The list includes officials who took early retirement (there is a significant bonus added to the normal retirement allowance for doing so) and those transferred to other agencies upon retirement. In 1998, 946 bureaucrats found post-retirement jobs, a figure that declined to 788 in 1999 and 781 in 2001. These numbers constitute only about 3 percent of the 30,000 or so non-career bureaucrats who retire every year. Non-career bureaucrats from the Ministry of Posts and Communications constituted 25 percent of the total *amakudari* registered during this three-year period – 639 out of 2,515 – while the Ministry of Construction accounted for 21 percent and the Ministry of Transport an additional 19 percent. These three ministries accounted for 1,655 of the total placements or two-thirds of all non-career bureaucrat *amakudari*. The Ministry of Finance was placed a distant fourth.

Reform?

The government is fighting an uphill battle to regain the public trust it has squandered since the early 1990s. Measures aimed at reforming *amakudari* and reporting more openly about this practice are designed to mollify critics, although they often contain loopholes. For example, in 1998 a new system for private-sector *amakudari* recruitment was introduced. Private-sector firms submit requests for former bureaucrats through a business association that transmits the request to the NPA. The NPA then matches the requested qualifications with retired or soon-to-retire bureaucrats. Although this new system is aimed at eliminating direct job offers that might arouse suspicions, it does not apply to officials seeking jobs in the private sector more than two years after their retirement.

Efforts to curtail *amakudari* are being made by the Koizumi administration. Koizumi has lambasted officials for seeking jobs in sectors formerly under their jurisdiction and then extracting favors for their new employers from the agencies they formerly worked for. This systemic corruption has eroded public confidence in the government and generated suspicions that the system is rigged for the benefit of the well-connected. The lure of lucrative sinecures also deprives the government of experienced officials who are under implicit pressure to resign before mandatory retirement to allow promotions for their juniors. This in turn creates pressures to secure *amakudari* to lure these officials into early retirement. In order to break this cycle, the government has announced a broad range of reform proposals aimed at eradicating *amakudari*.

Reform measures proposed by the administration include performance pay, modification of retirement allowances, privatization of the *tokushu hojin*, greater transparency in divulging information about *amakudari*, full monitoring of post-retirement employment of bureaucrats and further restrictions on their re-employment, and imposition of a binding code of ethics. These proposals will no doubt face determined opposition from civil servants and any reforms achieved will be slow, diluted, and incremental.

Nonetheless, the momentum behind reform will be sustained for a number of reasons apart from public outrage. The widening disclosures about *amakudari* and the troubled finances of the state-linked corporations, largely staffed by ex-bureaucrats, is undermining the defiant position of the bureaucracy. With the implementation of the information disclosure law in 2001, the practices and perks of *amakudari* are being dragged out into the open and negative reaction is spreading. Employees of the public corporations forced to take on so many overpaid and underworked bureaucrats are finding that their suspicions about gross discrepancies in pay scales are being confirmed. These blatant inequities rankle with long-term, loyal company employees or *haenuki* (native-born) workers and, at a time of budget cuts and privatization, their ability to oppose *amakudari* is increasing. Bureaucrats with little hope of landing the plum *amakudari* are also finding out just how rich their seniors are getting at public expense. Such rivalries will ensure that frustrated and envious bureaucrats and employees from within the system will be working to undermine *amakudari* abuses; whistleblowing and selective leaks can have an impact. *Amakudari* is also a juicy target for politicians and the media who have their own reasons for wanting to trim the wings of the bureaucrats and curb the institutionalized fleecing of taxpayers by the mandarins. After all, it is not often that politicians find a target more disliked than themselves.

Nonetheless, the main threat to *amakudari* is an informed populism. As the veils over the workings of the bureaucracy and special corporations are peeled back, one can expect calls for tighter restrictions more effectively implemented, and demands for fuller disclosure and a process that will force ex-bureaucrats to meet public expectations about their conduct. There is also an element of self-interest here. As it stands, the excesses and poor judgment of the few are tarnishing the reputation of all bureaucrats and it will be in the interests of the majority to ensure that their colleagues abide by higher standards of conduct. This situation may encourage improved self-policing, as bureaucrats have a vested interest in restoring public confidence. To the extent that officials are satisfied that new rules are clear and evenly applied, most bureaucrats will follow approved procedures.

Another major threat to *amakudari* is privatization. The dismal state of public finances and the need to trim outlays will influence how the *tokushu hojin* are run. The salad days of the *amakudari* system are coming to a close and there will be fewer cushy sinecures because, privatized or not, the special corporations are facing closer scrutiny and tighter budgets. They will no longer receive the privileged and unmonitored access to the public trough that they now enjoy and that has underwritten the *amakudari* system in the past. The flow of funds to these quasi-public entities is becoming more transparent, making it difficult to continue old practices. While at present they enjoy a blanket exemption from information disclosure, this situation will become increasingly untenable in a climate of growing transparency and demands for greater accountability.

High life

Thousand-dollar bottles of wine, $2,000-a-night suites at the finest hotels, kickbacks, and turpitude of the highest order; haughty and naughty mandarins living it up and enjoying the high life while the nation gapes in wonder and outrage at their brazen behavior.[2] This is one face of Japan in the new millennium. The myth of duty, sacrifice, and austerity endured for the good of the nation has been exposed in the media as a flagrant lie obscuring the seamy reality. Since the 1990s, the public has been treated to the spectacle of arrogant bureaucrats caught with their hands in the till, their pants down, and living way beyond their means. A cascade of scandals, each topping the last, has alienated a public confronted with cases ranging from the excesses of errant clerks caught up in the humdrum routine of government work to million-dollar scams perpetrated at the highest levels of the bureaucracy. More shocking than the audacity and criminality of their actions was the realization that such practices were not only well established, but could only have persisted because they were implicitly condoned by the public service establishment.

Lifting the lid on this culture of pervasive corruption prompts many questions. How could the cult of Mammon be so widespread in the hallowed halls of Kasumigaseki? How long had it been going on and why did the media take so long to start reporting what they must have long known or suspected? In Japan, reporters are attached to specific ministries and agencies and pooled in press clubs where the line between reporting and socializing is indistinct. In such an environment, the whiff of scandal and damning information must have been in circulation for some time.

Perhaps the single most telling example of this corporate malfeasance was the massive embezzlement perpetrated by a Foreign Ministry official over several years during the 1990s. Matsuo Katsutoshi is suspected of having defrauded the government of some ¥800 million (approximately $6.7

Figure 4.2 Matsuo Katsutoshi, convicted of embezzling massive sums from the Ministry of Foreign Affairs. (Photo: Mainichi Newspapers)

million) between 1993 and 1999 by inflating the costs of hotels and travel
arrangements for overseas trips by prime ministers and their entourages, and
submitting fake receipts for expenses that were never incurred. As director of
the Overseas Visit Support Division, the logistics bureau in charge of such
arrangements, Matsuo was able to swindle the government out of vast sums
of money by drawing on a clandestine slush fund that was not carefully monitored. His ill-gotten lucre was used to purchase racehorses, a luxury condo-
minium, and lavish gifts for his girlfriend, and to fund a lifestyle associated
with 'high rollers' rather than 'grey suits.' In the end, Matsuo pleaded guilty,
issued a public apology, repaid ¥300 million of the money he had stolen and
promised to spend the rest of his life repaying the balance. In 2001 he was
found guilty of embezzling some ¥500 million between 1997 and 1999, and
sentenced to seven and a half years in prison. Investigators failed to examine
the entire period of his tenure due to missing documents and (most likely) a
desire to wrap up the unseemly case as soon as possible. Colleagues

apparently attributed his new-found wealth to a large inheritance he invented to cover his tracks.

The massive fraud perpetrated by Matsuo undermined already shaky public trust in the government and raised a number of questions about the moral character of officials and lax oversight within ministries. The fact that he went undiscovered for so long suggested that the government was at the very least remiss in monitoring how public money was spent and far too tolerant of the expensive tastes that, it emerged, were the norm for top Japanese diplomats. Assuming senior officials did not condone Matsuo's actions, it is amazing that such a massive embezzlement went undetected for so long. Essentially, there are two scenarios, both damning. Either Matsuo's scheme followed standard practice in the ministry and was known to others who went on to make him a sacrificial lamb, or it is an indictment of lax bureaucratic procedures and controls.

The Matsuo scandal and other revelations taught taxpayers what diplomats in other countries had known for some time: Japan's diplomacy is conducted on a champagne budget, but yields beer-budget results. Although Japan's coddled diplomats may have known their way around the high-priced wine lists at the best eateries in Europe, they were not highly regarded by their counterparts for their diplomatic savvy or local knowledge. In short, Japan was punching well short of its weight in international fora and its pampered diplomatic corps have been accused of being ineffectual and out of touch.[3]

In the wake of Matsuo's massive embezzlement, investigations revealed similar, but smaller-scale, swindles by other officials charged with providing logistic support for international conferences. It emerged that padding accommodation and transport receipts for reimbursement was standard practice, but tolerated because departments squirreled away the extra funds for discretionary use, often for welcoming and departure parties, gifts, taxi vouchers, and other items not covered by the official budget. The problem was that officials engaged in systematically pilfering the Foreign Ministry's discretionary fund to amass slush funds for their respective departments, came to draw on these funds for personal use. In addition, officials charged with selecting venues for international conferences were wined and dined at plush hotels (sometimes with their girlfriends) in exchange for lucrative conference accounts. An internal investigation determined that at least 70 departments in the Foreign Ministry had amassed secret slush funds, reinforcing the perception that such frauds were rife. A Board of Audit investigation carried out in the closing months of 2002 discovered that the amount accumulated in the slush funds was over ¥450 million ($3.75 million), more than twice the sum uncovered by the ministry's internal investigation, raising questions about how seriously the ministry has taken the matter and how such vast sums could be accumulated without raising any flags. Wild bon voyage parties and vintage wines notwithstanding, it was hard to guess what could possibly justify sequestering such princely sums of taxpayer money and then covering it up. Yet again, by botching the internal investigation the ministry demonstrated a low sense of responsibility and an embarrassing penchant for public relations gaffes.

As a result of these revelations about the systemic abuse of the public trust and misuse of public funds, both the media and politicians have put pressure on government ministries to more carefully monitor expenditures and tighten oversight of officials. The Foreign Ministry has had to defend its clandestine budget, accept cuts, move ordinary expenses to other budget categories, impose tighter monitoring controls and issue new rules about entertaining visiting dignitaries at overseas embassies. Apparently overseas diplomats dipped into the slush funds to entertain visiting Diet members and even inspectors charged with curtailing just such abuses – hardly consistent with the allegedly clandestine information-gathering activities used to justify the massive discretionary budget.

From 2003, all such Foreign Ministry expenditures are to be subject to strict reporting requirements, review, and open disclosure. While this may not totally eliminate such abuses, it will certainly make it more difficult to commit them with impunity. It also appears that ranking officials at overseas consulates have been pocketing public money for personal use; unannounced and far more rigorous inspections are now being instituted. Thus, across the board, the Foreign Ministry is establishing stricter standards, tighter monitoring of disbursements, and setting a precedent for more disclosure – important steps towards better governance that will motivate other ministries to follow suit. Now that the media recognizes the power of freedom of information in generating front-page stories, and can report government scandals with impunity, the veils of secrecy that have allowed abuses to flourish are likely to be pushed back still further.

The Foreign Ministry's own investigation had shown that roughly ¥200 million in slush funds had been accumulated by 71 out of 100 departments. However, there was no effort to determine individual responsibility, no penalties were imposed, and investigators dug back only six years even though it was clear that diversion and misappropriation of funds had a much lengthier history. Information disclosure requests by the media unearthed memos suggesting that the investigation was conducted in a half-hearted manner, more as an exercise in public relations than an attempt to determine the extent of abuses and hold officials accountable for their ethical lapses. The skeptics were vindicated by the subsequent Board of Audit report. The ministry's own documents reveal a primary concern with maintaining harmony among officials, meaning that real efforts to pin blame were never attempted. The use of public money for personal projects appears to have been routine among officials at the ministry, as were attempts to generate paperwork meant to conceal such activities. In many respects, these revelations of abuses in the central government echoed the *kan-kan settai* and *karashutcho* scandals at the local level exposed by information disclosure activists in the mid-1990s; in both instances, creating slush funds proved to be accepted practice and an area of considerable bureaucratic skill. This was business as usual for a ruling class that had lost its bearings and ethics.

The Foreign Ministry has a reputation for being a 'gentlemen's' club, a high-class milieu within the bureaucratic ranks where family connections and 'breeding' count and second- (and third-) generation employment is more tolerated than in other ministries. The haughty bearing of top-ranking officials, their social pretensions and tin ear for political realities have made them suitable figures for the soap opera of national politics. The media have delighted in exposing their excesses and foppery, and the public has taken great pleasure in seeing them dragged through the mud.

Low life

Matters came to a head with the appointment of Tanaka Makiko as Foreign Minister in April 2001. Dropped into a cesspool of scandal and botched cover-ups, her brief was to sort out the ministry's problems and institute meaningful reforms. As she was the daughter of Japan's most notorious backroom fixer and the man credited with systematizing cash-and-carry money politics, there were resounding ironies in choosing her to wield a broom in the troubled Foreign Ministry. In addition, she speaks like a truck driver, has a strong grassroots appeal, and, at the time she was appointed, was the most popular politician in the country. For the bluebloods at the ministry she was a nightmare come true, a hard-nosed populist unyielding in her demands and uncompromising in her stance. Instead of looking to their tattered reputation, the mandarins fixed their attention on what they saw as their nemesis: Tanaka became a lightning rod for the contempt and anger of men unaccustomed to being hauled onto the carpet and forced to explain their actions.

After Tanaka's appointment – certainly not made on the basis of any foreign policy expertise – she wasted little time in alienating her subordinates by freezing all personnel rotations and promotions. This dramatic and unprecedented action was aimed at conveying her displeasure with some recent appointments and demonstrating that under her leadership it would no longer be 'business as usual' at the ministry. She was serious about rooting out corruption and made it clear that the freeze would remain until information about the scandals was forthcoming. Thus, she played a key role in forcing the ministry to come clean about practices that it would have preferred to sweep under the *tatami* mat. Far from gaining credit for trying to restore public confidence by coming clean on rampant abuses, her airing of the ministry's dirty laundry earned her the bitter enmity of her colleagues. They never seemed to realize that it was their own gaffes and poor judgment that had brought them low.

Aware of Tanaka's popularity with voters, Prime Minister Koizumi was hesitant to confront her, but a series of public spats about personnel shuffles and appointments during the first few months of her tenure made her

Figure 4.3 Tanaka Makiko, the popular Foreign Minister sacked in 2002 by Prime
Minister Koizumi. (Photo: Mainichi Newspapers)

departure only a matter of time. In addition, she aired some personal
disagreements with official policy, committed a number of gaffes that
included revealing the secret hideout of senior US government officials in the
wake of the events of September 11, 2001, and demonstrated that she was
generally ill-suited to diplomacy. Her enemies in the ministry, in connivance
with the Hashimoto faction in the LDP, leaked private comments made to
visiting dignitaries in order to embarrass and discredit her and give ammuni-
tion to her enemies in the Diet.

The media had a field day. From the revelations of corruption to the public
tiffs in the ministry, Japan was treated to an unprecedented spectacle: a
popular woman taking on the Establishment and giving as good as she got.
The revelations of abuses kept coming and, in revenge for a series of leaks
designed to embarrass her, Tanaka took her officials to task for reserving
over-lavish rooms for her on a visit to China. Defending this as standard practice did the ministry little good and, in the battle of public relations that raged
around her, she was making her ministry look every bit as bad as the

(Roger Dahl)

muckraking weeklies. However, as more and more commentators pointed out, being foreign minister involved more than waging a campaign against her own ministry, and concerns about her penchant for miscues led the Diet to impose humiliating travel restrictions that kept her from attending international meetings.

This impasse was finally resolved by her dismissal in January 2002 over allegations, supported by her own vice-minister, that she had lied in the Diet about an incident involving a notorious LDP politician Suzuki Muneo. Tanaka had accused Suzuki of pressuring the Foreign Ministry to bar an NGO activist from attending a conference on rebuilding Afghanistan. She refused to back down and repeated her allegations, which were verified by a senior official in the ministry, but Suzuki also repeated his denials. Finding the opportunity for which he had been waiting, Prime Minister Koizumi sacked both Tanaka and her vice-minister, while Suzuki escaped apparently unscathed by relinquishing his position on a foreign policy committee in the Diet. This astounding drama ended with the sacking of the nation's most popular politician, despite polls indicating overwhelming public support for her version of events. Suzuki gloated to the media that he was very happy with the outcome.

However, the tables were soon to be turned. In the ensuing months it emerged that Suzuki had indeed intervened in barring the activist from the Afghanistan conference on the grounds that he had voiced skepticism to the media about the truthfulness of government officials. This proved to be just the tip of the iceberg. Suzuki exerted enormous influence in the ministry in exchange for championing its budget and interests in the Diet. He was a virtual shadow foreign minister, especially with regard to Japan's policy towards Russia. In the disputed northern territories – a number of islands off the coast of Hokkaido seized by the Soviet Union in the closing days of World War II – Suzuki played a powerful and corrupt role in development projects. A native of Hokkaido, he regularly awarded contracts to local

Figure 4.4 Suzuki Muneo, a politician with close ties to the Foreign Ministry, is notorious for battles with Tanaka Makiko and his arrest for bribery. (Photo:
Mainichi Newspapers)

construction firms that had been generous with their campaign contributions.
He also intervened in promotions and rotation of personnel in the ministry,
received regular briefings, was privy to classified documents, and shaped
negotiations with Russia over the future of the northern territories. Suzuki's
contacts in the ministry allowed him to tap into the Official Development
Assistance (ODA) budget and he used this influence to leverage donations
from firms eager to win contracts.

Investigations revealed a number of irregularities that suggested he was
trading favors for money and he was eventually prosecuted and jailed after
being kicked out of the LDP. Tanaka's successor at the Ministry of Foreign
Affairs, who commissioned an inquiry into Suzuki's influence at the ministry,
termed his actions 'perverse' and made it clear that such destructive political
meddling would no longer be tolerated. So it was that Suzuki, one of the
biggest fundraisers in the largest faction (Hashimoto) in the LDP, a man
feared for his fiery temper and powerful connections, was brought low by an

activist from a small organization called Peace Winds. This tumultuous year in the Foreign Ministry provided the Japanese with a window on shenanigans in high places, unseemly mud-flinging, corruption on a massive scale, fraud as standard practice, and political meddling that revealed the ugly underside of the Iron Triangle.

The Suzuki case exposed influence-peddling as one of the major problems of a highly regulated economy. Corruption and collusion are built into the parliamentary system: *Zoku-giin* (Diet members who act as patrons of particular ministries) regularly meddle in policymaking, contract bidding and regulatory matters on behalf of those who make it worth their while to do so. Diet members develop an 'expertise' in a certain area and form close ties with bureaucrats in the relevant ministry who provide them with information, access and opportunities to influence policy outcomes for the benefit of their political supporters. The problem is not the interaction between politicians, bureaucrats and corporations per se, but rather the corruption and disregard for ethics that permeates such relationships. But as the autonomy of bureaucrats wanes and their decisions and policies become subject to public review, the risks of collusion are rising. Growing transparency will mean less room for rampant corruption. In Suzuki's case, information disclosure requests yielded documents that were used to expose his activities and led to his expulsion from the party and subsequent prosecution on charges of bribery. Thus, information disclosure has become a weapon not only for citizens and the media to hold bureaucrats accountable, but also for officials who can wield it to expose and deter political meddling.

Tanaka herself was also brought low and resigned her seat in the Diet in August 2002 following allegations that she misappropriated funds related to her secretary's state-paid salary. While this practice of diverting funds for other uses is a fairly routine practice, Tanaka was a marked woman. Suzuki's colleagues had their revenge while foreign ministry bureaucrats could not refrain from savoring a taste of *Schadenfreude.* One former subordinate commented to the press, 'She dug her own grave. I am sure some people will appreciate her role as the catalyst for Foreign Ministry reform, but most of us still hold a deep grudge for the way she lorded it over us.' Ironically, the reported amounts involved in the case were small change for such a wealthy legislator, reminding people of her father's conviction over a relatively modest bribe involving the purchase of Lockheed aircraft in the 1970s.

Lessons and consequences

The lessons to be learned from bureaucratic scandals point to the benefits of transparency and the problems that brew under the cloak of secrecy and unaccountability. The media tapped the new information disclosure law to force revelations that otherwise would not have been forthcoming. Government ministries were forced to confront their own attitudes and policies regarding accountability and transparency and improve on both fronts to quell public anger and to meet rising expectations about what constitutes good governance.

The bureaucracy is learning that the rules are changing in the twenty-first century. Whether it is *amakudari*, systematic defrauding of the government, influence-peddling, or 'compensation,' the bureaucrats' business is becoming the public's business and, as information about the workings of government become public knowledge, this is having an impact on how officials conduct themselves. For all its shortcomings, the information disclosure law is proving to be surprisingly effective in enabling the media and citizens to hold their officials accountable and bring them to justice in cases of malfeasance. Even in these early days, the media has proved itself resourceful in forcing disclosure and pressuring the bureaucracy to be more open.

It has long been assumed that real power in Japan resides in the bureaucracy and is exercised by bureaucrats with modest input from politicians. Although this remains true, there are four crucial factors that are slowly eroding the power, authority, and autonomy of the bureaucrats and restoring greater balance in the polity. The keys to bureaucratic power have been wide-ranging discretionary authority, power of the purse, control over information, and a high degree of immunity. Merely listing these pillars of power indicates how much has changed in recent years and to what degree the bureaucracy's wings have been clipped. Although it remains *primus inter pares*, the bureaucracy's power is in decline and the trend looks set to continue.

Let us examine these pillars of power in turn. *Gyosei shido*, the power of 'administrative guidance,' which facilitated the imposition of policies and actions based on bureaucratic fiat rather than the law, is now formally banned. Although this does not mean that such practices have been eliminated, it does mean that they are subject to penalty and censure should they become public knowledge. This is bound to have a dampening effect on the exercise of such discretionary authority, especially in an age of greater transparency and compulsory information disclosure. What used to be pervasive and unassailable now carries risk and the potential to jeopardize a promising career.

The bureaucracy's power over public spending remains, but it too is now subject to greater scrutiny and public disclosure. Spending practices that cannot meet public standards and expectations are more likely to result in sanctions than in the past. What used to be standard operating procedures have now been explicitly forbidden: lax oversight and a failure to ensure that money is spent on what it is intended for are now subject to rebuke and possible prosecution.

Those who transgress the new rules can no longer hide behind 'established practices' or expect superiors to cover for them. Taking care of such problems 'in-house' and covering up the embarrassing details, standard official practice until recent years, has become far riskier. The revolution in information technology and the information disclosure legislation have permanently undermined bureaucratic power to control events, processes, and outcomes by managing the flow of information. Citizens now have access to multiple information sources and can bypass traditional media outlets and the government to create their own networks of information and mobilization. Moreover, the government now governs in the knowledge that its actions and omissions can be second-guessed as a result of the information disclosure law. Actions that might once have passed muster under the cover of inaccessibility no longer make sense for bureaucrats whose record follows them throughout their career.

Finally, the high degree of immunity enjoyed by bureaucrats is fast disappearing. The media is publishing more about official abuses and letting the public in on some of the bureaucracy's tawdry secrets that have usually been kept under wraps.[4] With greater transparency comes greater accountability and less leeway for avoiding responsibility. Information disclosure means that bureaucrats no longer enjoy carte blanche to wrap themselves in the flag of national interest, or the need for discretion, and thus hold off inquiries and prosecution. Those who fail to serve the public interest or otherwise abuse the public trust now risk exposure and legal consequences. This will ensure that bureaucrats act with greater concern for the public welfare. The days of systematically favoring producers over consumers are numbered because now the public is in a position to access relevant information, expose official bias, and secure remedies. While there will always be strategies for avoiding oversight and disclosure, the risks and penalties are rising. Bureaucrats will come to trim their sails to the prevailing winds and that means accepting the logic and dictates of greater transparency, higher standards, greater accountability and much less insulation from scrutiny and punishment. The system that allowed bureaucrats to profit from the activities they control is in decline. They are being goaded to change, to set aside blanket secrecy and adopt policies that will regain public trust. Thus the crisis in the government's legitimacy that has resulted from the scandals has become also a force for change.

The decline in the autonomy of the bureaucrats is restoring balance to Japan's stunted and sclerotic civil society. The extensive regulatory and policymaking powers and autonomy enjoyed by bureaucrats under what is termed the '1940 system' are receding. This system of wartime powers, reinforced by the US Occupation authorities, left a legacy of distorted government, incomplete democratization, and few channels for citizens' input or oversight. The remaking of Japan by administrative fiat during the Occupation, imposing democratic reforms through undemocratic means, influenced the nature of Japan's polity and stunted the development of civil society (Dower 1999). The government was insulated from the exposure to public opinion that is part of the democratic process and endowed with sweeping powers to implement policies and regulations at its own discretion. While this streamlined the policymaking process and accelerated the pace of government decisions, and perhaps economic growth, it was achieved at the cost of losing touch with the people. Moreover, in pursuing high-speed growth at all costs the political economy of Japan came to systematically favor producers; the government saw its job as promoting the interests of the companies who were generating growth, jobs, and wealth. In doing so, the distinctions between oversight and boosterism were blurred and consumers' interests were neglected.

The power and autonomy of the bureaucracy are being further undermined by wrenching economic changes and prolonged recession that are transforming Japan's political economy. Privatization of state-owned enterprises and deregulation are proceeding as expected – slowly, fitfully, and incompletely. Restructuring of companies that compete in international markets, however, is proceeding with greater vigor as their survival depends on rapidly adapting to the demands of globalization. This more rapid pace of transformation in the private sector is generating pressures for change in the public sector and shaping how it governs; transparency, the rule of law, and other international norms are high on the agenda, reinforcing existing trends in Japan. So too the surge in foreign direct investment (FDI) is generating pressure for change. While levels remain small by international standards, the growing involvement of foreign investors and companies in Japan is making it ever more difficult to maintain the closed shop and 'old boy' network. In 1999, incoming FDI stood at $13 billion, up from $3 billion in 1998.[5] As more and more international companies come to operate in Japan they will lobby ever more effectively, often with the support of Japanese counterparts, for good governance, transparency, deregulation, acceptance of international norms, the rule of law and an end to favoritism. The strong support within the Japanese business community for sweeping judicial reforms and information disclosure – driven by enlightened self-interest – is consistent with changes favored by foreign companies and governments. The opaque and subjective ways of the current system are seen to be detrimental to business and one of the reasons for Japan's prolonged malaise.

Changing how the bureaucracy governs and reducing its autonomy are necessary to reinvigorate Japan's 'bonsai' civil society. For too long the branches of citizen input have been too rigorously pruned and overshadowed by the overgrown branches of bureaucracy. As NPOs develop and grow to more effectively channel citizen input on setting the nation's agenda, shaping policies, and monitoring outcomes, civil society will benefit from greater levels of public participation. Institutionalizing such participation in NPOs is crucial for them to develop the strength and expertise to become effective partners with government organizations. This process of transformation and reinvigoration of civil society will take decades and patience will no doubt wear thin as progress proves painfully slow. The reinvigoration of civil society is not a foregone conclusion and everything depends on how people respond – how they use their new powers and institutions, who they choose as their political leaders, and how committed they remain. Civil society is a delicate bloom that requires constant nurturing; it is easily blighted by apathy.

Threats to reform are evident in many quarters. As we have seen, the media has played a crucial role in lifting the lid on official corruption and gaining public support for more open government and, inter alia, reduced bureaucratic autonomy. As the public grows impatient with the slow pace of reform and the benefits they expect from it, sustained focus in the media on continued abuses of power and the public trust will prove crucial. This is why the government's frustrated efforts in 2002 to muzzle the media and deter whistleblowers under the pretext of a human rights bill are so alarming. An active and vigilant press is vital to the ongoing quiet transformation and, if silenced, could derail the entire process.

Will the sense of crisis and low morale in the bureaucracy generate internal pressures for reforming the government and open more space for civil society? Probably not quickly or thoroughly enough to meet rising public expectations. As much as recent initiatives are welcome signs of reform, the weight of institutional inertia and engrained habits of governance suggest a slow process rather than an abrupt shift to greater openness and accountability. Although bureaucrats have been stung by their battered reputation and the series of revelations that have alienated the public, they show little sense of urgency about the need to change their ways.

In 2002 the government commissioned a poll of 500 civil servants around the country, the first such survey undertaken and a rare insight into their troubled state of mind. It amounts to a searing indictment of the bureaucracy by the bureaucrats. More than 80 percent admitted that their elitist perspective prevented them from considering issues from the standpoint of the general public, while more than 70 percent admitted that intraministerial turf wars were more important than the national interest. While the report candidly admitted that the bureaucracy has failed to live up to public expectations, it offered little hope of reform if bureaucrats are left to their own devices. It presented a picture of an institution suffering from deeply engrained elitism, a sense of entitlement, little sense of public duty, and a failure to recognize that established patterns and practices had aided its own demise. In short, the bureaucrats seem at least to be aware of the public's opinion of them even if they abjure what the public expects of them. The bureaucrats emerged from the survey as reluctant reformers, responding only grudgingly and out of self-interest rather than out of a sense of duty. Thus, it appears that external pressures will be crucial to maintaining the momentum of reform and that the fragile prospects of restoring balance in the polity will remain dependent on informed and committed citizen participation.

Citizens' organizations and the media have played a key role in waking people up to the dangers of apathy and the benefits of transparency and accountability. Reporting on various scandals has been crucial in gaining public attention and support for more open government and, inter alia, reduced bureaucratic autonomy. In realizing the long-term goal of reinvigorating civil society, the self-inflicted wounds of the bureaucracy detailed by the media have been crucial in convincing more people that assuming the burdens of nurturing civil society is worthwhile and desperately needed. As we have seen, the struggle to promote open government has not been easy, but the strengthening of civil society through judicial reforms, information disclosure, and NPO activism is generating momentum for greater transparency. The initial successes in recent years are encouraging, but also demonstrate just how closed the business of government remains and how grudgingly bureaucrats accept the principle of the people's right to know. Clearly, transforming transparency and accountability into habits of those who govern remains a tremendous challenge.

5 Downsizing the construction state

Every valley shall be filled and every mountain and hill brought low; the
crooked places shall be made straight and the rough ways smooth.

Luke 3:5

First there is a mountain, then there is no mountain, then there is.

Old Zen koan

The country is in shambles, yet the highways extend far and wide.

Nabeshima Keizo, *Japan Times*, December 16, 2002

The term *doken kokka* or 'construction state' is popular shorthand for the huge
'cement industrial complex' that commands so much economic and political
power in contemporary Japan. Critics credit the *doken kokka* mentality with a
dysfunctional overbuilding of Japan's infrastructure since the 'Income
Doubling Plan' announced by Prime Minister Ikeda Hayato in 1960. In the
ensuing years, Japan has been criss-crossed by roads and expressways; rivers
have been concreted, dammed, and straightened; mountains have been
leveled, tunneled, sculpted, denuded, and concreted; wetlands have been
paved over; and bridges have spanned rivers, lakes, estuaries, and seas in an
archipelago that has the highest per capita cement consumption in the world.
While many of these infrastructure projects were necessary and beneficial,
the logic of the construction state does not rest on need and its benefits are
enjoyed most by a select few.

Pouring so much of the nation's wealth and energy into grandiose construction projects that are impoverishing both the treasury and the environment,
while ignoring small but necessary initiatives to improve the quality of life, has
led to what Alex Kerr (2001) refers to as Japan's failed modernization. For
Gavan McCormack (1996), the poor quality of life enjoyed by citizens in such
a rich country reflects the emptiness of Japanese affluence; so much wealth has
translated into so few benefits and left a squalid and money-draining legacy.
The nation's leaders have relentlessly defaced what was once a beautiful
country with concrete baubles that reflect the poverty of their imagination and
the depravity of their acquisitive ways. In doing so, they have burdened future
generations with mountains of debt. This mortgaging of Japan's natural bounty

Figure 5.1 Cherry blossoms above a concreted river bank. (Photo: Andreas Seibert/ Lookat)

and its economic future reflects an institutional myopia and pervasive corruption. While those who have fed at this golden trough of cement-mania have done well for themselves, others have been left to foot the bill for their profligacy. For both Kerr and McCormack, and the millions of Japanese who support their analysis, the squandering of vast sums of money on environmentally destructive and economically unnecessary projects for the benefit of the construction industry and its political patrons is an indictment of Japan, Inc. and all the more reason to cheer its demise.

As we have seen, the events of the Lost Decade revealed the flaws of Japan's postwar system and discredited the practices associated with it. Ironically, the 1990s proved a boom-time for the construction state as the government boosted public works spending in a failed attempt to revive the economy. Ever vaster sums were poured into construction of roads and tunnels to nowhere and dams and bridges without a purpose, adding to the mountain of debt already piled on the shoulders of today's and tomorrow's taxpayers for the benefit of yesterday's men. Between 1992 and 1999, a series of economic recovery packages totaling some ¥120 trillion was spent, boosting the total debt of central and local governments to a staggering ¥666 trillion by 2002. About ¥70 trillion of this ¥120 trillion, equivalent to nearly 90 percent of the national general account budget for 2002, was spent on public works projects. Although this pump-priming exercise was justified as a means to create jobs and soften the hard landing of the economic implosion, in reality it further distorted the economy, made more people dependent on an already unsustainable sector, and did nothing to resolve Japan's fundamental economic woes. Although administering the steroids of public works spending postponed the day of reckoning, the adverse impact of such injections on the economy is already evident. As the priming of the construction pump has fallen off, so has the number of jobs, while construction companies of all sizes are going bankrupt.

This disastrous policy of subsidizing and artificially inflating the construction industry meant that at the turn of the century it employed over 6 million workers, many in make-work jobs that could never be sustained. The construction industry accounts for more than 20 percent of Japan's GDP compared with 10.4 percent in the USA, 7.6 percent in the UK and 8.9 percent in Germany. About 8 percent of the US national budget is spent on construction, while in Japan it is 40 percent. In terms of the workforce, about 1 percent of Americans are employed in construction while in Japan the figure is about 12 percent. This helps explain why a country the size of California lays as much concrete as in the entire USA, and has cemented some 60 percent of its coastline.

In 2002, Japan had 586,000 construction firms each with an average of 12 employees, the result of a law passed in 1966 mandating that central and local governments award public works contracts to small and medium-sized local firms. As a result, contracts awarded to such firms rose from 26.8 percent in the 1966/67 financial year to 41.6 percent in 1999/2000. This situation also reflects the fact that most municipal and prefectural governments have rules that exclude non-local firms from bidding on public works contracts. As a result, the number of small, local road-paving firms has skyrocketed from 479 in 1966 to 41,867 by 1985, and 90,096 in 2001. This system has led to absurd distortions in the market. In general, these local contractors carry out little of the work they contract; after winning the bid they subcontract entire projects to large national construction firms after deducting a 'finder's fee.' The legal requirement favoring local firms has been a mechanism for influence-peddling, bid-rigging, price-gouging, bribes, and under-the-table contributions to political campaign funds. It has also resulted in Japanese taxpayers paying up to 30 percent more than market rates, often for work that was unnecessary to begin with.

Public works spending has thus been exposed as a quack remedy for the ailing national economy. Revelations of systematic bid-rigging, payoffs, faked demand projections, inflated contract prices, and political machinations have tainted the *doken kokka* and convinced an increasingly skeptical public that it is all a scam being run at their expense. Politicians are sensing this shift in voter perceptions and are increasingly running against pork-barrel projects as fiscally and environmentally irresponsible – elections have been won on this platform in a number of recent gubernatorial contests. While such reversals constitute only a tiny minority, they reflect a shift in mood that would have been unimaginable in the early 1990s. The perversities of the construction state detailed by McCormack and Kerr are now regularly featured in the mass media. Its defenders are reviled by Prime Minister Koizumi, and the press, as the 'forces of resistance' and condemned as obstacles in the path of reform. These so-called 'road tribe' (*dorozoku*) politicians are widely dismissed as relics of a bygone age, anachronisms who are standing in the way of Japan's economic revival and imperiling the nation's future. They are heavily implicated in the triangle of collusion involving public works bureaucrats, politicians and contractors. In the early years of the twenty-first century, their considerable power and influence is waning, heralding a paring back of the construction state in coming years.

However, environmental activists remain skeptical, pointing to the scant gains won against the cement juggernaut that has rampaged throughout Japan over several decades. It is hard for them to imagine that the *doken kokka* has mixed the cement of its own undoing and has built an archipelagic sarcophagus commemorating the folly of politicians more interested in votes and money, and bureaucrats more committed to turf and budget than the public interest. Although even a major scaling back of the *doken kokka* will still leave Japan with a bloated construction sector, most critics would concede that if ever there was a case where less is more, this is it; the pork will be trimmed not eliminated and some progress is better than none. And there are signs of clear, if limited, progress. The public rows over cuts in construction spending and subsidies have alerted people to the extent of accumulated indebtedness and environmental destruction wrought by the sector. And the declining autonomy of the bureaucracy due to information disclosure and the rise of the NPO sector should give citizens more influence on setting priorities and challenging agendas set by the vested interests of the construction industry. Privatization will also introduce market mechanisms into the assessment of large-scale road and bridge construction projects and impose a discipline that may curtail some of the current excesses. Now that the former Environmental Agency has become a more powerful institutional actor as a full-fledged ministry, it has successfully opposed some pork-barrel projects and can be expected to build on these successes. Finally, the Ministry of Land, Infrastructure, and Transport (MLIT – a combination of the former construction and transport ministries) is seeking to 'green' its budget, undoing some of the destruction it has caused – albeit for the usual bureaucratic motives of turf and budget. In a climate where fewer roads to nowhere can be built, it makes sense to

Figure 5.2 Some 60% of Japan's coastline is concreted, often with massive tetrapods like these. (Photo: Stuart Issett)

legitimize budget proposals in a way designed to meet public expectations and win kudos for a beleaguered ministry.

Thus momentum is building for the advent of the 'deconstruction state' – a renewed Japan built on the detritus of the *doken kokka*, involving large-scale environmental reconstruction projects such as decommissioning dams and nuclear power plants, restoring coastline by removing environmentally destructive concrete blocks known as tetrapods, restoring rivers to their natural state, and undoing the reclamation of wetlands. Restoration will be a far more welcome and legitimate way to justify public works spending on make-work jobs and help divert at least some of the destructive power of the *doken kokka* into environmentally friendly projects. Undertakings such as conservation projects, natural flood-control initiatives, and measures aimed at preserving biodiversity are already happening on a small scale. Although initially this may amount to little more than window-dressing, the experience of Europe and the USA in mounting comparable efforts will inspire Japanese planners eager to justify budgets, generate employment, and regain the public trust. Once it becomes clear that there there is money to be made and votes to be had out of 'deconstruction,' human nature will become an ineluctable force behind environmental restoration and preservation. Thus, in part for the wrong reasons, there is cause for guarded optimism about the prospects for strong political and institutional support for redirecting the *doken kokka* and dealing with some of its more egregious daubs on Japan's landscape.

Last hurrah for the *doken kokka*?

> There are no roads in this country worth investing in because none of them will be profitable. If the four road-related public corporations are to be privatized, all other money-losing road projects should be terminated as well.
>
> Japan Highway official, November 2001

There are four reasons why the construction state has passed its zenith and faces significant downsizing in coming years. First, the government's chronic fiscal crisis dictates sharp budget cuts, and road allocations are too tempting a target to ignore. Second, privatization of the expressway-related public corporations and elimination of their government subsidies will make economic viability the key criterion in any decisions affecting highway construction. (Based on this criterion, there are no highways worth building.) Third, privatization of the Post Office will eventually limit access to its savings accounts that fund the *zaito* (the so-called second budget, also known as the fiscal investment-and-loan program), where road spending is concentrated and subject to only cursory monitoring. Once the Post Office is privatized it will screen loan requests and unprofitable road-building projects are unlikely to receive funding. Finally, as we have seen, environmental concerns about the devastation caused by overbuilding the nation's infrastructure are translating into cancelled projects, successful anti-pork-barrel political campaigns, and a shift towards 'greening' of public works projects. Supported by national NPOs, and armed with the weapons of information disclosure, referendums, and lawsuits, local citizen groups eager to preserve the environment and curb spiraling debt will increasingly gain the confidence to take on the vested interests of the construction state – and may even sometimes prevail.

Downsizing the construction state will take time, but the moat has been breached and the siege continues. The construction state will persist because the massive revenues designated for road building (nearly ¥6 trillion per annum) are well protected by *dorozoku* (politicians who lobby for the *doken kokka*), whose political careers depend on literally cementing their base of support in the rural districts they represent. But, with tighter budgets and the rising fiscal demands of social welfare programs for an aging society, it is likely that in coming years more of these revenues will be channeled to the general budget, further closing the spigot of taxpayer largesse that has kept the cement flowing. Construction outlays will be subject to closer scrutiny and tougher evaluations as the government juggles priorities. Naturally, with so much money at stake the battles will be fiercely contested but, as Japan renovates its civil society, the balance of power is shifting away from the bureaucrats and politicians who champion the construction state. Competition for a slice of the budget pie will gradually lead to a redivision of the spoils, with other vested interests gaining at the expense of the road lobby.

Cash and carry

The *doken kokka* is based on the three Cs – cement, corruption, and cash. Because Japan is running short of the latter, the *doken kokka* is living on borrowed time – at least on its present grand scale. Aside from soaring budget deficits and the consequent need to trim outlays, the *doken kokka* is also discredited because it is associated with the postwar system widely blamed for the prolonged economic slump gripping Japan. As we have seen, during the 1990s the government engaged in massive public works spending to prime the pump and boost the economy out of the doldrums. But, far from rejuvenating the economy, these huge supplemental public works budgets have only exacerbated the government's fiscal woes while saddling taxpayers with mountains of debt for several generations to come. The architects of this failed policy are champions of dated policies that are no longer adequate to deal with the challenges facing Japan. They are identified with the corrupt practices and smoke-filled rooms where deals are cut, favors doled out, and the public is sold out. In short, the *doken kokka* is now viewed as a significant part of the problem – a juicy target for budget cuts and ambitious politicians eager to distance themselves from the practices of the past that are haunting contemporary Japan.

Bid-rigging is one of the most pervasive abuses of the *doken kokka*; while it maximizes profits for the firms that practice it, it also boosts the costs of construction projects to the state and the taxpayer. Bidding on most public works contracts is restricted by government authorities to designated firms that meet established criteria. The *dango* system of bid-rigging allows construction industry associations of such designated firms to unofficially pick the winners of public works contracts through a system of rotation based on size and track record. This cartel arrangement avoids ruinous price competition and spreads the spoils around. Knowing in advance the supposedly secret contract ceiling established for each project, the designated winner submits a bid close to that ceiling while the other firms submit higher bids and so price themselves out of the competition. Studies indicate that this rigged system results in contract bids that are almost always improbably close to 95 percent of the contract ceiling. In areas where there has been closer monitoring of *dango* practices and competition is opened to non-local firms, contract bids are usually only 70–85 percent of the proposed ceiling, meaning that in fair competition with no leaking of secret bid information, public works contracts can be far less costly. Since firms can still turn a profit at the lower bids, the difference no doubt represents the amount of money diverted to bribes, campaign funds, and other scams. Bid-rigging is tolerated by officials as it is an effective means to ensure that budget allocations are used up and cuts avoided in the following year. This is the dark side of the construction state, involving a collusive nexus between officials, businessmen, organized crime, and politicians that inspires comparisons with practices prevailing in southern Italy until recent times (Samuels 2003).

It is estimated that a vast majority of bids on Japan's public works contracts are rigged – or at least they were before the government started clamping down and the statute of limitations on prosecution was lifted. The rules of the game seem to be changing as even high-ranking politicians, including two former Construction Ministers and two prefectural governors, as well as several top executives at construction firms, have been arrested since the mid-1990s for bid-rigging and bribery.

In the wake of this spate of high-profile scandals reaching to the very top of the construction state, in 2001 the Diet enacted legislation requiring central and local governments, as well as public corporations, to disclose more information about contract bids and awards. They are now obliged to reveal the names of all bidders and winners of each contract, the amount of the winning bid and the criteria for determining which firms qualify for bidding. The new legislation also calls on the Cabinet to improve bidding procedures to eradicate bid-rigging. Other provisions include a ban on the practice of *maru-nage* (throw-it-all) whereby local contractors win bids, take a cut, and subcontract the project to large national firms. The bill also urges prefectural and municipal governments to refrain from imposing geographical restrictions that ensure local contractors face little competition in bidding. However, this latter measure is not mandatory and lacks punitive sanctions. Since the dominant LDP is dependent on local construction firms for campaign funds and votes, the prospects for meaningful reform in this area seem remote as long as it stays in power.

The collusion and corruption that this legislation was designed to counter is abetted by the system of ostensibly favoring small and medium-size contractors from local areas. For example, under national government guidelines drawn up in 2001, 45 percent of all national public works contracts were designated for such firms. This system has encouraged the growth of small, inefficient firms and heightened competitive pressures among them to win contracts. This makes them dependent on favors dispensed by well-connected politicians and bureaucrats responsible for allocating contracts, and so vulnerable to corrupt practices. With so much money designated for such firms, the temptations are commensurately large. While the number of road-paving firms more than doubled between 1985 and 2001, the number of registered construction firms also rose steadily in the 1990s, reaching the staggering figure of 600,980 in 2000. Although the 1990s saw a decline in private-sector construction contracts, the government's pump priming measures boosted the number of small construction firms looking for a handout or a boondoggle.

The unhealthy ties between contractors and politicians were reinforced by a change in the electoral system in the mid-1990s. The new system of single-seat constituencies enables the sole member in a given district to monopolize political patronage and direct contracts to local firms in exchange for campaign funds and mobilizing votes. Contractors who balk face the prospect of being frozen out of the bidding. This system was introduced during the surge in public works spending and, not surprisingly, coincided with a spate of influence-peddling, bribery, and bid-rigging scandals. However, this state of affairs is no longer going unchallenged: information disclosure ordinances enacted by most municipalities and prefectures have produced a new transparency and accountability that are exposing the sleazy pillars of the construction state and promoting reform.

Defining dysfunction

The political economy of exploitation that prevails in contemporary Japan is subjected to a devastating analysis in Gavan McCormack's 1996 book *The Emptiness of Japanese Affluence*. McCormack presents a face of Japan that is often left obscured in the shadows. This is a Japan where webs of collusion and corruption are endemic and the bad still sleep well. Whereas a few years ago the author might have been accused of Japan-bashing, his central arguments are now widely accepted: his views have become almost mainstream as Japanese people increasingly vent frustration with a dysfunctional system that has soured beyond anyone's worst nightmares.

What is empty about Japanese affluence? For most Japanese this is a nation that boasts wealth without prosperity. The collapse of the bubble economy has left the scars of a sustained recession and revealed just how much a chimera the miracle has been. Corruption and gross incompetence have left an ugly rubble of bankruptcies and bad debts. McCormack's analysis of the absurdities and destructiveness intrinsic to the construction state is a compelling indictment of such practices.

McCormack also underlines the importance of construction to the ruling elite. Many of the six million Japanese workers employed in construction live in the politically important countryside where votes count more than in the under-represented cities. Delivering public works projects to local companies is how politicians have been able to mobilize votes and extract campaign funds in these areas. The construction industry also means power and turf for bureaucrats with opportunities for personal gain, especially through well-paid post-retirement sinecures. It is the basis for a cartel system that inflates prices to ensure that profits are fat and skimming is the norm. As McCormack points out, the big loser in all this is the taxpayer:

> taxpaying citizens are in this way innocent victims of a high level extortion racket, but the reality is even more pernicious. Not only do citizens pay an involuntary, secret, and illegal levy on every project and on the public-works industry as a whole, but to a large extent the money is extracted both from tax-based regular state income and also from the special deficit bonds, and the accumulated deficit has risen to an astronomical sum that weighs more heavily on the shoulders of citizens
>
> (McCormack 1996: 39)

Figure 5.3 Pine-shrouded islet surrounded by tetrapods. (Photo: Jeff Kingston)

And this assessment was made even before the late 1990s surge in public works spending.

Even though there is a growing consensus that this kind of pump priming has not solved Japan's economic problems, and only postponed the day of reckoning, the government keeps piling on yet more debt, mortgaging the future to sustain a discredited system. With per capita construction-related debt topping ¥8 million, the consequences will not be pretty. In some respects the construction state is Japan's equivalent of the US military-industrial complex – except that it spends more than the Pentagon! McCormack compellingly argues that the *doken kokka* is 'sucking in the country's wealth, consuming it inefficiently, growing like a cancer, and bequeathing both fiscal crisis and environmental devastation' (McCormack 1996: 43).

The public works 'industry' has created a powerful group of vested interests and a political dynamic that cloud the prospects for reform and reviving civil society. The damage done to the environment is a powerful indictment of the system and a bitter legacy for future generations of Japanese who will pay higher taxes to repair the follies of a corrupt elite who sacrificed the environment for their own materialistic interests. Japan's impressive natural wonders are now all too often found encased in concrete or marred by cement monstrosities. Mist-shrouded islets nestled along pristine coastlines, with gnarled pine trees improbably straddling precarious outcrops, are a classic image in Japanese art and poetry, but now only accessible through skillful use of Photoshop and judicious cropping; what the tabloids don't reveal is that Japan has been surrounded by an invading army of giant concrete tetrapods that cover more than half the coastline and actually accelerate the problem of erosion they were intended to arrest. As McCormack explains, the system is dysfunctional because 'too much of the energy, capital and skills of the Japanese people has been appropriated, mobilized, and focused in a political economy of exploitation, both human and material, that ultimately exhausted both the people and their environment' (McCormack 1996: 65).

In his book *Dogs and Demons: Tales From the Dark Side of Japan*, Alex Kerr (2001) passionately laments the ugly-fication of Japan that has resulted from infrastructural involution and the bureaucratic obsession with taming nature and building large-scale monuments that deface the environment. Drawing on a Chinese parable, his title refers to the difficulty of depicting commonplace things (dogs) as against those that are gross and extreme (demons). Dogs symbolize 'the simple, unobtrusive factors in our surroundings that are so difficult to get right,' such as burying electric wires, municipal zoning, sign ordinances, and preserving historic neighborhoods and traditional dwellings. 'Demons,' conversely, are the grandiose projects such as bridges, highways, cultural halls, museums, and other expensive shrines to bad taste and poor judgment. In Kerr's Japan, the bureaucrats are likened to 'terminator robots' that cannot be stopped from laying waste to all around them. And just as depicting demons is straightforward compared to rendering the everyday details of society, Japan's architects and planners have ignored the details that enrich a society and serve its people, and instead have poured their money and souls into dams, bridges, and highways that threaten to bankrupt Japan's natural bounty as well as its coffers. In his view, the prospects for change are limited because the system is ossified and powerful defenders of the status quo are thick on the ground. As he said in a newspaper interview: 'Although I am skeptical of Japan's ability to change – the very roots of the tragedy lie in systems that repress change – in my heart I dream of change.'[1]

Whither Japan? Those in charge of reforming Japan are those who have benefited most from the existing system, a situation that understandably raises doubts about prospects for change. In the face of determined opposition from politicians and bureaucrats Prime Minister Koizumi has quixotically forged ahead with plans for privatization of public corporations, charging that they are a burden on the government and economy. These tentative moves towards privatizing key institutions in the *doken kokka* suggest at least a slowing of the construction juggernaut. Against the odds, diluted versions of his proposals have been approved and, as of 2005, Japan's expressway-related road corporations are slated to be reorganized and privatized. While the way in which this will be implemented will certainly fall short of reformers' hopes, merely making some form of privatization an inevitability is a major accomplishment and will set in motion forces and changes with significant implications for the construction state.

Cutting the umbilical cord through privatization

As of fiscal year 2002/03, the Japanese government stopped injecting taxpayer money into the Japan Highway Public Corporation to the tune of ¥300 billion per annum. This is the quasi-state-owned body responsible for building and managing Japan's network of national expressways. Its total debt of ¥25 trillion as of the 2000/01 financial year is equivalent to nearly 30 percent of the government's annual budget and ten times its annual operating income. This interest-bearing debt is projected to balloon to roughly ¥34 trillion by 2020. Every year, Japan Highway repays more than ¥920 billion in principal, plus about ¥560 billion in interest. As a result of opaque accounting practices and pooling of revenues and expenses, it is hard to determine where the losses are mounting most quickly.[2] What is clear is that there are no incentives to take the profitability of any individual expressway into account; the few moneymakers subsidize the white elephants imposed for political reasons. While the corporation is protected from the intrusions of national information disclosure legislation and has become a haven for MLIT *amakudari*, privatization hearings during 2002 provided some sense of the size of its problems and how large they may become without significant changes in the way it does business.

In principle, new highways are built from money borrowed from the fiscal investment and loan program (FILP), also known as the second budget (*zaito*). The money for FILP comes from the postal system, where Japanese place their savings and pay their insurance premiums. These funds total some ¥360 trillion, roughly one-quarter of the nation's aggregate personal financial assets. From 2003 these funds will be managed by a postal corporation established to oversee the process of privatizing the postal system. Previously, these funds were managed by the Finance Ministry's Trust Fund Bureau which decided where this money was invested and lent, ranging from government bonds and overseas development assistance programs to road construction projects. Highway-related loans and interest are supposed to be repaid from toll levies but, as toll receipts have fallen short of projections, the government has had to make up the difference – totaling some ¥500 billion a year as of 2001.

The cut in these subsidies reflects the government's plan to privatize by 2005 the four expressway-related public corporations: Japan Highway Public Corporation, Hanshin Expressway Public Corporation, Metropolitan Expressway Public Corporation, and the Honshu-Shikoku Bridge Authority. These are all large loss-making state enterprises and thus slated for privatization as a means to trim Japan's huge budget deficits. Together they have racked up some ¥40 trillion in debt, equivalent to half of the Japanese government's general account budget for 2002 and more than 1.2 times Russia's gross national income of $253 billion. According to the government's current privatization plan, the four operators would be privatized into five regional units while their assets and debts would be transferred to a public holding company. The privatized entities will lease toll roads from the holding company and pay for the lease with toll revenues collected from operating the expressways. Ten years after the privatized entities are established, they are scheduled to raise money from a share offering and purchase the express- ways from the holding company, presumably generating sufficient cash to retire accumulated debts. While this is the plan, it remains to be seen how privatization proceeds in the face of both economic and political headwinds. There is certainly a possibility that the anti-reform forces in the Diet will stall for time and wait for more propitious circumstances.

Comparison with the experience of Japan National Railway (JNR) suggests that privatization will not be a panacea. When JNR was reorganized and privatized in 1987, its accumulated debt was about ¥28 trillion and, compared to the highway corporation, the proportion of loss-making routes was smaller, its assets were more valuable, its debts were equivalent to only six times its operating revenues (as opposed to ten) and Japan's economy was in far better shape. JNR was divided into six regional entities. One of these, JR Tokai, started out with debt equivalent to six times annual revenues and also held valuable real estate assets. When JNR was privatized, the settlement corporation was supposed to sell off assets to dispose of about ¥25 trillion in debts; however, mismanagement led to an increase in its debt to ¥38 trillion by 1998 and it seems likely that taxpayers will be paying off this tab until the middle of the twenty-first century. Thus privatization does not seem a way to cure the nation's debt woes, only postpone them. Although doubts along these lines were voiced in 1987, it was more expedient to assert that debts would be retired by asset sales and push any problems into the future.

Privatization is about fiscal discipline and assigning responsibility for cutting costs, capping losses, and inserting a cost–benefit analysis into the process of expressway construction and maintenance. Now that Japan Highway must take account of how it is assessed in the market, its performance matters much more than in the past. In order to make Japan Highway an equivalently attrac- tive investment with a shot at profitability, its debts would have to be pared to a maximum of ¥10 trillion, leaving ¥15 trillion to be dealt with in some fashion, probably at the taxpayers' expense. Some of the projects that the corporation has inherited are bound to be liabilities. When JNR was privatized, it avoided the conundrums that Japan Highway now faces, as unprofitable local lines had already been built. The remaining routes the corporation plans to build for political reasons are almost certainly going to be money-losers and thus, to the extent that it proceeds in completing the entire network, its debts will rise and its appeal to investors will decline. Certainly these are not auspicious circum- stances for privatization.

Emerging information about the effects of privatization in the UK reinforce these concerns. Although most privatized entities seem to be surviving, there have been some notable failures. Railtrack Group PLC, which owns tracks, signals, and stations in Britain, was declared insolvent in 2001 and effectively renationalized through a public–private partnership. British Energy PLC is also in trouble and its future prospects are not bright because of the burden it faces in decommissioning nuclear power plants. While the gains of privatization in terms of efficiency and price competition have been realized in many cases, the experience of the UK suggest that not all public corporations are suitable for privatization.

In considering the prospects for privatization in Japan, however, the potential success or failure of a given venture may not be the most important criterion in deciding to proceed. Political pragmatism will be a much more potent factor as officials and politicians seek to postpone the day of reckoning by privatizing, in effect making the debt woes of the public corporations someone else's problem. Thus even if privatization is not the magic bullet, its principle virtue may lie in avoiding some of the hard decisions now and hoping that something works out in the meantime. This wishful, muddle-through approach is consistent with the government's track record in the 1990s as it failed to come to grips with various crises.

Privatization is imperative because Japan's public debt is conservatively estimated at some 150 percent of GDP and, as a result, its credit rating has been progressively downgraded by the international rating agencies; in 2002 its bonds were ranked alongside those of Malta and Botswana. In order to restore international confidence in Japanese government bonds, the government needs to rein in its deficits. This means plugging the budgetary blackholes in the special public corporations by privatizing them. Unlike the situation in the 1980s when Japan privatized its telecommunications entity, NTT, and its rail transport entity, JNR, following ideological trends in the UK and USA and entertaining vague hopes for greater efficiency, Japan is now in a fiscal position where it has little choice. No other OECD member nation has government debts exceeding 100 percent of GDP – while Japan is vaulting its way towards 200 percent. This is an unprecedented crisis and is forcing the government's hand.

The government's dilemma is well illustrated by the case of the Trans-Hokkaido Highway. In 1995, a 50 km portion of the planned 694 km highway opened at a cost of ¥90 billion. This route, paralleled by a toll-free national highway, averages fewer than 1,000 cars a day. This low level of demand has translated into losses of ¥134 for every ¥100 it makes, with only 7 percent of the planned road completed. Despite this poor record, approval has been given to commence another 412 km of the highway at a cost of ¥1.5 trillion. This situation is the outcome of the 'balanced development' approach to infrastructure-building advocated by the LDP's 'road tribe.' Japan Highway takes its orders from MLIT secure in the knowledge that the government will pick up the tab for whatever it builds; this is the system that has saddled Japan with so many loss-making highways. Back in 1987, at the height of the bubble, the government yielded to the demands of the road tribe and agreed to a vastly expanded network of expressways that would nearly treble the existing length of the national expressway system by the early twenty-first century. This huge increase was based on falsified demand projections and political meddling by influential Diet members. This explains why Japan keeps building highways few people need and why there has been such a political furor over freezing construction; stopping now will hurt the politicians who have waited in line for their share of the spoils in their own districts.

In preparing the ground for the privatization of expressway-related public corporations, the government is constricting the umbilical cord of taxpayer money that has helped sustain these economically unviable projects. Reduced access to the public trough will lead to a downsizing of the construction state. Once privatized, planned expressway projects that cannot pay their way face cancellation as private entities will no longer be able to rely on generous subsidies and unfettered access to the treasury. Politically motivated 'white elephant' projects are likely candidates for the chop. Naturally, the Diet members who head the 'road tribe' are fighting privatization, freezes on road construction and any attempts to thwart planned road projects. For them, as we have seen, viability resonates rather differently; public works spending on roads brings home the pork, improving their prospects for re-election and enrichment. Furthermore, in Japan's depressed rural districts, highway construction has long been a significant source of employment and revenues. Cutting their access to the central government's coffers is a prospect that threatens political bosses and is represented as harmful to local economies. However, many local governments are already staggering under the debts they have accumulated by participating in central government infrastructure projects, and are unwilling to further mortgage their futures.

Privatization is aimed at exposing projects that make no sense. At the end of fiscal 2002, 6,959 km of Japan's national expressway network has been completed out of the 9,342 km in the master plan. While the remaining 25 percent is slated for completion over 20 years, for projects that are not yet underway the prospects for completion are becoming much less favorable. The unfinished expressways are thought to be the least needed and thus unlikely to meet market criteria for funding and construction. The government simply can no longer afford such a heavy drain on its depleted resources and is thus looking to market forces to tame the vested interests that have grown accustomed to slurping loud and long at the public trough.

Japan's grid of planned highways is based on inflated traffic projections, risible toll revenue estimates and old-fashioned politics. The road business is run like a high-stakes con game and Japanese taxpayers are the unsuspecting mark. Drivers pay twice for the privilege of driving on a vast majority of Japan's money-guzzling highways, forking out for high tolls while the government subsidizes loss-making highways with their tax money. And with the mountains of debt amassed by the expressway-related public corporations continuing to grow, taxpayers may even be dunned a third time. Privatization offers a small chance that taxpayers may avoid this fate as the corporate entity responsible for highways will be tasked with both asset management and debt repayment, the latter staggered over 50 years.

Privatization is about fiscal discipline and making sure that some entity has a stake in cutting costs, capping losses, and inserting a cost–benefit analysis into the process of expressway construction and maintenance. Until now, Japan's expressway-related public corporations have been told what to build, where and when, and given a carte blanche to carry on; they are only a bailout and subsidy away from solvency and have powerful voices making sure that the taxpayer's check is in the mail.

The battle over privatization is being fought so tenaciously because the stakes are so high. For the LDP old guard, the full 9,342 km of highways has become the Holy Grail – a figure ordained for their own purposes rather than the public interest. They rally their core constituencies by asserting that this is a sacred promise to the electorate that must be fulfilled at all costs, even if it means mortgaging the future of Japan and burdening future generations with their profligacy.

Yet public opposition is mounting. When the Ministry of Land, Infrastructure, and Transport (MLIT) revealed for the first time in August 2002 that the government has poured ¥4.36 trillion of taxpayers' money into the construction of toll roads that were supposed to be paid for by toll revenues, the media had a field day. These subsidies are in addition to government loans that are serviced through toll revenues. The simultaneous funding of highway projects with government loans and subsidies is euphemistically dubbed the 'incorporated construction system.' It has been a common way to quickly fund and build unprofitable roads to meet the demands of road-tribe politicians. Of the nation's 60 toll roads, 39 have been funded in this way to the tune of ¥3 trillion, while an additional six routes under construction have already sucked in ¥1.36 trillion. These revelations have heightened public concerns about the huge waste of taxpayers' money, and have also raised doubts about the proposal to sustain tolls on a permanent basis as a means to facilitate privatization. Certainly it has emboldened drivers who have been refusing to pay tolls, a form of civil disobedience that is gaining popularity in Japan. In some cases, government subsidies constituted 90 percent of the total construction costs. In principle, once government loans are paid off by toll revenues, tolls are supposed to be eliminated. In cases where highways are paid for by taxes, tolls are not supposed to be levied at all. In practice, as the MLIT's figures reveal, these principles have been routinely ignored.

Pressure to change the system sometimes takes indirect forms. In August 2002, the government's privatization panel recommended that the central and local governments bear a larger share of proposed and ongoing highway construction costs. By demanding that local governments contribute more funding, the panel effectively suggested canceling construction of toll roads in the Tokyo and Kansai regions. Although the panel stopped short of calling for a politically unpopular freeze of highway construction, its demand for greater funding input from central and local government amounted to the same thing. Neither is in a position to do so even if strongly pressed by vested interests. This 'if you want to call the tune, pay the piper' approach has focused public attention on the glaring gap between rhetoric and reality that animates the debate shaped by road-tribe elders. Until now, paying for road expansion was an apparently painless exercise, but with stricter fiscal restraints and heightened competition for scarcer resources, the panel is trying to force governments and political leaders to prioritize. In order for privatization to succeed, or at least have a chance, the panel advocates capping the debts of the four expressway-related public corporations at the current ¥40 trillion; repaying this massive debt to the financially strapped central government becomes the politically appealing priority. The entity or entities that will eventually take over the assets and debts of the impecunious four will, in theory, service these debts and ensure that ongoing losses are minimized, a reassuring departure from current practice. Subject to market scrutiny, individual projects will come to be assessed on their merits and viability rather than the pull of their promoters.

The expressway crisis has left local governments in especially dire straits. In the past, they have relied on nationally funded public works to keep their localities afloat and are thus not interested in having to pay more for them. Pork-barrel advocates at the local level are now portrayed as mortgaging the district's future for dubious purposes and diverting allocations from other pressing needs. Moreover, Japan's rising number of elderly are not natural constituents for more highways and will support politicians who channel limited resources to meeting their needs.

The Koizumi administration has trampled on several road-tribe taboos, including efforts to divert road-related taxes to purposes other than road construction. By law, revenue from several taxes, including gasoline taxes and automobile weight taxes, are restricted to construction and repair of roads. In the budget for the 2001/02 financial year, this amounted to ¥5.8 trillion, or about half of all public spending on road construction.[3] This amount exceeds the national defense budget of approximately ¥5 trillion. The *doken kokka* has marched ahead because it can draw on vast segregated tax revenues designated purely for road building. These various tolls and taxes assessed on road users have proven to be a relatively stable funding base for the industry, despite the prolonged recession. In short, roads are built because there is budget to build them and there are politicians committed to guarding such revenues from the attentions of the Finance Ministry. In the past, efforts to divert some of the road taxes into the general budget have always been vigorously and successfully opposed by the LDP's road tribe. In 2002/03, however, the government for the first time diverted 10 percent of proposed highway allocations, drawn from vehicle weight tonnage taxes, to the general budget. Although this ¥280 billion is a comparatively small amount, shifting these funds undermines the principle of segregated road revenues and sets a precedent for fungibility.

To reiterate, the moat of the *doken kokka* has been breached and the prospects for a successful, if prolonged, siege are relatively good. Over time it will become ever more difficult to justify segregating road revenues from the general budget and make it easier to divert further funds for other purposes.

Reality check

Since the late 1990s the government has canceled a number of dam and road projects, large and small, a move that signals a growing disquiet about the logic and costs of the *doken kokka*. In 2001 the ruling coalition announced the cancellation of 233 projects, slated to save taxpayers some ¥2.8 trillion, a rather large drop in the bucket of infrastructure spending and significant in that the government now feels that it has to make such gestures. Having whet the appetites of the media and public for cost cutting, and demonstrated the seriousness of Japan's fiscal crisis, the government will come under pressure for further savings. And, for the same logical reasons that projects have been canceled, more will be. Although skeptics dismiss these project cancellations as mere window dressing, expectations have been aroused and pressures are building. As information disclosure leads to greater transparency, difficult questions will be asked about why a particular project is needed, why skewed projections were not scrutinized, why more cement needs to be poured, and so on. Once such questions and doubts are raised, and convincing responses are not forthcoming, the powers and discovery mechanisms of an increasingly dynamic civil society will make it more difficult to proceed with unwarranted projects.

The recent cancellations are partly a response to the large number of public-works projects that have been buried under snowballing debts. Many of these projects were built based on wildly optimistic demand projections that have, in many cases, proved totally divorced from reality. Planning for dams and roads assumed robust rates of economic growth that have not materialized. Former officials openly admit that they faced political pressure to come up with inflated numbers for projected water demand and road traffic that would pass muster at the Finance Ministry; in this way many questionable projects won approval based on manipulated data. In addition, the battle to maintain or expand budgets encourages bureaucrats to engage in creative accounting; the common practice of overestimating demand leads to a general inflation of projections. For example, on 42 out of 58 toll-charging highways constructed by Japan Highway the traffic volume has been less than projected and, in 1998, 26 of them lost money. Such practices continue: planners project a steady rise in traffic volume until 2030 that conveniently justifies completion of the planned national expressway network while Japan's population is expected to peak in 2006 and decline thereafter. With the rapid aging of society, and a higher percentage of elderly motorists, the

Figure 5.4 Celebrants at the last water festival to be held in Kawarayu Onsen, a village in Gunma that will disappear underneath the reservoir created by the giant Yanba Dam. (Photo: Greg Davis)

prospects of increased long-distance traffic seem remote except to those in charge of justifying further road construction.

The Aqualine toll expressway is a good example of the distorting impact of political meddling in the road-building sector, with the taxpayer as usual footing the bill. The route, which includes an undersea tunnel and bridge on Tokyo Bay, opened in 1997 and has never even come close to projected traffic volumes. Its breakeven volume is 33,000 vehicles a day, safely and reassuringly below the projected 2001 traffic figure of 45,800 vehicles a day. However, the actual traffic volume of 13,300 vehicles a day in 2001 shattered this rosy scenario. The losses accumulated by this extravaganza are staggering and show no sign of abating; in 1999 alone the revenues it generated of ¥14.42 billion came nowhere near offsetting the ¥45.87 billion spent on interest and facility management. Media attention to such stories of colossal mismanagement stokes public skepticism about the construction state and the wisdom and ethics of those who control it.

Other arms of the *doken kokka* also have spotty records on projections, notably the Water Resource Development Corporation (WRDC). In 1978 industrial and tap water demand was projected to reach 131 million m^3 per day by 1990, but in fact only reached 78 million m^3, a 40 percent margin of error! This huge – and deliberately engineered – gap between projections and actual water usage led to the building of many unnecessary dams. While numerous reservoir dams were planned to meet rising water consumption, a dwindling population in rural districts, the decline of industrial consumption

Figure 5.5 Two ladies looking grim at a party in 2002 celebrating the final agreement to complete Yanba Dam, after two decades of local resistance. (Photo: Greg Davis)

in some areas and the reluctance of town officials to assume more debt have all forced reconsideration of these facilities. Although in 2003 the WRDC operates 44 dams and is involved in planning or building 20 more, it is faced with scaling back and is investigating decommissioning some of its miscues.

Since 1996, plans to build 92 new dams have been scrapped – and this at a time when the government was lavishing money on any sand-and-gravel project with even the most feeble rationale. These cancellations came about because projected water needs never materialized. Reduced water demand and economic torpor have scaled back the need for dams, while cash-strapped local governments no longer see benefits in putting up their share of the financing. In addition, some projects could be eliminated because other cheaper methods of water management have been implemented. Despite all this, more than 400 dam projects are either being built or are planned

Figure 5.6 The $4 billion Miyagase Dam is an extravagant example of unnecessary public works spending. The grandiose scale exceeds by far its ostensible raison d'être (and the actual need) of providing flood control for the small Nakatsu River and drinking water for Yokohama. (Photo: Jeff Kingston)

nationwide. Although the fate of such projects is uncertain, especially now that money is being allocated far more parsimoniously, it is likely that further significant cancellations are on the drawing board. Not that Japan is short of dams for water storage and flood control; as of 2001 there are 2,704 dams of at least 15 m height scattered around the nation – an average of 57 per prefecture. As a result, while devastating floods are now rare, existing water storage capacity is well beyond what is needed.

It is significant that in contemporary Japan so much damning information about incompetence, mendacity, and corruption is so widely circulated. It was not always so; fleecing taxpayers in backroom deals and inside the impenetrable ministries has kept the public in the dark. Now that the lights have been turned on, the gross venality is visible for all to see. People involved in using smoke and mirrors to justify projects are candidly explaining to the media how the scams were concocted. These illuminating exposés of standard practices in the construction state constitute a searing indictment, making it clear to citizens that government officials were in cahoots with the construction firms, politicians, and special corporations in justifying and proceeding with unviable projects. This has stoked outrage, further eroded flagging public trust and contributed to the crisis of legitimacy that besets the government in the twenty-first century. Having betrayed the people and squandered their taxes the government can expect to face the consequences thereof and find its actions much more carefully examined for fraud, waste, inefficiency, and corruption. Activists lawyers, NPOs, and the media are making it their business to poke around and expose what they find, sending the magnates of the construction state scrambling for cover and desperate to make gestures that show they have mended their ways.

The good old days are gone. The MLIT research institute predicts that by 2010, annual construction 'investment' could fall 25 percent from its level in the year 2000. Firms and politicians that have grown fat at the public trough face difficult times, while the *amakudari*-seeking mandarins will find their sinecures harder to come by, less comfortable, and more demanding. The number of registered construction companies is dropping – by over 15,000 in 2001 alone – and this is where downsizing will pinch most; there are just too many inefficient companies in a sector that has a dim future because the government enticed them with misguided policies. Consolidation and unemployment will take a heavy toll on these victims of a dysfunctional system. A bolder media is lifting the lid on corrupt practices, and politicians, aware of growing disillusion with the construction state, are shifting ground and running against pork-barrel projects. This is a sign of the times and an ill omen for the *doken kokka*.

Electoral implications

Supporting transparency and running against the *doken kokka* has become smart politics in the early twenty-first century. Around the country, advocates of greater transparency and open government have generated a groundswell of popular concern about dysfunctional government practices and put information disclosure on the nation's political agenda. In several prefectures, candidates in gubernatorial elections backed by mainstream political parties have been defeated, often by political neophytes with no organization and limited campaign funds. In recent years voters have elected governors eschewing party affiliation in Akita, Chiba, Miyagi, Nagano, Tokushima, and Tochigi. Their opposition to the *doken kokka* has been a keystone of their campaigns. These newcomers have effectively tapped public anger against a rigged system that is widely viewed as a major obstacle to Japan's recovery from a prolonged economic slump.

Until the economic implosion of the 1990s, voters tolerated the peccadilloes of their politicians as long as they delivered the goods. The system of bid-rigging (*dango*) revealed in a series of scandals in the 1990s exposed the systematic plundering of the public purse by unscrupulous businessmen and their political sponsors. Some of those involved were dismissed, or received jail terms or fines, reflecting the change in public tolerance of corruption. Information disclosure laws were essential to gathering evidence on bid-rigging on sewer systems in particular and, armed with this experience, activists are expanding their investigations into other misappropriations of taxpayer monies, often estimated at more than 20 percent of the value of typical public works contracts.

Just as the public was outraged by exposés of lavish entertainment spending and falsification of expense claims by bureaucrats, so the squandering of far larger sums of money involved in the *doken kokka* has influenced public perceptions of their elected and non-elected government officials. They emerged as co-conspirators in a massive fraud at a time when people were feeling the economic slump and growing anxious about possible loss of jobs and security. The anger and sense of betrayal that spread in the 1990s translated into growing disaffection with the status quo and those who represent it. In the early twenty-first century this anger catapulted into power a collection of governors who made clear their opposition to the 'roads and bridges to nowhere' mentality that underlies the *doken kokka*. They ran against dam construction, against paving over wetlands, against unnecessary roads and the other infrastructure projects that were nothing more than status symbols for politicians on the take.

One of the most visible of the new-style governors is Tanaka Yasuo, a famous novelist and commentator who won an unexpected electoral victory in 2000 against the handpicked successor of the outgoing governor of Nagano. Tanaka ran on a simple platform of more open government and 'no more dams.' He also benefited from public outrage over dubious spending on the Nagano Olympics (1998) and the destruction of related documents that could have been used to indict officials. His stance on dams also won him kudos from environmental activists. Not content with simply thumbing his nose at the political establishment's backroom dealing, upon taking office Tanaka installed himself in a literally transparent office in the lobby of the prefectural government building and publicized an open-door policy for citizens to drop in. This novel openness to his constituents, combined with frequent town-hall-style meetings and his stance against

Figure 5.7 Tanaka Yasuo, Governor of Nagano, known for opposing further dam
construction, promoting transparency in government, and criticizing Juki
Net. (Photo: Andreas Seibert/Lookat)

environmentally destructive, wasteful spending has ensured him high
approval ratings.

Following his election, Tanaka has been at loggerheads with the prefectural assembly over his flamboyant political style and willingness to
publicly confront the construction state through his opposition to dam
construction. His cancellation of two large ongoing dam projects in June
2002 brought tensions to a head. Local politicians countered his concerns
about the adverse environmental impact of these dams by arguing with
classic *doken kokka* logic that, were the projects to be canceled, the central
government would need to be repaid the money already spent on them – so
it would be better to complete them. By portraying themselves as fiscally
responsible, and asserting that cancellation was the impecunious course,
dam advocates ignored the costs involved in completing the projects and
the ongoing maintenance and staffing of the facilities. Meanwhile Tanaka
fought back, preaching the virtues of replacing dams with natural and
sustainable flood-control projects, and dismissing the claims of his opponents that his policies would boost unemployment by arguing that such
conservation efforts are labor-intensive.

In July 2002, the assembly turned against Tanaka and forced him out of
office with a no-confidence motion, setting up an electoral showdown over
the fate of the dams and the obsession with public works that has left
Nagano one of the most heavily indebted prefectures in Japan.[4] Its debt of

some ¥1.6 trillion works out to nearly ¥10 million per voting-age resident, much of it incurred during the frenzy of building roads, a high-speed train line, and high-tech sports facilities in the run-up to the Nagano Olympics. The election campaign for governor that followed was extraordinary: none of the candidates claimed a party affiliation and all sought to distance themselves from endorsements or connections of any kind with the political establishment in the prefecture. In what was effectively a referendum on Tanaka's stance on the public works debate, none of the candidates cozied up to the assemblymen who brought him down. Tanaka's strong opposition to dam-building also went unchallenged: no candidate spoke in favor of more public works spending and none sought to curry favor with voters by indicating that they could bring home more pork. Tanaka's landslide victory, outpolling his nearest rival by more than two to one, was a vote of confidence from the people and public vindication of his anti-*doken kokka* policies.

Another candidate who eschewed party affiliation and ran against ready-mix politics was Domoto Akiko, one-time Lower House representative in the national Diet. In 2001 she became the first governor of Chiba prefecture (on the outskirts of Tokyo) for two decades not to have come from the LDP. As she promised during her campaign, she canceled a reclamation project that would have resulted in destruction of the Sanbanze tidal flat adjacent to Tokyo Bay. Her victory came on the heels of an obscure gubernatorial candidate's victory in neighboring Tochigi prefecture against a sixteen-year veteran with party backing.

The new logic of Japanese politics means that campaigning against large-scale public works is likely to figure more and more on the agendas of ambitious politicians – a marked turnaround from the time when bringing home pork-barrel projects for their constituencies was their single most important obligation. This new logic has led most politicians to support reform, however vaguely defined, even producing some unlikely converts among conservative dinosaurs who have risen through the ranks precisely because of their access to the public trough. The new logic means rejecting the practices of the political establishment and advocating greater public access to government documents and participation in government affairs. To do otherwise in a climate hostile to the old guard and its discredited ways has become increasingly risky politics.

Local electoral results in the early years of the twenty-first century thus provide a basis for limited optimism about the downsizing of the construction state. It is telling that mainstream political leaders at all levels of government are now embracing 'green growth' and 'green budgets' while slamming wasteful public works projects for doing more harm than good. While they remain a distinct minority, their successes are generating momentum for repudiating the worst excesses of the *doken kokka*.

Biodiversity: one step forward

These days, Sanbanze is how environmentalists in Japan spell success. In September 2001 Chiba's new governor, Domoto Akiko, announced the cancellation of plans to reclaim the Sanbanze wetlands on Tokyo Bay, marking a major victory for activists who had campaigned to save one of the last refuges for migratory birds passing through the area; more than 90 percent of Tokyo Bay's coastline is developed. This is the second major wetland reclamation project to be canceled in recent years, following the decision in 1999 to abandon plans to convert Nagoya's Fujimae tidal flats into a garbage dump. Chiba government officials first hatched plans to reclaim the Sanbanze wetlands in 1991, and in 1993 announced a development plan that would have covered 740 of the 1,200 ha of mudflats that lay between the Edo and Ebi rivers. Facing a barrage of criticism for this grandiose scheme, in 1999 officials reduced the area planned for reclamation to 101 ha. In 2001, Domoto ran for governor against the party machine and pulled off a stunning victory, in part due to her pledge to cancel the Sanbanze project.

It is a sign of the times that Governor Domoto's decision was applauded by the Environment Ministry; not so long ago it would have been unimaginable for the government to actually welcome local resistance to the imperatives of the construction state. But in early 2001 the Environment Ministry weighed in on the Sanbanze controversy and urged the Chiba government to review the reclamation project, citing changes in population growth and public sentiment. The reclaimed land was slated for urban development, including a sewage-treatment center and a new coastal expressway; the ministry lobbied for preserving the tidal ecosystem and placing the planned highway underground at an additional cost of some ¥100 billion. Now that the project has been canceled, the ministry has allocated budget to restore the natural environment, reflecting a growing appreciation of wetlands' role in filtering water and serving as spawning grounds for marine organisms as well as feeding and roosting areas for migratory birds. It is another sign of changing times that the prefecture is involving citizens and NPOs in working to reverse the degradation of these troubled shoals and the surrounding ecosystem. Citizen participation is a theme Domoto emphasizes in her efforts to rebuild civil society and transform Japan's dysfunctional political system – one that got her elected.

Japan's 'discovery' of biodiversity and the importance of preserving it is having a salutary impact on a nation ravaged by the construction ethos. Although Japan is a signatory to the 1971 Ramsar Convention on Wetlands, it has only thirteen sites designated as wetland preservation areas under the terms of the convention, making it an ecological laggard compared to other industrialized nations. England, for example, is half of Japan's size but has 130 Ramsar sites. However, the Environment Ministry is now planning to double the number of sites as soon as possible, and is relaxing its criteria for designation in line with Ramsar guidelines. In 2002 the government added the Fujimae wetlands, and a small lake site in Hokkaido that serves as an important stepping-stone for migratory birds, to its Ramsar sites. In addition to increasing Ramsar sites, the Environment Ministry is expanding its nature restoration projects, both in pursuit of its brief and as a way to increase its funding in a time of tighter budgets.

In March 2002 the government approved a new national biodiversity strategy that calls for enhanced environmental monitoring and a stricter system of controls to keep foreign species from ravaging domestic wildlife. This initiative reflects the government's commitment to the Convention on Biological Diversity adopted at the 1992 Earth Summit. The government is establishing 1,000 monitoring points around the country to gather data on various ecosystems with a view to informing new preventive policy initiatives and heading off problems before they become intractable. The new strategy aims to go beyond environmental preservation and endorses extensive restoration of damaged areas. These efforts will build on pilot projects targeted at rebending of a river and restoring wetlands in Hokkaido. Given the amount of damage inflicted, the list of candidates for such projects is long and will keep restoration experts busy for much of the twenty-first century. Moreover, in terms of budget politics, although the Environment Ministry is a clear winner, other ministries are expected to submit their own green plans to recast their roles in the 'deconstruction state.'

One step back

Despite this impressive catalogue of successes, the saga of the Isahaya Bay Land Reclamation project, adjacent to the Ariake Sea off the island of Kyushu, has been less encouraging. Although the project was scaled back, even the modified plan is causing significant environmental problems in the Ariake Sea. This development has all the hallmarks of an ill-conceived construction-state project that has lost whatever potential it may once have had to confer benefits on the people who pay the taxes to fund it. The price tag of this coastal blight has skyrocketed from initial projections of ¥135 billion to ¥249 billion, a typical example of cost controls in the construction state. As the *Asahi* newspaper put it, 'It is graphic evidence of the government's inability to terminate a project that has gone badly wrong.'[5] A series of dams, dikes, gates, and sluices has been built across Isahaya Bay to isolate some of it from the sea and reclaim the wetlands for use as farmland. While this may have been a good idea in the 1960s or 1970s, it is a silly and wasteful notion in a country where prime agricultural land lies fallow and the government pays farmers to grow less rice and other crops. In Nagasaki Prefecture alone, where Isahaya Bay is located, some 6,000 ha of arable land stands idle – there is hardly a compelling need for an additional 1,400 ha of reclaimed wetlands. In addition, would-be farmers face the high expenses and lag time of boosting the fertility of newly reclaimed land.

Figure 5.8 The construction industry tries to soften its image. (Photo: Jeff Kingston)

One unanticipated impact of the Isahaya project has been the deleterious effect on seaweed cultivated in the Ariake Sea. Since the sea-gates were closed in 1997, about 3,000 ha of tidal flats along the bay have been destroyed, robbing the Ariake Sea of this natural water purifier. It is believed that the stagnant water drained from the reservoir that forms behind the gates is responsible for raising levels of phytoplankton that have caused a red tide damaging to the local seaweed crop. The seaweed farmers' harvest is discolored and yields are below normal levels. This is an area renowned in Japan for its prized laver seaweed, causing a high-profile crisis that resonated throughout the nation's kitchens and sushi bars.

In 2001, a government committee recommended that the gates be opened for a sufficient period of time to permit a thorough three-phase environmental impact assessment. The Agricultural Ministry agreed to open the moveable gates and endorsed a short-term study. However, the two months allowed was too short a time to gather the necessary data or permit a return of the partially drained site to its natural state – suggesting that the ministry was more interested in public relations than a rigorous assessment. It appears that the ministry backed down under pressure from the Nagasaki prefectural government and other vested interests that want to see the project completed on schedule in 2006. The truncated environmental assessment also highlighted the ministry's lax oversight of the project and failure to gather data about possible consequences before building began. This construction-state mentality of building first and asking questions later means that information that might delay or force cancellation of questionable projects is pushed aside until too late. It is interesting that advocates of the Isahaya project now tout its virtues in terms of flood control and protection against typhoons; even they seem to acknowledge the flaws of the old rationale and so are busy formulating new ones that are nearly as unconvincing.

The devastating consequences of this heedless reclamation project were clearly spelled out by prominent Canadian environmentalist C.W. Nichols in an interview with the *Japan Times* in 2002: '[T]he Isahaya Bay project in Nagasaki is criminal. I went there before they started building and was amazed at the number of seabirds and migratory birds on those mudflats. I have never seen so many shellfish. It's so rich. OK, they've had floods there, but that method of flood control [by constructing raisable gates across the mouth of the bay] is ridiculous. Its obvious to anyone with an ounce of fisheries knowledge that it would kill the fisheries of the Ariake Sea. And why? To make more rice fields! A quarter of the rice fields in Nagano Prefecture alone are lying dormant and it's the same all over Japan. But what can you do when a fisherman signs off his fishing rights and local politics is so dirty.'[6]

While local *nori* farmers have staged sit-ins and blocked access roads in last-ditch efforts to force reconsideration of the project, the balance of forces is unequal. The weapons of the weak are a poor match for the juggernauts of construction and it is these farmers and their customers who will pay the consequences for the folly of those who are enriching themselves at public expense. The dazzling marine life of the Ariake Sea will be remembered nostalgically in coming decades while grandparents try to explain to puzzled youngsters why a sea-wall was constructed to provide reclaimed land nobody wanted.

Assertive citizens

The potential and limits of citizen power to tame the construction state is well illustrated by the bitter controversy that has erupted over a ¥100 billion dam project in Tokushima. Plans for a dam on the Yoshino River were formulated as early as 1982 and called for replacement of a 250-year-old *daijuzeki* (a barrier made from large rocks) in the river by flood-gates. Local citizen groups oppose this plan as wasteful, a threat to water quality and destructive of a local heritage site and instead are demanding repairs to the *daijuzeki* and the creation of improved embankments. In order to promote their alternative plan, citizens organized a referendum in 2000. Tokushima residents overwhelmingly voted against the Yoshino dam project while less than 10 percent of voters supported it. However, the government argues that the referendum is not legally binding and has ignored the unfavorable results. The battle continues, but the government's attitude has infuriated locals and given a boost to organizations fighting the dam.

Like the *nori* farmers of Isahaya Bay, Tokushima residents have been frustrated in their attempts to challenge the construction state. However, the government has been damaged by its blithe disregard for citizens' views and, in coming years as more citizen groups mount similar challenges, the political costs of ignoring public opinion will rise. The crisis in the government's credibility stems from examples of myopic arrogance such as these that make people realize just how little citizens count in the work of government. As referendums become a more common strategy, the government will have to learn to listen rather than riding roughshod over the people and treating them as an annoying obstacle to be overcome. To the extent it remains deaf to the voice of the people, it risks alienating them and further undermining its shaky reputation. As the political pendulum swings towards greater citizen participation, the inclination to exclude and impose will come into increasingly sharper focus as an anachronism society can ill afford.

The courts are another avenue that citizens are using to do battle with the construction state, albeit with mixed and dilatory results. Citizens affected by air pollution from vehicle emissions near roadways have filed injunctions to hold the government responsible for lowering airborne particulate emissions. Cases in Kawasaki and Amagasaki during the 1990s symbolize the power of citizens to assert their rights through the courts and to hold governments accountable for factory and automobile pollution.[7] More recently, in 2002, an out-of-court settlement of a class-action suit originally filed by Nagoya residents in 1989 awarded damages to the plaintiffs, and the government promised to curb vehicle emissions. Earlier, the government had rejected a decree by the court that it enforce limits on emissions and was able to evade accepting liability for health problems allegedly related to air pollution near highways. However, as air pollution cases multiply around the country, the government is feeling increased pressure to do something about the problem. Thus, even if court cases are not always being won, plaintiffs are effectively promoting their agenda through the courts and forcing the government to adopt measures it would not have taken without such pressures. As a result, the government has imposed stricter nitrogen oxide emission limits and is working towards other environmental goals such as phasing out diesel fuel in trucks and buses, lowering emissions from government vehicles, and establishing green belts along roadsides. The pollution cases are also raising questions about the continued emphasis on accommodating automobile traffic and the failure to use road taxes to offset the environmental damages caused by vehicle emissions and aid other efforts to improve air quality and the urban environment.

So on this front, too, the construction state faces challenges from an increasingly assertive citizenry no longer content to acquiesce to the government's dictates and the logic of the *doken kokka*. The courts are demonstrating an encouraging sympathy towards air pollution victims that raises issues of liability for highway operators in urban areas. Such legal challenges will undoubtedly grow as media coverage, and favorable settlements, encourage others to file suits. Those who build and operate highways thus face yet another constraint on their activities beyond budget cuts, debt woes, and market discipline – one that will gain impetus from the rejuvenation of civil society where the voices, and interests, of citizens will come to matter.

Prospects

While the downsizing of the construction state is not inevitable, given the forces arrayed against its advocates and beneficiaries such an outcome seems ever more likely as time goes on. Public works spending in the 2002/03 financial year is down ¥10 trillion, or 28 percent, from the 1995 peak when public works contracts amounted to ¥35.7 trillion, and further spending cuts are in the pipeline. Large-scale projects are being scrapped and for the first time a crack has appeared in the nation's 'cover-it-in-concrete' waterway policy. The Kumamoto prefectural government announced in 2002 that it plans to dismantle a relatively small hydroelectric dam in 2010, a decision driven by economic and environmental factors that has set a precedent for the nation's aging dams. The significant liabilities of keeping such dams in operation are now better understood, especially as budgets are carefully scrutinized and trimmed, a trend that suggests growing momentum for the 'deconstruction' state. The nation's overbuilt infrastructure faces an aging crisis that will require governments to devote scarce resources to maintaining a growing pool of crumbling white elephants. In this sense, the nation's over-dammed rivers, over-bridged waterways, and over-concreted coastline will yield a rich bonanza of decommissioning and dismantling opportunities. Downsizing the construction state will allow politicians to garner public support for environmental restoration projects, yield contracts for local construction firms, and generate sustainable benefits for local communities.

Proponents of the *doken kokka* have suffered a number of setbacks in the twenty-first century. The position of the road tribe is becoming less tenable and it is difficult to imagine that its members can successfully deflect the combined onslaught of privatization of the expressway-related public corporations and the Post Office; the imperative of budget cuts; the logic of cost–benefit analysis; the growing institutional and electoral support for environmentally sound policies; expanding transparency in government; greater accountability for those involved in road construction projects; and the changing priorities of an aging society.

The bitter political battles over downsizing the construction state are part of the larger confrontation between vested interests and the forces of reform that marks an era of transition in Japan. At the close of 2002, the battle has been truly joined as Prime Minister Koizumi's highway reform panel recommended suspending further highway construction, terminating access to *zaito* funds and implementing a strict timetable for privatization and repaying loans, with provisions to prevent backsliding. In response the LDP, with backing from the MLIT, issued a plan to raise ¥16 trillion to ensure that the

Figure 5.9 Prime Minister Koizumi Junichiro rolls up his sleeves trying to convince voters he is serious about reform. (Photo: Andreas Seibert/Lookat)

entire national highway network will be completed as planned. This is equivalent to nearly eighteen times the annual budget of ¥900 billion currently allocated for highway building projects. There are already 40 trillion reasons why the construction state is being reconsidered and downsized, and it is hard to make a compelling case for adding 16 trillion more. Despite such marked differences of approach, there does at least seem to be agreement on launching privatization in 2005. The reformers' plan to cap debt at the current ¥40 trillion, and require the private entities to pay it back in full over forty years, means that it will be virtually impossible to build the remaining 2,300 km of planned expressways. The road tribe's answer is more debt, more unnecessary highways, looser repayment terms, and a vaguer timetable on privatization. As the outcome is negotiated, one can expect a compromise somewhere between these two positions – but even that will mark an important step towards downsizing.

One of the key developments in the impending demise of the construction state is the simultaneous reform of the postal system and the public corporations. As we have seen, the massive 'second budget' or *zaito* financed by the postal system provides the wherewithal for public works projects, while the public corporations – scarcely monitored and politically manipulated – provide the channel for disbursement of funds. The bureaucracy goes along with this system of dual budgets because it increases their discretionary authority and is the lifeblood of the special corporations, where cushy sinecures await. Privatization is aimed at undoing this Gordian knot of vested interests by monitoring funding, increasing transparency, and replacing institutionalized corruption with market discipline.

Is privatization a panacea for what ails Japan? Can it lead to meaningful reform of the *doken kokka*? The jury is still out on these questions and only time will tell. Certainly the vested interests are not idling while their turf is being invaded and subjected to the whims of privatization and market forces. As we have seen, the government is planning to create a public holding company whose primary task will be to repay the debts accumulated by the privatized road corporations with revenues from the leasing of expressways to their private successors. Despite the fact that this new corporate entity will be shielded from external interference by legal mandate, few skeptics think this will be an insurmountable obstacle for those who have long made it their business to influence decisions that affect infrastructure projects. The quasi-public entity that is set to become the administrative agency for the expressway network is based on a plan proposed by the LDP's 'road tribe,' and many of the senior officials who will staff the new agency have long-standing links with their former ministry colleagues and these politicians. This cozy *amakudari* network will no doubt be an avenue for influencing the new agency's veto power over new projects and spending.

Thus, while privatization has possibilities to facilitate the downsizing of the construction state, these are not ineluctable and will depend on how carefully the activities of the new agency are monitored, how the laws protecting it from outside interference are enforced, and to what degree the collusive practices of the *amakudari* system can be curbed by information disclosure and transparency. These are substantial hurdles to achieving the stated goals of privatization and will certainly be a significant test for the forces favoring civil society. While past experience provides powerful reasons for skepticism, the less imposing basis for optimism are the intertwined and mutually reinforcing forces favoring accountability, transparency, and a more dynamic civil society. In addition, Japan's economic malaise also favors those who are eager to downsize the bloated and inefficient *doken kokka*.

Privatization will lead to greater disclosure and open accounting systems, in both the new postal and highway agencies that will be managing the process. To the extent that such practices are implemented, decisions about investing and lending money involved in highway projects will become far more transparent than they have ever been. The firms (often led by ex-highway mandarins) that have close ties with Japan Highway Public Corporation, and are dubbed the 'family enterprises,' have already been singled out by the highway reform advisory commission as a source of waste and fraud

(*Asahi Shimbun*)

inimical to the public interest. Such enterprises symbolize the clubby relationship that prevails between the private sector, bureaucrats, and politicians involved in the construction industry, and the costs of such collusive relations. The gross inefficiency, corruption, and opaque accounting practices that marked the operations of the highway corporations will draw far more careful scrutiny under privatization. Although the abuses and excesses will not disappear overnight, the risks and penalties will be higher, representing significant if small steps in the right direction. The bad will still sleep well, but may now face bouts of insomnia and nightmares that will make life more uncomfortable.

While privatization will hasten the end of collusion and corruption in the industry, the quest for greater efficiency and more productive use of resources is likely to prove more difficult. Advocates of privatizing the highway corporations may hope for cost cutting, better service, and lower tolls but, if the privatization of the railway network is any indication, such benefits will remain elusive. The cost of rail travel in Japan is ruinously expensive by international standards and seems set to remain so. Given the level of indebtedness of the highway corporations, it is probable that the lease arrangements with private operators will reflect such costs – meaning that tolls will be charged in perpetuity and remain onerous. This will put added pressure on the toll-free road networks, resulting in further congestion and pollution in more densely populated areas. It also then becomes a rationale for expanding such roads to meet the increase in demand; such is the tortured, self-perpetuating logic of the construction state.

The powerful institutional, political, and economic forces that have sustained the construction state are now confronting a growing challenge on several fronts and are coming under pressure to make concessions. It has taken four decades for the public to awaken to the damage inflicted by construction excesses, and it will take far longer to work free of the troubled legacy of debts and environmental devastation handed to future generations. The seemingly relentless, yen-guzzling *doken kokka* juggernaut is sputtering because it is running out of gas; the cash crunch has exposed the vulnerability of a system that depends on high-octane spending. The inefficiency of construction as an engine of growth is glaringly apparent and citizens will increasingly be inclined to support more efficient uses of their scarce resources. In an era of rising transparency, greater accountability, spreading NPO networks, a supportive judiciary, and more engaged citizens, the prospects for unfettered growth in ready-mix politics are not good. While the apparatus of the construction state remains powerful, the changing political and economic context of society, coupled with the needs of an aging society, suggest a downsizing is in the offing. More troubling than cutting the *doken kokka* down to size will be dealing with its impoverishing consequences. Figuring out how to rectify the concrete follies of the late twentieth century will be one of Japan's great challenges in the twenty-first century.

6 Bad blood

The betrayal and infection of Japan's hemophiliacs

I inject [the product] every day, thinking there is a toxic substance in it.
> Dr. Abe Takeshi, June 1983, at the first meeting of the
> government AIDS research panel he chaired

The need to worry about AIDS is slight ... All of you are being saved because of blood products.
> Public proclamation of safety issued in 1983 by the Ministry of
> Health and Welfare's AIDS research panel chaired by Dr. Abe Takeshi

Japan is lenient on people with authority.
> Comment by Diet member Kawada Etsuko, whose
> hemophiliac son developed AIDS from tainted blood products,
> on the acquittal in 2001 of Dr. Abe Takeshi

Systemic failure

In the 1980s, some 40 percent of Japan's 5,000 registered hemophiliac patients developed AIDS (Acquired Immuno-deficiency Syndrome) as a result of transfusions of tainted blood. (For comparison, about 10,000 of the estimated 20,000 hemophiliacs in the USA suffered a similar fate.) Although many of the Japanese victims filed suit, a large number died before advocates managed to win a settlement and extract an admission of wrongdoing from the government in 1996. Since then, some of the individuals responsible for the scandal have been brought to trial and convicted, although the most notorious figure associated with this chilling saga, Dr. Abe Takeshi, was found not guilty of criminal charges.

The case of the poisoned hemophiliacs, and the outbreak of an AIDS epidemic among them, sheds light on how Japan has treated one of its most vulnerable and marginalized groups. Their interests were shelved for more than a decade as a result of the collusive ties that unite bureaucrats and the businessmen they oversee in placing corporate concerns before the interests and welfare of the public. Perhaps no other scandal of the 1990s eroded public trust in the bureaucratic elite more than this case, which has led to Japan's 'best and brightest' becoming subject to greater scrutiny. In this sense, the suffering endured by hemophiliacs spurred challenges to patterns of conduct that have made it far too easy for officials to avoid accountability in the past. The HIV hemophiliac scandal was one of many cases that have aroused public support for greater transparency in government and, in particular, for the national legislation on information disclosure passed in 1999.

Hemophilia, a condition wherein blood does not easily coagulate, is a debilitating disease found almost exclusively among men. While women may pass on this genetic disorder to their offspring, only very rarely do they show signs of the easy bruising and bleeding that impairs the lives of those who suffer from this incurable malady. As a result of recent medical advances many sufferers are able to care for themselves at home, administering regular self-injection of clotting agents extracted from plasma. These blood products have freed hemophiliacs from frequent and time-consuming hospital outpatient visits for transfusions and have enabled many to lead lives far less constrained by their condition than was the case until the 1970s. However, from the 1980s these 'lifesaving' products, many derived from imported blood from the USA, became the conduit for an epidemic of HIV (Human Immuno-deficiency Virus) among hemophiliacs all around the world.

In March 1983, a warning was issued by the US Center for Disease Control in Atlanta, which suspected that a new virus was being transmitted via blood transfusions to hemophiliacs. In the same month, the US Food and Drug Administration authorized use of heat-treated blood products that sterilized the blood and thus ensured safer transfusions. Both these developments came to the attention of officials responsible for monitoring blood-related health issues at Japan's Ministry of Health and Welfare. This was the same year (1983) that the Japanese government authorized national health insurance coverage of self-injected blood products for hemophiliacs, easing the heavy financial burden of treatment and giving more patients access to these life-transforming clotting agents. It was an unhappy coincidence, as the bureaucratic and business forces that had lobbied for this expanded insurance coverage were suddenly confronted with information that threatened their interests.

The development in the USA of safe heat-treated blood products meant that the epidemic among Japan's hemophiliacs was not inevitable. While some of the HIV transmissions occurred prior to 1983, those that occurred after mid-1983 could have been avoided. This failure was largely due to hesitancy on the part of the MHW to move expeditiously in introducing heat-treated blood products. The various strands of this saga have been brought together by Feldman (1999), who places the blame on systemic failure rather than individual negligence or venality. In his view, by focusing on individual culpability and neglecting the institutional causes of the tragedy, similar catastrophes could recur as long as the structural causes remain unaddressed. For Feldman, the incestuous relationships between pharmaceutical companies, doctors, medical experts, and the bureaucrats of the MHW, fueled by immense medical profits and driven by the dictates of business, explain why so many hemophiliacs became infected.

The initial reaction of the blood-products industry was one of responsible caution. In June 1983, Travenol, the Japanese subsidiary of US-based medical products company Baxter International, contacted Gunji Atsuaki, the director of the Biologics and Antibiotics Division (BAD) of the MHW, and announced the company's voluntary recall of a range of blood products in the USA after a single blood donor had developed symptoms of AIDS shortly after donating blood. At this meeting there was also discussion of gaining fast-track approval for imports of the new heat-treated blood products already being used in the USA.

In the 1980s, Japan imported large amounts of blood plasma from the USA. Because plasma is derived from the pooled blood of between 2,000 and 25,000 paid donors, just one infected donor could infect an entire batch and the blood products processed therefrom, including the clotting agents used by hemophiliacs. It was the reliance on imported blood from the USA that placed Japanese hemophiliacs at risk, especially in the early stages when the dangers were less well understood and often minimized. At the time, it was widely believed among medical professionals that the risk of contracting AIDS from blood transfusions was a one-in-a-million chance, a wildly sanguine view in retrospect. Many hemophiliacs paid for this unfounded optimism with their lives.

After the meeting with Travenol in June 1983, the MHW established an AIDS research panel chaired by Dr. Abe Takeshi. Abe was one of Japan's leading hematologists, a vice-president of Teikyo University and a prominent advocate for expanded national health insurance coverage for hemophiliacs using self-injected clotting agents. While BAD Director Gunji did not inform the panel of Travenol/Baxter's recall of unheated blood products believed to be tainted by the HIV virus, it seems that he initially voiced support for emergency imports of heat-treated blood products. However, some time between July 4 and July 11, 1983, he had a change of mind. In a memo dated July 4, Gunji made three recommendations: he suggested that heat-treated blood products be imported on an emergency basis; that Travenol be urged to file an application for urgent approval of its heat-treated blood products; and that MHW use its 'administrative guidance' to direct businesses not to distribute unheated blood products imported from the USA. However, on July 11, Gunji reversed his position on all three points. These two memos, 'discovered' in 1996, have been the basis of suspicion that intensive lobbying by domestic drug firms lay behind the government's failure to take measures that would have protected hemophiliacs from infection with HIV. The firms involved stood to lose money since they had acquired large stocks of unheated blood products derived from US plasma in preparation for the anticipated rise in demand related to expanded insurance coverage for transfusions of blood products. They had also invested in developing the production capacity needed to meet the expected surge in demand. Moreover, since domestic drug firms had not yet developed a heat-treating process for sterilizing blood products, there was concern that fast-track approval would erode their market share and permit foreign competitors such as Travenol to gain a dominant position. In their own defense, MHW bureaucrats pointed to reasonable doubts about the efficacy of heat treatment, and asserted their duty to confirm the safety of treated products before authorizing widespread use.

One of the most disturbing aspects of this case was the government's attempts to stonewall hemophiliacs seeking information about its deliberations regarding blood products. From 1989, when HIV-positive hemophiliacs initiated litigation against the government and drug firms, until January 1996, the government denied any wrongdoing and negligence and claimed that relevant documents were 'lost.' However, when MHW bureaucrats carried out an investigation ordered by the new Minister for Health and Welfare, Naoto Kan, when he assumed office in January 1996, Gunji's incriminating memos were found within three days. Once the ministry's dirty laundry was made public, a settlement was quickly cobbled together. By this time, 536 of the nearly 2,000 infected hemophiliacs had already died from AIDS.

The failure to take steps that would have protected hemophiliacs from infection with HIV, and the subsequent cover-up, spoke volumes about the government's priorities. A number of key recommendations made by members of the panel established by the MHW in 1983 to cope with the risk of HIV transmission were rejected: stopping distribution of unheated blood products; granting of fast-track approval for imported heat-treated blood products; and the use of safer, but more expensive, cyrogenic blood products derived from just a few domestic donors. Reportedly, the chairman of the panel, Dr. Abe, heatedly intervened against such proposals and insisted on a full one-year trial period for the heat-treated blood products while opposing any restriction on further distribution of unheated blood products.

In July 1983 the panel acted to quell public concerns by refusing to acknowledge that a hemophiliac was the first Japanese to die of AIDS – despite knowing that this was the cause of death. It was only in May 1985 that the victim was retroactively recognized as having died of AIDS, after a homosexual Japanese man, resident in the USA, returned to Japan and was diagnosed as Japan's 'first' AIDS patient. Since AIDS was viewed as a gay men's disease, and something restricted to foreigners, it was important to publicly reaffirm this association by selecting a homosexual – and one who reassuringly lived overseas – as the 'first' official AIDS case. His infection could be blamed on his risky lifestyle and traced to foreign origins, encouraging public complacency about risks at home and reinforcing discriminatory attitudes towards homosexuals and foreigners. It was their problem, not ours.

The denial of the risks and incidence of HIV and AIDS among hemophiliacs ensured that the disease spread. In September 1983, Dr. Abe sent blood samples from 48 of his patients to the US for analysis and 23 came back HIV positive. Certainly this should have set off alarm bells and encouraged him to use his clout with the government to institute emergency measures. The link between transfusions and such high infection rates would not have been lost on one of Japan's leading blood experts and, at the very least, should have led to public health advisories about the suspected risks. Instead, Abe failed to inform his patients of their test results and continued to insist on a full one-year testing of heat-treated blood products, despite good initial results after six months. He also continued to administer unheated blood products to all of his patients and publicly backed their general use.

The failure of physicians to inform patients of the diagnosis of a serious illness was relatively common in Japan in the1980s: doctors felt that it was better to spare the patient the bad news. At the time, as was the case with government information, open disclosure was viewed as neither helpful to those concerned nor a duty on the part of the practitioner. In following this practice with his patients, Dr. Abe placed their loved ones at risk, with the result that some contracted HIV. Had he acted on the information he had at his disposal, and warned those most affected about the risks involved, it is likely that fewer Japanese would have contracted HIV. The tragedy of Japan's hemophiliacs thus hinges on a policy based on denial and suppression of information.

In Japan, it is still widely assumed that those in positions of authority or with expertise in a particular field will act ethically – to question them is considered both rude and strange. Doctors are rarely questioned and seeking a second opinion is considered almost unseemly. In recent years there have been some changes in public attitudes towards doctors, and also within the profession, and they are now becoming more informative and open about what they prescribe or diagnose. But in 1983 old habits prevailed and patients did as their doctor advised – it was a matter of trust.[1] In this context, professional reassurances given to skeptical or suspicious hemophiliac patients, who had some knowledge of developments related to AIDS in the USA, created a tense situation. The experts were minimizing the risks while at the same time extolling the benefits of plasma treatment, a therapy newly covered by national health insurance. Under these circumstances, while hemophiliacs and those who cared for them might harbor doubts and anxieties, to openly state such opinions, refuse treatment or insist on different treatment, was nearly inconceivable.

Kawada Etsuko, whose son contracted AIDS in 1986, recalls attending a summer camp for hemophiliac children in 1982 where one father raised questions about the safety of imported blood products. This was the time when the first reports of Gay-Related Immuno Deficiency (GRID), later renamed Acquired Immuno-deficiency Syndrome (AIDS), were beginning to reach Japan. Kawada later quarreled with her husband after he too voiced concerns about continuing with transfusions in light of the heightened risks of transmission of HIV. In retrospect, she wishes she had been more questioning and assertive and blames herself for having placed her trust in the

Figure 6.1 Kawada Ryuhei, a hemophiliac infected with HIV and a leader in the campaign for accountability and compensation. (Photo: Mainichi Newspapers)

'experts.' After further disagreements with her husband about joining the hemophiliac lawsuit against the government and five drug companies that followed the breaking of the scandal, her marriage unraveled and the couple finally divorced in 1993. Shortly afterwards Kawada and her son joined the lawsuit in an effort to secure justice and accountability. Her son Ryuhei became one of the most prominent victims, going public when many hid their identities, leading demonstrations and holding press conferences. Given the strong social taboos against both hemophiliacs and AIDS sufferers that made victims reluctant to come forward, his decision to 'go public' helped win a sympathetic hearing from both the media and the public.

Kawada ran for office, largely to advocate for AIDS-infected hemophiliacs, and as an elected member of parliament she has not been shy in voicing her criticisms of those involved in the scandal. She accused Dr. Abe of conducting experiments on live humans. She also is bitter about the delay in availability of heated blood products, pointing out that even after their approval in July 1985 many hemophiliacs still had no access to the safer products. And doctors continued to reassure their patients about the safety of unheated blood products while knowing that they could be infecting them with HIV. Her son Ryuhei expressed the frustration of all the patients: 'Every week, every day, some of us have been dying. It's not that we are dying like everyone else; we're being murdered' (*Asia Week*, August 15, 1997).

It took seventeen years – from 1983, when the first evidence of HIV transmissions to hemophiliacs was produced, to 2000 – before Dr. Abe was brought to trial on charges of negligence. In March 2001, in a controversial and unpopular court decision, Abe was acquitted. In court the prosecutors presented an array of evidence in support of their contention that he was professionally negligent in the death of one of his patients who contracted HIV from tainted blood in mid-1985. The prosecutors argued that, at that time, it was beyond doubt that HIV could be transmitted via unheated blood products. They asserted that, as a leading blood specialist, Abe must have known that he was placing his patient at risk by injecting unheated blood-clotting agents, pointing out that many of his patients had been infected with HIV and two had already died of AIDS at the time of the 1985 injections. The prosecution further accused Dr. Abe of delaying approval of heat-treated blood products in order to protect pharmaceutical giant Green Cross, a company that had donated some ¥18.5 million ($75,000 at that time) to a foundation he had established to promote self-injection of unheated blood products by hemophiliacs. Prosecutors pointed out that Green Cross lagged in developing a process for heat-treating blood and had invested substantial sums in unheated blood products, and suggested that this explained Abe's opposition to fast-track approval for Travenol's heat-treated blood and the placing of restrictions on unheated products. Green Cross's involvement was also invoked to explain the withdrawal of MHW 'administrative guidance' concerning use of unheated blood products. The media weighed in and turned up a damaging personal connection, reporting that in the 1960s Dr. Abe was a research assistant to Naito Ryoichi, the founder of Green Cross and a former member of the notorious Unit 731 that had conducted vivisection and biological warfare experiments in China during the 1930s and 1940s.[2]

Although acquitted in a court of law, Abe was condemned in the court of public opinion: the media accused him and found him guilty, portraying him as a heinous tool of the pharmaceutical industry, abusing his power and ignoring the welfare of his patients. The prosecutors appealed his acquittal but abandoned the case in 2004 due to Abe's health. For the media, this was yet another case of arbitrary, negligent, and unaccountable abuse of power. As Kawada ruefully commented to reporters after the trial, 'Japan is lenient on people with authority.'

In his assessment of the significance of the Abe trial, Japanese lawyer Awaji Takehisa (1997: 581) put his finger on the crucial issue: 'Although heated-and-safe blood products were already available from the USA, government approval in Japan was deliberately delayed for almost three years while local pharmaceutical companies developed the products.' As we saw, Abe's forceful stance in the deliberations of the MHW's AIDS panel played a major part in its recommendation favoring the continued use of unheated blood products. Awaji sought to explain Abe's motives:

> It is suspected that Abe was influential in leading the research team to such a conclusion, and that he considered the interests of a domestic pharmaceutical firm with which he had a connection. Thereafter, the use of unheated blood products mushroomed, partly because home use had been brought within the coverage of national health insurance and partly because the [medical] companies vigorously sought to increase sales by discounting the price.

Even after domestic firms developed a heat-processing treatment for plasma, and official approval for the use of heat-treated blood products manufactured by both domestic and foreign firms was granted in July 1985, shipments and use of unheated blood continued unabated. Drug firms failed to recall already distributed unheated product despite the known risks and continued shipping them even after safe blood was made available.[3] It seems that the steep discounts offered by US suppliers of unprocessed blood made this economically compelling. In addition, since the compensation received by Japanese doctors and hospitals was based on the price of Japanese-made blood products, which was far higher than the price of imports, the medical insurance system was set up to financially reward distribution of imported blood products. Such structural flaws in the medical system help explain why, even after approving the heat-treated blood products – a measure aimed at safeguarding the nation's blood supplies – the MHW failed to order a recall or ban further distribution of unsafe, unheated blood products. The business of blood was the undoing of its consumers.

Kan Naoto

The hero of this dismal saga is Kan Naoto, one-time NGO activist and a maverick politician who joined the small New Party Sakigake in 1994 as a committed reformer. Kan headed the research group on HIV infection through tainted blood products set up by the party and was aware of the MHW's stonewalling of plaintiffs seeking information on bureaucratic deliberations. Although he was well known for his critical views of the bureaucracy and commitment to more open government, as a member of a small fringe party his stance was not taken seriously. However, when the New Party Sakigake joined with the conservative LDP in coalition government, and extracted the MHW portfolio in return for its cooperation, Kan was suddenly catapulted into a position of power over the officials he was famous for castigating. Although he told the media he felt 'like a coconut bobbing in the ocean,' he belied this image of helplessness by ordering an immediate investigation into

Figure 6.2 Kan Naoto, Minister of Health, who exposed the ministry's wrongdoing in the HIV hemophiliac scandal. (Photo: Mainichi Newspapers)

the case of the hemophiliacs – an investigation that produced damning results in less than 72 hours. Kan was a man of the people and, unlike many other budding reformers who found their wings effectively clipped by bureaucrats skilled in the art of infighting and neutralizing adversaries, he succeeded in outmaneuvering them, to the applause of a grateful public.

Personal virtues aside, Kan's timing was impeccable. In January 1996, the three-party ruling coalition – the LDP, Sakigake, and the Social Democratic Party – was wrangling over a common policy platform in a bid for re-election. The need of the LDP to get the junior partners on board provided an opening for Kan, then head of his party's policy research council, to insist on inclusion of two issues on the parties' joint policy platform: investigation into hemophiliac HIV infections to determine the extent of government responsibility, and a review of finance sector regulations. Since these issues would appeal to voters in a climate of rising skepticism towards the government and banking world, the LDP acquiesced. This desire to broaden its popular base of support was reflected in the LDP's resistance to MHW lobbying against inclusion of the hemophiliac investigation. In need of Sakigake support to retain the post of prime minister for itself, the LDP also agreed to name Kan Minister of Health and Welfare despite misgivings among the health bureaucrats and their LDP supporters in the Diet. This was a price Prime Minister Hashimoto Ryutaro was willing to pay, perhaps reflecting his confidence that he could use his position as premier, and longstanding ties in the MHW where he had served as minister, to blunt Kan's reformist zeal.

Hashimoto's hopes were to prove unfounded. On assuming his ministerial post, Kan immediately unveiled the cover-up surrounding the tainted plasma and brought the incriminating evidence to light. He took a wry pleasure in undoing his bureaucrats by appealing to their sense of professional pride. As he observed to reporters, 'When a bureaucrat is given a job to do, he cannot refuse. It is his nature to carry out an assignment to the best of his ability. I thought that once the investigation team was created, the chances of finding those memos were pretty good.' Gunji's missing memos proved beyond doubt that the MHW had permitted HIV-tainted blood products to be administered to Japan's hemophiliacs long after the fatal risks were known. The government's complicity in their deaths and negligence in carrying out its duties were plainly documented. Like their colleagues in France and Germany, they were to be held responsible for failing to prevent an unnecessary tragedy.

As *Asia Week* (March 4, 1996) commented, Kan 'had lifted the veil of secrecy on his own ministry, revealing a pattern of incompetence, insensitivity, and dissembling.' Given their own secretive inclinations, the ministry bureaucrats could not comprehend Kan's commitment to open government and transparency and wrongly assumed that the missing files would be edited before being released for public consumption. The so-called 'Gunji files,' named after the director of BAD in mid-1983 when the government had rejected emergency imports of heat-treated blood products, reveal that government officials took account of the potential economic impact on domestic pharmaceutical firms if imports were approved. It soon became public knowledge, and an enormous embarrassment to the MHW, that Japanese hemophiliacs had been sacrificed to protect the market share and future profits of domestic drug firms. When releasing the files, the MHW stressed that this disclosure of government deliberations was a special case and not intended to set a precedent – a none-too-subtle attempt to resist the principle of open government. Given the extent of the tragedy that was unfolding on the national stage, it is not surprising that the public and media took the opposite view, arguing that transparency is the basis of accountability and thus responsible governance.

But the new minister did not stop with disclosure. The next shock for beleaguered officials was Kan's insistence on making a public apology and acknowledgement of government wrongdoing. After years of denial and stonewalling, it was inconceivable to officials that, having already disgraced the MHW by airing its dirty laundry in public, its own minister would further 'betray' the organization by admitting negligence and taking responsibility for this. *Asahi* journalist Itagaki Tetsuya (1996: 27) neatly summed up the official position: 'Bureaucrats saw as their ultimate responsibility opposition of the plaintiff's claims and protection of the government's coffers from undue financial loss, rather than ensuring justice.'

The legacy of Kan's tenure is hotly debated. Some argue that he helped nudge at least some bureaucrats towards the principle of transparency as the only means to regain public trust and remove the tarnish of accumulated scandals and cover-ups. Others suggest that, in the wake of the affair, officials are merely more scrupulous about what they commit to writing and what they shred. For Kan, the hemophiliac tragedy was a powerful demonstration of the need for information disclosure legislation: 'Japanese bureaucrats have held onto their powers by monopolizing information. They hide essential information, and what was worse, they do not take any responsibility for their actions. I think this is the biggest problem festering in the bureaucracy. The key to solving the problem is to establish a system of information disclosure' (Itagaki 1996). He also suggested strong restrictions on *amakudari*, arguing that those who regulate industries should not be allowed to retire into firms that have been under their purview. While information disclosure legislation was subsequently approved, as we saw in Chapter 4 the practice of *amakudari* and the conflicts of interest that accompany it remain widespread.

Settlement

The plaintiffs did not get the satisfaction or sense of justice provided by a court judgment or decree. Instead, a settlement was suggested by the Tokyo High Court and accepted by interested parties in March 1996, less than two months after Kan Naoto blew the whistle on his own ministry. Although the basic provisions of this settlement were on the table as early as October 1995, proceedings stalled due to the government's refusal to admit any wrongdoing. This position became untenable with the release of internal documents and memos that irretrievably compromised the government's denials.

Despite its failure to hand down penalties, the court provided some solace in affirming that government negligence was responsible for the epidemic. It asserted that the MHW could not plead ignorance of the link between hemophilia and AIDS:

> Since early 1983, the United States government issued numerous recommendations about measures to protect hemophiliacs from AIDS, among which was a suggestion to reject blood donors belonging to high risk groups. [The court] finds that the director of the Biologics and Antibiotics Division at the Health and Welfare Ministry knew of the foregoing situation in the United States, for he had started collecting information on AIDS and hemophilia around the beginning of 1983.
>
> (Awaji 1997: 593)

The court went on to assert that the risks of transfusions to hemophiliacs were already common knowledge to scientists by the summer of 1983. Despite this, defendant drug firms continued to sell their products and failed to completely recall unheated blood products that were responsible for the outbreak. Taking the government to task for failing to take simple counter-measures, the court concluded: 'it is difficult to deny that this delay in taking action resulted in the spread of a tragic injury, HIV transmission to hemophiliacs in Japan.'

The sudden exposure of the ugly truths about why hemophiliacs were infected with HIV, mostly involving bureaucratic negligence and connivance with drug firms to protect them from foreign competition, undercut the defendants' position and at the same time clarified their responsibility. The terms of the settlement involved several wide-ranging determinations: a lump sum payment of ¥45 million ($360,000) per person (40 percent from the government and 60 percent paid by the five drug firms named in the lawsuits); a monthly maintenance payment of ¥150,000 ($1,200) per month for those with AIDS symptoms; full insurance coverage for healthcare costs; disability status for purposes of securing social welfare payments; a commitment on the part of the drug firms and the government to improve healthcare for HIV sufferers; establishment of a HIV research and treatment center; and a promise to make every effort to ensure that a similar tragedy would never occur again.

In addition, both the government and drug firms made public apologies to the victims. Minister Kan made a powerful statement of apology on behalf of his ministry, which included withering references to both the negligence that allowed the tragedy to occur and the subsequent cover-up that prolonged the victims' suffering and ensured that 536 hemophiliacs died before vindication was achieved in the court-ordered settlement. In February 1996, shortly before the settlement was finalized, Kan met with 200 plaintiffs and their families to deliver an emotional apology. 'Representing the ministry I make a heartfelt apology for inflicting heavy damage on the innocent patients. I also apologize for the belated recognition of the ministry's responsibility for the case. I understand the delay has tormented the victims.'

In one of the more telling scenes of this unfolding drama, the president of Green Cross issued a public apology at a gathering of victims and their families that was deemed too perfunctory. He said, ' We deeply regret that our products created a serious situation that resulted in pain and grief.' One mother who had lost her son hurled abuse at him and upbraided him for not demonstrating sufficient contrition and remorse for depriving families of their loved ones. The president walked over to her and bowed so deeply that his head touched the floor – a gesture that might have been more convincing if he had not spent the better part of seven years denying responsibility and hiding information that exposed his firm's dealings in bad blood.

By international standards, the terms of the settlement were generous. Even though the plaintiffs did not get the satisfaction of a guilty verdict, the

Figure 6.3 Green Cross executives apologize to hemophiliacs and their families for distributing HIV-tainted blood despite knowing of the deadly risks and then denying any responsibility for nearly a decade. (Photo: Mainichi Newspapers)

settlement brought speedy relief and comprehensive measures covering all of the victims. For many of them, there was simply not enough time to wait for lengthy appeals and prolonged negotiations. Most importantly, the settlement provided far more generous remedies than is permitted under the Japanese legal system. Under Japanese law the courts are only allowed to order single, lump-sum compensation payments and have no recourse to the ongoing periodic payment options and non-pecuniary research and treatment measures involved in the settlement. By contrast, in the USA the search for justice by hemophiliac victims was derailed by a court decision against their federal class action suit, forcing them to seek individual redress.

Profits before safety

The HIV hemophiliac scandal was animated by corporate greed, political sleaze, collusion, and personal profits – indicating that not much has changed over the years. The blood industry has never had a very positive image in Japan and was depicted at its lurid worst in Oshima Nagisa's film *The Sun's Burial* (1960). It seems that the lure of blood money still brings out the worst in those involved in the business.

In early 2000, three drug company executives were sentenced to prison by the High Court in Osaka for their roles in the infection of nearly 2,000 hemophiliacs with HIV. The judge accused the defendants of 'putting profits before safety' by distributing and then failing to recall unheated blood products, despite knowing the dangers of infection they posed to hemophiliacs. The three executives, who all served as president of the now defunct Green Cross, were sentenced to prison terms ranging from fifteen months to two years for professional negligence. Although these sentences appear relatively light given the charges, and were harshly criticized by victims and their relatives, these men are the first senior executives of a pharmaceutical company ever convicted of crimes related to drug sales in Japan.[4]

The case of Matsushita Renzo, president of Green Cross between 1983 and 1988, highlights the cozy ties that still prevail between businesses and the bureaucrats that oversee them.[5] He joined Green Cross after retiring from the MHW and was the handpicked successor of the firm's founder. Matsushita sought to shift at least some of the blame for the scandal onto the government. Responding to allegations that the company continued to sell off its inventory of suspect blood, he told the Associated Press that the reason Green Cross kept selling unheated blood products, even after heat-treated blood products were approved and available, was because the government failed to prohibit such sales. It seems that tainted plasma continued to be shipped for ten months after Green Cross announced that it had halted such sales in 1985.

Not all of those with close involvement in the scandal were punished by the courts, however. Dr. Abe Takeshi, often portrayed in the media as the arch-villain in the HIV hemophiliac case, was more fortunate than Matsushita; in March 2001 he was acquitted of the death of one of his patients who had been infected in 1985. Before the trial, Dr. Matsuda Juzo, a professor at Teikyo University where Abe served as vice-president, testified in the Diet about the case. He stated his belief that former MHW officials employed at Green Cross had pressured Abe to delay imports of heat-treated blood products to protect corporate interests. These collusive interests formed the core of the prosecution case against Abe. In July 2000 prosecutors argued at the Tokyo District Court that 'his victim was tragically infected with the AIDS virus because of his grave and malicious negligence. He has no sense of responsibility or ethics required of a doctor.' They argued that by September 1984 Abe was fully aware of the high risks of administering unheated blood products to hemophiliacs but continued to use them because of his close ties to domestic drug firms from which he had received some ¥43 million ($180,000 at that time). The prosecutors alleged that, in his position as head of the MHW panel on AIDS, Abe had delayed approval of heat-treated blood products to prevent domestic drug firms such as Green Cross, which controlled about 50 percent of the domestic blood products market in the early 1980s, from incurring huge losses on their large stocks of unheated blood products.

Professional pride also played a part in the tragedy. The prosecutors alleged that Abe had rejected other doctors' recommendations to suspend

Figure 6.4 Dr. Abe Takeshi, after Diet testimony regarding his central role in the HIV epidemic among Japan's hemophiliacs. (Photo: Mainichi Newspapers)

administering the unheated blood products. As evidence, the prosecution produced transcripts of Abe's own statements made during the course of their investigation. He had said: 'I didn't stop using [potentially HIV-contaminated] unheated blood products. I admit my mistake.' Asked why he kept using these products despite knowing the risks, Abe replied, 'I gave my pride [as expert] priority. [If I had stopped using them] it would mean admitting my professional mistake.' He admitted having rejected the advice of junior colleagues to approve the importation and use of heat-treated blood products, 'because to do so would have meant that I was wrong. In retrospect, their advice was correct.'

The judge acquitted Abe, despite these frank admissions. In his ruling the judge argued that although Abe had been aware of the danger of HIV infection, he could not have anticipated the consequence of the disease because so little was known about AIDS at that time. The judge also dismissed the testimony of two of Abe's colleagues who had recommended the use of safer clotting agents, suggesting that their testimony against Abe was self-serving. Oddly, Abe's financial ties and motivations were not covered in the ruling nor did the judge address his self-incriminating statements.

In contrast to the Abe acquittal, the Tokyo District Court convicted Matsumura Akihito, a former top official at MHW, of causing the death of a blood-transfusion patient by failing to prevent his infection with HIV from transfusions of tainted blood products. He was convicted of negligence in the death of a liver patient in 1995 and given a one-year sentence suspended for two years. Despite the suspended sentence, this was a landmark ruling as Matsumura became the first public servant in Japan to be held personally accountable for failing to act to prevent harm to an individual citizen. He was, however, acquitted of further charges relating to the death of a hemophiliac who became infected with HIV in 1985.

The judicial assessments of negligence in these two cases were complex. The guilty ruling hinged on the judge's opinion that Matsumura knew in early 1986 that using unheated blood products carried an extremely high risk of HIV infection. Despite this knowledge, the MHW section manager approved continued use of the risky blood products and forbade use of alternatives. By failing to halt sales of unheated blood products or order their recall, Matsumura was judged to be negligent in his duties and responsible for fatally infecting the liver patient. By contrast, Judge Nagai Toshio, who earlier in the year acquitted Abe Takeshi of infecting a hemophiliac, also acquitted Matsumura in the death of a hemophiliac patient on the grounds that a majority of doctors in 1985 were unaware of the danger of unheated blood products. Prosecutors in the case had argued to no avail that, as a qualified doctor and director between 1984 and 1986 of the Biologics and Antibiotics Division (BAD) in the ministry's Pharmaceutical and Medical Safety Bureau responsible for ensuring the safety of blood products, he must have been aware of the dangers.

Convoluted and odd as the guilty ruling in the Matsumura case may have been, its implications are considerable. It has rekindled debate over whether individual officials should be held criminally liable for their actions and omissions. Although many top government officials are experts in their field, the policymaking process tends to be collective, collaborative, and opaque. Under such circumstances where various ministries, agencies, and officials formulate policies, determining individual responsibility is extremely difficult. In previous cases involving the side effects of drugs, such as thalidomide in the early 1960s and the outbreak of SMON (subacute myleo-optico-neuropathy) in the 1970s, lawsuits did not focus on the criminal liability of officials. One of the lawyers involved in the hemophiliacs' legal action, Suzuki Toshihiro, expressed forceful opinions on the issue: 'Bureaucrats usually have extensive knowledge and strong influence over the general public. They should be required [by law] to shoulder the utmost responsibility for citizens' well-being and convicted of professional negligence should they neglect this responsibility. ... It's time for the country to set specific moral standards for individual experts and to create a [legal] system to try them when they neglect such standards.'[6]

Others disagree with this position and assert that, given the collective nature of policymaking, trying to pinpoint individual responsibility is more akin to a witch-hunt than justice. Uemura Eiji, a law professor at Seikei University, favors information disclosure as a means of preventing negligence and tragedies like the hemophiliac case, rather than prosecuting individual officials. He asserts that bureaucrats will develop an increased sense of responsibility and feel compelled to meet public standards if they know that their actions are open to scrutiny. 'If even the slightest misjudgments by bureaucrats are visible to the public, they will become more cautious when making decisions.' However, Otani Fujio, a former MHW official whose struggle to reform government policies towards leprosy patients is discussed in Chapter 7, is less hopeful. He warns that the bureaucratic mentality is essentially conformist and thus not inclined towards reforms. Drawing on his own experience, he commented in an interview: 'Making changes usually makes more trouble for your colleagues as well as industries that have benefited from existing policies. If you do it several times you are classified as a troublemaker and your career prospects are no longer bright.'

Otani's comments hint at an unholy alliance between the MHW and drug firms that is especially evident in their hiring practices. In its issue of April 6, 1996, *The Lancet* medical journal reported that an estimated 100 former high-ranking officials of the MHW's Pharmaceutical Affairs Bureau were working as advisers or executives of drug companies. Prosecutors investigating the HIV infection case discovered the involvement of five top executives at Green Cross who were former MHW officials. *The Economist* expressed this aspect of the case succinctly in a story published on April 6, 1996: 'It illustrates the unhealthily close connections between doctors, the Ministry of Health and Welfare and the drug companies they were supposed to be regulating.' Commenting on the foot-dragging that impeded imports or approval of heat-treated blood products, *The Economist* continued: 'Humanitarian and health considerations seem to have played no more than a minor role. In Japan, doctors make most of their money by prescribing drugs. They stood to make more money from prescribing unheated products – which they could buy cheaply – than from expensive imported ones.' Sakurai Yoshiko (1994), an investigative journalist, reported that between 1983 and 1985 unheated blood imported from the USA was sold to Japanese drug companies at 40–50 percent discounts, indicating the extent to which drug firms and doctors distributing risky blood profited from this trade.[7]

Lessons and implications

In 1999, ten years after the hemophiliacs' first lawsuit was filed, a monument commemorating the victims was erected after nearly three years of wrangling over the inscription to be placed on it. The government refused to inscribe a pledge to eliminate negligence and prevent similar tragedies from occurring in the future; instead, it agreed to 'do its best' to prevent such accidents.

Despite this undertaking, Japan has experienced a rash of cases eerily reminiscent of the hemophiliac tragedy of the 1980s. The anti-cancer drug irinotecan is a case in point. In August 1997, the MHW admitted that it had known about many more deaths from the side effects of irinotecan than it had previously disclosed. The revelation was ironic in that the ministry had recently abolished the tainted Pharmaceutical Affairs Bureau that had been responsible for both industry promotion and drug safety, drawing sharp criticism of a conflict of interests. A government spokesman explained that while the ministry had not concealed the number of known deaths from side effects caused by irinotecan, neither had it publicized the high number of fatalities. But in the court of public opinion 'sins of omission' are no excuse, and the ministry's 'defense' has further battered its reputation.

Further scandals involving blood products have also surfaced. In October 1999 it was reported that two patients who had received blood transfusions were infected with HIV from blood collected by the Japanese Red Cross through its domestic blood donation drive. A similar incident was reported in 1997. It is suspected that the donors had only recently contracted AIDS and, since it takes about three weeks for the body to produce the telltale antibodies, typical screening procedures did not detect the presence of the virus. Although more sophisticated tests can detect the virus within 11–16 days of infection, it seems that these more expensive procedures were used selectively for screening donors in certain areas of Tokyo. Yet again, the price of safety was deemed too high and the government has been slow to issue stricter guidelines on screening blood.

In 2002, a drug firm with ties to the defunct Green Cross[8] was sued for distributing a blood-clotting product, fibrinogen, linked to an outbreak of hepatitis C in the late 1980s. Plaintiffs in the case argue that the risks of contamination were known, as fibrinogen's approval had been revoked in the USA in the 1970s.[9] They assert that if the government had regulated the sale and use of the product, and the drug companies had provided patients with proper information, the tragedy could have been prevented. Hepatitis C is a liver illness mainly contracted through the blood. Although its acute symptoms are relatively mild compared with other types of hepatitis, it tends to become chronic and can develop into cirrhosis and liver cancer. An estimated 1.5 million people in Japan have hepatitis C, and medical experts suspect that many were infected through tainted blood products administered to patients giving birth or during operations. Yet again, profits were put ahead of patients and the Green Cross has come to symbolize an avoidable health calamity.

The Japan Red Cross, which is solely responsible for collecting and distributing blood, announced in 2003 that about 6,400 units of blood used in transfusions between 1995 and 2003 may have been tainted with syphilis, hepatitis, HIV, and other viruses. Many blood donors during this period had tested negative at the time of donation, but have more recently tested positive for various viruses. There is concern that these viruses may have been incubating at the time of donation in the 'window period' and were not detected. This potentially large-scale transmission of viruses through transfusions further eroded confidence in the nation's blood banks. Never again? Yet again, patients learned that they are vulnerable to inadequate safeguards.

The tragedy of Japan's hemophiliacs highlights the dangers of allowing the government to escape public scrutiny and permitting cozy relations between businessmen and the bureaucrats who monitor their activities. The widespread practice of *amakudari* creates a conflict of interest that undermines public confidence in those who govern and conveys the impression, true or not, that public welfare is systematically sacrificed on the altar of profits. The hemophiliacs' tragedy exposed the downside of collusive relations between business and government, generating public anger and strong support for reforms such as the 1999 information disclosure law. Citizens learned the hard way about the need for government transparency and the risks of 'business as usual.' A people who were accustomed to revere their mandarins learned that their trust was not fully justified or reciprocated. Disgust with the bureaucracy is reflected in a new term, *yakugai*, meaning harm (*gai*) caused by *yakusho* (government offices) or *yakunin* (government officials). Japanese hemophiliacs are only too well acquainted with the consequences of *yakugai*.

The HIV hemophiliac tragedy was exacerbated by a political practice all too common in Japan, whereby those with a financial interest in the outcomes of the government policymaking process have significant input in crafting those policies. The hemophiliac scandal, one of a series uncovered in the 1990s, contributed to a change in the political climate in Japan, eroding the edifice of power and generating support for accountable government and popular sovereignty. The struggle of the hemophiliacs, battling popular prejudice against both their genetic inheritance and an added infection born of negligence and greed, demonstrated that people can make a difference, that laws can be used with effect and that the quality of democracy depends on citizens exercising such rights. And the intervention of Kan Naoto in exposing the misdeeds of government officials showed that some individuals can make a real difference; his success is an object lesson in the power of principled leadership. This case also highlights the importance of timing – both Kan and the litigants were able to exploit public indignation aroused by the collapse of the bubble economy and the discrediting of government officials and businessmen caught up in related scandals. Citizens' tolerance of public corruption had evaporated. Above all others, the hemophiliacs' case broke the façade of the government's *kanson mimpi* (bureaucratic arrogance) – the powerful were brought low, if not to justice, by the weak and marginalized. The outpouring of sympathy and support orchestrated by an episodically sensitive media helped break down discriminatory attitudes and left behind a legacy of increased tolerance in a society notorious for its intolerance. The

HIV hemophiliac saga has changed Japan in a variety of ways, belying common perceptions of a stagnant society impervious to change.

Minamata redux?

The images of Minamata victims bearing the telltale deformities and vacant stares of those irrevocably poisoned by mercury have been seared into our consciousness by the photos of Eugene Smith. These photos of the limp naked bodies of children bathed by their forlorn mothers shocked the public and galvanized support for compensation and tighter environmental standards.

It is tempting to look back at the shocking tale of mercury poisoning that affected poor fishing households from the village of Minamata in the 1950s and 1960s and draw invidious comparisons suggesting that little, after all, has changed. As with the hemophiliacs, the confluence of government and business agendas conspired against public welfare. There too, 'the national interest' and corporate profits were valued above people's health and human rights. There too, there was a sustained cover-up and amends were made too late for many of the victims. There too, citizens eventually 'won' something resembling justice, using the legal system and sympathetic media coverage to triumph in the court of public opinion and pressure the government to arrange a settlement. There too, the words 'never again' raised hopes that people's suffering was not in vain, that the disabilities and premature deaths would be offset by the knowledge that others had been spared a similar fate, that society was listening and connecting the dots.

The story of Minamata is a heartrending one. Beginning in the 1930s, industrial effluent laced with exceptionally high levels of mercury was dumped by the Chisso Corporation, heedlessly and relentlessly, into the bay adjacent to the village of Minamata on the south-west coast of Kyushu. One grasps a sense of just how high the concentrations were, and just how low a company could stoop, in learning that Chisso established a subsidiary to mine the seabed and extract the mercury for sale, while simultaneously denying that mercury poisoning had occurred and that the company was responsible for it and should clean it up. Although many of the victims have been awarded settlements and Chisso is now defunct, the scars remain. Eugene Smith, the photojournalist beaten by company goons, died of injuries sustained while working to publicize the plight of the victims. His stark photos linger in the memory, reminding one of the enormity of what was visited on the marginal fishing communities stricken with the same neurological trauma that made the local harbor cats dance in a frenzy before dying, the first sign that something was terribly amiss.

The victims' struggle to hold the government and Chisso accountable for their negligence is the subject of a study by George (2001). In his view, the story of Minamata is the story of citizens making democracy work through their sustained and persistent efforts to exercise their rights. Creating civil society is a struggle to be won, not something that governments bestow. In fighting against the odds, in peeling back the layers of denial, suppression, censorship, and brute power that drove the cover-up for so long, the people were able to give meaning to the rights they were eventually able to claim as their own. By refusing to give up the struggle for justice, they forced the government and Chisso to admit wrongdoing and make amends, however inadequate, for the suffering they inflicted on people who did not really count.

On the face of it, Chisso's actions were little short of a crime against humanity. Why did the company actually increase its dumping of industrial waste even after its own internal investigations had alerted it to the consequences of dumping untreated effluent into the bay? For Chisso, larger issues were at stake: increasing production was necessary to qualify for larger government subsidies, and thus there was a twisted logic to its degradation of the environment. The government for its part was loath to take the side of the people because it was preoccupied with industrial development regardless of the costs. Lamentable as destruction to the environment and health of local villagers may have been, their suffering could not be allowed to derail the larger national interest of pell-mell industrial expansion. The dictates of economic planning at the time pushed aside considerations of sustainable development, while the people were expected to sacrifice their individual welfare for the greater good and wealth of the nation. The local government also stood on the side of Chisso because it was the largest taxpayer and employer in town, while the townspeople were divided between those who sought justice – a lower-class minority – and those who dismissed their agitation as selfish, greedy, and destructive to municipal interests, generating negative publicity and making it hard to find spouses.

Did Minamata make a lasting difference? There is evidence on both sides of this question. Certainly the hopes of 'never again' have been betrayed by subsequent events and the vibrancy of Japanese democracy seems to lie more in its potential than reality. Time and time again, collusive relations between business and government have generated scandals and aroused public ire, but such patterns persist. Perpetrators often seem to escape judgment and are infrequently punished and all too lightly. The impunity of polluters and the difficulties of securing judicial remedies are still notable features of contemporary Japan.

So is there a Minamata legacy? The name is a powerful symbol of what went wrong with Japan's economic miracle and continues to serve as a reminder of the costs of environmental degradation, corporate immunity and opaque governance. The Minamata settlements negotiated over the years changed the rules of the game. Progressively they became more inclusive and generous, and established the principle that even the most powerful and well connected can be held to the rule of law. Corporate impunity is no longer the norm and no longer do the courts consistently act as rubber-stamps for Japan, Inc. A precedent has been set and the brief for victims steadily improved: the prolonged and progressively more generous settlements enacted form part of the context for litigation and settlement in the HIV hemophiliacs' case. Minamata has served both as an inspiration and a model, blazing a legal trail for others to follow. In this sense, the hemophiliacs' case is part of a larger continuum, part of the struggle to infuse the legal process and constitutional guarantees with real meaning and to assert the rights of those who 'do not count.'

Both the Minamata and the HIV hemophiliacs' cases have set important precedents in Japan. Their wider significance is evident in the successful litigation of Hansen's disease sufferers to reclaim their constitutional rights, as discussed in the following chapter. Over the past few decades what was unusual – standing up for one's rights against the powers that be – has become acceptable and normal. The recourse of the most vulnerable members of the community to legal redress, and their success in obtaining it, is an object lesson in the nature of sociocultural transformation in Japan – always slow, incremental and haphazard. Although the system has at times been dysfunctional, dilatory, and inconsistent, if one judges a society by the way it treats its marginalized peoples, there are some encouraging signs. If in the 1960s the struggle of Minamata victims seemed quixotic, the hemophiliac and leprosy cases reveal how far public standards have evolved; it became a matter of decency to treat the victims with respect and dignity, and those that failed that test met with public condemnation. The hemophiliac and leprosy cases have rattled the edifice of bureaucratic power and privilege. While bureaucratic arrogance will undoubtedly linger in the halls of power, the assumption of immunity from individual responsibility is no longer sacrosanct. Such blatant examples of government negligence and corporate connivance have slowly fueled public support for transparency and taught painful lessons about the dangers of impunity. This awakening to the inherent possibilities of democracy is the legacy of Japan's modern tragedies.

Another of the legacies of Minamata has been the incorporation of environmental issues into the political mainstream. Environmental pollution, at one time seen as a necessary cost of economic development, used to be an issue monopolized by actors on the political fringe. The introduction of environmental politics onto the national political stage and the adoption of 'green' issues by the mainstream, pro-business LDP was a major political shift that has been elucidated by Broadbent (1998). By the 1970s, it had become smart politics to demonstrate a commitment to protecting voters by protecting the environment. The Diet enacted environmentally progressive legislation because the costs of not doing so – politically, economically, and environmentally – had simply become too high. The Japanese public has learned that when it mobilizes to raise the costs of inaction or negligence, the government tends to respond, however reluctantly.

The HIV hemophiliac case is one of the legacies of Minamata. Ordinary people stood up to the powerful vested interests in government and industry, challenged an elite medical establishment and fought to hold them accountable for their actions. The media and public supported the victims in their struggle, despite being burdened with the twin taboos of hemophilia and AIDS. By the 1990s, the foundations of Japan, Inc., based on collusive relations between bureaucrats and businessmen, were widely seen to be detrimental to the public interest. An older inclination to sweep scandals under the national *tatami* mat is giving way to a willingness to expose public abuses and sustain pressures for reform. Airing the government's dirty laundry is now regarded as politically astute – one response to public disaffection with 'business as usual.' The mantra of reform and deregulation that echoes through the archipelago, or at least in the media, is a reflection of a desire for change and recognition that the status quo is no longer tenable. Neglecting and mistreating the weak and vulnerable has belatedly become risky business.

7 Dignity denied

The 1990s was a time when we began to regain our dignity as human beings and rights as citizens.
                                      Suzuki Koji, 78, leprosy patient, May 7, 2002

At the beginning of the Showa Era we were treated like scum. Now, we are human beings again.
                            Tsutsumi Ryozo, responding to the Kumamoto court ruling
                                in favor of Hansen's disease sufferers, May 11, 2001

Put a lid on something that smells.
                                                          Japanese proverb

The way in which a society treats its most vulnerable members offers valuable insights into its norms and values as well as the nature of the relationship between ordinary citizens and those who govern. This chapter continues the story begun in our discussion of the Minamata pollution case and the HIV-infected hemophiliacs in the previous chapter. The common thread is the story of citizens acting in concert to hold those responsible for these public health disasters accountable for their actions – persevering in the face of adversity, hostility, and obstacles both legal and institutional in their pursuit of something resembling justice. Each of these cases is about citizens trying to make democracy work, struggling to make their voices heard and have their suffering addressed. The victims of these various tragedies held a mirror up to society that revealed some ugly truths and, at the same time, appealed to the collective conscience and sense of compassion. In each of these cases, victims who had been deprived of their dignity sought to regain it by challenging authority and asserting their human rights, whether through the courts, on the streets or in the media. Such struggles have helped to shape and revitalize Japan's fledgling civil society.

The history of those suffering from leprosy, now commonly referred to as Hansen's disease, is a grim tale – until recent decades, they were treated as pariahs by every society. In Japan, government policy towards lepers was inspired by the European example, resulting in compulsory isolation, institutionalized discrimination, and legal apartheid since 1907. A Leprosy

Prevention Law passed as late as 1953 reaffirmed the government's policy of forced isolation. It was only in 1996 that leprosy quarantine laws were finally repealed, some forty years after effective drug treatment was discovered. Thus although Japan was not the first country to isolate lepers, it maintained legal constraints through most of the twentieth century and for far longer than other nations. Unbelievably, leprosy sufferers had to wait until the dawn of the twenty-first century for a change in their fortunes. In 2001 a district court in Kumamoto, Kyushu, ruled in favor of a large group of Hansen's disease victims who had brought a lawsuit against the government. The court ruled that the 1953 quarantine laws had infringed on their constitutional rights and had created an atmosphere that encouraged discrimination against them in society. The judge went on to order the government to pay compensation to the victims. To the surprise of the whole nation, newly elected Prime Minister Koizumi Junichiro rejected the advice of officials and opted not to appeal the decision. Instead, he admitted that the government had been wrong in its treatment of victims, apologized, and acted to halt the suffering of these unfortunate people, most of whom were in their seventies. As a result, Koizumi's credibility as a reformer was solidified and his popularity soared. This decision was both astounding and encouraging because, unlike the stratagem used against the hemophiliacs, the government did not try to evade legal responsibility for its mistreatment of this vulnerable and shunned community.

The struggle of Hansen's victims in Japan is a story about coping with a debilitating and disfiguring disease while living with the legal apartheid and social stigma attached to this notorious illness. It is about the state belatedly trying to make amends and a society reluctantly facing up to the enormity of what it had wrought in ostracizing the weak.

Leprosy

This chronic disease, sometimes referred to as 'humanity's burden of misery,' has visited discrimination on its victims from time immemorial. Leprosy mainly affects the skin, peripheral nerves, and mucous membranes, mostly as a consequence of immune reactions triggered by a bacterial infection known as Mycobacterium leprae. Most people do not develop symptoms from exposure to the airborne bacillus and it is not easily communicable. Mild cases are marked by numbness and disfiguring skin lesions, while in more severe cases progressive loss of extremities such as the nose, ears, fingers, and toes occurs. Ancient Indian and Chinese medical texts describe this disease as early as the fifth century BC. Leprosy is referred to in both the Bible and Koran, where it is associated with ritual impurity and the need for segregation. Less well known, or at least less widely practiced, is the religious exhortation to compassion for the victims.

Exclusion from society or any normal life has been the fate of lepers throughout the ages. They have been shunned out of fear of contagion and the unsightly disfigurement that progressively ravages the extremities and faces of those who fall ill. In Europe during the Middle Ages regulations were imposed to isolate lepers because the disease was thought to be highly contagious. It seems that, with the exception of endemic areas like Norway and certain places around the Mediterranean, the disease began to recede in Europe in the eighteenth century – but not before it had been transmitted to the New World and other far-flung territories affected by colonial expansion.

Effective treatment for the disease was slow in coming. Following the lead given by Louis Pasteur's research on bacteria in the mid-nineteenth century, in 1873 a Norwegian physician, Armauer Hansen, succeeded in isolating the bacillus Mycobacterium leprae as the micro-organism responsible for the disease that now bears his name. While his discovery provided a scientific basis for institutionalizing discrimination and isolation, difficulty in cultivating the bacillus in the lab or in animals rendered the search for a cure elusive. The era of treatment dawned in 1941 when an American doctor, Guy Faget, resorted to treating patients with a sulphone drug. Subsequent advances in drug treatment have produced more effective and rapid cures, and the world medical community is confident of eliminating this disease as a public health problem in the early decades of the twenty-first century, much as smallpox was eliminated in the twentieth century.

Hansen's disease in Japan

As elsewhere, the history of leprosy in Japan is a grim tale. Following common practice in Europe, Japan established a quarantine policy in 1907 on the advice of Mitsuda Kensuke, a leading medical expert who warned of the dangers posed by allowing diseased people to roam freely, exposing others to what he considered to be a highly contagious disease. More than 10,000 patients were committed for treatment under the aegis of this law in Japan before World War I; they were forcibly removed from their homes by police (alerted by local doctors) and sent into permanent exile. Internees who tried to escape were often placed in solitary confinement and could legally be denied food as punishment. As a consequence of the Leprosy Prevention Law passed in 1931, all patients were eventually rehoused in fifteen leprosaria scattered about the country in remote areas – suggesting that the government wanted patients out of the public view. Indeed, one of the reasons for justifying quarantine and institutionalization was the embarrassment of having such unsightly beggars clustered around temples and shrines visited by foreigners. As in many other areas, Japan's acute sensitivity to Western opinions, real and imagined, and the urgent desire to appear 'modern,' led to a reform modeled on Western practice.

Figure 7.1 Suzuki Koji, leprosy activist, discussing his life and his struggle to be treated with dignity. (Photo: Jeff Kingston)

Family life

From the 1930s, people diagnosed with Hansen's disease were taken from their families and incarcerated at one of the nation's fifteen leprosaria. Usually, patients were kept in the dark about the precise nature of their affliction and were not told that a diagnosis of leprosy was the equivalent of a life sentence. Patients often expressed confidence that they would return to a normal life after being cured of their mysterious numbing ailment, never imagining that they would be permanently separated from their families. The illness was reported by doctors to local authorities in order to process their rapid transfer to distant facilities.

Suzuki Koji (b. 1923), a farmer's son from Akita, was diagnosed with the affliction at age 16 and bundled off to faraway Gunma a few days later, never to return. He was told nothing about his illness nor what lay in store for him. According to Suzuki, families who were spared disclosure of the diagnosis to the local community were fortunate, since in such cases they could be chased out of their village or their homes might be burned down. The best that could be hoped for was temporary evacuation so that the premises could be sprayed with disinfectant. Even so, families of leprosy patients would have to cope with being shunned by neighbors in isolated rural areas where participation in the community was essential and desired. The threat of *murahachibu* (ostracism) of families with a diseased member was real and, even six decades after their enforced exile, many elderly patients remain reluctant to return home due to concerns about embarrassing the family, stirring up prejudice against relatives, and causing trouble with neighbors. Suzuki, who has remained in a national leprosarium called Kuryu Rakusen-en in Kusatsu, Gunma since 1940, explains the reason for his own decision: 'I couldn't go back … it would be too embarrassing for everyone. For me it would be like Urashima Taro [a famous character in Japanese mythology who reappears after a long disappearance to find everything unfamiliar]. I can never go back … they took my home away from me forever.'

The national leprosaria practiced a grotesque eugenics regime. While marriage was permitted, men were required to have vasectomies (some were castrated) and women were forced to have abortions if they became pregnant. Prior to World War II they were routinely sterilized. More than 4,000 castrations and abortions were carried out on the tens of thousands of patients who were forced into sanitariums nationwide between 1907 and 1996. Only very recently has the government owned up to this shameful history: on May 28, 2001, Shinozaki Hideo, head of the Ministry of Health, Labor, and Welfare's Health Bureau, testified in the Diet that the policy of forced abortions – euphemistically termed 'eugenic operations' – persisted until the 1960s. Shinozaki referred to the duress patients were put under: 'Patients were given the option of consenting to eugenic operations at the very latest by the mid-1960s. Before then, we understand that eugenic operations were basically forced on them in a number of ways.' Patients who developed the disease after giving birth were institutionalized with their children, but lived separately. The children were raised in dismal circumstances and received a low level of care.

Living conditions in the state institutions were cramped. Couples lived communally, with three couples sharing one twelve-mat *tatami* room (one mat measures 173 cm by 88 cm) with limited scope for privacy. Now that institutionalized patients are dying off from old age, and newly diagnosed patients receive outpatient treatment, there is more room in the remaining leprosaria for the survivors and each patient now has a private six-mat room. As a result, the staff now outnumber the patients and the facilities have come to resemble elderly rest homes.

The absence of children means that virtually all of the patients have opted to remain institutionalized even after it became possible for them to move out. They literally have nowhere to go. Having grown used to living at the facilities, unaccustomed to the 'outside' world, with no children to support them and fearful of discrimination, they have come to regard the leprosaria as 'home.' The bitter fruit of their forced removal from their homes and compulsory childless marriages is their inability to reintegrate into society and leave the places that served as their prisons for so long.

Forced labor

Patients who were able to work were forced to do so, apparently in some cases without pay, and could legally be committed to solitary confinement and denied food to compel them to work. Because Hansen's is a progressive disease and many develop tuberculosis, a related disease, younger men were pressed into hard labor while still able to perform it, sometimes with fatal consequences. Suzuki Koji, who suffers from a chronic back ailment he attributes to this hard regime, recalls the heavy labor imposed on him as a daily task: he would walk 11.5 km to pick up three bundles of coal weighing a total of 40 kg and then return uphill with the heavy load strapped to his back. In 1940 when he was committed he was only 16 and, since he was raised on a farm, was used to hard labor. But even for him at an early stage of Hansen's, the regime was exhausting and he could not imagine how others were able to endure it. During the war he was shifted to forced, unpaid labor in a nearby iron-ore mine, working alongside Chinese and Korean workers who arrived and left the mine in manacles. Although this was difficult and dangerous work, oddly enough Suzuki felt proud that he was helping in the war effort and saw his work as patriotic service.

Suzuki recalls that those who refused to work were locked away and deprived of food. In his view this treatment was designed to dispose of recalcitrant patients: 'patients may not be the right word since the overall purpose of the leprosarium was to hasten our deaths and keep us out of public view until the embarrassment [constituted by the patients] disappeared.' Towards the end of the war, conditions worsened at the facility and patients were given the difficult task of extracting fuel oil from pine-tree roots.

During parliamentary hearings on the treatment of leprosy patients held in 2001, Eda Yasuyuki, a Komeito party Diet member, commented: 'They were only called sanitariums, but I have heard that they were really concentration camps. Inmates were forced to perform heavy labor such as cremations and sewage disposal. I wonder if the government really wonders how much it violated these people's human rights.'[1]

Personal glimpses

In his book *The Inland Sea* (1971), Donald Richie recounts a visit to the islet of Oshima off the coast of Shikoku in the early 1960s, where he had an unanticipated encounter with a leper colony of 702 residents.[2] Struck with the unspoiled beauty of the place, Richie (1971: 78) noted sadly that 'Lepers are often sent to beautiful places, as if in compensation for the ugliness of their disease. Or, perhaps, it is just that, being sent to places far away, they naturally live where the hand of man has not as yet completely destroyed natural beauty.'

Landing at the pier, Richie was immediately drawn to the sound of bells attached to poles carried by old men and women, bells that would help locate them if they strayed. They were all blind and disfigured: 'the men have ears that were blackened at the edges, crinkled like leaves, as though charred. Several of the old people had no noses, just two holes in their faces. Their hands were like bird's feet, the fingers drawn clawlike to the palm.' Observing a young man who suffered from a virulent form of the disease, Richie imagined the coming years when 'The hairline will recede; the eyebrows will disappear; the nose will collapse, flatten, leaving the nostrils staring; the lips will retract and at the same time the face will widen, furrows growing until the skin is a folded mass around the mouth of a snarling animal – the dread lion face. The change will be very gradual.'

At the time of his trip, Richie noted that patients were being successfully treated by the local doctor, and sent home if possible. Although it was common knowledge in the medical community that the disease was not particularly contagious – certainly less so than tuberculosis – leprosy patients were still forced to live apart from family and society. Richie met a girl of nineteen from Kyoto who had been cured and was therefore eligible to leave the island. However, leprosy had made her a permanent outcast: 'Her family has disowned her. She has no place else to go. They did this because disease is a disgrace. If it became known that she was a leper, her sisters could not make proper marriages, her brothers could not find proper employment. Her name has been removed from the family register. To the outside world it is as if she never was. And the law is strict. If you have no place to go, no one to take you, then, even though you are cured, you cannot leave. So, for the rest of her life, this healthy and beautiful girl will remain on the island, looking as now, toward the distant land.'

Despite their shattered lives, Richie found that the leprosy victims on Oshima accepted their lot: 'They are not despairing but neither are they cheerful. They are dignified.' Some 30 years on, he told me that the translation of his book into Japanese had omitted the section on leprosy as well as his references to *burakumin* (a minority group also suffering discrimination) – reflecting the publishing world's knowledge of the prejudices of their audience and their preference for keeping taboo subjects at arm's length.

Regaining dignity

At the end of World War II, Suzuki's leprosarium in Kusatsu was visited by a delegation from the JCP (Japan Communist Party) that investigated the forced labor regime at the institution and publicized its findings in the Diet and media. As a result, forced labor was ended at Kuryu Rakusen-en and the other leprosaria. Patients began to achieve political rights at this time, too: as a result of the intervention by the JCP, and with the helping hand of GHQ, Hansen's patients won the right to vote in elections. Suzuki recalls that this was the first time he came to realize his rights and power as a citizen. It was also the first time that outsiders had treated him with respect and expressed concern about his situation. Reeling from the shock of Japan's defeat in the war, and wondering if his efforts in the iron-ore mine had all been in vain, Suzuki recalls finding hope in finally becoming a citizen.

But the struggle for patients' civil rights had only begun. The introduction in the 1940s of effective medicines for the treatment of Hansen's led most governments able to afford the costly treatment to abandon their policy of segregation by the early 1950s. However, in Japan, the same Dr. Mitsuda who had originally established the quarantine policy in 1907 strongly advised against abandoning this regime and the government acted on his advice in crafting the new Leprosy Prevention Law of 1953. Thus the policy of forced isolation persisted. Mitsuda, one of the nation's more highly decorated physicians (he was awarded the Order of Culture in 1945 and the Grand Cordon of the Order in 1957 for his work on Hansen's disease), also advocated forced sterilization for sufferers.

Armed with a new sense of power and encouraged by the promises of democratization, Hansen's patients founded a national association and campaigned for their rights, including street demonstrations and sit-ins at the Ministry of Health and Welfare. This struggle for their civil rights led to a gradual improvement in conditions at the sanitariums and, from the mid-1950s, patients cured of the disease were permitted to rejoin society. However, in the absence of sustained government assistance in securing employment and housing, the lingering stigma meant that leaving institutional care was not a viable option for most. Public ignorance about the disease persisted, fueling prejudice against patients who were thus doubly victimized.

From the patients' perspective, the government had failed to raise public consciousness about their disease and instead encouraged ignorance and prejudice. When the national patients' association petitioned the MHW to abandon mandatory segregation during the 1960s, they were told that responsible medical science still required isolation. It was telling that a senior official of the MHW, on concluding negotiations with the patients' group, chided them for leaving their facilities to lobby for their cause, claiming that it was a regrettable action from a public health perspective.

However, one government official was to prove a staunch champion of leprosy sufferers and their rights in society. Otani Fujio, a former president of the International University of Health and Welfare, worked for nearly 25 years at the MHW (1959–83). During these years as a civil servant, he worked to improve living conditions and human rights at the leprosaria. However, Otani now regrets these efforts, believing that such palliative measures as were taken only served to prolong the fundamental injustice of the state's quarantine policy and made the denial of patients' civil rights more palatable. After retiring, he worked to establish the Museum of Hansen's Disease in the suburbs of Tokyo so that this sordid chapter in Japan's history will not be forgotten. Otani believes that the long struggle endured by victims for dignity and civil rights contains important insights for the Japanese. In a newspaper interview given in 2000, he said:

The decades-long suffering of the leprosy patients is a result of administrative indifference and irresponsibility by which the government failed to make necessary and rightful changes. It is Japanese people who blindly follow existing values or systems no matter how wrong they are. To learn the history of the disease is to learn the mentality of the Japanese – and is also the only way that society can compensate for the patients' suffering.[3]

Otani recalls telling colleagues in the early 1960s that Hansen's was not highly contagious and there was no need for isolation, but his advice fell on deaf ears. The men of the MHW clung to their misinformed belief that it was incurable, highly contagious, and thus required isolation. Not only did they want to avoid contact with lepers, they could not even be bothered to find out the facts about the disease.

Suing for justice

In the late 1990s, the frustration of Hansen's patients over a continuing lack of civil rights resulted in their initiating several lawsuits against the state. In suing the government, sufferers focused on the fact of enforced segregation even after the government knew it was no longer medically necessary. In 1960 the World Health Organization had decreed that there was no need to segregate leprosy patients from society. In its defense, the government maintained that it was not until 1981 that reliable drug treatment became available and thus, until that time, the quarantine policy was reasonable. However, the 1953 Leprosy Prevention Law was not repealed until 1996, meaning that according to the government's own criteria patients' human and constitutional rights had been violated for at least fifteen years. Moreover, the patients challenged the government's defense that reliable drug treatment did not become available until 1981, arguing that the 1953 law was both unconstitutional and ill-conceived in the light of contemporary medical knowledge. They maintained that between 1953 and 1996 their rights had been systematically violated at the government's behest – a 43-year nightmare that had ruined their lives.

In April 1996 the Minister of Health and Welfare, Kan Naoto, pushed through repeal of the 1953 Law on the Prevention of Leprosy. His action effectively ended this chapter in the saga of legalized discrimination and isolation inflicted on Hansen's patients. This law was subsequently judged to have infringed on the constitutional rights theoretically guaranteed for all citizens, but systematically denied for Japan's lepers.

In July 1998, following repeal of the Law, Hansen's patients from two leprosaria in Kyushu filed a suit for compensation, followed by a similar suit filed in Tokyo in March 1999. The court concluded the Kyushu hearings in January 2001, and in April of that year a nonpartisan group of lawmakers in the Diet was established to promote a final resolution of the various issues involving the Hansen's disease patients. The Hansen's lawsuits were about defending the human rights of the vulnerable and setting a precedent that would deter similar actions by the state in the future. According to a report in the *Japan Times*, lawyers representing the plaintiffs in the Hansen's case asserted that 'public indifference to the plight of minorities allowed the enactment of the AIDS Prevention Law in 1988, which was designed to prevent the spread of the syndrome at the expense of the human rights of people with HIV or AIDS. They [the plaintiffs] say that failure to restore the dignity of people who had Hansen's disease would make it highly likely Japan will make similar errors in the future.'[4]

In October 1999 Otani Fujio testified at the Kumamoto District Court on the hardships endured by the Kyushu patients. 'We must learn from their experiences. We must learn that we must fully respect the rights of minorities and the socially weak. Otherwise, we will make another mistake again, as seen in the recent HIV debacle involving hemophiliacs who received tainted blood coagulants.'

After the hearing of the first case in Kumamoto, Kyushu, nearly 400 former patients joined various suits scattered around the nation's district courts. However, at first only a small minority of patients joined the lawsuits, about 10 percent of the total institutionalized under the mandatory isolation policy, reflecting differences of opinion on how best to proceed. Opponents of the action argue that it would only generate a backlash against them and heighten prejudice. Fujita Sanshiro, head of the patients' association at Kuryu Rakusen-so, expressed concern that the court case might stir up latent prejudice and cause more trouble. In addition, he was fearful that a vindictive government might retaliate in some way against the patients, undoing the improvements in their welfare won over the past few decades.[5]

The plaintiffs disagreed with Fujita's assessment and argued that principles and dignity were at stake. As Kodama Yuji, a leader of the Kuryu plaintiffs' groups, asserted: 'The very fact that they cannot put the highest priority on their human rights is the most tragic result of the 90-year history of prejudice and discrimination.' And Fuyu Toshiyuki, a 65-year-old patient from the leprosarium in Tama, added: 'Hundreds of former patients are now dying of old age. Unless we take action now, our suffering will merely be a page in the history books.' For Suzuki Koji, the lawsuit was a means 'to win full recognition of all the wrongdoings and injustices imposed upon me for almost my entire life.' Aside from monetary compensation, the plaintiffs demanded an official apology and acknowledgement of wrongdoing.

Belated justice

On May 11, 2001 the Kumamoto District Court ruled in favor of the plaintiffs, agreed that the 1953 Leprosy Prevention Law denied them their constitutional rights and fanned prejudice against them, and ordered the government to apologize and pay compensation. The plaintiffs were jubilant, the media relished the David vs. Goliath scenario presented by the judgment, and the government sought ways to limit the damage.

In a commentary published in perhaps the most conservative of Japan's mass-market daily newspapers, the *Sankei Shimbun*, Otani Fujio welcomed the court's landmark decision and the government's decision not to appeal the ruling.[6] In his view, the government had subjected sufferers to wholly unwarranted discrimination and ruined their lives through policies of isolation, forced labor, and sterilization. What the court ruling did not clarify, however, was the individual responsibility of those involved in this institutionalized system of discrimination – the bureaucrats, lawmakers, doctors, and various association members who had established, sustained, and implemented this cruel system over the decades. Otani underlined the importance of devising

> ... ways of preventing future lawmakers and government officials from making the same mistakes. Otherwise, similar human-rights violations are likely to occur. The problem had its roots in the views held at the time by medical experts, which fanned fears that the disease was contagious. It must be determined how these individuals failed to fulfill their social responsibilities, and the lessons thus learned must be reflected in the education of medical and welfare experts from now on.

In his view, the constitutional rights of Hansen's patients were trampled on for so long because the courts and the media failed to fulfill their responsibilities. Moreover, the prolonged discrimination against them reflects 'the widespread tolerance of discrimination,' suggesting that this case is a symptom of deeper social problems in Japan.

For Otani, the case showed that Japan was lagging behind other advanced nations in the human rights field. 'I feel that Japanese fail to give serious consideration to human-rights problems. Westerners would not have tolerated the kind of discrimination that was practiced against Hansen's disease patients in Japan. The problem would never have arisen if Japan were a civilized nation that honored basic human rights and democratic principles. At the root of the Hansen's disease problem are the ills of postwar Japanese society.' He concluded his piece by emphasizing that it is only by determining responsibility, holding individuals accountable for their actions, and raising public awareness about the plight of Japan's lepers that society will come to appreciate 'the importance of human dignity.'

In his summing up in the Kumamoto District Court, presiding judge Sugiyama Masashi argued that the government bore a grave responsibility for the consequences of its isolation policy and for failing to modify that policy after reliable drug therapy had become available. In his view, the government should have allowed patients cured through drug therapy to return to society by 1960 at the latest, and there was no justification for continued isolation. The judge held the Ministry of Health and Welfare responsible for implementing misguided policies, and lawmakers for failing to carry out necessary legal revisions in a timely manner. His ruling stated in part: 'It was obvious in 1960 that the law stipulating the isolation of patients was unconstitutional. It is appropriate to note that [the Diet] failed to reverse, or revise or scrap such a stipulation.'[7] The court ruled, however, that when the 1953 Leprosy Prevention Law was first promulgated, its provisions for mandatory isolation were reasonable given contemporary medical knowledge.

In its ruling, the court also rejected the government claim that the patients had waived their right to sue based on the twenty-year statute of limitations enshrined in the Civil Code. The government argued that since it was more than twenty years since the isolation policy was adopted, the statute of limitations should apply; however, the court recognized that the policy had not been abandoned until 1996 and the plaintiffs' right to sue was upheld. The court also awarded damages ranging from ¥8 million to ¥14 million to the former patients depending on length of institutionalization. (The average annual salary for a 30-year-old college graduate in 2000 was approximately ¥5 million, about $40,000.)

The former patients were jubilant at the comprehensive ruling in their favor. One of the plaintiffs, Tamashiro Shige, recalled her forced abortion: 'This is my revenge [against the state] on behalf of my child.' Another plaintiff, Shimura Yasushi, raised a clenched fist on hearing the ruling and told reporters, 'We are recognized as human beings at last. The seeds sown by our comrades who died while protesting have blossomed into big flowers. They can finally go back to their birthplace.' He added that the ball was now in the government's court and the fight would go on until the government addressed all leprosy-related problems.

The ruling immediately led to media speculation about a government appeal and the prospects for a negotiated settlement. Senior government sources were quoted to the effect that Minister of Health and Welfare Sakaguchi Chikara would recommend to Prime Minister Koizumi that he proceed with an appeal as a prelude to negotiating a settlement. However, this media speculation proved off the mark. Dr. Sakaguchi made it clear that he personally opposed an appeal and threatened to resign if the government made one. His party, Komeito, publicly stated the government should not appeal the ruling. Komeito was part of the ruling coalition and Dr. Sakaguchi was its only Cabinet representative. Indeed, before the prime minister had formally decided against an appeal, Sakaguchi made the first admission of government wrongdoing. One week after the court ruling, he stated at a Diet committee meeting: 'It is true that the [1996] abolishment of the [Leprosy Prevention Law of 1953] law [that forced the isolation] came too late.'[8] He added that the ruling was correct in its assertion that the ministry bore a grave responsibility for failing to alter its segregation policy at least by 1960, when drug therapy enabled patients to return to society. His remarks contradicted the public position taken by his own ministry – a rare instance of political courage, given that ministers usually defer to senior career officials from the ministries they oversee.

Thus Prime Minister Koizumi came under considerable pressure from Sakaguchi, a doctor by training, to refrain from appealing the court's decision even though the bureaucrats within his own ministry favored proceeding with an appeal.[9] One unnamed ministry source told the media, 'For the time being, we should appeal the decision, then probe a settlement using the same methods taken in the AIDS blood poisoning suit.'[10] The logic of the ministry's position lay in a reluctance to set a precedent that would open a floodgate of similar lawsuits. Narita Norihiko, a professor at Surugadai University, criticized these efforts to pursue an appeal: 'I can only think it seems like government bureaucrats don't like having their responsibility for their actions questioned. It is a bureaucratic way of saving face. It's like they're saying, "We'll pay the money, but we don't want to take responsibility."'

Meanwhile, dozens of former patients were ratcheting up the pressure by demonstrating in front of the prime minister's residence and demanding a meeting with him to express their opposition to an appeal. On the third day of their vigil the prime minister met with them and that evening announced he would not pursue an appeal. For Koizumi, recently elected as a reformer ready to tackle vested interests and sweep away the corrupt practices of the past, this was his first real test as a leader. When he announced on May 23, 2001 that the government would not proceed with an appeal, his popularity soared. Merely by refusing to add insult to injury in this sad case, he burnished his reform credentials and showed himself to be – at least on this occasion – a man of the people guided by a sense of justice and principle.

In acting as he did, Koizumi threw out the script and wrong-footed all the other actors accustomed to playing their familiar roles and waiting for the usual cues. Explaining his decision not to appeal, he said: 'We reached the decision because we believe that we have to finalize the issue as soon as possible.'[11] He added a clear apology: 'We now admit that the policy segregating Hansen's disease patients violated their rights. The government sincerely reflects upon its actions and apologizes for the patients' pain and plight.'[12] His apology was somewhat vitiated, however, when the government simultaneously issued a statement citing legal problems with the Kumamoto court ruling. Despite its decision not to appeal, and the prime minister's apology for the prolonged mistreatment of these unfortunate citizens, the government hedged by quibbling over the issue of legal responsibility for its actions and policies. While the bureaucrats and lawmakers were ready to admit – albeit grudgingly – that they were wrong, they were unwilling to shed the cloak of immunity. Anticipating such a response, the court and plaintiffs had pointed to the 1985 Supreme Court ruling holding that government officials could be held legally responsible for their actions in egregious cases of misconduct or failing to act to prevent wrongdoing.

The government rapidly moved into damage-control mode. In an attempt to avoid setting a precedent, the Cabinet issued a statement asserting that the decision not to appeal was a special case reflecting the advanced age of the former patients and the need for a speedy resolution. The Cabinet statement

(Roger Dahl)

also questioned the right of the judicial branch to monitor the actions of the Diet and hold it responsible for failing to act in a timely manner. It also argued, in a clear challenge to the judgment of the court, that the award of redress for damages sustained over a forty-year period ran counter to the Civil Code limit of twenty years. In issuing such a statement on an individual court ruling, the Cabinet indicated how seriously it viewed the implications of the leprosy case and the judgment holding the government responsible. The Cabinet also indicated that under normal circumstances it would have appealed the ruling. According to a report in the *Japan Times*, 'The government cannot approve of the ruling's interpretation of the State Redress Law, which it says excessively restricts Diet members' activities. The interpretation contravenes a previous Supreme Court decision that lawmakers cannot be held responsible unless they intentionally pass laws that conflict with the primary interpretation of the Constitution.'[13] Thus, the landmark court ruling and the surprise move for reconciliation by Prime Minister Koizumi were offset by bureaucratic and political reluctance to assume responsibility for their part in the scandal.

From the state's viewpoint, the model for the leprosy case was the HIV hemophiliac case and its many predecessors – wherein the government files an appeal against an unfavorable lower-court ruling and, while the appeal is pending, negotiates a compromise settlement. The government favors this scenario because it has a better track record in upper-court decisions, no doubt reflecting political influence on senior judicial appointments and career prospects. Time is also on the side of the government as victims die off and legal costs mount. Moreover, plaintiffs, knowing that the odds are stacked against them, usually regard a settlement as an acceptable compromise and preferable to an interminable stalemate: a monetary damage settlement is awarded, apologies are forthcoming and the victims are vindicated in the court of public opinion. The government is allowed to save face and, more importantly, evade a precedent-setting ruling of legal responsibility that might unleash a flood of similar suits.

Figure 7.2 Sakaguchi Chikara, Minister of Health, agreeing to compensation for lepers following a 2001 court ruling in their favour. (Photo: Mainichi Newspapers)

On June 7, the Diet passed a resolution apologizing to former leprosy patients and admitting that it had been wrong to prolong their suffering by needlessly keeping them quarantined. The lawmakers agreed that their dilatory response to the plight of the patients had made them liable to censure, but stopped short of accepting that they could be held legally responsible, referring in their resolution to the 1985 Supreme Court decision that limited this to extreme circumstances. Having evaded legal responsibility, they then passed legislation on June 12 to compensate current and former leprosy patients who suffered under the state's segregation policy. Under the terms of the bill, an estimated 5,500 people were made eligible to receive ¥8–14 million, depending on the length of institutionalization. However, many of those affected were not entitled to redress under the terms of the legislation, including surviving families of deceased former patients and Hansen's disease sufferers who were not quarantined. Although other lepers claimed that they still suffered discrimination as a result of the government's isolation policy, the compensation covered only those who were still alive and had been kept in state facilities.

As late as September 2001, MHW Minister Sakaguchi reiterated the government's decision not to extend the redress measures to cover those patients who had not been isolated in government facilities, nor the bereaved families of patients who had died, despite a recommendation from the Kumamoto court to do so. However, on Christmas Day 2001, the government relented and agreed to settle with those who had not been forced into quarantine, in effect acknowledging their claim that the government policy of isolation had set the tone for how all lepers were treated in society. The settlement was based on damages related to the cost of medical treatment denied to those who had not been institutionalized (ranging from ¥5–7 million each). In addition, the government settled separately with bereaved families (ranging from ¥5.5 million to ¥14 million, depending on length of institutionalization).

Finally, on January 28, 2002 the government agreed to settle a separate damages suit with former leprosy patients and their bereaved families, ending the epic court battles for justice and dignity. In this agreement, the government explicitly admitted that its forced isolation policy had helped foster public prejudice against Hansen's disease sufferers, even those who had not been forcibly segregated, and agreed to pay compensation to them. In addition to taking responsibility for promoting prejudice towards sufferers, the government also issued an apology and committed itself to paying damages.

Aftermath

Although this most recent settlement brought a degree of closure, former leprosy patients feel that only the first hurdle has been cleared and are calling on the government to do more than undo the wrongs of the past. They have asked the government – at both national and local levels – to institute welfare policies aimed at helping leprosy survivors to live a normal life and to educate people about the disease in order to eliminate prejudice and inform the public about the implications of their case.

In 2001, a study conducted among Japan's 4,300 surviving Hansen's disease patients indicated that fewer than 2 percent wanted to leave the sanitariums and return to their old homes, reflecting the consequences of their long-term isolation, fears of lingering prejudice, and anxieties about the impact on relatives of a possible return. As most of the patients are now in their seventies, they lack the experience to survive in society and have no children to depend on. Many are handicapped, having lost limbs as well as their sight, while others lack the skills and resources to survive in the outside world. In their view, the legal victory does not mean that the social stigma has been erased.

One activist in the campaign for reparations emphasizes the need to challenge the authority that stripped patients of their agency. When I asked Suzuki Koji what lessons could be learned from the struggle for dignity by leprosy patients, he replied: 'You must act on what you believe to be right. You must persist and remain true to your principles.' He recalled learning the need to question authority after virtually forcing his doctor to alter his drug treatment because of severe side effects. Throughout the 1950s he was put on a drug regime that cost him his sight, his hair, and his teeth, without any significant improvement in his symptoms. He constantly ran a temperature of 40° C and felt wretched. Then during a New Year's holiday, the nurse responsible for giving him his drugs left to visit relatives without making arrangements for continuing his drug treatment. His fever subsided and he immediately began to feel much better. After this, he refused to resume drug treatment and had a series of confrontations with the doctor in charge of his case. Forty years later, the feeling of bitterness has not subsided, nor the satisfaction in finally getting the doctor to back down and administer a much weaker dosage. By standing up to officialdom, Suzuki regained his eyesight, lost his fever, and his symptoms showed marked improvement.

Feeling that in his wretched state he had nothing to lose, Suzuki had successfully challenged authority and in so doing experienced a strength and dignity as a human being that had been denied him during his incarceration. He suddenly felt as if he was in charge of his life and realized that only through struggling against the injustice of his situation could he be redeemed. As a result of this experience he joined other patients in the 1960s in fighting for better treatment and basic human dignity, sticking with the cause right up through the landmark ruling in 2001. He participated in many demonstrations and even a sit-in at the MHW headquarters in an attempt to force government officials to confront the consequences of their inhumane policies. In Suzuki's view, this could not be described as a struggle for justice because there could never be justice for people who had lost their entire lives. For him the court ruling was vindication of the value of being true to one's principles; it was this that made all the sacrifices worthwhile.

Suzuki is keen to ascribe credit for the reforms to the right quarter, believing that the role of politicians and media coverage in securing redress for leprosy sufferers has been exaggerated. In his opinion, it was the people who joined with the patients and supported their cause who made it happen – ordinary citizens asserting their rights as members of a democracy whose voices became so loud that the media and politicians were forced to listen. For a man with every reason to have lost faith in humanity, Suzuki is uncommonly gracious both to his former opponents and to those who helped the lepers' cause for no other reason than compassion and a desire to fight discrimination and injustice.

Suzuki concluded the interview with a message – and a warning – to the future: 'Japanese people tend to be pliable and do what others want them to do – they don't question authority. This is the sad lesson of what happened to us and this is why young people need to know about our story. We are old

and soon will die, but to give meaning to our struggle we want coming generations to reflect on the nature of discrimination and the problem of conformity. People can make a difference by their choices if they want to. This is
what Japanese democracy needs.'

8 Mad cows and ocean cockroaches

After seeing the results of investigations conducted in Europe and other areas since the outbreak of mad cow disease in Japan, I cannot say confidently that there are no problems in how we are dealing with the situation.

Takebe Tsutomo, Agriculture, Forestry, and Fisheries Minister, responding at a press conference to criticisms that the government was negligent in preventing the outbreak of BSE, December 1, 2001

This is what whales in the waters surrounding the Japanese archipelago would say: Our numbers have increased a bit too much, we have to scramble for fish, as things stand now we're worried if we, whale species, will be preserved for the future, it may seem a radical measure but we were wondering if someone would balance up the situation by whaling.

Hara Taira comment in advertisement sponsored by the pro-whaling Institute of Cetacean Research, *Japan Times*, June 16, 2003

Outbreak

September 11, 2001 is the day after which the world would never be the same for Japan's cattle and beef industry. On September 10, the Ministry of Agriculture, Forestry, and Fisheries (hereafter referred to as the Farm Ministry) announced Japan's first case of BSE (bovine spongiform encephalopathy), popularly known as mad cow disease. This was the first outbreak outside Europe and the repercussions have been powerful. Consumers rapidly lost faith in beef products and consumption went into a tailspin, forcing fast-food outlets to switch to non-beef products and leaving the nation's *yakiniku* and *gyudon* beef restaurants empty and reeling in shock. Farmers and beef producers suddenly faced a steep drop in revenues. The nation has paid a high price for the total of nine Holstein dairy cows (six of which were born in the spring of 1996) that had been identified with BSE by November 2003.[1]

Despite timely warnings from the European Union, the World Health Organization, and Great Britain, the Farm Ministry had utterly failed to prevent the outbreak. Its inaction has raised serious questions about bureaucratic negligence, incompetence, and the government's inclination to protect producers at a high cost to consumers. The BSE scandal has served as a microcosm of what ails Japan, revealing collusive relations between LDP politicians, Farm Ministry bureaucrats and producers. It also reveals a disturbing lack of common sense among all involved. The fallout of the mad cow scandal continues to drift over Japan as the media have detailed how beef processors tried to scam a government subsidy program aimed at curbing their BSE-related losses. By repackaging cheap imported beef as expensive domestic beef eligible for the buyback program, the nation's leading meat-processing firms sought to turn the program into a profit-spinning venture. It has since emerged that false labeling of food is endemic in Japan. Thus, this is not only a story about the failures of bureaucrats, the meddling of politicians, and the low level of corporate ethics, but also of seriously alarmed consumers.

Anatomy of a debacle

The postmortem on the mad cow outbreak has revealed a shabby record of policy miscues, inadequate laws, negligence, and complacency on a grand scale. In April 2002 a government advisory panel composed of non-bureaucratic experts issued a withering indictment of the nation's food safety mechanisms and pilloried bureaucrats in the Farm Ministry for having failed to heed repeated warnings about the need to ban imports of products potentially tainted with derivatives from BSE-infected cows. The report details the complacency of Farm Ministry officials to the possibility of BSE infection, despite the sobering experience in Europe where the epidemic nearly wiped out a once-thriving industry. The *Japan Times* (April 5, 2002) expressed the sense of outrage aired in the media: 'The report is a woeful reminder that the government initially had little or no real sense of crisis about BSE, much less a plan of action to prevent it. Bureaucrats failed to learn from the mistakes committed by European nations in allowing the disease to spread as it did. In other words, the government showed itself to be incompetent as well as negligent in coping with the crisis.'

The blistering tone of the postmortem report is highly unusual for a government advisory panel and underscores just how blatant the errors were and how urgent is the need for action. The panel's interim report had already raised hackles in the Diet by singling out LDP politicians in the *nosuizoku* ('agricultural tribe,' lobbyists for agrobusiness interests) whose meddling in policymaking led to the failure to prevent BSE. These collusive relations between bureaucrats and politicians resulted in what the panel wryly described as an 'opaqueness in policymaking' that contributed to the blunders and miscues that have dogged government efforts to restore consumer trust in food safety and in the officials responsible for ensuring it.

The panel called for creation of a food safety agency and an overhaul of food safety regulations in order to better protect consumer interests and reduce the pro-producer bias in the regulatory framework. According to the panel, the BSE crisis was exacerbated by inadequate coordination and communication between the Farm Ministry and Health Ministry; it advocated a single watchdog agency free of interference or control by either ministry. The experts also noted that an extensive legal overhaul is long overdue: the existing legal framework for food safety dates from a time of early postwar food shortages and is thus geared to promoting production rather than safeguarding consumers and ensuring high levels of food safety. This producer-first mentality has also been promoted by the LDP's *nosuizoku*, reflecting their close ties with farmers, agricultural cooperatives and agrobusiness interests.

Responding to the panel's recommendations, a food safety law was enacted in May 2003 and the Cabinet Office established a Food Safety Council in July 2003 with authority to issue advisories to relevant ministries regarding a wide range of food products and food-related materials. The panel of seven food scientists and experts must be approved by the Diet. Critics complain that there is no provision for including consumer advocates on the panel. The Farm and Health Ministries retain joint responsibility for food safety risk management measures and industry oversight, perpetuating the division of authority that was identified by the panel as a major hurdle to improved safeguards. A new bureau for food consumption and safety has also been established in the Farm Ministry, part of a restructuring effort aimed at restoring public confidence.

Meat-and-bone meal

On September 18, 2001 the government finally decided to close the barn door after the cows had been infected, by prohibiting feeding cows with meal made from dead cattle. This meat-and-bone meal (MBM) is made by supplementing cattle feed with the ground-up carcasses of slaughtered cows to provide additional protein. However, it is suspected that BSE-inducing prions from slaughtered cows with the disease can be passed on to animals that eat the feed. This tainted meal was probably the main culprit in the spread of mad cow disease in Europe. Exposure to BSE can give rise in humans to a variant of Creutzfeldt-Jakob disease (vCJD), which has killed more than 100 people in Europe, mostly in Great Britain where the BSE outbreak first struck in 1985 and where there have been the most cases of infected cows. It is believed that this disease, which slowly destroys the human brain and for which there is no cure, is contracted by eating BSE-infected meat products.

The response of the Japanese government to the well-publicized dangers of MBM was one of complacency leavened with corruption. In February 1990 the British government sent a report to the Farm Ministry detailing its reasons for banning MBM cattle feed, but this warning was not heeded. The British government had already banned MBM in 1988 as a result of strong scientific evidence linking widespread use of MBM to the BSE epidemic. At that time the USA, Germany, and France had also banned the import of MBM. In September 1990, the Paris-based Office International des

Epizooties (OIE), a body specializing in the containment of epidemics and animal husbandry issues, issued a similar warning to the Farm Ministry that also went unheeded.

The alarm bells continued to ring in the halls of Japanese bureaucracy. Despite unambiguous warnings about the dangers of importing MBM from European producers, which were issued by the World Health Organization in March 1996 and the European Union in June 1996, and a concurring opinion from a panel of Japanese experts, the Farm Ministry failed to ban such imports. Instead, in that same year it issued a legally non-binding document under 'administrative guidance' that merely urged the industry to refrain from using the feed. In the view of the government panel, this failure to heed the repeated warnings of experts and learn from the European catastrophe doomed Japan to a preventable tragedy, leading them to term the ministry's action (or rather non-action) a 'grave blunder.'

As bureaucratic advisory panel reports go, this constitutes a bare-knuckled indictment that goes well beyond the normally carefully hedged language of deferential and hesitant reproach. The ministry's reluctance to impose an outright ban reflects the entrenched preference of bureaucrats to rely on flexible 'administrative guidance' rather than rigid legislation, thus preserving their assumed right to subjective discretion. This inclination to preserve bureaucratic power acts to undermine the rule of law and has been the source of charges of favoritism and malfeasance in this case as in many others. In this case, it appears that the 95 domestic manufacturers of MBM, who together produce some 400,000 metric tons per annum, called on the *nosuizoku* to exercise their influence to prevent a ban that would have driven them out of business.

One known source of imported infected feed was Italy. In the mid-1990s, new techniques were developed to remove the BSE-causing bacteria called prions from cattle carcasses and render MBM safe. However, one of the producers in Italy that was exporting its MBM to Japan lacked the requisite sterilizing equipment. Even though the European Union warned the Farm Ministry about this state of affairs, imports from the producer in question inexplicably continued. As a result, in February 2001 the EU warned that Japan was at risk because it had imported potentially tainted MBM from Italy. A 1998 EU inspection had found that removal of brains, where prions are often concentrated, had not been done thoroughly at Italian meat disposal centers that also lacked the necessary equipment to neutralize prions present elsewhere in the carcasses.

The Farm Ministry has also had to explain why one of its officials wrote an article in 1996 promoting use of MBM in the journal *Dairy Japan*. Since the dangers of MBM were already well known and it had been banned in the UK eight years before, this strong backing for MBM was embarrassing and inconvenient. To make matters worse, this was the same year that it was reported that humans had developed a variant of Creutzfeldt-Jakob disease from eating BSE-infected beef.

It was not until October 2001, after infected cows had been found in Japan, that the government bowed to scientific opinion and consumer sentiment and banned use of MBM altogether. In addition to the 400,000 metric tons produced domestically, Japan had been importing approximately 170,000 metric tons of MBM per annum from European producers. The Farm Ministry had dragged its heels on imposing a total ban, arguing that MBM is safe as long as it is not fed to cows and that domestically produced MBM was clean. Until the total ban was imposed, MBM was also commonly used in feed for chickens, pigs, and fish, and to produce pet food. It was feared that in the absence of a total ban some MBM would still find its way to the cows' feeding troughs.

Subsequent investigations by the government into the issue of MBM revealed discrepancies in how animal feed is fortified in Japan. Investigators uncovered the existence of unlicensed feed dealers in Hokkaido who fortified cow feed with steamed bone meal. Because the steaming process does not eliminate the prions that cause BSE, the use of this feed is potentially dangerous if the bones are from infected cows. Such instances indicate how lax the government's inspection practices have been, and how passive its monitoring role, despite the catastrophe in Europe.

After the imposition of a total ban, the government was left with the problem of disposing of massive stockpiles of MBM. The solution adopted has no doubt brought a wry smile to the lips of critics of Japan's notorious *doken kokka* (construction state). Burning the MBM was ruled out as there were inadequate incinerator facilities to handle the huge task, difficulties in igniting the material, and concerns about possible effects on neighboring communities and the incinerators themselves. The nation's cement companies have come to the rescue by copying techniques developed in Europe to use the MBM in cement production. This process has been in use in Germany, France, and Belgium, where cement benches enriched with MBM have become the latest accessory in city parks. According to the Japan Cement Association, the MBM is mixed with cement and heated to 1,450° C to sanitize the mix and render it safe. The nation's largest producer, Taiheiyo Cement, began production in March 2002 and the Environment Ministry has authorized production at sixteen plants nationwide. No glitches, or complaints about the benches, have yet been reported.

Crisis mismanagement

The story of the government's attempts to manage the crisis makes a sorry tale, one where the interests of consumers were systematically sidelined in favor of producers, and their supporters in government and the bureaucracy. In June 2001 the government blithely ignored an EU report about the likelihood of a BSE outbreak in Japan, not long after it had effectively banned beef imports from the EU by imposing rigorous testing requirements. The EU, whose member countries have suffered through a massive epidemic fed by myopia, complacency, and poor coordination among member states, was seeking to encourage international cooperation in eradicating BSE. It conducted a BSE risk-assessment report on countries that imported MBM from the EU, concluding that Japan's risk was relatively high. When the EU requested further information from the Farm Ministry to conduct a more detailed study, it was turned down and pressured to shelve the report. (Oddly enough, it was the Farm Ministry that first requested such a study back in 1998.) Finding that the report's conclusions did not mesh with existing policy and views, the ministry stopped further cooperation with the EU in June 2001. Following the outbreak, and facing a ban on exports of Japanese beef products, in December 2001 the ministry tasted humble pie, not for the last time, and requested the EU to continue with its risk assessment. Otherwise, the EU had warned, Japan would be placed in a high-risk category that would have effectively resulted in a ban on Japanese beef-product exports to EU countries. While the government was not so concerned about a ban on beef exports, it did fear domestic repercussions should Japanese consumers learn of the EU risk assessment and the government's uncooperative attitude.

The blunders in crisis management continued with the country's first case of BSE infection on September 10, 2001. The Farm Ministry announced that the infected cow had been put down and incinerated, only to retract this statement four days later when it discovered that the infected carcass had in fact been ground into meat and bone meal. So much for the safety of domestic MBM. The government was at fault in three areas: it failed to take sufficient steps to prevent the disease, actively contributed to the outbreak through its inaction, and then responded ineptly even when faced with a certain health threat. According to the advisory panel established to look into this question, the government lacked a sense of urgency and demonstrated an absence of preparation and skills needed for effective crisis management.

The inept handling of the crisis revealed an unseemly saga of cursory inspections, cozy relations between inspectors and producers, and a bureaucracy where the same officials charged with ensuring food safety are also involved with promoting the food industry. This blending of the roles of risk management and industry promotion creates an intrinsic conflict of interest that has often worked in favor of producers.[2] The system of *amakudari*, wherein bureaucrats retire into well-paid sinecures in organizations they previously monitored, generates strong incentives to 'play ball' with future employers and so pay less attention to consumer interests.

The government's actions to contain the outbreak also revealed its lack of preparedness for such a crisis. Despite government plans for a nationwide testing program for all slaughtered cows, only 6 of the nation's 47 prefectures announced that they were ready to implement the plan in 2002.[3] A shortage of animal husbandry experts and veterinarians is hampering efforts to impose rigorous testing and therefore making it difficult to restore consumer confidence. In addition, cash-strapped prefectural and local governments lack the resources to meet the costs of implementing higher standards. It is thus feared that infected animals may make their way undetected into the food chain and onto the tables of unsuspecting consumers. The discovery that one infected cow failed to display any of the external symptoms of the disease (such as stumbling) has underlined the insidious nature of BSE and the difficulties that will be faced in eradicating this threat.

Transmission

In November 2001, believing that MBM was the source of the infection that had produced the BSE outbreak, the government conducted a survey that indicated that in the nation's 47 prefectures some 5,129 cattle in 15 prefectures had been fed MBM. These cattle were purchased by local veterinary associations with government money, inspected for BSE, and then incinerated. None tested positive, confounding expert opinion about how cows become infected. To add to the confusion, interviews with farmers whose cattle actually *were* infected with BSE suggested that they had not been fed with MBM.

In the absence of definite incriminating evidence against MBM, the source of mad cow disease was tentatively traced to a skimmed powdered milk substitute fed to calves in their first seven weeks. This is a solid feed consisting of artificial powdered skim milk, beef and pig tallow, sugar, and other ingredients. It is believed that there were cases in Great Britain, where BSE was first detected in 1986, in which calves were infected from a milk substitute containing MBM. One of the ingredients in the Japanese milk substitute, beef tallow, was imported from the Netherlands and it was suspected that BSE-inducing prions were present in the tallow. The milk substitute that has been linked seven of the nine known outbreaks of mad cow disease in Japan was produced by the Scientific Feed Laboratory in Takasaki, Gunma. Rather than MBM, the initial suspect in transmission and probably the main cause of the epidemic in Europe, powdered milk fortified with infected Dutch tallow was initially identified as the source of Japan's BSE infections.

Questions persist, however, about the role of MBM in BSE infections and the future of Japan's MBM producers. The isolation of powdered milk as the source of BSE infection has disturbing parallels with another food scandal, the 0157 (E. coli) food poisoning outbreak that hit schools in Sakae city in 1996.[4] Despite significant evidence that tainted beef was the culprit, the government determined that *kaiware daikon* (white radish sprouts) were the source of transmission. This conclusion met with skepticism from medical experts, given that 0157 is a bacteria found in feces and is likely to occur in beef that has not been butchered under sanitary conditions.[5] In 1998, a chance meeting with an official in the Sakae city government confirmed suspicions of a cover-up, a perspective echoed in various internet forums at that time. It appears that the school lunch contracts were controlled by firms with *yakuza* connections that had imported cheap 'grey market' beef (in other words, not USDA-approved) from the USA that was not intended for human consumption. Fingering the beef as the culprit might have had severe repercussions on the government for conducting business with the mob. Moreover, a beef-based food poisoning scandal raised the specter of an expensive bailout similar to Britain's experience in the wake of the mad cow disaster. Far cheaper to blame (and then compensate) the radish sprout farmers rather than cast a pall over the entire beef industry. This solution had the additional merit of avoiding a damaging row with the USA, given already tense trade relations and the prospects that US beef exporters would suffer from this revelation.

Thus the hapless radish sprout farmers were made the convenient and affordable scapegoat in the 0157 affair, and were served up accordingly. Is powdered milk substitute the *kaiware daikon* of the mad cow scandal? In an atmosphere of misleading and contradictory reports, and revelations about a culture of complicity with producers prevailing in the Farm Ministry, levels of distrust and skepticism are justifiably high. For officials who did not heed warnings about MBM, and the 95 MBM producers, powdered milk looks appealingly blameworthy.

However, in August 2003 the farm ministry reinstated MBM as the main suspect in the outbreak. The investigating panel was unable to confirm the origin of the tainted MBM, but did express doubts that the powdered milk substitute was the source of the infection. The Dutch tallow in question apparently was not tainted and there have been no cases of BSE transmission in the Netherlands from substitute milk.

The cost of incompetence

Since the 1960s Japanese per capita beef consumption has risen fourfold to 10 kg a year, two-thirds of which is imported. This sharp rise in beef consumption is startling, considering that in the early 1980s the government was maintaining that beef exporters were faced with stagnant markets in Japan because Japanese have trouble digesting beef due to their longer intestines. Now they are having even more trouble digesting revelations about the government's role in this avoidable catastrophe.

To the extent that Japan's outbreak of mad cow disease can be attributed to bureaucratic bungling, official incompetence has exacted a high cost. On October 19, 2001 the temporary ban on beef sales was lifted and bidding prices immediately plunged to as low as 50 percent of their levels before the BSE infection. It was not until August 2002 that prices and sales volume recovered to pre-outbreak levels, adding up to nearly a year of steep losses. Although this recovery has been more rapid than anticipated based on the European experience, the mad cow scare has served as a wake-up call for Japanese consumers who have taken for granted that food is safe and that labels are reliable. They have learned the hard way what consumers around the world have also learned to their regret: lax regulations on food safety are an invitation to deception and dangerous practices.

The affair has proved extremely costly for all parties. As of 2002, the down

(Roger Dahl)

payment for the mad cow disaster came to ¥365 billion ($2.76 billion). At the farm gate, revenues slumped by some ¥131 billion (over $1 billion) in the year after the first BSE infection was announced, while meat sales fell some ¥160 billion ($1.2 billion). In addition, takings at Korean barbecue beef (*yakiniku*) restaurants fell by as much as ¥90 billion. Clearly the fall-out of the mad cow scare has been expensive as consumers initially shunned beef and lost confidence in food safety standards. In order to alleviate the consequences, the government distributed some ¥100 billion to compensate farmers for their losses in the 2001/02 financial year and set aside an additional ¥206.4 billon for BSE-related compensation in 2002/03. Of this latter figure, ¥178.5 billion is earmarked for farmers while ¥23 billion is for disposal of MBM stockpiles.

In the wake of the mad cow scare, dozens of firms in the beef industry have gone belly up. McDonald's, one of the largest fast-food outlets in Japan, estimated an 81 percent plunge in profits during the first half of 2002 and a near halving of net income for the full year. However, it appears that consumer concerns have declined rapidly compared to other BSE-affected nations and meat consumption has rapidly recovered; a 2003 survey indicates that beef consumption rose to 86 percent of pre-outbreak levels. This is a surprising twist in the mad cow experience, indicating that anxieties over and awareness of the dangers of infection are not very high among Japanese consumers. By August 2002 beef prices in wholesale markets had recovered to normal levels and the Japan Yakiniku Association reported that sales in the summer of 2002 had rebounded to pre-outbreak levels. Yoshinoyu, the nation's leading *gyudon* (savory sliced beef on a bowl of rice) chain, also overcame an initial downturn and reported increased sales of 10 percent in 2002.

How much mad cow disease will ultimately cost the government, producers, and consumers is anyone's guess – although a comparison with post-BSE Europe suggests that it may be staggering. Perhaps some Japanese see this as a price worth paying to break down the cozy relations and collusive practices that allowed this eminently avoidable debacle to occur, and to overhaul the nation's food safety administration.

One scapegoat at least has been sacrificed in the wake of the scandal: at the end of 2001, the Farm Ministry's Vice-Minister Kumazawa Hideaki resigned to take responsibility for the outbreak of mad cow disease. He had played a crucial role in the crisis by failing to formally ban the use of MBM despite expert warnings to do so.[6] After assuming his duties in January 2001 as vice-minister, the highest non-political position in the bureaucracy, Kumazawa had ultimate responsibility for rejecting EU warnings, refusing cooperation in the risk assessment study, and applying pressure to shelve the EU report issued in June 2001. The offer of a job with the meat industry following his resignation added to speculation that his close ties with industry officials and *nosuizoku* politicians had compromised his duty to protect the public interest. In the end, Kumazawa turned down this *amakudari* position – but only after a weekly magazine had publicized his pending sinecure with a beef association run, appropriately enough, by a former senior bureaucrat with the Farm Ministry.

What's in a label?

In Japan, Snow Brand used to conjure up pristine pastoral images of Hokkaido dairy farms. This conglomerate, which originated in a Hokkaido dairy products sales union established in 1925, is a leading player in the food-processing industry with a range extending well beyond milk products to include meat packing, pharmaceuticals, and other product lines. Its famous snow-flake symbol, redolent of natural purity, was first tarnished in the summer of 2000 when some 13,000 people in the Osaka region fell ill from drinking milk containing high levels of bacteria. Investigations of the firm's milk processing plants around the nation found that sanitation problems were widespread in its facilities and that, even after managers became aware of the problems, they continued to ship tainted milk derivatives. Apparently, in order to maintain production and cut costs, the firm systematically cut corners that led to unsanitary conditions at the plants. The media mercilessly excoriated Snow Brand for this blatant disregard for food safety and consumers' health. A leading name brand, which the firm had worked hard to establish over decades, was devastated overnight and its loyal customers melted away. Product loyalty is high in Japan and Snow Brand had squandered its large customer base by failing to spend small sums of money to ensure proper levels of hygiene. This corporate policy of reckless endangerment resulted in loss of public trust and plummeting sales, and the company was forced to close down several plants and lay off hundreds of workers.

Snow Brand's fortunes took a further dive when it became embroiled in the BSE scandal. In early 2002 it was revealed that the company's meat packing subsidiary had falsely labeled imported beef as domestic product so that it would qualify for a ¥10 billion government beef buyback program aimed at alleviating the impact of the BSE scare on beef sales. It has emerged that the repackaging scam originated in a directive from Snow Brand's Tokyo headquarters. Revelations about the false labeling of imported beef were followed by reports that the firm had withheld domestic beef that was supposed to be disposed of through the government buyback program. The domestic product was held back to avoid incurring losses, suggesting that the firm planned to sell the potentially tainted meat at a later date when the furor over BSE had died down and prices had recovered. The fraudulently labeled Australian beef had been purchased for ¥900 per kg while the buyback price was set at ¥1,060 per kg, enabling the firm to generate a small profit. However, domestic beef had been purchased at prices ranging from ¥1,600 to ¥2,500 per kg, meaning that delivering the beef to the buyback program would incur significant losses.

This crass manipulation of the buyback program indicates that company executives sought to defeat the food safety thrust of the program for what amounted to small change for a large firm such as Snow Brand. The government's countermeasures were intended to ensure that potentially infected beef, slaughtered before the government imposed stringent testing measures on October 18, 2001, was kept off consumer tables. The buyback program has come under criticism from the government's own audit bureau for sloppy practices and squandering of taxpayers' money. This scheme, instigated at the insistence of *nosuizoku* Diet members, is also seen to reflect the prevailing pro-producer bias in government and the endemic neglect of consumer interests. The government planned to incinerate some 12,600 metric tons of beef it purchased under this program. Although the price offered by the government was below market rates, the scheme was designed to limit losses, not eliminate them altogether, and certainly not to generate profits for firms selling cheap imported beef disguised as domestic product. By withholding some 20 metric tons of beef butchered before the nationwide testing initiated on October 18, 2001, Snow Brand demonstrated a crass disregard for consumer safety and government efforts to safeguard food supplies. It turns out that Snow Brand had also been misleading consumers about its pork products since at least 1999, selling imports as domestic pork, again at a markup.

The Snow Brand subsidiary involved in the scam, once the nation's sixth largest meat packer, went bankrupt and the firm's image, along with its stock price, took a further nose-dive. Again, consumers' faith in the company was shaken and the new scandal indicated that the company's management had failed to mend its ways and had learned nothing from the tainted milk case.[7] Contracts with school lunch programs, prepared food producers, and retail outlets were canceled in the wake of the scandal, ensuring the firm's demise.

Snow Brand risked its reputation and its bottom line in attempting to scam the government out of a paltry ¥196 million ($1.6 million), a drop in the bucket for a firm of this size. Since one has to deduct the costs of the imported Australian beef from this total, the actual 'profit' received amounted to some

¥20 million ($160,000). In considering that the cost of liquidating its meat subsidiary alone ran to ¥25 billion (nearly $200 million), not to mention the loss of customer goodwill and a trustworthy name brand, it is astounding that corporate executives were prepared to risk so much for so little. Far from being the action of a rogue employee, the decision to proceed with the scam was based on a directive from corporate headquarters. What kind of working environment and training could produce such a monumental blunder? What lessons were learned?

It seems that the prospect of easy money from government coffers was an irresistible temptation that led executives to take leave of both their senses and ethics. After the Snow Brand fiasco, the government began investigating warehouses where the beef under the buyback program was stored and discovered further evidence of conspiracy and fraud by industry executives. In August 2002 a meat-packing subsidiary of Nippon Ham, an Osaka-based giant in the food processing industry, was caught in a bid to scam the government's beef buyback program similar to Snow Brand's label-doctoring fraud uncovered earlier in the year. Adding to the firm's woes were revelations that top-level management knew about the scam and conspired to cover up the ensuing scandal. They did so by falsifying documentation and later inciner-ating the evidence (mislabeled foreign beef) that it had retrieved from the industry association warehouse where it had been delivered as domestic beef eligible for the buyback program. The scam was revealed when an anony-mous whistleblower faxed incriminating documents to the Farm Ministry's regional bureau, prompting a series of interviews that convinced the govern-ment that Nippon Ham was concealing some shady dealings. Investigations revealed that 1.3 metric tons of cheap Australian beef had been relabeled as domestic beef eligible for the buyback program, nearly three times the amount that company officials had first admitted to. Investigators also found evidence that the scam was not the sole responsibility of the one manager who claimed he had acted on his own initiative. Other industry players were also involved in the scandal. The Japan Ham and Sausage Processors Coop-erative Association has come under fire for colluding in a widespread cover-up of mislabeled beef and allowing Nippon Ham to cart the meat away for incineration before government inspectors could seize it as evidence.

The corporate ruse to make money off the government's emergency beef buyback program has shaken public trust in the entire food industry as new revelations of unethical practices, fraudulent labeling, and an apparent indif-ference to consumer interests have emerged. It is a classic case about how prominent and once venerable companies in the food industry have destroyed their image and brand name by engaging in deceptive practices that raised questions about their corporate ethos and the extent of possible corruption. Understandably, these self-inflicted wounds have shaken the public's confidence in food safety and the veracity of labeling. The scandals prompted retailers across the nation to pull these firms' meat products – not just beef – from store shelves, and contracts with other institutions have been canceled. What is astounding is that the firms involved risked such immense damage to their reputations and overall revenues for the small amount of money involved in the scams. Executives at these meatpacking firms now face court proceedings that will lead to fines and possible imprisonment. The *Asahi* (August 1, 2002) described how it had all gone so badly wrong: 'Those who tried to gyp the government out of undeserved subsidies face criminal prosecution. … Revelations of corporate efforts to cheat a program intended to help beef producers have made it impossible to fulfill the goal of eliminating consumer anxiety about domestic beef.'

Like Americans shaking their heads at the shenanigans at Enron and Worldcom, the Japanese public cannot quite believe what is going on in corporate Japan. It is all the more shocking because Japanese corporations have enjoyed a large degree of respect and are expected to play a paternalistic role. In this sense, the meat packers are a symbol of a corporate betrayal that has gathered momentum since the 1990s, cutting a swath through prevailing myths and revealing a world of ruthless practices and cold-hearted decision-making more often associated with US-style market-oriented capitalism. Any illusions about the beneficence and reliability of corporate Japan have been shed since the 1990s, mirroring fading faith in the nation's mandarins. The mad cow disease and false labeling scandals reflect poorly on the officials who were responsible for food safety, reinforcing public perceptions that in crisis after crisis, the bureaucrats were caught either asleep at the wheel or driving the getaway car – a record of negligence and complicity that has undermined the government's legitimacy and left its officials' reputations in tatters.[8]

Food safety

In 2002, a number of food-related scandals forced the government to take action to improve food safety. In addition to the BSE outbreak and the false labeling scams, there have been extensive media reports on high levels of pesticide residue found in imported vegetables, and deaths and illnesses caused by Chinese dietary aids. In a bid to alleviate consumer anxiety, in 2003 the government established an independent commission run by experts to advise the government on food safety and associated health risks.

A new basic food safety law introduced in 2003 places responsibility for food safety squarely on suppliers and creates more opportunities for consumer groups to have input on government decision-making in this area. The law also mandates risk analysis before the government decides on any food-related measure. The food safety commission is charged with implementing such measures based on scientific methods and criteria. The law also mandates the commission to take prompt action to avert any food-related crisis and to adopt appropriate risk management measures if deemed necessary from a preventive viewpoint. The commission is also charged with evaluating health risks and hazards presented by foodstuffs, excluding drugs.

One of the key tasks ahead will be separating the risk management and industry promotion roles that have created incentives for government officials to overlook consumer interests in favor of producers. The active involvement of *nosuizoku* in shaping food safety measures raises concerns about further meddling and more 'opacity in policy-making.' While the government advisory panel's recommendation to overhaul the entire food safety structure remains an elusive goal, the reform of the legal framework is an encouraging harbinger of change.

In response to the bogus labeling scams, the Diet passed legislation providing for stiffer fines and prison terms for perpetrators. In addition, to allay concerns over mad cow disease and gauge the extent of the problem, a new law requires cattle farmers to submit for BSE testing all carcasses of cows that die at age 24 months or older, beginning in April 2003. Another bill strengthens supervision of beef distribution by requiring farmers to register identification numbers assigned to all cows. This law further obliges wholesalers and retailers to label all beef products with these same numbers.

Retailers are responding to consumer fears by introducing computerized traceability in selected products, giving consumers instant access to the origins of a particular product. For example, by punching in the 10-digit label on the price tag of a joint of domestic beef, customers can view a scanned copy of the cow's breeding history and its BSE-free certification on a nearby computer screen. Retailers are planning to widen the scope of this program so that consumers can trace the path of food items from point of production to their shopping cart. Although this system is designed to promote greater faith in food safety, it is not foolproof and, like labeling, is open to manipulation. To gain credibility, the databases need to be meticulously maintained and producers must maintain reliable records, two major challenges that will determine the success of traceability. In the wake of the labeling scandals, winning over consumers and allaying their suspicions will be difficult. The scandals have raised concerns about the murky nature of food distribution channels that will not be dispelled by a display on a computer screen.

In order to facilitate a smooth transition to traceability, the government has agreed to underwrite the tagging of some 4.5 million dairy and beef cows. In the future, producers will have to bear these costs and pass them along. In addition, since 2000 a traceability project involving rice, tea, and soybeans has been run by Zenno, the National Association of Agricultural Cooperatives. Traceability has a promising future in Japan owing to the government's preliminary agreement to adopt international standards for monitoring genetically modified organisms. This will give impetus to the program and put pressure on producers to meet international standards as they will face external monitoring of their record-keeping.

Traceability may also lead to altered purchasing habits by consumers as they become more alert to the origins of the food they buy. Japan is heavily dependent on imported foodstuffs, accounting for some 60 percent of its caloric consumption. Consumer advocates suggest that providing information about the freshness of produce may increase demand for locally produced foodstuffs that have a shorter and more direct route to supermarket shelves and are less likely to be treated with preservatives. Japanese sensitivity to such information can be gauged from reaction to the high levels of pesticide residue detected in frozen vegetables imported from China, the subject of saturation media coverage in early August, 2002. Overnight these frozen vegetables were shunned and the Japanese I spoke to at the time made a sour face at the mere mention of frozen Chinese *edamame* (soybeans), a popular summertime snack. What the media failed to point out is that pesticide use is extraordinarily high in Japan as well, and that spinach and tea produced in Saitama have been found to contain high residues of carcinogenic dioxins.

The new regulatory regime is already having an impact on the politics of organic farming and food production. An organic farmer in Gunma told me that Japan's farmers fear a deluge of cheap Chinese imports and that highlighting the toxic dangers of Chinese food is an important strategy in encouraging Japanese to ignore cheaper imports and pay more for domestic produce. In his view, the more information that customers get about food products the better business will be for organic farmers; Japanese farmers cannot compete on price and so must differentiate their products by stressing their relative safety. There are lessons to be learned from the credibility crisis suffered by organic vegetable farmers due to a lack of strict labeling criteria. In response, the government tightened the criteria by mandating screening of producers to qualify for government certification. Without this certification producers are not allowed to label their produce as 'organic' and violators face sanctions. This has helped curb violations and should eventually buoy consumer confidence in organic labeling.

International context

In Europe, more than 6 million tests conducted on slaughtered cattle up through 2001 indicate that BSE infection is far more widespread than experts had anticipated. At the same time, fears of widespread transmission of the brain-wasting disease to humans have not yet eventuated. In 2001 there were only 23 new cases in Great Britain of the variant Creutzfeldt-Jakob disease that affects humans, and one each in Hong Kong and France. Since the disease was first identified in 1995, there have been a total of 113 cases as of 2001, and 105 fatalities, all but four occurring in Great Britain. At this point, scientists are unsure if the apparently low transmission rate reflects a long incubation period, natural immunity, or exposure to prions below the level that constitutes an infectious dose. Expert projections of the human death-toll vary considerably, ranging from a minimum of hundreds to a maximum of 40,000.

The incidence of the disease in cattle has been much higher. In 2001, there were 755 new cases of BSE reported outside Great Britain, with 202 in

France, 115 in Germany, 75 in Portugal, 71 in Spain, and 37 in Italy. Britain, the nation with the highest levels of BSE infection, reported 526 cases in the first nine months of 2001, marking a substantial drop from the 37,000 cases recorded in 1992 when the epidemic peaked. Overall, since the outbreak in 1985, Great Britain has recorded 180,000 cases of BSE infection. Japan joined the club of mad cow countries in 2001, along with the Czech Republic and Slovakia.

The EU imposed a total ban on MBM only in 2001, after it appeared that a partial ban prohibiting its use for cattle feed was proving ineffective. Disposing of the red powder has been difficult as hundreds of thousands of tons have been stockpiled, and its use as fuel in cement plants and as a constituent of concrete benches has not kept pace with supply. The EU estimates that the cost of disposing of the surplus MBM adds up to some $5 billion a year, including environmental restoration and buying alternative plant proteins to fortify the cattle feed. Between 2001 and 2006, the EU also plans to buy up and destroy surplus beef to offset projected losses to the tune of $2 billion.

The future of food safety in Europe is threatened by bureaucratic wrangling and national rivalries. EU governments have still not established a European Food Safety Agency – regarded by everyone as an essential development – not because of disagreements over the mandate, but because of competition among member states to host this new institution. Squabbling between member states and finger-pointing over the best way of dealing with the BSE epidemic have contributed to failures in cooperation, coordination, and communication, and facilitated the spread of mad cow disease in Europe. Certainly this is not a distinguished record of timely response to a major crisis.

The food scandal circle continues to widen, and the consequences of Japan's meat woes have hit producers in Europe, the USA, and Australia. It is estimated that the decline in beef consumption in the wake of the mad cow scare cost American beef exporters, who send about half of all their exports to Japan, some $2 billion. The ripples of the crisis have also reached the shores of Denmark, one of the few nations in the world to run a trade surplus with Japan, mostly due to pork sales. It is estimated that Danish producers lost some $500 million as a result of the labeling scandals that hit Nippon Ham and other large customers of pork products, demonstrating the complex vulnerabilities generated by fragile confidence.

Ocean cockroaches

Collusion between government and commercial interests, and the mislabeling and contamination of food products likewise play a leading role in the widening circle of scandal surrounding the Japanese whale meat industry. In an attempt to defend Japan's 'scientific whaling' and interest in resuming commercial whaling, Japanese government officials regularly describe whales as 'ocean cockroaches,' a phrase designed to rob these marine mammals of the appealing image they have gained in the West. The scavenger image refers to the huge appetite for fish that whaling advocates – and whaling advocates alone – believe is the reason for the depletion of world fishing stocks. The campaign to resume commercial whaling, and end the international moratorium that has successfully prevented some species from becoming extinct, is yet another example of bureaucratic commitment to a policy that does little to further the national interest at considerable expense.

Since the international moratorium on whaling was imposed by the International Whaling Commission (IWC) in 1986, Japanese consumption of whale meat has declined markedly, the commercial whaling fleet has all but disappeared, and consumer interest is negligible. Nonetheless, the government spends considerable sums underwriting 'scientific whaling,' campaigning for a resumption of commercial whaling, and subsidizing sales of whale meat supplied from scientific whaling. In this mind-boggling boondoggle, the nations' officials have decided to splurge on securing a product few people want, advertising it to encourage more people to want it, and subsidizing the purchase of it for the few who actually do want it. These costs are compounded by increasingly frayed relations with anti-whaling nations and a reputation for pursuing a diplomacy of high-risk brinksmanship for minimal benefits. However, since the mandarins have articulated whaling as an issue involving preservation of cultural diversity and a nationalistic rebuff to US ecoimperialism, the prospects for reconciliation and compromise are remote.

Whale wars

Why is the Japanese government pursuing a policy on whaling that seems to cost so much and promise so few benefits? What is the logic of risking international disapprobation by urging the harpooning of whales when there is more interest even among its own citizens in watching them frolic? In a word, nationalism. The consumption of whale meat has become a powerful touchstone for a country that perpetually views itself as a victim of international pressures and prejudices. Japan is often portrayed in the nation's media – in stark contrast to international coverage – as constantly giving in to international demands and making sacrifices for the sake of international harmony. It is also saddled with an uncomfortable legacy that produces pressures to support US foreign policies that are seen to run counter to Japan's own national interests. As the world's only victim of atomic bombing it would be logical for Japan to play a leading role in promoting test bans and nuclear disarmament; but by virtue of its alliance with the USA, it has to watch with gritted teeth as Washington ignores such concerns. Thus, on issues that Washington deems paramount, Japan is forced to give way. Under these circumstances, lesser issues serve as pressure valves for the bilateral alliance and an opportunity to regain lost pride and self-esteem, especially for government officials.

Whaling is a made-to-order touchstone for nationalists of all stripes as well as gadfly gourmets anxious to assert cultural values: 'We are a whale-eating nation so don't presume to impose your preferences on us.' It is telling that, although a majority of IWC member nations oppose commercial whaling, it is the USA that stands out as the main culprit and punching bag in the Japanese media. Bashing the USA over its stance on whaling provides an opportunity to vent well-justified frustrations with an overbearing and insensitive ally that pursues bilateral relations as if Japan were still under occupation. Of all the issues on which the USA and Japan disagree, the relatively minor question of whaling has proved to be one of the more persistently and emotionally divisive ones.

There are some resounding ironies in these contemporary bilateral temper tantrums over whales. In 1853 when Commodore Matthew Perry was sent to Japan, he was instructed to secure better treatment of shipwrecked American whalers who were routinely beheaded or imprisoned. Whaling was a fairly significant US industry at the time and the USA saw Japan as interfering with its whaling interests. Later, during the Occupation it was General Douglas MacArthur who argued Japan's case for resuming whaling in the Antarctic over the protests of allies who still bore grudges from World War II. At that time, whale meat provided impoverished and hungry Japanese with a reasonably cheap source of protein that was regularly served up in school lunch programs. During the 1950s, whale meat constituted some 50 percent of Japanese protein intake, slipping to an estimated 30 percent by the 1960s and less than 1 percent today. In the new millennium, demand among young people is negligible while for their elders it is all about culinary nostalgia. The slump in demand for whale meat has left some 30 percent of government stocks unsold, and the government has provided further subsidies to lower prices by 20 percent in an unsuccessful effort to boost sales. The declining popularity of whale meat has undercut official propaganda aimed at preserving cultural diversity, especially for younger Japanese who show scant interest in reviving whaling let alone eating the fruits of such scientific research. It is also difficult to portray as a deeply ingrained cultural tradition in that, outside of coastal communities, consumption of whale meat did not become popular until after World War II.

International Whaling Commission

The IWC was founded in 1946 to conserve whale stocks and promote sustainable commercial whaling. By the late 1970s whale stocks had been badly depleted by over-fishing and some species were at the brink of extinction. In 1982 the IWC convinced member nations of the need for a temporary moratorium on commercial whaling that commenced in 1986.

'Temporary' is the key condition of the moratorium and the term at the center of the controversy that has enveloped the issue. The consensus on maintaining the moratorium has ebbed in recent years as scientific evidence mounts that many species have recovered sufficiently to safely resume carefully monitored whaling. The issue of resumption of commercial whaling is hotly contested with a mixture of scientific logic, simplistic science, fierce emotion, nationalistic grandstanding, and concerns by the conservation lobby that, once the door is opened, sustainable management practices will go out the window. While lifting the moratorium requires support from three-quarters of the 49-member IWC, the 2002 vote against Japan's Revised Management Scheme indicates that opposition to whaling remains strong. Japan's position is that other IWC members are flouting the international convention agreed to by the members since it is aimed at responsibly managing whale stocks, not ending whaling.

One of the problems of bridging the angry gap between pro- and anti-whaling nations is that politically, on both sides, it is a no-lose issue. Taking a stand against the anti-whaling nations plays well in Japan's political theater, while condemning whaling as barbaric and irresponsible is a surefire way to galvanize support from green voters and contributors to environmental causes in anti-whaling nations. Thus the incentives to find common ground are often ignored in favor of sanctimonious posturing.

The 54th IWC Conference (2002) was held in the Japanese city of Shimonoseki, a port with a long whaling tradition, and featured the usual polarized rhetoric and mudslinging, punctuated by some particularly ugly displays. The unofficial highlight of this set piece was the grand opening, timed to coincide with the arrival of conference participants, of a new fast-food outlet featuring, naturally, whale meat. Whale dogs, whale cutlets, and other tasty whale dishes sold like hotcakes, as the restaurant Kujiraya reaped the benefits of the conference hoopla and publicity from a media desperate for a human interest story that did not feature frothing delegates ranting about perfidious opponents. The stage for this farcical interlude was set by advocates and opponents exchanging salvos on banners and t-shirts adorned with slogans such as 'Save Them, Eat Them,' 'Whales Increase, Fish Decrease. People are in Trouble,' and 'We Japanese don't need contaminated whale meat and blubber.'

Despite all the drama, prior to the conference there had been some signs of a meeting of minds. The influential environmental lobby World Wildlife Foundation Japan (WWF) had recently modified its no-whaling-under-any-circumstances policy to acceptance of sustainable whaling, provided it was justified by scientific data and accompanied by rigorous monitoring. The shift in stance by the WWF reflects its concerns that Japan's growing catch under its self-allocated quotas for research, coupled with other nations' whaling activities, is creating the conditions for a de facto resumption of unmanaged commercial whaling and the trade in whale meat. It is increasingly recognized that the tense standoff in the IWC is undermining the organization, and WWF Japan is one of a number of anti-whaling advocates moving towards a carefully monitored resumption of whaling with strict safeguards in order to avert a free-for-all. Greenpeace Japan has also stepped back slightly from its strident anti-whaling position.

However, at the 2002 meeting these encouraging signals were quickly pushed to the side by the less compromising stances of delegates out to score points. The Japanese delegation presented its familiar position that scientific data confirmed that whale stocks had recovered enough to allow selective fishing, and cited the similar conclusion adopted by the IWC Scientific Committee. Drawing on the findings of a recent book by Morishita Joji, deputy director of the Far Sea Fisheries Division at the Fisheries Agency (Morishita 2002), the delegation attributed the recent spate of whale beachings to overpopulation and starvation. Predictably, they blamed the decline of world fishing stocks, usually attributed to commercial over-fishing by humans, on gluttonous whales scarfing down an estimated 500 million metric tons of fisheries resources compared to the 90 million metric tons consumed by people. The USA was also accused of first embracing an anti-whaling stance during the Vietnam War as a means to deflect criticism away from its use of environmentally hazardous defoliants in Vietnam.

At the IWC conference, critics countered the Japanese charges with some of their own, accusing Japan of using overseas aid to gain support for its positions on whaling – a practice that an official at the Fishing Agency had once described as a legitimate strategy. (Japanese delegates countered that Australia had also brandished aid as a way of browbeating Papua New Guinea into supporting its own positions.) Rather than support a resumption of whaling, New Zealand, Australia, Brazil, and Argentina lobbied for expansion of whale sanctuaries into the South Atlantic and South Pacific. Arguing that there is no scientific justification for sanctuaries, Japan rejected these proposals. The strongest arguments mounted by anti-whaling critics focused on an exposé by a former executive of a Japanese whaling company that detailed systematic evasion of controls by underreporting of whale catches and taking of undersized whales. This report implies that estimates of whale populations used by the Japanese government to support resumption of whaling may be inaccurate. It also highlights the dangers of illegal trade and poaching. Concerns were also raised about the mislabeling of whale meat for sale at markets in Japan that was uncovered by DNA testing, also suggesting that Japan was harvesting and selling animals prohibited even under its scientific whaling program. Critics also dismissed claims that whales are responsible for depleted fishing stocks: the simplistic assumption that fewer whales eating fewer marine resources means more fish for human consumption cannot be squared with the complex ecosystems characteristic of oceans. As one environmentalist quipped, this is the scientific equivalent of claiming that to save a rainforest we must cut down the tallest trees.[9]

Since the moratorium began in 1986, Japan's self-allocated quota of whales for purposes of scientific research has come under heavy criticism by anti-whaling advocates. They argue that Japan is not whaling to conduct research, but rather is conducting research to provide an acceptable cover for whaling. The scale of the program has grown considerably, from 300 whales in 1987 to a projected 700 in 2003. Critics point out that the scientific research has produced paltry results, with only a small number of papers published in internationally refereed scientific journals. The WWF has also charged Japan with exploiting a provision of the Whaling Convention that permits small-scale scientific whaling in the Antarctic whale sanctuary. The selection of whales for research also seems to reflect consumer preferences for certain species rather than others, undercutting the claim that scientific whaling is directed towards responsible fisheries management.

In May 2002, an international group of eminent scientists took out a full-page ad in the *New York Times* that cast serious doubts on the scientific validity of Japan's research whaling. The text took the form of a letter signed by a distinguished group including three Nobel prize winners:

> We are concerned that Japan's whaling program is not designed to answer scientific questions relevant to the management of whales; that Japan has refused to make the information it collects available for independent review; and that it lacks a testable hypothesis or other performance indicators consistent with accepted scientific standards. Most of the data being gathered by Japan's 'scientific whaling' are obtainable by nonlethal means. ... The commercial nature of Japan's whaling program conflicts with its scientific independence ... These commercial considerations create a profit incentive to kill whales even when no scientific need exists. Japan has announced that it will soon begin killing sei whales, an internationally listed endangered species, ostensibly to determine the whale's diet ... There is no reasonable likelihood that killing additional sei whales now will add to what is already known about their diet. By continuing to fund and carry out this program, Japan opens itself to serious charges that it is using the pretense of scientific research to evade its commitments to the world community.[10]

In addition to these trenchant criticisms, skeptics have pointed out that the volume of whales harvested exceeds what is needed for research, adding to claims that science is being used as a convenient cover for maintaining a declining industry with a dwindling clientele.

Another stumbling block to resumption of commercial whaling is Japan's spotty record on wildlife management. Reports of rampant poaching and sales of whale meat under false labels do not inspire confidence. Whaling advocates recently lost an important ally when C.W. Nicols, a prominent Canadian environmentalist based in Japan and staunch defender of its whaling program over the years, reversed his stance due to the evidence of fraud, fudged data, and misreporting. This turnaround is a major blow to advocates in Japan who have long relied on Nicols to make a credible and objective scientific case in support of whaling. Hammering out a mechanism for monitoring both whaling and the trade in whale meat is necessary to allay fears that the whalers will again run amok. Traceability is emerging as a crucial factor here. The Japanese proposal in 2002 for a resumption of

Figure 8.1 Komatsu Masayuki, pro-whaling advocate, representing Japan at IWC
2002 in Shimonoseki. (Photo: Mainichi Newspapers)

whaling lacked provision for an international whale DNA register, one of
many reasons why delegates voted it down by 25 to 16 (with three
abstentions). Anti-whalers stress that a DNA register could help curb
poaching and allow officials to check meat on the market against the DNA
'fingerprints' taken from captured whales to determine if the meat has been
legally acquired. It was the use of this method that led to revelations that
illegal whale meat was being sold in Japanese markets, raising suspicions
about Japan's reluctance to support a DNA register. Conference delegates
also rejected Japan's call for a secret ballot rather than the current practice of
a public show of hands, reflecting suspicions about Japanese vote-buying and
a preference for transparency.

The 2002 IWC conference concluded on a sour note, with the Japanese
delegation lobbying support to deny Russian and American indigenous
peoples their existing exemption from IWC restrictions that enables them to
conduct coastal whaling. This effort was in retaliation for the IWC denial of
Japan's bid to resume coastal whaling, a tit-for-tat initiative that reflects the
increasingly ill-tempered exchanges at the forum. Japan has argued that the

USA is hypocritical in denying Japan's traditional whaling communities the right to engage in coastal fishing while at the same time supporting an exemption for native American Inuits. The latter's annual quota of 60 bowhead whales comes from an endangered species whose numbers are estimated at less than 7,000 and produces as much whale meat each year as Japan takes in its research program. The US proposal sought to grant a five-year extension to the American and Russian aboriginal whalers on their exemption from the moratorium, involving a total take of 279 bowhead whales during that period. The USA defends this exemption as necessary for the Inuit to maintain their traditional way of life. Nearly 10,000 Inuit in Alaska in ten coastal villages rely on whale meat and blubber for 80 percent of their protein and for protection against the severe cold – the blubber helps them cope with temperatures of 70–80° F below zero. Subsistence whaling by the Inuit is conducted without commercial considerations, as the locals consume the whales themselves and use their bones and oil as part of traditional rituals and practices. Moreover, the 6–8-man motorized skiffs used in Alaska's coastal waters are a quaint reminder of the days when whaling was a truly dangerous undertaking. Nevertheless, since the USA has invoked protecting Inuit culture, Japan contends that the principle of respecting cultural diversity should not be selectively applied. It also counters US claims of a simple difference between whales for supermarket shelves and subsistence consumption by arguing that for Japan's coastal whaling communities, commercially oriented or not, whaling is an established way of life and therefore the IWC should not support a double standard. In the end, 10 other nations joined Japan in voting against the extension and thus succeeded in killing the exemption by denying the 32 supporting nations the necessary three-quarters majority.

In sabotaging the proposal to allow an extension of subsistence whaling by the Alaskan Inuit and the Russian Chukotka, Japan gained a Pyrrhic victory and did itself little good by publicly gloating over the outcome. Komatsu Masayuki, deputy director of the Japanese delegation, basked in the shock value of the decision, calling it 'a sunny day for Japan.' Success in this case meant empty larders for subsistence whalers. Reveling in their 'victory' made Japan appear petty and vindictive, taking much of the gloss off its argument that its stance is based on science. In terms of public relations, Komatsu's ranting appearances on television and jubilation at the expense of indigenous peoples looked less like a blow against double standards than the frenzied behavior of a self-aggrandizing official enjoying his fifteen minutes of notoriety in the limelight.[11] Later in 2002 at a follow-up meeting in the UK, away from the glare of domestic media, the Shimonoseki decision was overturned and the exemption for subsistence whaling by aborigines was extended.

(Roger Dahl)

Whale business

The Japanese whaling industry owes its survival to a close network of commercial and government interests. Since 1987, nine whaling ships belonging to Kyodo Senpaku, a private fishing company with 300 employees, have conducted Japan's whaling research expeditions and hunting of mostly minke whales. The company's main source of revenues is the Institute of Cetacean Research, a foundation established in 1987 following imposition of the whaling moratorium, and the Japan Whaling Association, a trading body, which contribute $45 and $10 million respectively for the expeditions. After conducting tests, the research institute sells some 2,000–3,000 metric tons of the whale meat to the Japanese government, which in turn distributes it to prefectural governments (with the exception of Okinawa), which sell the meat on to regional fish markets. These sales effectively pay for the costs of the whaling expeditions. The central government retains one-fifth of what it buys from the research institute to promote whale consumption. These close ties between the government, a trade association, a private whaling company, and a government-sponsored research institute that generates research, advertising, and a slick propaganda campaign suggest a determination to sustain a commercial whaling capability despite an indifferent public and diplomatic contretemps.

A 2002 newspaper cartoon lampoons Japan's stance by showing a whaling ship returning to port with its catch lashed to the foredeck. Asked about the whales, the captain responds, 'Useful scientific research, invaluable biological data – and lunch!' To the chagrin of whaling advocates, however, very few Japanese think of whale when they think of lunch. In 2001, 30 percent of the 725-metric-ton catch went unsold, reflecting high prices and a shrinking clientele. The Fisheries Agency hopes to boost consumption both by subsidizing the price and by importing cheaper stocks from Norway, which pulled out of the IWC after the moratorium was imposed. It catches about the same number of whales on a commercial basis as Japan does in its scientific whaling program and is eager to commence sales of whale meat to Japan, as maintaining frozen stockpiles in warehouses is expensive. And now there is the stumbling block of contamination to deal with, a test that threatens to imperil the future of whaling altogether.

Oops

While no one is surprised when the right and left hands of the bureaucracy get out of synch occasionally, eyebrows are certainly raised in Japan when one ministry undercuts another by siding with NGO activists. In June 2002, the Health Ministry, reeling from a series of revelations that it sacrificed consumers' health to protect producers' interests, startled whaling advocates by drawing attention to the health risks of whale consumption and mooting restrictions, if not an outright ban. The ministry indicated that it had long been concerned about the high levels of mercury in whale meat and also reports of PCB (polychlorinated biphenyl) contamination.[12] It has announced that its options include banning whaling and imposing restrictions on the trade in whale meat. Three environmental groups – Greenpeace, Safety First, and the Environmental Investigation Agency – have pointed to research indicating that whale meat and blubber contains extremely high concentrations of mercury and PCBs. Mercury poisoning resonates powerfully in Japan as a result of the Minamata saga, and there is rising concern about PCBs due to suspicions that they are carcinogenic and an endocrine disrupter thought to impair fertility. The Health Ministry's announcement came soon after the prestigious *New Scientist* magazine issued a report indicating that whale meat was so contaminated with mercury that just one mouthful could cause brain damage and put human fetuses at risk. In January 2003 the ministry released findings that high levels of toxins had been detected in meat from particular whale species and reported that 10 percent of whale meat is mislabeled. It also revealed that meat from some of the highly toxic species has been sold as the less toxic minke whale. However, the ministry sought to ease public fears by stressing that, since whale meat is not an everyday item on most Japanese menus, the likely ingestion of toxins falls within established guidelines and does not constitute a public health risk. Very reassuring.

This announcement by the Health Ministry places the Fisheries Agency in a delicate position as it continues to spend taxpayers' money to promote both the supply and demand for a product that scientific research now shows to be dangerous for human consumption. Since the agency has staked out a position that rests on the logic of scientific data, these latest findings are particularly inconvenient. Ecotoxicologist Tanabe Shinsuke has carried out extensive research on the safety of whale meat; he was so disturbed by his findings that he has barred his own children from eating it. Tanabe argues that the probable cause of the increased incidence of whale beachings is increased levels of marine pollution, not overpopulation or starvation as the government asserts. Pollutants impair immune functions and make whales more susceptible to viral infections that leave them weakened. His research shows that whales and dolphins are susceptible to contamination because they are at the top of the ocean food chain and, unlike people and other land animals, retain high levels of toxins because they lack enzymes that work to break them down. Tanabe reports that some of the whales caught in Japan's research program contained such high levels of mercury that they were not put on the market, citing sperm whales caught in the North Pacific. He welcomes the Health Ministry's review of whale consumption, as mercury and PCB standards were last set in the 1970s and fail to address the problem of chronic toxicity or cumulative exposure. In light of these findings, and based on the experience of Minamata, people in whaling villages who regularly consume internal organs of whale are particularly at risk. According to Tanabe, consumers would benefit from more detailed and reliable labeling information, as coastal and toothed cetaceans tend to have higher concentrations of mercury and PCBs than other species. It is also disturbing that dolphin meat is sometimes labeled as whale meat, as dolphins tend to have higher contamination levels. Japan's annual dolphin and porpoise catch of 17,700 animals, the world's highest by far, is thus a matter of concern for public health authorities. While there is no international ban on hunting these marine mammals, Japan operates under a self-imposed quota system. This was established after a species-threatening 46,000 dolphins were killed in 1988, a sharp rise attributed to the 1986 whaling moratorium.

Lessons from the food front

The cases of mad cow disease and advocacy of whaling do not at first blush seem to hold many parallels. However, in both cases false labeling aimed at evading health regulations has deceived consumers and put them at risk. Consumers have also been let down by officials who seem to have lost sight of the public interest and show a cavalier attitude to public health concerns. Both cases reveal cozy government–business relations where producer concerns have come first, no matter how shortsighted. It is also evident that the Japanese government's reputation has suffered, first by ignoring warnings and cooperative initiatives by the EU to rein in the BSE epidemic and in the second instance by acting ungraciously, even vindictively, when its flawed plan for a resumption of commercial whaling was voted down. In both cases, the reliability of Japanese scientific research remains suspect and compromised by revelations of fudged data, misreporting, and deceptive practices endemic to the industries involved. In order to regain public trust and allay justifiable concerns about health hazards, government officials need to set high standards and ensure that they, and those they are entrusted to monitor, live up to them. Safer beef and sustainable whaling depend on earning and maintaining this trust.

It is encouraging that the BSE outbreak and fraudulent labeling scandals have spurred moves towards significant reforms of the food safety administrative framework and legislation. These scandals have raised consumer awareness about the need for greater vigilance and placed the government and industry on the defensive in trying to regain public trust. With long incubation periods for BSE of up to eight years, it remains uncertain to what extent fears of a vCJD outbreak are justified, especially in light of the low death toll experienced in Europe thus far.

The trend towards building civil society promised by Japan's third transformation is influencing ongoing reforms in the food industry, raising hopes and expectations for still further measures to safeguard the rights of consumers. Again, it is the failure to protect the public interest that has exposed and undermined the patterns, practices, and relationships that have endured too long in postwar Japan. This negligence is generating powerful forces favoring change and reform inimical to the old guard and its ways. While the public health disasters discussed in this chapter have led to a loss of trust and confidence, they are also heralding a new era and forcing the pace and breadth of transformation.

9 One hand clapping
Currents of nationalism in contemporary Japan

The sort of Japanese identity which nationalists and neo-nationalists strive to restore, rooted in tradition and blood, and distilled in the person of the emperor, is undermined most not by confrontation with the dark recesses of war memory, but by the global market itself, which desacralizes and commodifies everything, including Japanese culture and 'Japaneseness' itself.

Gavan McCormack (2000: 261)

In a more transparent and accountable, and competitive and harsher, Japan, the presence of the state will further diminish in the Japanese mind. This is no recipe for the revival of nationalism.

Tamamoto Masaru (2001: 40)

Nationalism

The revival of nationalism in Japan has been reported with some regularity over the years as if it is a new phenomenon, and one that reveals something significant about the national psyche. Taboos and embarrassment associated with overt displays of nationalism do appear to be progressively eroding, giving rise to anxieties that Japan might revert to the war-making and dissent-stifling ways of the 1930s and 1940s. The acute sensitivity to such signs of resurgent bellicosity, both in Japan and overseas, is one of the legacies of the Pacific War. In contemporary Japan, one need not look hard for signs of a renascent nationalism. Politicians' speeches and actions, government-approved textbooks, commentators in the mass media, popular *manga* (cartoons), best-selling books and the ubiquitous sound trucks blaring patriotic pabulum all offer aggressively packaged evidence that nationalism is a critical influence in twenty-first-century Japan. It has been for some time. Thus, while there is no point in denying that contemporary Japanese people are less reticent about embracing nationalism, we need to ask what this shift signifies. If indeed nationalist sentiments have been fairly widespread over recent years, what are the merits of examining Japan from this particular angle and what makes this phenomenon somehow more threatening in Japan than elsewhere?

There is a widespread misperception that any revival of nationalist sentiments will inexorably place Japan on the slippery slope back into the 'valley of darkness,' the term coined by progressive Japanese scholars to describe the nation's experience in the 1930s and early 1940s. Given the horrific consequences of Japan's rampage through Asia in those years, it is understandable that concerned commentators carefully scrutinize national attitudes for any signs of 'infection.' Going beyond this attitude of vigilance, however, there appears to be an implicit assumption that Japan cannot handle nationalism nor stop itself from going too far, almost as if the image depicted in Frank Capra's film *Japan: Why We Fight* (1945) is the unadorned truth. Improbably, the wartime propaganda about a nation hardwired for militarism and drunk on nationalist grandeur remains embedded in the collective pysche. Why, after half a century of alliance with the USA, do suspicions about Japan still linger and images of the Japanese indulging in nationalist displays signify an imminent peril? Do the tub-thumping statements and actions of Japan's ruling conservative elite indicate a latent, virulent and bellicose strain of nationalism? In short, no.

Legacies

Japan continues to live under the cloud of its wartime conduct and a perceived failure to make an unambiguous accounting for its record of atrocities and excesses. Critics are still waiting for an unequivocal and sustained demonstration of sincere contrition and state reparations for the damage Japan visited on its neighbors between 1931 and 1945. While there have been leaders of goodwill eager to make amends, their initiatives have been vitiated by other prominent Japanese who favor vindication over expiation. This seemingly unrepentant attitude has left the country a prisoner of its past, arousing animosity and suspicion in the region. To some extent this is a self-inflicted wound. However, the issue of nationalism in contemporary Japan is more complex than the media has portrayed it, and again suggests the need to unwrap and examine monolithic views of Japan and the assumptions on which they are grounded.

Concerns about a revival of militarism in Japan, both domestically and internationally, explain why signs of renascent nationalism are so carefully scrutinized. At the core of this perception is the notion that the Japanese are somehow predisposed to militarism and that Japan's dreams of ruling Asia have not been eradicated, but merely lie dormant. Hence, the nationalistic impulses, displays, and symbols common in other countries reverberate more menacingly in Japan. Thus media headlines trumpet the 'Resurgence of the Japanese Right' with a predictable regularity, even though the long-dominant political party, the LDP, serves as an umbrella organization that encompasses mainstream conservatives along with a rich array of ultra-nationalists, xenophobes, jingoists, mobsters, and others of a rightist bent. What is meant in this context by 'resurgence,' given that these groups have been closely connected to those in power for much of the postwar era without transforming the incubus of nationalism into something more

Figure 9.1 Tokyo Governor Ishihara Shintaro, known for his ardent nationalism and discriminatory comments about non-Japanese residents in Japan. (Photo: Greg Davis)

menacing? Is there something uniquely dangerous about Japanese nationalism?

Some are in no doubt that this is indeed the case. Lee Kuan Yew, the founding father and long-time ruler of Singapore, has compared the prospect of Japan's participation in peace-keeping operations under the auspices of the United Nations with giving a liqueur-laced chocolate to a recovering alcoholic: an unnecessary temptation that might lead the Japanese to revert to their bad old habits. In his view, the Japanese people are given to do whatever they do both diligently and excessively – part of the reason they have been such an economic success, but equally reason to be concerned about them adopting any kind of overseas military role. While peacekeeping seems innocuous and praiseworthy in itself, in Lee's view Japanese participation carries the seeds of an inexorable revival of militarism. Thus more than a half

(Roger Dahl)

century after World War II, some neighbors still worry out loud that Japan has not learned its lessons and could well become a regional rogue in the future if its nationalistic impulses are not tightly reined in.

It seems that in the case of Japan, the term 'nationalism' is code for 'militarism,' xenophobic patriotism and right-wing zealotry. The success of ultra-right-wing parties in Europe has been termed the European disease. Is Japan suffering from the same virus? In Europe, it appears that immigration and the challenges of multiculturalism have fueled a recent rise of right-wing nationalism. In Japan, however, the conservative LDP has ruled Japan for almost the entire period since it was established in 1955. There has been no sudden sharp rise in nationalism, no sudden sharp spike in support of militarism and no driving issue such as immigration or ethnic tensions to drive voters into the arms of ultra-conservatives. While some chauvinists – such as the governor of Tokyo, Ishihara Shintaro – have a strong personal following, this does not mean that most Tokyoites subscribe to his reactionary agenda or agree with him that the Rape of Nanking never happened. Some factions within Japan's leading political party have made no secret of their desire to undo many of the liberal reforms enacted by the USA during the Occupation (1945–52). Some factions have also been keen to revise the Constitution, especially Article 9, so that the nation can develop what some conservatives view as a 'normal' military capability commensurate with Japan's interests and aspirations. (This view runs counter to polls indicating strong attachment among the Japanese people to the Peace Constitution.) Since September 11, 2001, the government has also embraced a more clearly defined and expanded military role in conjunction with the USA, amounting to what many domestic critics suggests is a de facto abrogation of Article 9. Moreover, many of the old guard in the LDP would welcome an enhanced role for the Emperor in the Japanese polity. Thus, although there is no shortage of signs of a renascent nationalism in terms of agendas, pronouncements, and initiatives, interpreting their real significance is a complex matter.

Figure 9.2 Japanese protesters take to the streets in opposing the war in Iraq. (Photo: Andreas Seibert/Lookat)

The mainstream dominant party in postwar Japan is a party of the right and one that is unabashedly nationalistic and generally unrepentant about the grisly record of imperial excesses in the 1930s and 1940s. As late as 1995, the Diet was embroiled over a war apology resolution that issued an expression of contrition so flaccid that it veered closer to justifying than apologizing for imperial excesses. It is no secret that, in the aftermath of World War II, the USA made common cause with Japanese conservatives to revive the economy, impose political stability, and integrate Japan into a supporting role in US wars in Asia and, more recently, the Middle East. The legacy of this bargain, negotiated in terms of Cold War politics and never openly questioned in Washington, has been surprisingly strong continuities with Japan's discredited wartime past. Why have these longstanding continuities suddenly become so sinister? Put another way, given that large segments of Japanese society continue to contest pressure for an enhanced security role, resist revision of the Constitution, and oppose a stronger monarchy – thus acting as a constraint on the more avid nationalists – why is there still an assumption that Japanese society cannot handle the normal strains of democracy?

The nationalist impulse in Japan has also grown out of a sense of grievance. It reflects simmering dissatisfaction with six decades of deferential adherence to US foreign policies and a bilateral relationship that seems forever locked into the asymmetry established during the Occupation. In this sense, Japanese assertion of nationalism is a normal, and some might say healthy, reaction against Japan's prolonged subordination. Certainly the media has played a role in highlighting crimes committed by US troops stationed in Japan and emphasizing how the USA seems to take its ally for granted except when browbeating it to adjust its policies to suit Washington's agenda. Relations have been troubled for much of the postwar era. In the 1960s and 1970s, tens of thousands of Japanese took to the streets to protest the bilateral security treaty and the Vietnam War, while the twin 'Nixon shocks' (normalization of relations with China and abandonment of the gold standard with no prior consultation) left lingering scars and undermined trust. In the 1980s, vivid television images of Americans smashing Japanese-made products, overseas criticism of Japanese real-estate investments in trophy properties, and tensions fueled by trade imbalances further eroded goodwill between the two nations and raised the specter of 'yellow peril' redux.

This uncomfortable partnership helps explain why politicians, intellectuals, activists, and others routinely voice their suspicions, resentment, and criticism about America. In 2003, overwhelming public opposition to the war in Iraq expressed in opinion polls and rallies drew on a healthy reservoir of anti-American sentiment, while Prime Minister Koizumi's strong support for the Bush Administration reflects the power realities that have alienated so many Japanese.[1] While such reactions have not drained the bilateral reservoir of goodwill, they highlight the normal tensions in US–Japanese relations and indicate how they have stoked Japanese nationalism. While ubiquitous displays of the national flag and schoolchildren reciting a pledge of allegiance to the nation are not evident in Japan, there is no denying that such echoes from across the Pacific leave an impression.

The past still casts long shadows over contemporary Japan, and time has not yet buried memories of the bloody history that continues to divide Japan from its Asian neighbors, especially China and Korea. Western observers have also pressured Japan to face up to its record of excesses and atrocities in Asia, often drawing on the scholarship of Japanese researchers who are at the forefront of investigation into this subject. While there is truth in the allegation that the Ministry of Education has encouraged a collective amnesia about Japan's record as imperial overlord and invader in Asia, it is also true that Japanese scholars, educators, politicians, and journalists have robustly challenged such efforts to whitewash the past. And while many Japanese may nurture a keen sense of victimization regarding the Pacific War that baffles its Asian victims, the very public debates about the past have forced the nation to confront inconvenient evidence and memories that undermine the more exonerating versions of this traumatic era. Bookstores overflow with studies of the period, the media runs a stream of stories and television specials, and the controversies over Japan's wartime record have been aired in the public domain over and over again. While zealots, chauvinists, and patriots gain considerable attention both within Japan and overseas, there are many scholars, writers, students, and readers who do not subscribe to their views and have made it impossible to give a hasty burial to the nation's unexamined, unflattering past.

Figure 9.3 Prime Minister Koizumi's support for the US invasion of Iraq was very unpopular among the Japanese. (Photo: Andreas Seibert/Lookat)

Indeed, the 1990s have been a time of reckoning when the past suddenly
caught up with the Japanese, largely unprepared by their schooling to
confront the unsavory truths of what the imperial forces were engaged in
when they were not 'liberating' Asians from the yoke of Western imperialism. Once Emperor Showa (Hirohito) died in 1989, the archives began to
yield their secrets, soldiers recovered their diaries and memories, and revelations about the horrors inflicted by Japan suddenly poured forth. Equally
important has been the sustained pressure applied from the late 1980s by
Asian activist groups seeking redress and a more accurate depiction of
Japan's sordid past involving abuses and atrocities such as the taking of
comfort women, the slaughter in Nanking, slave laborers, and the activities of
the notorious Unit 731.[2] As a result of these mutually reinforcing domestic
and regional developments, during the 1990s the Japanese learned more than
they were prepared for about the sexual enslavement of tens of thousands of
Korean girls, biological warfare, vivisection experiments on POWs, and the
Rape of Nanking. This sudden flood released from the cesspool of Japan's
history proved shocking and unsettling to a people accustomed to more

glorious and heroic versions of the past. Understandably there has been resistance to these revelations and efforts to deny, mitigate, justify, and otherwise shift responsibility for the more gruesome tragedies. However, during the cathartic 1990s the self-vindicating and glorifying narrative that focused on noble sacrifice and victimization of the Japanese people has been irreversibly discredited. While many will continue to prefer the more comfortable version of their history, the exhumed past is here to stay and cannot be reburied.

Pan-Asian fantasies

In Indonesian *merdeka* means 'freedom' but in Japanese, judging from the 2000 film of the same name, it translates as 'flop,' as in box-office disaster. This melodramatic film focuses on Japan's role in helping Indonesia win independence in 1949. However, it is only because the film asserts an exonerating, blinkered view of Japan's occupation of Indonesia between 1942 and 1945 that it received any attention at all.

Merdeka embraces an historical narrative of the Pacific War that has shown marked resilience in Japan and is undergoing something of a revival. This narrative emphasizes that Japan invaded its regional neighbors to liberate them from the yoke of Western imperialism. Japan's pan-Asian ideology ('Asia for the Asiatics') reserved it a special place in the hierarchy of Asian nations. Japan assumed the role of elder brother in recognition of its 'successful' modernization and militarization during the Meiji era, culminating in the first victory of Asians over whites in the Russo-Japanese War in 1905. Having fended off Western imperialism and bloodied a European nose, Japan indeed did serve as an inspiration for nationalists throughout Asia including Indonesia. Pramoedya Anata Toer, perhaps Indonesia's most acclaimed novelist, touches on this issue in *This Earth of Mankind* (1982), in which the protagonist expresses his admiration for what the Japanese had achieved, and the need to learn from their example.

Certainly in the 1930s and 1940s many Japanese were sincerely motivated by the principles of pan-Asian ideology and were hopeful of establishing an Asia run by and for Asian interests. Their hopes and subsequent disappointments were mirrored throughout the region. However, there is compelling scholarship on both sides of the Pacific that shreds the pan-Asian rhetoric and argues cogently that Japan invaded Southeast Asia for natural resources rather than political principles.[3] Nevertheless, like other imperial nations Japan has sought succor in a more appealing myth, and conservatives routinely refer to the noble goal of ousting Western colonial overlords as justification for Japan's fifteen-year rampage throughout the region between 1931 and 1945. Naturally, justifications of Japanese imperialism antagonize China and Korea, countries that understood all too well the realities of Japanese brotherly love. The rhetoric of Asian solidarity rang hollow among people who experienced the harsh realities of Japanese 'liberation.'

Ultimately, the nationalist aspirations of Asians were sacrificed or manipulated in service to the war effort, and the positive consequences of Japan's Asian interregnum – such as the gaining of independence – were largely unintentional, depending more on serendipity than imperial magnanimity.

Pride (1998), a film produced by the same company that made *Merdeka*, probed the theme of victor's justice and the 'martyrdom' of Tojo Hideki at the Tokyo War Crimes Tribunal. It also suggests that Japan played a significant role in Indian independence. As in *Merdeka*, the theme of pan-Asian liberation is invoked to restore a valorous view of Japan's aggression in Asia. This view has lurked in the shadows of a Pacific War narrative dominated by a valorous America fighting the good fight against 'beastly, blood-thirsty Japanese raping and pillaging' their way around the region.

Films such as *Pride* and *Merdeka* demonstrate the persistence of a nostalgic yearning among conservative Japanese for a more positive rendering of their shared past with Asia, one free of damning incidents and inconvenient interludes. 'Freedom' means escaping the burdens of a shaming past that weighs on contemporary Japanese and complicates ongoing efforts to portray Japan as the noble victim rather than loathsome victimizer. It seems only natural that many Japanese are uncomfortable with the burdens of such an unflattering history and the constraints that it still imposes. In these circumstances, the reactionary Dr. Feelgoods of Japanese history have found a gullible public eager for the vindicating and exonerating pabulum they serve up. Their views are featured in the mass media, in *manga* and most recently in a controversial junior-high-school textbook published in 2001 by the Atarashi Rekishi Kyokasho wo Tsukuru-kai (Japanese Society for History Textbook Reform), an organization that seeks to portray Japan's modern history in a more flattering light.

Books and films such as these unabashedly glorify the past in order to encourage Japanese people to feel better about their nation and to offset the flood of negative revelations that swept the country during the 1990s. Nishio Kanji (1999), head of the textbook reform society, asserts that young Japanese need a history that will give them pride in their nation. The so-called masochistic history that focuses on the atrocities and excesses of the Imperial forces undermines patriotism and cultivates what he views as an unhealthy shame. What is needed, according to like-minded conservatives, is a more inspiring history that nurtures pride in nation. It is uncertain how this particular brand of national pride will stir the patriotism and devotion to the state that the conservative revisionists are also seeking to instill.

Much of the action of *Merdeka* focuses on the Japanese establishing an Indonesian military force, known as PETA, and giving inductees spiritual, physical, and military training. Emphasizing the creation of Indonesian military forces buttresses the filmmakers' claims that Japan played a key role in Indonesian independence, for without these soldiers it is doubtful that Indonesia would have successfully resisted the reimposition of Dutch colonial rule during the 1945–49 revolution. Indeed, the national struggle for independence has imbued the term *merdeka* with powerful symbolism. Precisely because of its sanctity for Indonesians, the Indonesian Embassy in Tokyo protested the use of this word as the title and suggested an alternative title: *1,000 Days*, in reference to the duration of the Japanese occupation. The film also emphasizes the role of some 2,000 Japanese deserters who joined forces with their Indonesian 'brethren' and fought heroically at their side after releasing caches of weapons to them in defiance of Allied orders. In the film, these pan-Asian shock troops prove their sincerity by dying down to the featured platoon's last man, all with shouts of *sampai mati* ('until death' in Indonesian) on their lips. The film is silent on the much larger numbers of Japanese troops who worked with the Allies to restore peace and suppress the nationalist movement when the British arrived in 1945.

The real distortions in *Merdeka* occur not as a result of what is portrayed, but rather by what is left out. In a film that purports to trace the rise of the PETA there is no mention of the most famous incident in PETA history, their mutiny in Blitar against the Japanese and the subsequent executions of those involved. It seems that the PETA soldiers had turned to mutiny not only in protest against their own mistreatment, but also to vent their rage at the plight of the *romusha* (literally 'day laborer' in Japanese, but in this context referring to Indonesians who were compelled to work for the Japanese occupying forces). The film makes no mention of this grueling system of forced labor that involved an estimated 10 million Indonesians in various infrastructure and mining projects in Indonesia and overseas, most notoriously on the Death Railway linking Thailand and Burma where Allied prisoners of war (POWs) also served as forced laborers.[4] Indonesian estimates of *romusha* deaths run as high as 4 million, although recent scholarship suggests a figure closer to 1.5 million.[5]

Perhaps nowhere is the gap between the rhetoric and reality of pan-Asianism more yawning than in the miserable story of the *romusha*. Mobilized in the Holy War fought in the name of Emperor Hirohito, these unfortunate victims of war experienced the inequalities inherent in the pan-Asian hierarchy. 'Liberated' Asians served as chattels for the victors and were viewed as expendable. Allied POWs have consistently pointed out that however badly they were treated, the treatment of *romusha* was far worse, belying the solidarity of Asians trumpeted by Japanese apologists. Nor does the ennobling *Merdeka* shed any light on the plight of those made to serve as Imperial sex slaves. The brutal methods employed by the *kempeitai* (Japanese military police), ever vigilant for sabotage and espionage among the 'liberated' but apparently ungrateful Indonesians, claimed many more victims, while the military's confiscation of rice harvests bore heavily on a populace already close to starvation.

How are the Japanese remembered by Indonesians? Certainly with considerably less rancor than in Korea or China. Indonesians calmly recall 'unpleasant' incidents in a manner that suggests the past is not a festering wound. A former employee of Domei, the Japanese news agency that operated in Jakarta during the war, has written perhaps the harshest indictment of Japanese rule in Indonesia. Pramoedya Anata Toer's memoir *Mute's Soliloquy* (1999) recalls his days on the news desk and conveys horrific images of Japanese soldiers that expose pan-Asianism as a sham. The nostalgic imperialism and romantic familial brotherhood served up in *Merdeka* could not be further from Pramoedya's version of the shared Asian past. Like many Indonesians, the high hopes he held when the Japanese arrived were soon shattered by the arrogant and cruel oppression inflicted by the new colonial overlords. To say that they proved more of a disappointment than an inspiration would be an understatement.

Whether or not a glorifying version of history will succeed in restoring Japanese pride in their nation, it is ironic that the nostalgic nod to pan-Asianism embodied in *Merdeka* has had the effect of trampling on the pride and dignity of Indonesians, evoking the cruel realities of the time in ways the director never intended. Inevitably, films and books in this genre generate speculation about the potential for a revival of Japanese militarism in a way that Rambo does not seem to do in the USA. Perhaps this reflects the one-sided legacy of the dominant Pacific War narrative in which Americans were essentially good guys while the Japanese were (and potentially remain) 'blood-crazed beasts.' The corollary is that in some way the 'inscrutable Japanese' are hardwired for militarism and one must be vigilant for latent signs of nationalist-inspired aggression. Certainly one can sense the rising appeal of nostalgic nationalism in turn-of-the-century Japan and the rush of historical hucksters eager to fan and reap the rewards of such sentiments. Certainly many Japanese are frustrated with the current version of the war portraying them as uniquely guilty of various excesses. They no doubt welcomed the airing on television of recently unearthed archival footage in the UK that shows Allied soldiers committing the same barbaric acts against Japanese soldiers (*Hell in the Pacific*, 2001). It is no fun always being the villain and having to cope with perpetual ignominy. Public craving for a more palatable history (and the accompanying temptation to sweeten the unpalatable) is hardly unique to the Japanese and indeed is a key ingredient in the creation of the national (and nationalist) mythologies of countries around the globe. The jump from a selective, reactionary reading of history to a revival of militarism seems an awfully long and dubious leap.

The nostalgic nationalism that is proving so popular in Japan has become a catalyst for debate about an underexamined past. The deluge of revelations about wartime excesses and atrocities that followed in the wake of the Showa Emperor's death in 1989 caught an unprepared public by surprise. These revelations have sparked tentative revisions of the official version of the past that are now encountering a backlash from those who take comfort from a less damning account. For the moment the tide seems to be flowing with the reactionaries and their vindicating views, but it may be a mistake to exaggerate the importance and implications of this apparent lurch to the right. After all, the conservatives who have dominated postwar Japanese governments have long tried to orchestrate a collective amnesia about Japan's shared history with Asia – but with mixed success. Why is it suddenly dangerous or threatening that they persist in their efforts? While it is natural (if disturbing) that conservatives still cling to their version of the past, it is encouraging that their denials are subject to greater scrutiny both within Japan and by its neighbors. If the empty theaters showing *Merdeka* are any indication, it seems that relatively few Japanese are seeking solace in an exonerating history.

Yasukuni Shrine visits

If a single monument can be considered to be a focus for militant nationalism and Japan's failure to offer a convincing repentance for its war record, it is the Yasukuni Shrine, located in downtown Tokyo. The shrine is controversial not because it is a memorial to 2.47 million Japanese soldiers who died in past wars, but rather because it is a potent symbol of militarism and veneration of the Emperor. Before 1945 Yasukuni was administered by the army and navy, and those killed in action were honored there as living gods. Since 1978, fourteen convicted and executed 'class A' war criminals have also been enshrined there as 'gods.'[6] Since then, Yasukuni Shrine has been inextricably linked with the men held responsible at the Tokyo War Crimes Tribunal for Japan's bloody rampage through Asia during 1931–45.[7] Prime Minister Nakasone Yasuhiro was the last leader to visit the shrine in his official capacity as prime minister on August 15, 1985, the fortieth anniversary of Japan's surrender. His visit provoked an angry reaction from regional neighbors such as China and the Koreas, which remain extremely sensitive about Japan's reluctance to face up to its checkered past, come clean on its war crimes, and issue an unequivocal apology.

While Japanese attitudes to Yasukuni are complex, it has undeniably become a focus for an exculpatory version of the nation's wartime history. One of the reasons Japanese give for visiting the shrine is simply to honor all those who died during the war. Prime Minister Koizumi Junichiro, who has made several 'unofficial' visits to Yasukuni, has justified his actions on the grounds that it is unseemly to discriminate among the dead and thus he has honored all equally, including the war criminals. This perhaps reflects a widespread perception among Japanese that the Tokyo War Crimes Tribunal was a kangaroo court that served up a biased 'victor's justice.' Conservatives have long chafed under the victor's narrative of the Pacific War that denigrates Japan's pan-Asian aspirations during the war as empty rhetoric justifying its own imperial ambitions in the region. For many Japanese, the 'class A' war criminals put on trial were remote from the things of which they stood accused: they were not convicted of actually committing the atrocities, but rather were held responsible for crimes against humanity, for leading Japan into war and failing to prevent atrocities committed by soldiers on distant battlefields. Thus many Japanese consider that their

Figure 9.4 Nationalists gather at the Yasukuni Shrine. (Photo: Andreas Seibert/ Lookat)

convictions were unjust and that the tribunal failed to recognize Japan's legitimate reasons for going to war, including a variety of Western provocations and colonial domination of Asia.

Yasukuni is also a touchstone for domestic controversy because it is a Shinto religious facility and visits are interpreted by some observers as contravening the division between the state and religion enshrined in the Constitution. This is a sensitive issue because, during the war, state-sponsored Shinto was linked with Emperor worship and was used as a vehicle to inculcate loyalty to the government and mobilize popular support for the war. Shinto is thus tainted, in the eyes of some Japanese, by its dubious links with imperialism; and Yasukuni, as the focal point of wartime Shinto, is considered the temple of ultra-conservative nationalism where the most regrettable aspects of Japan's military past continue to be venerated.

Yasukuni is thus laden with symbolism that reverberates loudly and divisively both within and outside Japan. Powerful right-wing lobby groups ensure that the monument will never be forgotten. The Association of War-Bereaved Families (Nihon Izokukai) and the National Shrine Association (Jinja Honcho) are large conservative groups that pressure politicians to pay respect to the nation's war dead in exchange for well-organized electoral support and generous funding. Both have longstanding ties with the ruling LDP, and party leaders regularly serve as the president of Nihon Izokukai. Paying obeisance at Yasukuni is for such associations a litmus test of a politician's credentials – in the same way as abortion is for fundamentalist

Christian organizations in the USA. In both countries politicians consult their consciences and coffers, and act accordingly.

Visitors to the shrine are often struck by the large numbers of grey and black buses parked there, most of which are filled with members of right-wing ultra-nationalist groups known as *uyoku*. These buses can often be seen cruising the streets of Tokyo blaring martial music at high decibels and disrupting traffic, with the police turning a blind eye and deaf ear to their antics. The thugs who fill the buses hail from Japan's underworld, where cozy ties between the mob and right-wing politicians prevail. Their intimidating presence, and regular resort to violence against journalists and politicians who cross them, ensure that their views carry more weight than their numbers justify.

In 1975, Prime Minister Miki Takeo became the first postwar prime minister to visit Yasukuni on August 15, the anniversary of Japan's surrender, albeit in a 'private' capacity. His visit occurred shortly after an attempt on his life by a right-wing fanatic. Previously, prime ministers had visited the shrine during autumn or spring festivals. Three years later, in 1978, fourteen war criminals were enshrined in Yasukuni, ensuring the shrine's future as a potent talismanic symbol for unrepentant rightists. Subsequently, prime ministers have walked the Yasukuni tightrope by insisting that any visits they make to the shrine are made in a personal and private capacity. Although such explanations were intended (ostensibly, at least) to emphasize the absence of an official government imprimatur, this subterfuge has not succeeded in bamboozling either foreign or domestic critics. When Prime Minister Nakasone broke the taboo on official visits in 1985, the subsequent uproar led him to resume the fiction of personal visits. His successors have followed suit.

Despite this controversy, during his first three years in power Prime Minister Koizumi Junichiro (2001–) visited the Yasukuni Shrine four times, and has insisted that his visits will continue. These visits were conducted amid a media circus and provoked the expected rebukes from Beijing and Seoul. Ongoing efforts to promote reconciliation with the two nations that suffered most from Japanese wartime brutalities have been derailed by Koizumi's apparent nonchalance towards historical sensitivities. While his homage at a shrine that is indelibly associated with Imperial Japan was viewed as a foreign policy gaffe that fanned bitter memories in the region, his visits generally played well at home, especially among key LDP constituencies. Many Japanese shrug their shoulders about the visits and wonder what all the fuss is about. Some argue that such homage is *atarimae* (natural), because all nations commemorate the sacrifices of their soldiers who have died in past wars. Indeed, some ask why Japan is held to a standard regarding its war dead that is not equally applied to other nations.

It would be misleading, however, to assume that there is a national consensus on Yasukuni visits and that those who support, or at least accept, the visits by top politicians knowingly assume all of the attendant historical baggage. It is important to bear in mind that there is considerable domestic opposition to Yasukuni visits. Leading political parties such as New Komeito, a coalition partner in the Koizumi administration, publicly oppose the visits, as does the Japan Communist Party and the Socialist Party of Japan. New Komeito's support base is the Soka Gakkai, a Buddhist lay organization. State-sponsored Shinto has been associated with systematic discrimination against Buddhism since the Meiji era, and there is a lingering wariness about government ties to Shinto among the vast Soka Gakkai membership. The press also carries critical commentary about Yasukuni, especially the *Asahi* and *Mainichi*, but also NHK, the quasi-government broadcasting corporation, various weekly magazines, and English-language dailies such as the *Japan Times*. Thus, there is a rich array of countervailing views that belie simplistic notions of the Japanese nation monolithically defending Yasukuni visits and embracing a dangerous nationalism.

Unlike in Europe where fringe parties tend to be the standard-bearers for controversial nationalistic sentiments, visits to Yasukuni shrine are favored by the mainstream, dominant party. In Japan, the ultra-nationalistic fringe is a core constituency of the LDP and indeed one of the key figures in the party's formation was Kodama Yoshiro, a right-wing zealot, suspected war criminal, and gangster who came to prominence in the postwar period.[8] High-profile visits to Yasukuni are aimed at rallying core supporters and ensuring their continuing largesse in funding election campaigns and mobilizing the vote. As campaign financing comes under closer scrutiny and corporations have cut back on funding, wooing potentially rich sources of funds makes sense. In addition, the LDP is not as dominant as it once was, since 1994 having to form coalition governments, and thus it is eager to pursue policies that will attract voters.

Interestingly, even within the LDP there are reservations about the Yasukuni visits. One outspoken critic is Nonaka Hiromasa, a notorious and powerful backroom fixer who calls shots from the shadows rather than the limelight of power. He is one of the few members of the present LDP leadership who actually served in the army during the war and is also one of the nation's most prominent politicians of *burakumin* origins.[9] As a senior party member who has sought to cultivate close ties to China, he regards Yasukuni visits as undermining both these efforts at reconciliation and Japan's long-term national interests. Nonaka has publicly chided party members on the Yasukuni issue, but without demonstrable impact.

When Koizumi came to power in 2001, it was as a party maverick who promised a solution to Japan's economic problems and was not afraid to challenge the LDP old guard. He also made an explicit promise to visit Yasukuni Shrine on August 15, the anniversary of Japan's surrender. It is intriguing that his political mentor, Fukuda Takeo, was prime minister in 1978 when the remains of Japan's chief war criminals were enshrined at Yasukuni. The media also revealed that after this sanctification, Emperor Showa, the chief priest of Shinto and the man for whom so many war veterans had been prepared to give their lives, made no more visits to Yasukuni. For

Figure 9.5 Koizumi mania swept Japan in 2001. (Photo: Andreas Seibert/Lookat)

conservatives, this inconvenient symbolism and unspoken repudiation undermines their efforts to reconstruct an Emperor-centered national identity. Emperor Akihito has similarly confounded conservatives by failing to support efforts at constitutional revision aimed at restoring the Emperor to a more prominent role.

Koizumi's planned visit to Yasukuni stirred up an international furor. In the weeks leading up to August 15, 2001 the media plunged itself into a frenzy of debate and both South Korea and China issued stern, very public diplomatic warnings against carrying out the planned visit. In the midst of this political maelstrom, Koizumi visited the shrine two days early on August 13, a choice that displeased everyone. Right-wing nationalists claimed he had caved in to unwarranted international pressures – but could not have been too disappointed by his high-profile visit. However, in China and Korea both government and people expressed anger that the visit had gone ahead and were manifestly not mollified by Koizumi's decision to avoid the politically sensitive anniversary. Relations with these countries had already been soured in the spring of 2001 over the release of junior-high-school textbooks that whitewashed Japan's violent record of colonialism and military expansion at the expense of its neighbors. Japanese progressives also spoke out against the visit, making it clear that many Japanese also regard Yasukuni as a symbol of a shameful era of militarism.

Japanese prime ministers need not visit Yasukuni Shrine in order to commemorate the war dead. A viable alternative is the nearby tomb to the unknown soldier at Chidorigafuji, a secular monument to the war that now looks somewhat forlorn and draws relatively few visitors. Indeed, most Japanese are probably unaware of its existence. Each year on August 15, the government holds a ceremony at Chidorigafuji expressly to honor the war dead, and it is thus an ideal venue for a prime minister to pay his respects.[10] In an effort to assuage his critics, Prime Minister Koizumi has established a panel to explore other alternatives to Yasukuni; however, he remains unrepentant about his visits to the Yasukuni Shrine and has taken Korean and Chinese diplomatic rebuffs with a studied insouciance.

There has been a strong domestic reaction to Koizumi's actions. In the wake of his 2001 visit, more than 900 Japanese citizens joined suits against the prime minister across the archipelago, charging him with violation of the constitutional separation of state and religion. This is a sign that democracy is alive and well in Japan and that there are citizens willing to use the courts to hold the government accountable. The government was placed in the odd position of arguing that the visits were not official and thus the line of separation between religion and state had not been breached. In response to charges that the prime minister had signed the visitors' book with his official title, traveled to the shrine in an official car, and laid a wreath bearing his official title, the government disingenuously responded that these gestures were personal and private. In this case, 'personal' was certainly a flexible term as Koizumi was accompanied to the site by dozens of other lawmakers and the whole event had been given substantial prior publicity, ensuring a crowd of onlookers and blanket media coverage.

The court cases brought against Koizumi drew on similar litigation against Prime Minister Nakasone, the last Japanese leader to visit the shrine in his official capacity. In 1992, the nation's three high courts in Tokyo, Sendai, and Osaka all found that Nakasone's official visit in 1985 had been unconstitutional, thereby making it problematic for subsequent prime ministers to follow in his footsteps. Thus it is only by a political sleight of hand – maintaining the fiction that the visits are private and personal – that his successors have been able to visit Yasukuni and so galvanize their core constituencies.

The politics of Yasukuni ensure that it will remain an important symbol of Japan's militaristic past. Nationalists bridle at suggestions of alternative sites to pay respect to the war dead precisely because the issue is not the souls of fallen soldiers. The issue of the shrine is about national pride and reviving a more glorious, unapologetic narrative of Japan's past. However, some commentators are seeking to examine more deeply the issues surrounding commemoration of Japan's war dead. Ienaga Saburo, a noted progressive historian who led the fight against reactionary distortions of the nation's history for more than four decades until his death in 2002, argued that while the souls of the fallen soldiers must be honored, it should not be by deifying them. In his view, Japan must ensure that the mistakes of the past are not repeated by exposing the crimes of leaders who sacrificed these soldiers as cheap cannon fodder for unworthy reasons; only then will the war dead be truly honored. By conflating the issues of nationalism, patriotism, and filial piety, those who support retaining Yasukuni as the de facto national war cemetery seek to defend an outmoded and reactionary national ideology. However, the whole issue may die a natural death. As Tamamoto (2001: 40) reminds us, 'Soon, Japanese old enough to remember the spirits enshrined at Yasukuni will fade away, and few are ready to inherit their care.'

Visits to Yasukuni by prominent politicians are driven by a volatile mix of fears and uncertainties. These fears stem partly from Japan's economic decline and China's rise as a world player, while politicians desperate for votes and campaign donations fear alienating conservative voters who have been a bedrock of support for the LDP. There is also a real fear of political extremists – men who are ready to kill for their beliefs, as the mayor of Nagasaki (wounded in 1990) and an *Asahi* reporter (killed in 1987) experienced to their cost. Nobody wants to risk offending the goons of the right, nor do the police zealously pursue them. By invoking atavistic symbols of nationalism aimed at reawakening pride in nation, politicians are responding to a sense of fading glory, growing insecurity, and a loss of faith in the government.[11] They are also seeking to rally the public and cultivate a sense of shared purpose that has all but disappeared during the Lost Decade. In such an atmosphere it is not surprising that people and politicians seek refuge in reassuring symbols and gestures of nationalism. However, the leap from visits to Yasukuni to militarism and regional expansionism made by some foreign commentators borders on hysteria and seems grounded on a racist distrust. These siren songs from the past sound more like a last gasp than a call to arms.

Reconciliation tango

Economic stagnation and prolonged recession have taken a toll on the nation, generating concerns that Japan may be losing its position of regional dominance. These troubles and uncertainties are stoking Japanese nationalism as people search for a reassuring identity. At the end of the 1980s, more than a few Japanese basked in the glory of their economic success and displayed a degree of *Schadenfreude* at what appeared to be a declining USA. The juggernaut of Japan, Inc. made dreams of a Pax Nipponica seem within reach. However, the bursting of Japan's asset bubble in the early 1990s drove home a sobering and unsettling reality. The consequences for postbubble

Japan have been stark, with most banks and construction companies surviving on a government-funded life-support system. Unemployment has skyrocketed and incomes have declined due to lower bonuses and reduced overtime. The social and economic norms that guided Japan in the postwar era have been rapidly undermined, along with the lives of many workers and their families who depended on this system. The security and certainty of lifetime employment and seniority wages are fading, while reports of pay cuts, layoffs and coerced early retirement make people edgy. Bleak scenarios for the future are the grist of weekly magazines and bestsellers – it is as if the Japanese are oddly drawn to their own impending demise, masochistic spectators voyeuristically enjoying their painful slide into oblivion. What will be next?

This domestic unease has been readily translated onto the international front. Japan has shuffled painfully into the twenty-first century, still trying to come to terms with an uncomfortable past. For every occasion on which a leader apologizes to Japan's neighbors for past misdeeds – and they have done so frequently and with conviction – there is always an embarrassing incident or bellowing nationalist politician ready to undo any goodwill generated. Whether it is a question of denying the Rape of Nanking or publishing textbooks that whitewash Japanese atrocities committed against fellow Asians, there is always a sense that Japan is still trying to evade responsibility for its wartime misdeeds while emphasizing the suffering endured by its own people. Given that its rampage through Asia claimed some 20 million lives, it is startling to other Asians that Japan continues to portray itself as victim, with little sustained recognition of its role as brutal victimizer. While the atomic bombings of Japan may well have been an unpardonable sin, in no way did they wipe out or sanctify Japan's own war record.

Despite the uplifted voices of the reactionaries, reports about Japan's collective amnesia concerning its invasion of Asia during the 1930s and 1940s are exaggerated, misleading, and outdated. Prominent Japanese scholars and pundits have written some of the best work on Japanese excesses and atrocities during the 1931–45 era and have reached a wide audience. Indeed, Western scholars of this era openly acknowledge their debt to their Japanese colleagues. Today there is no monolithic Japan, and this is especially so when one discusses the wartime era. Interpretation of the causes of the war, what actually happened during the war, and the aftermath raises divisive questions in contemporary Japan. There is vigorous debate about this period, active media coverage of the controversies, and a high level of awareness about opinions in other countries. In this atmosphere, where right-wing defenders of Imperial Japan are regularly taken to task by progressive critics in various public forums, it is hard to imagine how 'collective amnesia' can be taken seriously as an accurate characterization of prevailing realities. Just because some groups in society favor airbrushing the inconvenient and unappealing aspects of Japan's wartime record does not mean that this is a widely embraced point of view. The exculpatory junior-high-school textbook

(Roger Dahl)

approved by the Ministry of Education in 2001 was adopted by fewer than 1 percent of junior high schools, reflecting the good sense that prevails.

As much as Japan may deserve the scathing criticism hurled at it by its neighbors, the Koreas and China are not above using the memory of wartime excesses for diplomatic leverage. Nationalistic fervor runs high in East Asia, and singling out Japan is a strategy adopted for more than purely historical reasons, justified as they may be. Keeping Japan on the defensive about its past, and its failure to come to grips with its record in the present, has proved to be an effective diplomatic strategy. Indeed, Japan's large economic assistance programs in China are widely viewed outside official circles as a form of war reparations. It pays to keep pressure on Japan regarding the past in order to ensure that the spigots of aid, grants, loans, and investment guarantees are kept open.

Rhetoric aside, on the Korean peninsula and in China there is scant inclination to get over the past and move on to a relationship with Japan oriented towards the future. Such a stance would be politically unpopular in countries where admiration for Japan's achievements is exceeded only by a love of Japan-bashing. In addition, a defensive Japan has been unable to assert itself politically in the region, deferring to its neighbors and remaining reassuringly allied to, and constrained by, the USA. Much as China publicly bemoans the US–Japan bilateral alliance and security co-operation, the alternative of an independent Japan developing its own nuclear weapons and beefing up its defense forces is hardly more alluring. Thus, hectoring Japan about its lack of contrition for the past has proved an effective way to hamstring Japanese ambitions in the region and, at least in the case of China, extract a continued flow of quasi-reparations in the form of concessionary loans and grants.

Symbols that divide

In 1999, while the economy languished and various social issues demanded urgent attention, the government devoted a great deal of time and energy to legally ratifying the national flag and national anthem as official symbols of Japan. Despite the reported misgivings of a large segment of the public, the flag-and-anthem bill was hurriedly and overwhelmingly passed in the Diet. Although the Hinomaru flag, a white field with a red circle in the center, and the Kimigayo anthem have long been national symbols, the passage of a bill giving legal sanction to this status is significant in a nation still divided over its past. While the sun flag is a minor issue for most Japanese, many consider Kimigayo ('Your Majesty's Reign') a throwback to the era when the Emperor was an absolute monarch and, as such, incompatible with the postwar Constitution where the people have been transformed from subjects to citizens. Moreover, the song is an unabashed paean to the Emperor and a reminder of a painful time when Japan was waging war throughout Asia in his name. To the extent that the anthem is reminiscent of Japan's militaristic past, it is rejected by progressive groups who feel the nation has done too little to atone for the past. While passage of the bill in the Diet by an overwhelming majority is indicative of the dominance of conservative political forces, polls reveal less enthusiastic support among the public. Although at the time high-school teachers expressed concern that the new legislation would force them to raise the flag and sing the national anthem at school ceremonies, the furor over the issue has subsided. While schools have complied under pressure from the Ministry of Education, many liberal educators remain distrustful of nationalism and its symbols. Whereas in other nations this controversy might seem like much ado about nothing, in Japan these national symbols reflect the political faultlines that exist between progressive and conservative forces.

The strong desire to venerate national symbols is of course not unique to Japan and emulates the emphasis that other nations, especially the USA, place on such talismans. Although the flag-and-anthem legislation constituted a significant victory for nationalists, the consequences have been muted. While there is now official sanction for symbols that have long enjoyed de facto recognition, it does not seem that the public views this development as particularly sinister or threatening. At most, it is a barometer of the rising assertiveness of the right-wing elements within the ruling conservative coalition of forces that govern Japan. The tepid reaction of political opponents reflects both their loss of power and the prevailing public nonchalance about a controversy that no longer resonates powerfully. Thus, a move that would have triggered massive demonstrations in 1960, and probably toppled a government, is now taken in stride. While honoring their nation through a national flag and anthem is taken for granted everywhere else in the world, Japan's perceived failure to come clean about its past has tarnished these symbols in countries that were once at war with Imperial Japan. Within Japan, the tarnish remains for those concerned about the revival of militarism, rising chauvinism and continued rule by conservative forces embracing a reactionary agenda. The mass-market daily *Asahi* has been the most persistent arm of the media in expressing such concerns and keeping them in the public eye. However, most Japanese seem indifferent to the controversy, belying exaggerated reporting that the flag-and-anthem legislation reflects a rising tide of nationalism. Not all supporters of the legislation are rabid nationalists and for many this development is natural (*atarimae*) – the way things should be, and accepted as a proper display of respect, no more and no less.

World Cup 2002

> What the machinations of FIFA politics had done was to throw two nations that despised each other into the arena together, but this time on the same side.
>
> Fred Varcoe (*Japan Times*, May 16, 2002)

The co-hosting of the World Cup soccer finals in 2002 by South Korea and Japan was remarkable for a number of reasons. This was the first time that two nations had been designated as joint hosts of the tournament and, given frequently prickly bilateral relations, a surprising choice foisted upon the two reluctant collaborators by the organizing committee. Two nations that have argued angrily and endlessly about a shared past, and have experienced usually sullen and frosty relations as a consequence, were suddenly thrust into a situation demanding compromise and cooperation. It seemed as if the organizers had either a tin ear for history or a wickedly twisted sense of humor.

The co-hosting surprise provided an unanticipated chance for the two countries to overcome their historical animosities and build a basis for warmer relations. At present, both nations have little incentive to change as clinging to slanted histories plays well on both sides of the Straits of Tsushima. Japanese leaders have grown exasperated with what they view as Korea's fierce clinging to old wrongs, while Korean ire is provoked by Japan's seeming rush to bury an unexamined history, downplay if not deny crimes involving the comfort women, and willful neglect of Korean sensibilities over the Yasukuni Shrine visits and new school textbooks that gloss over the worst aspects of Japan's colonial rule on the Korean peninsula (1910–45).

Breaking out of this pattern of recrimination and distrust required a level of courage, statesmanship, and vision that has proved far too elusive for too long. In the end, it was the son of Emperor Showa who showed the way forward by gazing unflinchingly at the past and emphasizing fraternal ties as the basis for a more fruitful relationship. In his annual message delivered in December 2001, Emperor Akihito caused a muted stir by publicly acknowledging for the first time that the Japanese imperial line is descended from Korean forbears. By confirming what scholars have long known to the

Figure 9.6 Japan's victory over Russia in the soccer World Cup 2002 prompts wild
  street celebrations. (Photo: Stuart Issett)

Japanese public, Akihito was seeking to set the tone for an improvement in
bilateral relations and make a case against ethnic chauvinism; they are we.
Interestingly, out of the major newspapers, only the *Asahi* carried this part of
his message and many Japanese, caught up in the end-of-year celebrations,
were blissfully unaware that the Emperor had spoken of his dynasty's Korean
lineage. However, his frank admission earned him warm praise in the
Korean press and was taken as a long-awaited olive branch. (Aside from
Asahi subscribers, other readers in Japan must have been bemused by subsequent reports concerning Korean praise for Emperor Akihito, since they had
not been informed about the ancestry comments that were so welcome.)
Clearly, this gesture is in line with a series of initiatives by Emperor Akihito
to express sincere contrition about the past and promote reconciliation
between Japan and its regional victims. The lost decade of the 1990s was a
time when the Imperial Household, despite constitutional constraints,
demonstrated courageous leadership in tackling the unfinished business of
World War II that has impeded improvement in Japan's regional relations.
Akihito has stepped forward as assertively as possible, and helpfully, to
undo the accumulated harm of neglecting, denying, and minimizing past
wrongs committed during his father's reign. His efforts to put Japan's inglorious past behind it in a manner acceptable to past victims stands in contrast
to the inaction of hesitant bureaucrats and opportunistic politicians who
have failed miserably in coping with the contemporary repercussions of
past misdeeds.

Partly as a result of the monarchy's efforts (Prince Takamado, who died in November 2002, was also actively involved in tournament-related bilateral diplomacy), the World Cup turned out to be far more than soccer at its best. It was also a showcase for a sustained bilateral cooperation that suggests the potential for overcoming the animosities that have built up between the two countries. During 2002, prior to the tournament, both countries organized a series of cultural exchanges aimed at breaking down negative stereotypes; Japanese media coverage was extremely favorable and sympathetic towards Korea. The impasse in relations at the government level, arising from disputes over textbooks and Prime Minister Koizumi's provocative visits to the Yasukuni Shrine, stood in stark contrast to warm grassroots exchanges and a determined effort by the Japanese media to portray Koreans in a favorable light. While internet chat-rooms featured some of the more familiar chauvinism, they also demonstrated that young people in both countries are not necessarily prisoners of the past, locked into the animosities that have defined bilateral relations for more than a century.

Polls taken during the tournament itself suggested that Japanese perceptions of Koreans had improved. My own experience in informally polling students, and watching a game with a group of farmers, artisans, and craftsmen in rural Japan, who all vocally supported the Korean team, confirms this. After Korea's controversial victories over Spain and Italy, many Western commentators complained about questionable calls and match-fixing, but the Japanese I spoke to viewed this as little more than sour grapes and obviously took a pan-Asian pride in Korea's surprisingly good showing. Even though Korea's team advanced farther than the Japanese team, the Japanese were good sports about their neighbor's success and supported them to the end. It appears that this goodwill was not reciprocated in Korea, however, as fans there made a show of supporting Japan's opponents and cheering its setbacks.

Perhaps most remarkable were the displays of feelgood nationalism that swept over the archipelago during the tournament. People spoke of little else, media coverage was obsessive, and Japan's better-than-expected performance, advancing to the quarter finals, was enthusiastically appreciated by a nation that has not enjoyed much good news for a long time. Even the prime minister acknowledged that he had taken time out to watch a match during work hours, joining millions of new fans caught up in soccer fever. The nation would brook no criticism of its team. When on the eve of the tournament Tokyo's Governor Ishihara dismissed the Japanese team's French coach, Philippe Troussier, as a typical third-rate foreigner and lousy coach who was taking advantage of Japan, he was loudly denounced by the press for his comments. Troussier's excellent coaching effort was widely seen as crucial to Japan's vast improvement and solid performance in the tournament, and thus Ishihara's jingoism backfired, making him appear both churlish and clueless.

During Japan's game against Russia, one that certainly carried the burden of past wars and current tensions, I misjudged the length of the half-time break and was out walking my dogs when suddenly every house in a usually placid enclave erupted with the full-throated voices of ecstatic supporters; it was not hard to guess which team had scored in the opening minutes of the second half. Previously, when Japan had tied with Belgium, Roppongi's bars emptied into the streets, disrupting traffic and testing the patience of the assembled riot police with an impromptu display of pandemonium. These wild street celebrations by Japanese youth with *hinomaru* (red sun on white background) painted on their cheeks, screaming with unabashed and unrestrained enthusiasm for the national team, were an unanticipated outbreak of mass hysteria, a moment of feelgood nationalism when flag waving and loud *banzai*s erupted from a people long reluctant to voice such sentiments. Newscasters bubbled with enthusiasm and television stations repeatedly ran the highlight reels, stoking pride in a team whose moment of glory was eagerly embraced by a nation desperate for an escape from the relentlessly bleak economic news. June 2002 was a month of mania, a time when it appeared very few Japanese were not caught up in the hoopla. It was a moment of liberation from the burdensome past, from looking over the collective shoulder at the outside world, and a time to shed inhibitions and ambivalence and let it all hang out. A normally buttoned-down citizenry was basking in the reflected glory of their national team and savoring the precious moments. Office workers slacked off and turned on televisions at work; many showed up at the office wearing team colors, some sporting the ubiquitous cheek-flag paste-ons, others wearing celebratory *happi*-coats. There was a happy feeling of shared exuberance, pride, and community.

I have described these displays of nationalism at some length precisely because they would hardly merit a mention in most countries under similar circumstances. When Japanese people engage in the celebratory gestures and displays common in other nations, it is somehow different. It is different because such unguarded moments are rarely displayed for external consumption. While the world watched, while the global media carried images far and wide, Japanese eviscerated more than a few stereotypes in laughing, yelling, high-fiving and having fun. The meek, self-deprecating, stoic, and terminally reserved and conformist automatons imagined overseas suddenly came to life, sporting various shades of dyed hair, diverse fashions, and a bubbly zest. These effusive displays of nationalism were reassuringly rooted in a decidedly internationalist context, and were thus unthreatening and shorn of any darker connotations. The tournament provided a healthy and cathartic release for a nation where nationalism and patriotism have been conflated with militarism and associated with past excesses and atrocities. This new 'nationalism lite' seems light years away from the valley of darkness.

The thaw in relations between Korea and Japan peaked in the final game held in the Yokohama Stadium where President Kim Dae Jung was seated beside Emperor Akihito – a revealing sideshow to the main event between Brazil and Germany. This was an image pregnant with meaning and ironies, one that only ten years ago would have seemed highly improbable. The maverick leader of the Korean democracy movement, once abducted in Japan by KCIA agents intent on killing him, was now the honored guest of an Emperor committed to reconciliation and laying to rest the ghosts of the past. Those in Japan who most strongly support a revival of the imperial system – a motley collage of ultra-nationalists, mobsters, and political extremists occupying the far-right spectrum of conservative politics – are also those who are least willing to support this Emperor's agenda of reconciliation. Their symbol of reawakened nationalism has inconveniently distanced himself from their own agenda, and promoted a humanitarian and pacifist sense of nationhood predicated on assuming responsibility for the past, demonstrating contrition and reaching out to past enemies. Nothing could more effectively dash nostalgic yearnings for – or fears about – the 'glory days' of *hakko ichiu* (literally, eight corners of the world under one roof) when a 'sacred' war was waged to impose a Japanese empire.

Unfinished business

In considering the implications of a rising Japanese nostalgic nationalism, one in which divergent groups embrace disparate dreams but share a visceral pride in nation, it is important to understand both why other nations remain so vexed by such a prospect and why Japan has remained so obtuse to its neighbors' anxieties. Although Japan has changed considerably since 1945, the legacy of the wartime era still means that perceptions have not progressed very far beyond the 'land of the Rising Sun.' This phenomenon is rooted in a fundamental and unyielding ethnic distrust shared by those who suffered from Japan's imperial ambitions, and is fanned by a potent combination of complacency, apathy, and ignorance in Japan about such concerns. Japan is seen to be shirking the burden of its history to the extent that it continues to embrace a self-vindicating narrative that casts the nation as victim and relegates competing narratives to the margins.

As we have seen, other nations continue to berate Japan for its collective amnesia in order to keep Japan on the defensive and wring concessions and assistance from it. There is also a racist element in some quarters: the Japanese are held to be militaristic in character and will revert to form in due course. Moreover, the depredations of the Japanese are more graphically depicted and lamented than those perpetrated by its adversaries precisely because it was a race war and remains so even in its aftermath – now the battles are over, how is the war to be portrayed and analyzed?[12] The valorous narrative of the victors draws both implicitly and explicitly on the damning narrative of the dehumanized enemy. As a result, suspicions about Japan and its intentions remain high and explain why evident changes are belittled or ignored. In the immediate aftermath of September 11, 2001, the comparisons with Pearl Harbor that were invoked revealed just how powerfully this damning image has been seared into American perceptions of

Japan. Not a few Japanese were taken aback by this reflex comparison and the sentiments it evoked.

Why has Japan clung so tenaciously to a whitewashed version of its past and only belatedly recognized – and that tentatively and intermittently – its role as victimizer? Surely Japan would gain stature in the eyes of the world, and facilitate its own regional integration, if it came clean about its devastating wartime record and stopped caviling about details that make it look eager to evade responsibility. The reasons for continuing denial are various. For many Japanese, the vilification of Japan and ceaseless demands for apologies reflect a double standard; many countries have committed horrible crimes on an enormous scale that they minimize or ignore. For younger Japanese people, the burdens of history seem unfair and irrelevant: grandfather did those things and that is his problem. For many older Japanese, the exoneration of Emperor Showa provides a convenient cover: if the man in whose name a sacred war was waged was able to avoid responsibility, why should anyone else be held accountable? For pragmatic government officials, there is no pressing need to take official responsibility and the tab for compensation could prove very expensive. And as we have seen, there is also a practical reason for avoiding controversy over the past: confrontations with the ultra-nationalists can provoke violent retribution.

In the postwar era, the US alliance and access to US markets effectively insulated Japan from the demands of it neighbors and made regional reintegration a choice rather than an imperative. In contrast, war-ravaged Germany faced the Soviet menace to the east and had no alternative to a reintegrated future with Western Europe. Germany thus needed to facilitate reintegration and could only do so by paying the price that history exacted. For Japan, the stakes of regional integration have been lower. Under the auspices of the USA, Japan could pursue reintegration at its own pace and on its own terms. However, with the end of the Cold War and the rising threats in a more dangerous neighborhood, especially those emanating from North Korea, this approach is ripe for reconsideration. Moreover, the specter of China as the future regional hegemon and its role as the great frontier for Japanese business interests are raising the potential rewards of integration. Thus, like Germany, Japan may also find that the costs of ignoring the burdens of history are becoming too expensive while the benefits of reassuring past enemies prove a compelling spur to change.

Identity

Who are the Japanese? National self-absorption with this riveting question sells millions of books in Japan. The rise of nationalist sentiments and the artful manipulation of the symbols, language, and regalia of nation at the turn of the century all point to a battle over identity. The national identity crisis has been exacerbated by the economic malaise and revelations about persistent bungling, negligence, and malfeasance by the nation's bureaucrats and civil

Figure 9.7 Uyoku (ultra-nationalists) making a speech from a bus on a busy Tokyo thoroughfare. (Photo: Stuart Issett)

servants. While in the 1980s the Japanese basked in the glory of Ezra Vogel's 'Japan as Number 1,' and in 1990 could feel proud of their nation's economic vitality, by 2000 they could only dwell on their nation's rapid decline. The economy having fallen so far so fast, it is understandable that the public mood is so gloomy. During the Lost Decade, Japanese also confronted the nation's 'secret' past and found much to be ashamed of. In response to the pervasive gloom and the damning history being uncovered, reactionaries have attempted to orchestrate a state-oriented national identity. They have done so by publishing hundreds of books and comic books that are aimed at cultivating a mass constituency in support of their agenda of restoring pride in nation. They have tapped into a deep-rooted sense of victimization among Japanese, conveying a sense that 'we' are embattled, isolated and belittled both within and without. They are waging a battle to wipe away the stains on the 'purity' of the nation that have unfairly besmirched it since 1945.

Perhaps, in constructing a glorious historical narrative, they may help the Japanese feel a little better about themselves and enjoy, for a change, the sense of being a victim of foreign perfidies. But will this vindicating history translate into a swaggering patriotic zeal for state-directed nationalism? It seems almost comical to imagine that the beleaguered Japanese public could be hoodwinked into fanatical support for the state that couldn't shoot straight. The lowly shenanigans of the nation's political and bureaucratic leaders and their responsibility for the nation's debacle are not lost upon the Japanese people. Legal sanction for the flag and anthem may please some conservatives, and pass with flying colors in the Diet, but in the country at large it has been received with all the excitement of a collective ho-hum. There is an air of desperation to the campaigns for reviving cultural nationalism waged by Japan's reactionaries that conveys their own sense of futility. As time marches on, they are realizing that they are ever more marginal and less influential. They are winning symbolic battles, but few hearts and minds. The diminishing power and prestige of the state, and the dubious image of the more extreme nationalists, suggests little cause for alarm that Japanese are seeking to fill the void of identity by assuming the mantle of patriotism. People may love their nation, but see little reason to sacrifice more than they must for a state that has lost so much of its credibility. The public is not awaiting some charismatic leader with a risky plan that departs too sharply from existing policies; there is greater comfort with incremental change and inertia. The emergence of civil society, fueled by skepticism towards the state, provides further reassurance.

Conclusion

Nationalism in Japan is no more, or less, dangerous than in other technologically advanced industrialized nations with significant military power and the capacity to develop weapons of mass destruction. However, both the Left in Japan and critics overseas remain anxious that a more assertive nationalism is emerging. As support for pacifism recedes and pro-nationalist taboos are cast aside, some observers perceive a danger that the ruling elite might gain enough confidence and power to take Japan down a more dangerous and threatening road.

The US State Department was sufficiently concerned about the portents of Japanese nationalism to sponsor a symposium on the subject held in Kyoto in October 2002. However, media reports indicate that the participants did not see much of a threat in Japan catching a dose of virulent nationalism, and historian John Dower was quoted as saying that the rise of US nationalism was probably a greater cause for concern.

Although the signs of renascent nationalism in Japan are certainly troubling, there is a risk of exaggerating their significance. Regrettable as Koizumi's visits to Yasukuni Shrine may be, it is folly to assume that they signal a consensus in Japanese society about how to honor the war dead, support for the war criminals enshrined there, or that they betoken an unqualified embrace of the ultra-nationalists' agenda. The nationalistic whitewashing of history in a government-approved textbook, lamentable as it may be, must be balanced against its nearly universal rejection by school boards all over the country. And are bad films vindicating Japan's wartime efforts truly a matter for concern? When former Prime Minister Mori Yoshiro evoked wartime memories in the summer of 2000 by referring to Japan as a 'land of the gods,' he was widely repudiated and depicted in the media as a buffoon.

The great majority of Japanese people do not identify with extreme nation-alism and do not want to become involved in overseas conflicts, nor do they wish to lend credence to imperial ambitions. Despite the increasingly asser-tive nationalism evident among political and opinion leaders in Japan, the mass of the population does not subscribe to their views, or the logical conse-quences thereof. Militant nationalism has reverberated in contemporary Japan with the silence of one hand clapping. There is no support at all for foreign adventurism, as the people and their leaders across the spectrum prefer to do the bare minimum required of Japan on the international stage, and then often in a grudging manner. On the international front, Japan remains a reactive and tentative state, one that does not seek to lead and is unwilling to assume the burdens and responsibilities that go with leadership. Unlike the situation in the 1930s, Japan is now one of the status quo powers that has more to risk than gain from projecting its military power into a wary region bristling with modern weapons systems. The dominant US military presence in Japan and its surrounding seas is also an important and decisive constraint.

It is further reassuring that the Right in Japan is not a monolithic entity with a uniform agenda. Japan boasts a dazzling array of conservative groups and they are deeply divided over many issues. At the apex of the Right is the LDP, an umbrella organization that encompasses a variety of often feuding political factions drawing on diverse constituencies for support. Assuming that they have a common set of goals and agreed means to achieve them requires a vivid imagination. Indeed, the LDP is often in disarray over the need to balance the competing and conflicting agendas among its supporters and constituencies. As an umbrella organization it represents a spectrum of conservative interests ranging from corporate lobby groups to the ultra-right-wing, and maintains ties with organizations as various as the mob, the War-Bereaved Veterans Association, doctors' lobbyists, and Shinto Shrine associ-ations. While some conservatives favor dismantling the Peace Constitution and becoming a 'normal' nation with commensurate military abilities and proclivities, others cling to Article 9; some bristle under the US alliance while others extol its virtues. Thus, the prospects of right-wing forces in Japan making common cause appear remote. Just as the US theater of politics pushes Republicans to make gestures aimed at mollifying fundamentalist Christian supporters without realizing their entire political agenda, the LDP is also motivated and constrained by the demands of its constituents and need to galvanize its support base and keep the campaign funds flowing. It would thus be a mistake to assume that the mass of Japanese, or even their conserva-tive leaders, actually identify with, much less support, extreme nationalism. The *uyoku* (ultra-right-wing) sound trucks are blithely ignored by passers-by and the police, no mean feat given the deafening sound levels emanating from their speakers and the traffic-impeding size of their bus corteges.

Another way to look at this phenomenon is to remember that the contexts in which taboos have been observed and later shrugged off has changed considerably. Leftists who cut their teeth on politics during the heady days of the 1960s and 1970s are naturally perturbed by the apathy and insouciance of the younger generation. To this aging group of progressives, the current dominance of conservatives and the virtual eradication of left-wing political influence has been a bitter pill. It seems that all that they fought for has been lost and they are just as appalled by the legalization of the flag and anthem, Yasukuni visits, the infamous textbook, Prime Minister Mori's mutterings about a divine nation, growing military cooperation with the USA, and other signs of a refulgent nationalism as are foreign critics. They have invested such issues with a talismanic significance that no longer resonates among Japanese people. This does not mean that their concerns are no longer relevant, but rather that people no longer get terribly excited about gestures and rhetoric that once defined the key political faultlines of society. This does not mean, however, that people are embracing the right nor that they are hopelessly naïve in their apathy.

One can argue that civil society in contemporary Japan is far stronger than it was in the days of violent political confrontation in the early 1970s and that, as a result, the constraints on conservative leaders are no less effective. This is a cumulative consequence of the sustained struggle by progressive forces in Japan that have labored, with some notable successes, to address the inglorious past and challenge various conservative initiatives. Japanese youth are not as apathetic as some critics suggest, as their volunteer activities in the aftermath of the Kobe earthquake bear witness. Citizen groups and NPOs are tapping into this energy and idealism and making civil society a reality. There is far greater transparency in government now than at any time in the past, and a broad spectrum of people motivated to hold the government accountable for its actions. While the ruling elite can still ride roughshod over its opponents and critics, it is now more heavily constrained by the costs of such actions. And while conservatives still hold most of the trump cards, they remain beholden to political realities. When the Defense Agency was caught snooping on citizens exercising their right to information disclosure, the resulting furor handcuffed the government and revealed just how robust civil society has become in Japan. While old taboos may no longer hold much sway, that does not mean that they have disappeared entirely and there are no obstacles to a revived nationalism. Rather than manning the barricades, citizens, NPOs, and the media are applying the rule of law, participating in and influencing open public debates, and exercising their rights to counter government excesses. In such initiatives, they are gaining support from a public that is increasingly skeptical and suspicious of those who govern. The declining legitimacy of the government and the lingering allergy to bellicose nationalism are reassuring signs that the radical fringe will not be able, as they did in the past, to hijack the nation and impose their own marching orders.

It is also well to bear in mind that, just as the Right in Japan is divided and fragmented, nationalist sentiments and gestures carry quite different meanings and resonate in various ways among contemporary Japanese. There is no monolithic NATIONALISM to excite alarm, there is no consensus on what it signifies and what it entails, and it does not carry a unifying meaning that mobilizes disparate groups in society to act in unison. The flag-waving football fan basking in national glory, like the vast majority of Japanese, has little in common with the thugs in the buses. There are nationalists of different stripes and hues, reflecting the diversity that exists in contemporary Japan. There are nostalgic nationalists, feelgood nationalists, hardcore *banzai* nationalists, recession nationalists, anti-globalization nationalists, anti-American nationalists, opportunistic nationalists, left-wing nationalists, reactionary nationalists, fashionable nationalists – the varieties are endless. The fact that, in the twenty-first century, they are all less reticent about expressing their particular brand of nationalism is less a matter for concern than a sign that the 'postwar era,' along with its sensibilities, patterns and taboos, is drawing to a close.

10 Social transformations

Family, gender, aging,
and work

The old and rigid order – symbolized by seniority, lifetime employment, and
omnipresent bureaucratic control – is to be replaced by a more liberal, open,
fluid, thus harsher order. A Japan that abandons long-cherished notions of
harmony and predictability is in the making.
Tamamoto Masaru, *World Policy Journal* (fall 2001): 33

You could file criminal charges against your husband for domestic violence
but the court is not likely to hear your case unless, of course, you were to die.
Judge's comments to a woman submitting a
medical report on her injuries. *Asahi*, May 27, 2002

We have patrols in various parts of the city. We have lots to do these days.
Tokyo is not as safe as people think and there is a lot more theft and violence
these days. Young people set houses on fire just for fun. Even in daytime
people are robbed at knifepoint.
Guardian Angel, Kichijoji (western Tokyo suburbs), November 2002

Japan conjures up images of stable families, dedicated workers, paternal employers, traditional gender roles, social harmony, and respect for the aged.
These images linger despite sweeping changes that are transforming Japanese
society. A nexus of powerful trends involving family, gender, aging, and
work is shaping and driving fundamental social transformations in the emerging Japan. This chapter examines a number of significant and interrelated social changes – innovations in the structure of work and the family, the
changing roles of women, demographic changes including the growing needs
of the elderly, the impact of divorce, suicide – and argues that they constitute
the birth-pangs of a new society that is struggling into the light of day. They
are signs that the patriarchal and authoritarian rules of Japan are no longer
adequate to maintain a viable social order, and the nation ignores them at its
peril.

In the postwar era, many Japanese people came to enjoy a relatively high
degree of security and stability that is now in the process of unraveling. The
twin pillars of this fixed social order have been work and the family;
however, beginning in the 1990s, both have become less secure and less

stable. A confluence of transitions is creating a riptide that is eroding the foundations of these pillars with alarming rapidity. The graying of the nation – Japan's demographic time-bomb – is generating significant pressures for change in policies affecting women, the family, and the employment system. This is forcing reconsideration of gender roles and stirring debate about how to help families balance the demands of work and home. In this transition era, the gap between prevailing social realities and existing policies, values, and patterns is adversely affecting the family. People are increasingly challenging the patriarchal biases that are limiting women's careers, lowering the birth rate and shortchanging society. These streams of social change are merging with broader currents of reform. Both the public and private sectors, with increasing input from citizen groups, are seeking to reinvent Japan and create a society more in tune with the needs and aspirations of its people. The consequences of such fundamental changes, and the anxieties that accompany them, are everywhere evident in contemporary Japan and are further evidence that tectonic shifts are underway as the nation stumbles into the twenty-first century.

Nowhere is Japan's contemporary crisis more apparent than in the labor sector. The country's nearly four million unemployed, some 6 percent of the workforce, know just how insecure jobs have become and how poorly prepared the government is to handle their problems. Work just isn't what it used to be: the three most prominent features of Japan's employment paradigm – lifetime employment, seniority wages, and enterprise unions – are fading away while the breadwinner model, based on the notion that the husband provides for his family's needs, is giving way to two-income families, which account for some 60 percent of all households. The relatively privileged core labor force is shrinking as firms pressure older workers into early retirement and impose wage and benefit cuts on many who remain. Firms are hiring less secure and lower-paid temporary or part-time workers to slash labor outlays and avoid costly, long-term employment commitments. As a result, the government is having to cope with the decline of what was in effect a corporate-sponsored welfare system (*kigyo chushinshugi*). Now that workers are being laid off, companies downsized, and factories shut down or shifted overseas, unemployment has risen massively and the government is faced with problems never experienced during the prolonged era of employment stability. The proliferation of non-standard work arrangements (part-time, temporary, and contract jobs) – constituting nearly 25 percent of the workforce as of 2002 – has serious implications for pensions, unionization, tax revenues, and social welfare policies designed for regular employees.

Looming over these immediate problems are the medium- and long-term implications of stark workforce demographics: Japan's low birth rate means a rapidly aging society, more pensioners depending on fewer worker contributions, and an impending labor shortage. These projected changes resonate throughout the industrialized world and carry implications both for the family and for the whole structure of society. Given these circumstances, there is a perceived need to boost women's participation in the workforce and to develop policies that will make this viable and rewarding for them and their families. In addition, projected labor shortages will generate increasing pressures to permit more immigration – a potential force for revitalizing the economy, but one with risks for dividing society.

This demographic time-bomb presents Japan with a number of policy challenges and is serving as a catalyst for social transformation. The scale of Japan's aging problem underscores the failure of past policies regarding the family and women, and the urgency of reform. An extensive overhaul of policies in areas such as taxation, medical care, pensions, work, and family leave is already underway and the resulting reforms will have significant consequences for the quality of life, the state of the economy, and the government's credibility. Here, it is argued, as fare women so goes the future of Japan.

Yet women are being asked to shoulder the burden of increased participation in the workforce at the very time when changes to traditional workplace practices have made them most vulnerable. The family is being buffeted from all sides by rapid changes and growing strains in the social fabric that highlight the unrealistically high demands and expectations imposed by the government, employers, and the prevailing ideology. These pressures are taking a toll that falls most heavily on women and their children. The prevalence of domestic violence, divorce, juvenile delinquency, suicide, and alienation are some of the disturbing signs of the times.

Hidden scourge

The incidence of child and spousal abuse has exploded in Japan since the mid-1990s, with reported cases for fiscal 2001 reaching 18,804, up 60 percent from the previous year. This is the second year in a row that the number of reported cases rose by 60 percent, reflecting both the growing scale of the problem and a greater willingness on the part of friends, neighbors, teachers, and doctors to do something about it. In 1990, for comparison, only 1,101 cases were reported. Yet reported cases represent only the tip of the iceberg because many victims are reluctant to involve the authorities in what is viewed as a family matter. This reflects not only the fear of social stigma, but also the lack of adequate counseling facilities. Japanese people have been forced to confront the uncomfortable reality that what they had long regarded as exceptional is in fact an everyday reality for many children and their abusers. With a numbing frequency in recent years, heartrending tales of child abuse have raised public awareness and led the government to pass the Child Abuse Prevention Law (2000). It would be a hard-hearted person who could read the story of a young boy bound, beaten, verbally abused, burned with cigarettes, and left to starve to death – in a case involving both parents and grandparents – and not decide that something should be done to stop this hidden scourge.

Publicity of this kind is creating the conditions for social change. The belief that 'family problems are best dealt with in the family' is fading under the sustained pressure of activist groups and heightened media scrutiny. Japanese society is slowly and painfully emerging from a long period of denial. Bullying of students, corporal punishment, neglect, and suspicious deaths, along with spousal, child, and sexual abuse, have all been swept under the national *tatami* mat – taboo subjects that could not be openly discussed until recent years. In 1989 Japanese television aired a CBS *60 Minutes* segment about child abuse in the USA. At the conclusion of the program the Japanese television commentators looked aghast, shaking their heads in disbelief and expressing relief that Japan did not have such problems. Such attitudes of wishful thinking and denial are fading. Now people cannot avoid looking into the mirror held up by the media, and have been collectively horrified by a social problem that is far worse than most people had imagined.

Proactive measures are being taken to confront the problem. It appears that there has been both an actual increase in child abuse, linked to rising unemployment and other economic problems experienced during the 1990s, and higher levels of reporting. The new child-abuse legislation makes reporting mandatory for teachers, physicians, and social workers, which will boost the statistics still further. In addition, starting in 2000, the government is obliged to include all abuse consultations in its statistics on child abuse in addition to those cases in which the child welfare center takes action. The shift from denial and 'privatization' of domestic abuse to mandatory government involvement has been astoundingly rapid. The challenge now is to match the state's legislative initiative and heightened public awareness with sufficient resources for overburdened child welfare offices; many victims are given too little information and there are too few staff to provide adequate counseling and assistance. Nara prefecture, for example, has only one child welfare official per 132,900 people, the lowest rate in Japan, whereas Aomori leads the nation with one official per 26,900 people – an indication of the scale of additional resources needed everywhere to tackle the problem. Child-support advocates also argue that government authorities must go beyond identifying and punishing offenders by working with NGOs, support groups and other activist organizations to improve systems to help both victims and their abusers to re-establish their lives.[1]

Some commentators link the increase in child abuse with social changes affecting women; they argue that today's young mothers face more stress in raising children because they more frequently shoulder the burden alone – especially in urban areas, where three-generation households are increasingly rare. Living in crowded isolation in large anonymous housing complexes, many young mothers are overwhelmed by their responsibilities and lack access to community or family support. Public care facilities are limited for infants and preschool children, and especially so for mothers who are not working. In addition, many parents may have been treated harshly as children and in turn subject their own children to the patterns of discipline and punishment that they grew up with. Social norms are changing in Japan, as elsewhere, and what once passed as acceptable may now be dubbed abusive. As contemporary American attitudes towards children's welfare are transmitted through films, television programs, and news stories, Japanese people have become more aware of what passes international muster and what must be judged excessive and abusive.

Violence against women is also gaining more attention and government authorities are taking legislative initiative to criminalize such behavior and give women legal recourse and protection.[2] In 2000 the Prime Minister's Office reported that some 20 percent of married women were beaten by their husbands and nearly one-quarter of those were victims of life-threatening violence.[3] About 40 percent of these victims of domestic violence never discussed their experience with anyone. About half also reported that they had been sexually molested in the past, while 7 percent had been raped. Also in 2000, an anti-stalking law was passed while a new law on protection of crime victims eliminated the statute of limitations on reporting rape. More significantly, legislation passed in 2001, the Law for the Prevention of Spousal Violence and the Protection of Victims, created a system for preventing and dealing with the consequences of domestic violence and includes provision for courts to impose restraining orders. The courts can force perpetrators to vacate premises (for two weeks) and refrain from approaching spouses (for six months) under certain conditions. Failure to comply with the court order can lead to imprisonment for up to one year and fines of up to ¥1 million. The law applies to all couples living together regardless of marital status, an important provision that reflects both changing social realities and values and the government's willingness to acknowledge them. Beginning in 2002, the government is providing funding for shelters for abuse victims and appears committed to continuing expenditure in this area.

While these legal reforms have been achieved principally as a result of pressure from advocacy groups, other social factors have also conspired to bring about change. The media has played a critical role in uncovering cases of abuse and giving a voice to victims and their supporters. Social advocacy groups have also welcomed the increase in women applying for the bar exam in recent years, arguing that more female legal professionals are necessary for the law to become an effective tool for preventing and redressing violence against women.[4] Thus, it is not just the legal framework that needs to be changed. It is widely believed that Japan's male-dominated legal system implicitly, and in some cases explicitly, favors patriarchal privileges; women seeking protection or recourse in domestic violence cases can only be reassured by the increasing numbers of women lawyers, prosecutors, and judges.

While the new domestic violence law may be revised to allow victims direct access to the courts, there is a widespread perception that the gender-biased attitudes of the police and court officials involved in abuse cases significantly influence the effectiveness of the legislation. Konishi Takako (2001) recounts a story in which a court mediator trying to talk a woman out of divorce asked, 'But there were no problems other than the beatings, right?'

The popular weekly magazines delight in showing how the consciousness of legal professionals, mostly men, remains antediluvian on issues of domestic violence. According to the Japan Federation of Bar Associations, the courts routinely privilege men over women and judges regularly betray their bias in comments such as: 'Men can't win in a verbal argument so they naturally tend to respond with violence,' or 'If you say something like that, anyone would want to punch you.'[5] Judges are also disinclined to believe that highly educated men with high-status jobs could be guilty of domestic violence. This tendency to associate domestic violence with the working class is yet another form of denial and bias that obscures the extent of the problem and inhibits effective responses. In many instances, women suffer degrading treatment from the police, lawyers, mediators, and judges involved in their cases. They are often confronted with comments such as: 'You are willing to divorce over such a trivial matter because you have a job,' or 'It is your responsibility to keep your husband from resorting to violence,' and 'It is natural for a husband to use a little more violence on his wife. Be more tolerant.'

Divorce

Rapidly rising divorce rates are another indicator of sweeping social change and the need for continuing adjustments to social policy. The divorce rate has been rising dramatically in recent years and in 2002 stood at 23 percent of all marriages, tying Japan with Germany at fourth place in global rankings. (The USA leads the world with a divorce rate of 41 percent.) Japan's contemporary divorce rates are nearly triple those reported in the early 1960s, and the 264,255 divorces recorded in 2000 represent a 33 percent jump from 1995. Although divorce is clearly becoming more common, there is no consensus as to why this is so. In the past, women endured bad marriages out of necessity since few earned enough to be economically independent and alimony was relatively rare, seldom compulsory, and generally insufficient. In addition, the social stigma attached to divorced women, and the probability of losing child custody, dissuaded many women from taking this route. These days working women are more financially independent and, at least in urban areas, no longer face enough social stigma, or care enough about it, to endure an unhappy marriage. In addition, as families have decreased in size and many women are only children, they have the option of falling back on their parents' resources.

Aside from these economic factors, it is clear that divorce is a much more acceptable option than it used to be. It is no longer universally condemned in magazines, television programs, and advice columns, which are beginning to convey positive images of divorcees and are contributing to society's grudging acceptance of divorce. It is now seen as a part of the fabric of life and something to be lamented and analyzed rather than an excuse for ostracizing the victims. In cities, neighbors are no longer scandalized by the divorcee next door, and even in more conservative rural areas divorce is increasingly accepted as a fact of life. Moreover, tolerance of male philandering and domestic violence is fading and such actions are no longer seen as a woman's cross to bear.

The reasons for Japan's rising divorce rates are keenly debated. Some conservative commentators suggest that young people have been spoiled and no longer have the social skills, patience, and mental toughness to cope with the ups and downs of married life. At the extreme is the 'Narita divorce syndrome,' a reference to new couples ending their marriage upon returning from their overseas honeymoon to Tokyo's international airport. Offsetting this perspective is the reality that older couples have some of the highest divorce rates. Older, retired husbands are frequently referred to as *sodaigomi* (large garbage that gets in the way) or compared to *nureochiba* (sticky wet leaves that are hard to brush off), indicating among other things a decline in respect for patriarchal values. When their husbands retire, wives are faced with spending a great deal of time with a demanding partner with whom they might never have developed a close relationship, someone who inconveniently imposes on their private time and space. As a result of long working hours and work-related obligations, couples can become estranged over the years and wives harbor accumulating resentments over loveless marriages, loneliness, and being left with the lion's share of child-rearing and household duties. It is not uncommon in Japan for husbands and wives to socialize separately and it is almost considered bad form to say kind things about one's partner. Older men will often bellow 'Oi, ocha' (Hey, tea) or demand in a peremptory manner some other service from their partner as their due. Wives who have grown accustomed to their spouse's long working hours and having the home to themselves openly admit that they dread weekends when their husbands are around and have to be taken care of; many welcome their disappearance for a day of golf or fishing. The sudden imposition of a retired husband is thus a trying experience for wives and more of these couples are splitting. If the kids are finished with schooling, and family resources are sufficient, increasing numbers of older wives are cutting their losses by dumping their men.[6]

The spike in divorces since the mid-1990s also appears related to the economic downturn. Media reports suggest that more middle-aged couples are calling it quits after husbands lose their jobs and cannot cover family expenses. In fact, the highest divorce rates are for couples who have been together for four to ten years. Some of the racy weekly magazines emphasize the selfishness of spoiled young women who abandon the relationship at the first sign of trouble. But the media wants to have it both ways and these women are also portrayed with some sympathy as rebelling against intolerable domestic servitude.[7] They are depicted as both silent victims and shrill despots who lord it over henpecked husbands and threaten divorce to get their way.

The prevalence of divorce is making it a more acceptable option for unhappy couples. However, the personal, social, and financial costs of divorce are as high in Japan as they are elsewhere in the world. Children have to deal with the consequences and have few emotional resources to help them cope with the emotional trauma involved. Despite the reduced social stigma, many children are reluctant to openly discuss their situation and have little access to counseling.

The costs of divorce are especially high for women. Single mothers have the highest incidence of poverty in Japan. Enforcement of alimony payments is sporadic, levels are insufficient, and inadequate informal settlements are common. Responding to this situation, in 2003 the Justice Ministry introduced a system aimed at forcing 'deadbeat dads' to pay assigned child support. The courts can now ensure child-support payments by garnishing the salary of the former spouse; these automatic payments from monthly salaries take precedence over deductions for any other purpose. Nevertheless, single mothers still face financial duress. Employment options are limited for many divorced mothers and poorly paid work, often on a part-time basis, ensures low incomes. The government has belatedly recognized the needs of the increasing numbers of struggling single mothers but, while it scrambles to create an adequate safety net and provide needed social services, many families are suffering the consequences of poverty in a nation that prefers to turn a blind eye to it. Moreover, the social stigma attached to welfare makes it difficult for single mothers to seek out the assistance that is available. Thus, the divided families bobbing in the wake of divorce face a host of difficulties that more and more Japanese will experience as the twenty-first century advances.

The larger social and financial implications of rising divorce rates are enormous, mainly because the policies and practices adopted by both government and employers have been predicated on a stable family structure. For example, care of the elderly almost always depends on a significant contribution by the family and is usually undertaken by wives. In the new situation, who will take responsibility for a divorced man's ailing parents? Who will care for childless divorcees? Employers have also assumed the presence of a stable home situation to support their regular male workforce. Indeed, as male employees reach their thirties it is expected that they will marry and settle down; a system of allowances and seniority-related salary increases is geared to meeting the increasing financial demands of raising a family. Corporate warriors have been able to work long hours and devote themselves to the firm because they have relied on the support of their wives to take care of household responsibilities, including child care and care of aging parents. For men, divorce entails assuming some of these household responsibilities and undercuts a single-minded devotion to work. The growing instability of the family thus threatens both the existing employment system and the attitudes towards the family that are intrinsic to it.

It is also clear that standard corporate practices involving the sacrifice of private and family life for the good of the company have contributed to the break-up of the family. The practice (known as *tanshinfunin*) of transferring husbands to branch offices while the mother and children remain in their home town places enormous pressure on marriages. Monthly visits are no substitute for a shared life. The gender division of labor is reinforced by the practice of sending the father away from the home where he can offer no assistance in child rearing or other household responsibilities. This practice also fails to recognize the growing prevalence of two-income families, and disadvantages working mothers for the benefit of their husband's company.

As in many other areas of Japanese society, the structure of work illustrates the widening chasm between prevailing practices and attitudes based on outdated assumptions, on the one hand, and emerging realities on the other. The challenge to be faced lies in finding ways to modify some of the key assumptions intrinsic to Japan, Inc. Under this system it has always been assumed that family life would have to accommodate to the dictates of a husband's job. This includes not only the work itself, but also obligatory long hours, after-work drinking and gambling sessions, weekend golf and hot-spring get-togethers, distant job transfers, and frequent business trips. Absentee husbands are par for the course. However, the costs of this system are painfully evident and have had a deleterious impact on the family.

As a response to daunting demographic challenges, Japanese policy-makers are wrestling with innovative programs and working arrangements designed to tailor the demands of work to family life – a reversal of priorities that reflects the seriousness of the situation. But if it is no longer desirable to treat families as an adjunct to work, it is also difficult to expect a sudden shift by corporate Japan, given how well the system has worked for employers in the past. The flexible, family-friendly policies needed to integrate women – who already shoulder multiple roles as wives, mothers, and care-givers – into the labor force are a world away from prevailing practices. In a time of prolonged recession it is unlikely that employers will shift their focus from the immediate bottom line and look closely at the larger, long-term implications of their employment practices. Japanese employers have adopted the flexibility of non-standard working arrangements primarily in order to save on wages and benefits – not as a means of reforming the relation between family and work. This is a failure of vision that Japan can ill afford.

Suicide

A further indication of turmoil within the system is the fact that Japan has one of the highest suicide rates in the industrialized world. Yet, as recently as 1994 Japan ranked 19th in the global suicide table and was on a par with Western European countries. At the turn of the century, 25.4 Japanese per 100,000 population commit suicide compared to 15.8 in Germany, 12 in the USA and 7.4 in Great Britain. Trends in suicide in Japan correlate with economic cycles; the recent surge in suicides is the third since World War II. In 2002, an average of 8 people a day took their own lives and since 1998 an average of some 30,000 people per annum have committed suicide, triple the toll from traffic fatalities and up 50 percent from the roughly 20,000 Japanese who killed themselves in 1990.[8] The most recent spike is concentrated among middle-aged men and has been attributed to depression caused by work-related stress and financial problems; nearly 75 percent of suicides involve men over 40.

Business restructuring has stirred anxieties at all levels: among those dismissed, those who remain and are pressured to produce more, and those involved in implementing the downsizing. The compact between employers and employees – in which job security was promised in return for loyalty to the company – is unraveling and this is generating high levels of stress among those who have risen through the ranks and are now at the peak of their careers. Management is abandoning lifetime employment and paternalism, generating new tensions between managers and those they supervise. Middle-aged employees who have been expecting to collect on their seniority now face uncertain prospects and feel a sense of betrayal. They are also weighed down by family responsibilities and stressed by the prospect of being unable to fulfill them. Unwanted workers are lost souls who feel not only betrayal, but also a sense of shame that they have failed. There is a widely reported phenomenon of sham workers – men pretending to go to work, leaving home and returning at the usual times, unable to bear the shame of disclosing their plight to families and neighbors. Their sense of self-esteem plummets in a society where hard work is a deeply ingrained value and people often identify themselves by reference to their employer: 'I am Honda's Tanaka.' Workers who lose their jobs also lose their identity and social orientation, something especially stressful in a society where belonging to a group is a core cultural value. The sharp decline in stock and land values also means that many workers approaching retirement (or facing retrenchment) have lost their nest eggs and must repay loans that exceed the value of their homes. Thus, for a whole variety of reasons, distressed middle-aged men find themselves staring into the abyss with no prospects and limited emotional resources.

Suicide in Japan has reached epidemic proportions. There is a forest near Mount Fuji infamous for large numbers of suicides, where the government has now placed signs aimed at dissuading those who are at the end of their tether. Many suicides are committed as a way of collecting on life insurance policies and so making a final contribution to solving family financial problems. Leading life insurance companies have responded by extending the nonpayment period from one year to as many as three years to discourage troubled breadwinners from making the ultimate sacrifice at their expense. In 2000, the National Police Agency reported that one-third of suicide victims left notes citing their economic woes. This report also noted that unemployed people were responsible for 47 percent of all suicides in 1999, accounting for 15,467 deaths.[9]

Japan's suicide epidemic reflects a general problem in dealing with depression. Seeking treatment for depression is still relatively rare and is considered a sign of weakness, especially among men. In addition, people undergoing mental health care incur a stigma that can harm their careers or even their children's marriage prospects. Suicide, on the other hand, is sometimes portrayed in Japanese culture as a noble and pure gesture, one steeped in samurai tradition that appeals to those with an ingrained sense of duty and obligation.[10] In 2001, the railway company JR East established a hotline in response to the surge in suicides on its tracks in the Tokyo region. There were 228 such deaths in 1998, up from 191 in 1997 and triple the total for 1987. In the first six months of 1999 an additional 125 took the plunge. These suicides cause serious delays on Tokyo's crowded transport network and families are charged large sums for the inconvenience; many jumpers favor lines charging lower fines out of consideration for their relatives.[11]

Japan's National Health Care system is partly to blame for the failure to come to grips with depression as a serious disease, as patients are funneled through local health clinics where doctors are either untrained or in some cases unwilling to diagnose the illness. Awareness of depression as a mental disorder is low in Japan and symptoms are often interpreted as malingering or evidence of a bad attitude. Very few patients receive counseling or appropriate drug therapies, while extreme cases are often institutionalized, with the attendant stigma, for excessive periods in facilities where therapy is rudimentary.[12] Thus, those who need counseling face obstacles in seeing clinical psychologists and are far too often left to their own devices, sometimes with tragic results.

This sorry state of affairs is beginning to change as both business and the government come to grips with the related phenomenon of *karoshi*, death from overwork. Family survivors are using the courts to seek redress from companies that they allege have overworked their relatives and thus sent them to an early grave. The suicide of a young Dentsu (Japan's largest advertising agency) worker caught national attention in 2000 when Japan's Supreme Court found the firm liable for his suicide in 1991 at the age of twenty-four. He had worked seventeen months without a day off, often well into the evenings, and his superiors were aware of his deteriorating health. Throughout the 1990s the media covered such cases of *karoshi* extensively, raising awareness of the problem and generating pressure on the government and companies to address the issue. This constituted a dramatic change from the prevailing work ethos in the postwar era, when employees were expected to sacrifice everything for their company and to *gaman* (tough it out) even when exhausted. This ideology inculcated a distinct set of values among many workers who regarded the ability to handle hard work, long hours, and lengthy commutes as a sign of masculinity.

However, unreciprocated loyalty has taken a toll on this corporate-centered ideology and led many Japanese to openly question such damaging work practices. In 1999 the Ministry of Health and Welfare revised its guidelines to permit compensation for work-related suicides, a move that is forcing firms to think more seriously and sympathetically about overwork and stress among employees – since they will have to compensate families and endure the resulting public opprobrium.[13] Subsequently, in 2001 the government relaxed the criteria used to define *karoshi*, leading to a rise in reported cases qualifying for compensation.[14]

Although the consequences of suicide on families are poorly understood, in 2002 it was estimated that nearly 120,000 young Japanese were trying to cope with the loss of a parent, usually their father. Given the stigma attached to suicide, it is difficult for those affected to discuss their loss and confide openly in friends or counselors. Ironically, the blame for suicide is often pinned on the legendary reluctance of middle-aged males to communicate emotional distress – a tragedy that leaves their surviving family members similarly constrained.

Troubled youth

The excesses of Japan's youth culture are widely covered in the mass media and predictably deplored by those who look at today's rainbow-haired youth and see a bleak future. Its grimmer manifestations include a proliferation of youth crime, delinquency, truancy, promiscuity, prostitution, sexually trans-mitted diseases, and the phenomenon of *hikikomori* ('withdrawal' – an esti-mated 500,000 to 1 million young men, and some women, rarely venture outside their bedrooms). However, it is apparent that today's troubled adoles-cents are not only contributing to Japan's social malaise, but their behavior is also a reflection of the welter of problems afflicting the family.

Young people seem to be poorly served by, and many are alienated from, the nation's crisis-ridden educational system (McVeigh 2002). The media regularly carry reports about violence, suicide, bullying, *gakkyo hokai* (class-room collapse, where teachers lose control of their students), and *toko kyohi* (school refusal, where students vote with their feet). Although educational reform has long been on the national agenda, this catalogue of troubles indi-cates just how little progress has been achieved. McVeigh (2002: 3) regards the prospects for meaningful reform as remote: 'There is a dark spirit plaguing the Japanese university classroom. It is the ghost of opinions suppressed, voices lost, self-expressions discouraged, and individuality restrained. The ghost is malevolent, and in its vengeance demands silence, self-censorship, and indifference from the students it haunts.' The problems of Japan's intellectually impoverishing education system are deeply embedded in existing social structures; they have been generally impervious to reform because the process has been co-opted by those who stand to lose most from an overhaul of the system. The numbing process of socialization that passes for education in Japan seems programmed to churn out disci-plined workers and listless and apathetic citizens. However, there are count-less exceptions who manage to overcome the shortcomings of their education, and it appears that they are finding more support and social space than in the past. Clearly, Japan needs such people more than ever.

Today's youth are very much the victims of Japan's current crisis and the social vacuum it has created. All that the postwar generation has striven to create seems to be in shambles, ruined by an imploding economy that, after all, was its raison d'être. If the economic miracle has been the source of Japan, Inc.'s legitimacy, and the Income Doubling Plan of the 1960s its clarion call, the collapse of the economy in the 1990s heralded the search for a new calling. Certainly, the generation that made Japan's rapid postwar recovery possible has much to be proud of, in particular a level of income equality and accumulated social capital that are the envy of other advanced industrial societies. However, such a pedestal makes an uncomfortable vantage-point for witnessing the loss of so much that has been synonymous with Japan, Inc., and scant comfort as the older generation looks towards retirement. Few aspiring pensioners feel confident that today's youth will be willing to shoulder the burdens of Japan's rapidly aging society. Young people are often described by their elders as 'aliens,' and the contrast between the stolid gray-suited salarymen reading their newspapers on the trains and the casually dressed, blond-haired, pierced, ear-phone wearing, *keitai* (cellular phone)-packing young has never been so vivid.

Of course such impressions are based on appearances only, and it is far from certain that today's 'rebel without a cause' will remain shiftless and alienated, shunning what has passed for success in postwar Japan – a stable job with a big company and a cramped house 90 minutes from the office maintained by an accomplished housewife bearing one or two children. After all, we have all seen how today's wild child becomes tomorrow's downtrodden conformist. Indeed, the prospect of the predictable, inescapable, and relentlessly stultifying life of the salaryman may well explain the displays and excesses of youth – a last gasp and groan before assuming the burdens of adult life. But then again, having grown up in isolated suburbs with absentee fathers and unhappy mothers, it is understandable, even encouraging, that contemporary Japanese youth do not seem to be plodding the well tramped paths to 'success' and the My Home Dream that inspired their parents' generation. Indeed, they have witnessed the betrayal of the social contract by corporate Japan and the costs of unswerving loyalty and devotion to the firm. It does not look like much of a life, and certainly not one to make sacrifices to emulate. Youth have little faith in the system and declining expectations for enjoying the stable employment conditions taken for granted until recently by many older Japanese. It is a less paternalistic, more competitive world of work that awaits today's young Japanese.

As much as elders look with dismay and undisguised loathing (and some disguised envy) at the exuberant lifestyles of contemporary youth, there are encouraging signs. More than one half of Japanese people now continue their education past high school and nearly all youngsters have acquired at least some internet savvy by virtue of *keitai*, the one accessory that all teenagers must own, if only to avoid social ostracism. Thus, compared to their middle-aged, *nasakenai* (clueless) fathers, many of whom depend on secretaries to make copies and send faxes – and hope they can retire before having to acquire computer skills – young Japanese are entering the labor market with considerably less technophobia.[15] Impatient, impetuous, informal, seeking personal fulfillment, and part of a far more cosmopolitan world than their parents knew, today's youth seem ill-suited for the rigidities and conformity of Japan, Inc. They will shape tomorrow's Japan and hopefully make it more appealing than the world their parents left behind.

However, even if we discount the conventional despair of parents over the new generation, there are clearly some less reassuring trends on the youth front. Violence is on the rise and a sensationalizing media has done nothing to diminish concerns about its prevalence. The surge in youth crime is one of the more alarming social developments of recent years and a number of particularly heinous and well-publicized cases have triggered public alarm. Not only are more of Japan's youth committing crimes, more are also becoming victims. Although this plague of delinquency is poorly understood, it is often attributed to violence on television and in computer games, domestic violence, divorce, economic woes, and declining social and communication skills. Elders lament that kids don't seem to know right from wrong – or do not care about the distinction. Bewildered families look to the authorities for solutions, while educators complain that too much of their time and energy is occupied by disciplinary problems, with too little to spare for teaching. Commentators point out that the loss of community bonds in large anonymous cities and suburbs creates a breeding ground for trouble, and that the popular media offers plenty of negative models for youth to emulate. Dysfunctional families, a breakdown in intergenerational communication and a permissive social environment are also seen to contribute to the problem.[16]

In addition to the litany of lesser delinquent acts such as stealing bicycles, sniffing paint thinner, or loudly revving motorcycles late at night on main thoroughfares, contemporary youth are beset by an array of more serious problems. Drug use is far higher than can be comfortably acknowledged: amphetamines are cheap and readily available, while designer drugs are an established feature of the club scene. Mugging and even killing for money is far more frequent now than in the past, and there have been numerous violent attacks on homeless men. Malicious acts of arson have increased dramatically while vandalism is common. Middle-aged men have been frequent targets of roaming gangs, often at train stations, sometimes for money, revenge for an imagined insult, or even just for sport. The currency of the term *oyajigari* (hunting of middle-aged men) for this particular form of violence indicates the extent to which it has become a problem. The government has responded by urging educators to place more stress on patriotism and respect for tradition – but such gestures offer little reassurance and reflect a stunning poverty of imagination.

Crimes such as these have always been part of the underbelly of Japanese life – Oshima Nagisa's 1960 film *Cruel Story of Youth* portrayed a society

Figure 10.1 Light My Fire: Alienated youth complain they live in a world without dreams. (Photo: Nara Yoshitomo/Koyama Gallery)

where young men use their girlfriends as sexual bait to entice middle-aged men, who are then beaten and blackmailed. The film presents a Japan where adultery, abortion, and predatory gangs are commonplace. While the pathology has not changed all that much, what was once simply shocking has become shockingly quotidian.

What is different in Japan in the twenty-first century are the worsened job prospects for youth and the unraveling of the reassuring myths that sustained Japan, Inc. in the recent past. Estimates of teenage unemployment range from 15 percent to 20 percent, meaning that contemporary youth are feeling the pinch more sharply than other age cohorts. Gone are the days when high-school graduates could choose between job offers and many could look forward to lifetime employment and a steady rise through the ranks. The jobs they once commanded are being taken over by college graduates, sacrificed to automation or downsizing, or exported overseas to places where labor costs are a fraction of what they are in Japan. The jobs on offer pay poorly and are usually part-time or temporary positions with scant prospects for promotion. Workers who skip from one part-time job to another have given rise to the term 'freeters' ('free arbeiters'), a romanticized concept conjuring up images of freedom and rejection of the rat race – images that mask the poverty, desperation, and dismal prospects that are the reality of freeters. They may have thumbed their noses at society, but at a price that takes its toll in alienation, self-esteem, and hardship.

The bleak prospects of contemporary youth are finding a mirror in art. Nara Michi, the leading turn-of-the-century pop artist in Japan, has a huge cult following among young Japanese. He explains that his often forlorn, cartoon-like figures resonate so powerfully among today's alienated youth because they see a reflection of their own pain and so feel less isolated.[17] The anomie he depicts draws on his own suffering as a teenager and captures the funk of the times. Nara is an inspiration to youth because, although he refused to play by the rules, he has still come out on top.

Generation Slump, as the youth of the recession-plagued 1990s are known, evinces little of the loyalty and dedication to their jobs that was once taken for granted. Growing up in the shadow of unrelieved gloom, they have emerged disillusioned with the practices, attitudes, and inclina-tions of Japan, Inc. A system that delivered rapid growth and prosperity for their elders is now seen as one stuck in the quagmire and widely discredited because the sacrifices of workers for their companies has been rewarded with betrayal. The layoffs, downsizing, pay cuts, and pressures to take early retirement imposed on their fathers, coupled with high-profile cases of corporate sleaze and incompetence, have undermined faith in the system. Younger Japanese are often criticized by their elders for being more indi-vidualistic, less willing to sacrifice their private lives and eager to get what they can as soon as they can under an increasingly merit-based pay system, but this is a logical response to the sundering of the social contract by corpo-rate Japan. The labor system is shifting away from lifetime employment to lifetime employability and from seniority-based promotions and wages to one relying more on performance. Employees are responding accordingly and in doing so are casting off attitudes and inclinations that have typified work relationships for much of the latter half of the twentieth century. Looking at how their parents' generation was stiffed by the system, it would be surprising if they were not more individualistic and looking out for them-selves. The rigidities of employment and lifestyles characteristic of that system no longer match the aspirations of, nor inspire dreams among, today's more curious and diverse Japanese.

Sexploitation

Another sign of Japan's ongoing social crisis is the growth of the sex industry and its increasing impact on the young. Recognizing this, in 1999 the government belatedly passed a law banning child prostitution and child pornography. The ban on sexual abuse of minors makes it a criminal offense for anyone in Japan, or any Japanese traveling overseas, to pay for sex with children under eighteen. The law also bans the production, distribution, and sale of pornographic materials featuring children. This legislative initiative was in part a response to Japan's allegedly leading role as a producer of internet child porn (80 percent by some estimates) and also represents an effort to discourage sex tourism. The law further targets the rise in *enjo kosai* (prostitution involving junior- and high-school girls) facilitated by *keitai*-based services and networks.[18]

However, it seems that the law is having little deterrent effect due to permissive attitudes towards pornography and sexual exploitation and the massive size of the sex industry. 'Soaplands,' a euphemism for brothels, can be found even in small rural towns, and red-light districts are common throughout Japan. Phone booths near urban train stations are often festooned with graphic ads for sexual services, and mailbox inserts offering videos, massages, and more leave little to the imagination. As a result of the economic downturn, students, dropouts, the unemployed, indebted *ols* (office ladies), and housewives have all joined the sex industry in droves. In this unpromising context, it is hard to be optimistic about the prospects for reform. As the *Japan Times* put it in a recent editorial:

> By inclination and tradition, most Japanese tend to view sexual exploitation of women and children as a benign evil. Even though prostitution has long been illegal, the proliferation of 'fuzoku' [the Japanese word for 'public custom,' but it is best read as 'sex'] business involving young and increasingly younger women is evident everywhere. ... It is up to the public to pressure the government to continue the campaign and to change its own attitude. After all, child prostitution and pornography are not just a matter of unsavory international reputation; they reflect the values of our own society.[19]

Parasite singles

Young unmarried working people remaining at home with their parents have been dubbed 'parasite singles.' This group, some ten million strong, delay or avoid family formation and are thus held to contribute to the declining birth rate. In addition, by refusing to set up their own homes and feeding off their parents' resources, they are blamed for depressing consumption and contributing to the recession. Among other 'sins,' these 'parasites' are also credited with eroding individual vitality, motivation, and the work ethic for reasons that remain unclear. They have become popular scapegoats for what ails Japan.

Why are young people continuing to live with their parents instead of jumping the nest? According to Yamada Masahiro, a sociologist who coined the term 'parasite singles' in 1999, the prospect of a significant decline in the quality of life is the main reason why children are staying at home well into their thirties. Calculating the costs of rent, and finding that affordable apartments are cramped, inconveniently located, and not 'serviced' by mothers, many young people opt to stay put. Postponing marriage and children is also motivated by the anticipation of lifestyle sacrifices and a lower living standard. Young women in particular balk at the sacrifices involved in becoming a wife and mother, including giving up their careers or, if they continue to work full-time, consigning themselves to a stressful existence that compares unfavorably with life as an indulged daughter. More permissive social attitudes also mean that they can enjoy casual relationships without the hassles of marriage. Thus, Yamada emphasizes that young people are staying put for the fun and the money.

Yamada's catchy phrase has caught the public attention in part because it appeals to many people who believe that modern women are failing to live up to their responsibilities as bearers of babies. This fits with the mass-media image of young women dashing off to European cities for shopping sprees in fashionable boutiques, dining at gourmet restaurants, and staying at ritzy hotels. Living at home and paying no rent, these women symbolize a 'gorgeous' lifestyle that is relentlessly promoted, analyzed, lampooned, and criticized by the media. Naturally, there has been a popular backlash motivated by envy and resentment – this audience finds the 'parasite single' analysis very appealing. By linking their choice of living arrangements with social problems such as the low birth rate and a sluggish economy, Yamada has struck a chord. The concept of parasite singles is rooted in 'proper' gender roles whereby women are expected to leave their own family for their husband's, and sons are expected to carry on the family line. Thus, the homebound son is in some way fulfilling his duty while the daughter is avoiding hers. This helps explain why single working men receive much less criticism in the media than their female counterparts – the real 'parasites' are all those self-indulgent young women who are putting off marriage and child-bearing.

The parasite singles argument is flawed in another way, too: there is no explanation of why living at home has suddenly become a barrier to family formation. It has long been common in Japan for children to remain at home until marriage, and there is no evidence that this practice resulted in low birth rates and delayed marriages in the past. Why is this now the case? It appears that Yamada has confused a consequence for the cause: it is more plausible to account for young people's choice to remain home in terms of their deteriorating economic circumstances. Young working women face continued job discrimination, which has worsened since the recession-hit 1990s, meaning that relatively few land well-paid, stable career jobs. For men, the 1990s has also been a difficult time as firms cut back on hiring and now prefer to hire part-time and temporary workers who cost less and lack employment security. More young people are staying at home not because they are selfish, but rather because alternatives are too expensive and job prospects are ever more uncertain. Moreover, if they do eventually want to get married and have children, living at home is a sensible way to accumulate the necessary resources, something that is more difficult to do in an era when incomes are declining. Some stay-at-homes may indeed be motivated by the desire for a glitzy lifestyle, but we should beware confusing media hype with mundane realities. Perhaps the situation is a sign that family relationships are not as tattered as one might assume from reading the news.

Ironically, for much of the postwar era staying at home was considered a proper demonstration of filial piety worthy of praise rather than condemnation. In Ozu Yasujiro's classic film treatment of the changing family, *Tokyo Story* (1953), the dutiful daughter worked in a local school and lived at home with her parents, while her less dutiful siblings ran off to the big city in search of a better life. In those days, the selfish ones were the migrants who left families behind and forgot their filial duties. Large corporations also commonly required their young women employees to live with their parents, implying that those who lived outside the family home prior to marriage were somehow undesirable and potentially a risk to the firm's reputation. Now women who work and live with their parents have become scapegoats for what ails society and the economy.

Challenging patriarchy

The status of women is another fiercely contested arena of public life in Japan. One of the battles of the sexes is being fought over whether or not women should have a legal right to retain their maiden name after marriage. Reformists argue that changing names is a time-consuming process and creates problems for women with existing professional and work identities.

In Japan the requirement for a married couple to share a single family name dates back to 1870, one of the many changes set in motion by the Meiji Restoration in 1868. Until that time, ordinary citizens were banned from using family names, although informally some families ignored this stricture. From 1870 the use of family names was legitimized and in 1871 the lineal family (Japanese *ie*) was established as the unit of registration for taxation purposes. As a result, related families, even if they lived separately, were registered under the name of one *ie*. The *ie* as the basis of the patriarchal family system was later enshrined in the Civil Code in 1898. It was also at this time that the eldest male in a family line was vested with a number of exclusive rights, including primogeniture, the right to approve marriages, and the right to decide the place of residence of married family members. The Civil Code required that a wife enter the *ie* of her husband, register in his *koseki* (official family register), and bear his family's name. Under the law, wives had no legal rights over family matters such as property. Marriage was by legal consent of the fathers of the prospective bride and groom, and the wife was absorbed into the husband's *ie* through marriage.

Naturally, not all couples followed the law and, especially in cases where permission to marry was denied, elopements and common-law marriages often resulted. Marriage was also more flexible in the late nineteenth century, with a high incidence of remarriage after the death of a spouse or divorce; in the 1880s the divorce rate per 1,000 people was approximately 3 compared to a contemporary level of 1.9.

The patriarchal *ie* system was overhauled by the postwar Constitution, enacted in 1946. The family head's right to approve marriages was eliminated and marriage became based on the principle of mutual consent. The Civil Code of 1947 stipulated that a married couple can choose either the husband's or wife's name with which to register the *ie* and maintain a *koseki*. This reform also recentered the *ie* on the nuclear family rather than the lineal system. Despite the option to choose either name, virtually all marriages in Japan are registered under the husband's name, reflecting the strength of even recently crafted 'traditions' and the persistence of patriarchal inclinations.

While surveys indicate a majority in favor of retaining premarital surnames, resistance in the LDP-dominated ruling coalition remains strong. Although recent efforts to table legislation have failed, it is clear that the government recognizes that social norms are changing. Some 27 million women work outside the home and many regard the mandatory name change as disruptive to their careers. Moreover, it is discriminatory since men do not face the same inconvenience: in 97 percent of all marriages it is women who change their names. Opponents argue that separate surnames would generate social turmoil and undermine family solidarity. However, the fact that one in every three new marriages ends in divorce suggests that family solidarity is already fragile and is not a problem that can be ascribed to separate surnames.

The name-change debate reflects wider changes in gender roles and relations. Advocates for reform point to the growing trend towards equality as the basis for marriage partnerships and growing acceptance of diverse living arrangements. Traditional marital relations were based on the husband working and the wife remaining at home, but this no longer reflects the changing reality of contemporary Japan. With more wives pursuing careers and developing professional identities, retaining the maiden name has become more important and practical. In recognition of this reality, both private firms and government offices have been allowing married women to use their maiden names in the workplace. However, in the absence of legal backing for separate surnames, women are experiencing problems in obtaining official documents such as identification cards, passports, drivers' licenses, and credit cards under their maiden name.[20]

The controversy over names is a microcosm of the larger debate and tensions in society caused by the changing roles of women. The fact that this issue has generated considerable political and media debate and resulted in draft legislation makes it a barometer of the times. The opposition of the LDP's old guard to legislation has been conducted in the face of majority public support and in opposition to the central government, whose bureaucracy effectively sanctions use of maiden names in the workplace in the interests of achieving a gender-equality society. Although this government goal remains distant, and progress in eradicating discrimination and harassment has been glacial, issues that were not long ago dismissed out of hand are now on the agenda. Pragmatic self-interest is compelling Japan, incrementally and fitfully, to move closer to the egalitarian ideal. Society is coming to take women's rights and grievances more seriously and the battle over names is part of the struggle to counter patriarchal bias. Since the government and people both think this is important, eventually politicians will come around.

There are other signs of a sea change in attitudes towards women that reflect a growing respect. In 1999 the government passed a law banning sexual harassment and in the same year the courts ruled against a major political figure for harassing one of his female campaign staff. 'Knock' Yokoyama, the once-popular comedian and ex-governor of Osaka, was hit with a large fine for sexually molesting a young woman working in his election campaign, and convicted of indecent assault. Public disapproval of his conduct forced him to resign from office in disgrace. Until recent years, prominent figures could expect suppression of such stories and to weather such controversies if they became public. Certainly there is no shortage of media stories about women who have suffered for trying to expose the predatory actions of co-workers and bosses, and surveys indicate that sexual harassment is disturbingly common. However, more men are facing censure and punishment for such behavior and they can no longer count on escaping responsibility. The implications of the Yokoyama case are likely to be far-reaching, sending a strong signal that the courts (and public opinion) will no longer tolerate the 'wink and nod' approach to dealing with abuses of women's rights, even if it involves powerful men. This may encourage more women to seek legal remedies and discourage men from risking their fortunes, reputations and careers by such behavior. As Japanese companies have learned from their operations in the USA, sexual discrimination in all forms is far too costly to tolerate. This is a lesson that Japanese courts are beginning to teach at home.

The new attitudes towards women have caused stirrings in the highest echelons of Japanese society. The birth of Princess Aiko in 2001 has spurred debate about the possibility of a woman succeeding to the Imperial throne. She is thus far the only offspring of the Crown Prince and, if no male sibling is born, would be in line to become Japan's ninth reigning empress. In order for this to occur, however, the Imperial Household Law would have to be amended to permit female succession. Since the enactment of the 1889 Imperial Household Law, women have been formally barred from succession, a situation that seems out of step with the Constitutional guarantee of equality for men and women. Clearly politicians are hoping for a male heir to avoid grappling with this thorny issue. However, surveys indicate that nearly 70 percent of the public has no qualms about the prospect of a princess ascending the throne. Should she do so, it would further erode some of the barriers against women and bring Japan in line with monarchies in Europe that have amended their laws to enable the eldest child of a sovereign to succeed to the crown, regardless of sex. Thus, by the middle of the twenty-first century, the nation's leading family may be in a position to set an example for society and reinforce women's rising status.

As in the West, the struggle to control fertility and reproduction is proving a key part of the women's movement. In 1999 the Ministry of Health and Welfare approved use of the birth-control pill for women, bringing an end to a campaign by women's rights organizations that had stretched over more than three decades. The government had withheld approval of the Pill since the 1960s on the grounds that its usage might promote promiscuity and an erosion of traditional feminine roles. The medical community also opposed the Pill, citing concerns about the effects on women's health and doubts about its safety. In addition, it is alleged that many doctors opposed introduction of the Pill as they derived substantial unreported income from performing abortions.[21] The lack of a reliable form of contraception – condoms and the rhythm method have been the most widely used methods – has led to many unplanned pregnancies. As a result, many women in Japan have resorted to abortions, with estimates running at 2 million per annum from the mid-1950s to the mid-1960s and remaining (by some estimates) at between 750,000 to 1.5 million per annum through the 1990s (Norgren 2001). Earlier government approval of the Pill was quashed when the rising threat of AIDS and other sexually transmitted diseases led to concerns that it would lead to a rise in unsafe sex. Feminists however allege that the ban on the Pill reflected male domination of politics and society. Some argue that concerns about Japan's declining birth rate also made bureaucrats reluctant to give women more control over their fertility.

The government's decision to approve the Pill is widely linked to its speedy approval of the anti-impotence drug Viagra, also in 1999. In this case, the government's acceptance of foreign drug trial studies undermined its earlier objections to the Pill based on the alleged need for further trials and the unreliability of foreign research findings. The fast-track approval for Viagra made the government's stance on the Pill increasingly untenable, opening it to a barrage of criticism over double standards. Despite the approval it had gained, few experts expect the Pill to be widely used because of publicity about adverse side effects. However, proponents argue that the main point of the campaign was to give families and women the right to make decisions about their reproductive life free from government interference and patriarchal prejudice.

As women have increasingly shrugged off ascribed gender roles, they have issued a challenge to a patriarchal society, especially to older males who are reluctant to lose their prerogatives. Over time there has been a slow unraveling of the patriarchal system and the attitudes, patterns, and practices that have sustained it. Although some women find fulfillment within traditional roles, a growing number are choosing to break the mold. The popular stereotype of meek, submissive Japanese women has long obscured the reality of their lives, status, experiences, and perspectives, and, at the advent of the twenty-first century, is no more than a condescending caricature. Recent opinion polls of women indicate that they do not feel particularly fulfilled nor consider that they are treated as equals in society or within the family. However, most agree that their lives are much better than those of their mothers and grandmothers and there is scant sentiment to return to darker days when young brides were at the mercy of the men and older women in the family. More importantly, more and more women are carving out roles in the economy and society that are not consistent with traditional ideals. They are also urging their daughters to be more independent.

The tension between lingering attitudes and the changing reality of women in Japan animates the debate on gender. Gender-relations is an area where Japan has made disappointingly little progress in eliminating discrimination. Society as a whole pays for this neglect because it perpetuates a situation where women's potential is far too often squandered as a result of outmoded patriarchal practices. As elsewhere, women want equal treatment, respect, and freedom from harassment, assault, and discrimination. They also desire a society free from constraints based on gender and one that provides support for the multiple roles they are taking on as wives, mothers, workers, and nurses for the elderly. For all that, women remain the fulcrum of the family and, despite the tremendous social transformation already experienced in Japan, they have helped maintain a degree of family stability that is the envy of other industrialized nations.

On strike

For various reasons, women are on strike, bearing fewer children and shying away from marriage. From a high point of 4.3 babies in 1947, the birth rate has dropped to 1.32 children per woman in 2002. This is well below replacement level and, in the absence of large-scale immigration, will lead to a shrinking population. This ongoing decline in the birth rate is certainly linked to the decision of more women to postpone marriage or to forgo it altogether.[22] Changes in the patterns of marriage and childbearing in Japan are ascribed to a number of recent social changes: an increase in women's participation in the labor force, rising women's educational attainment, increasingly attractive single lifestyles, reluctance to accept less opulent lifestyles owing to marriage, and a yawning gap between the sexes in attitudes to marriage and gender roles. Women's greater economic independence reduces their attraction to marriage and is effectively allowing increasing numbers of women to buy out of this option. Raymo (1998) suggests that the proportion of women who never marry will continue to increase. As of 1999, 54 percent

NEWS ITEM: JAPAN'S BIRTHRATE HITS ALL-TIME LOW

(Roger Dahl)

of women in their late twenties have never married, while 20 percent in their thirties have also remained single. As a result of the increasing numbers of women delaying or evading marriage, their average age at marriage has risen from 25.6 in 1970 to 27.9 in 1999. The percentage of unmarried men and women in the 35–39 age cohort rose from 6.1 percent and 5.3 percent respectively in 1975, to 22.6 percent and 10 percent in 1995. While the huge rise in the proportion of unmarried men is remarkable in itself, in terms of our discussion the doubling in the numbers of women withdrawing from the marriage market in the space of two decades carries enormous implications for the birth rate. In 2002, NHK reported that in the previous decade the percentage of unmarried women in their thirties had nearly doubled from 12 percent to 23 percent, a rising trend that looks set to continue. Given how few children are born out of wedlock in Japan, the surge in non-marriage suggests continuing declines in the birth rate and raises questions about the provision of care for these singles in their old age.

Women are on strike because they have found the costs of marriage and child-rearing to be unacceptably high, usually with negative impacts on their careers and lives. In 2003 the Cabinet Office reported that the projected lifetime loss of income for a typical working woman who quits her job to give birth amounts to a staggering ¥85 million, even if she later returns to work. Since raising a child through university is conservatively estimated to cost some ¥25–30 million, the high price of parenting constitutes a significant disincentive. This stark projection of lost income is significant, since two-thirds of Japanese women quit their jobs upon giving birth to their first child and shift their energies to taking on most of the child-rearing work. This happens because the labor market is structured in ways that discourage women's participation and also reflects problems in accessing childcare services. Overall, only about one out of four women with children under the age of three continues working. The rigidities of the employment system make it difficult for mothers to remain employed full-time and help explain why 40 percent of working women do so on a part-time basis and why so few become managers. The key point is that once women quit their jobs to raise children, most are effectively banned from good jobs thereafter. They are usually shunted onto the part-time, dead-end track of low-paying, insecure jobs. However, with divorce rates rising, the growing reliance of families on two incomes, and rising job insecurity for husbands, women are reconsidering whether they can afford to interrupt their paid employment and devote themselves full-time to child-rearing responsibilities.

Despite these pressures for change, attitudes toward women's 'proper' roles in society remain deeply ingrained and patriarchic.[23] Having babies means accepting significantly restricted freedom and much heavier household burdens. There are also strong social expectations that mothers will take care of their children until at least the age of three, meaning that they are expected to shelve their careers for this period. Effectively, this terminates many of their careers. Thus, it is not merely a problem of corporate or government policies, although these reflect and powerfully reinforce ascribed gender roles. It remains true that most of the unpaid work at home is done by women whether or not they are working. It is estimated that on average men spend 36 minutes a day on housework, while working women average nearly 4 hours on top of their commuting and jobs. Some 70 percent of surveyed men report that they never prepare meals or do washing. This imbalance at home makes it especially onerous for women to work full-time and helps explain why so many withdraw from working after giving birth. The general unwillingness of husbands to participate in domestic duties also helps explain why so many women are leery of marriage – and have simply gone on strike.

Childcare

The scarcity, inflexibility, and cost of childcare contribute to Japan's low birth rate, posing a hurdle that discourages some couples from having a family. While parents seem satisfied with the quality of public childcare services, there is not enough to go around. In some areas there are long waiting lists, while working mothers often complain that the drop-off and pick-up times are difficult to manage. Competition for places is so strong in some municipalities that couples plan their births to coincide with optimum times during the year for registering their babies for childcare. As of 2001, only 23 percent of children under the age of six are enrolled in public daycare facilities, and this low figure is one of the reasons why only 11.2 percent of housewives have full-time jobs. While private childcare options are available, they are relatively expensive.

The government has responded to this birth crisis by adopting a number of new policy initiatives aimed at improving access to childcare, encouraging firms to grant unpaid childcare leave to employees and paying a subsidy to workers who take up this leave. However, despite the good intentions of the

Childcare Leave Law (1991), the uptake among employees has been disappointing, especially among fathers. In response, as of 2003 the government is requiring local government offices and firms with more than 300 employees to draw up concrete action plans aimed at achieving participation targets of 80 percent for women and 10 percent for men. As of 2002, less than 0.5 percent of fathers are opting to take the leave to which they are legally entitled up until the child's first birthday, compared to 56.4 percent of women in enterprises with over five employees. A government allowance drawn from the unemployment insurance fund equivalent to about 40 percent of regular salary is payable when the leave is taken; leave-takers receive 30 percent of their usual pay during the leave period, and a 10 percent lump sum on returning to work. Under provisions of the law, firms are prohibited from dismissing employees applying for or taking the leave, and employees with children under six years of age are not required to work after 10 pm. A revision enacted in 2002 prohibits disadvantageous treatment of leave-takers and creates a new sick-leave system allowing parents to take care of ill children under the age of six, although this is not mandatory.

Compared to Europe, Japan provides very little support for child rearing. Exemptions for dependents and various forms of support for childcare amount to only 2 percent of a typical Japanese household's annual income, compared to an average of 10 percent in Europe. In addition, the Japanese system requires families taking childcare leave to forgo a significant portion of their income; this seems to be a major factor in limiting the number of parents taking advantage of the leave scheme and, by extension, depressing the birth rate. Not only do couples lose 70 percent of one of their incomes for the duration of the leave, they also forgo that wage earner's bonus payments and any overtime income. Advocates of more generous childcare-leave policies point to other countries that have focused on minimizing the loss of parental income and making leaves more flexible and shared. In Norway, for example, after a child's birth the parents are entitled to 42 weeks' leave at full pay or 52 weeks at 80 percent pay, divided as they wish.[24] In order to be eligible for this program, fathers are required to take at least four weeks of the paid leave. This stipulation has succeeded in boosting fathers' participation in the scheme from 4 percent prior to 1993, when it was imposed, to a level in 2003 of 80 percent.

A recent government initiative, dubbed Plus One (2002), focuses on shortening working hours and making firms partners in promoting childcare leave. This plan explicitly aims to improve parents' quality of life and adjust employment practices to fit more comfortably into the rhythms of family life. While the government had previously focused on establishing more childcare facilities under the auspices of its Angel Plan (1994), it has now opted to emphasize family-focused pronatal policies. Given the low rate of male participation in childcare-leave schemes, the 10 percent target set by the program for fathers' participation seems ambitious. According to government surveys, men fail to take up their childcare leave because they are too busy, cannot afford the reduction in income and often face unsympathetic employers. They are also worried about failing to get coveted promotions or losing their jobs through restructuring. Since men generally earn more than women, families trying to minimize their loss of income tend to favor the mother taking the leave. In addition, conventional notions of gender-role divisions remain strong among young couples raised in an environment where childcare has usually been considered the responsibility of women.

Because traditional attitudes about gender roles remain strong, male employees take childcare leave at some risk to their careers. Despite the need for fathers to shoulder increasing childcare responsibilities as greater numbers of women opt to work outside the home, they have received little encouragement from society and the government and are even penalized by their employers. Especially during times of economic hardship, firms look askance at employees who assert their rights without apparent regard for their fellow employees and the inconvenience to the company. Although the childcare-leave legislation requires firms to restore leave-takers to their former positions, this is not always honored in practice because of the difficulties involved in hiring temporary staff for many positions. In addition, established corporate practices and ingrained attitudes remain hostile to workers who assert their rights or seek treatment deemed special or accommodating. Employers have generally opposed childcare leave and the new mandates for numerical targets because they conflict with the need to extract maximum value from employees and cut costs. While employers may have a theoretical appreciation of the negative consequences of a declining birth rate and the need to nurture a future workforce, the government's pronatal policies are seen to have definite immediate costs and only uncertain prospects of subsequent benefits.

The government has tried to be a cheerleader for the childcare issue, a role played out most prominently in 1999 when train stations were plastered with posters stating that 'a man who does not take care of his children should not be called a father.' However, the music star featured in the ad subsequently divorced his equally famous spouse, introducing an unanticipated slice of ironic reality into the campaign. The poster also raised hackles among men who suggested an alternative slogan: 'companies that fail to support their male employees who want to participate more fully in raising their children should not be called a company.'[25]

Conventional attitudes about child rearing are blamed for the rising numbers of women who either decline to have children altogether or sacrifice their careers to raise a family. It is difficult for married women to reconcile the competing demands of work and the home, where they are expected to be the principal caregivers for children and aging parents. As a consequence, many married women with children give up on full-time jobs and work part-time in jobs that allow them the needed flexibility and time to juggle their heavy responsibilities. However, in doing so these women are abandoning relatively well-paid, responsible jobs with career potential for low-paying jobs with limited responsibilities and scant prospects for promotion. The relatively high percentage of highly educated women who give up work reveals just how much Japan is losing by failing to implement effective policies that would enable women to balance their lives and juggle their multiple roles.

Women and work

Although a series of legislative initiatives was launched in the late 1980s and 1990s aimed at improving women's position in the economy, these have not yet produced the desired results. While this legislation was intended to assist women in balancing the various roles they are expected to assume at home and in the workplace, this goal remains elusive. Despite the ratification of the UN Convention for the Eradication of all Forms of Discrimination Against Women in 1985, and enactment of such measures as the Equal Employment Opportunity Law in 1986, the 1991 Childcare Leave Law, the 1994 Angel Plan (expanding care facilities for children and the elderly), the 1998 Elderly Care Leave Law, and the 2000 Nursing Care insurance program, women still lag far behind men in the workplace in terms of job status and pay. In addition, the birth rate continues to slide and families face unprecedented strains because of the burdens piled on women's shoulders. These laws are an attempt to help the growing number of women who are taking on multiple roles, but face significant difficulties in assuming their varied responsibilities in the absence of adequate support mechanisms.

It is important to bear in mind that, in most families in Japan, both the wife and husband work outside the home as paid workers. Since the 1980s, more married women have entered the paid labor force and in 2003 fewer than 40 percent of families depend on the husband's earnings alone. However, the assumption that most married women are stay-at-home housewives lingers despite this changing reality. Wives' earnings are critical to family finances and thus not working is not a viable option for most married women. This is an important trend that has accelerated since the 1980s, leaving social attitudes and government policies regarding the family, daycare, elderly care, and welfare programs racing to catch up. The gap is narrowing, but working women often find themselves confronting frustrations and difficulties in balancing their various roles as wife, mother, caregiver, and worker because of the lag between their everyday reality and the social context in which they function.

Their situation is not eased by government tax and pension policies that encourage women to stay at home or limit themselves to part-time employment. For example, if a man's wife receives over a certain amount of annual income (¥1.3 million), she loses her special income-tax exemption and must pay social security, and the husband loses a dependent tax credit. Working women who pay social security are also penalized: while full-time homemakers who pay no pension premiums receive 75 percent of their husband's

(Roger Dahl)

pension in the event of his death, working wives must choose between the (usually smaller) pension to which they contributed or only 50 percent of their deceased husband's pension. This example illustrates how government policy penalizes women who choose to pursue careers and indeed seems designed to limit their employment. In addition, in many firms an employee's family loses some important benefits, such as a housing subsidy or dependent's allowance, if his wife works full-time.

Thus, in considering why women so often seek part-time work, it is important to bear in mind such factors as the tax penalty for working full-time, the potential loss of a husband's benefits, the cost of private daycare for young children, and the inadequacy of elderly care that forces many women to play the main role in caring for aging relatives. Hirao (2001: 429) puts the matter succinctly: 'These policies define the home to be the women's place, and expect family (namely women) to bear the social cost of childcare and elderly care.' These policies artificially depress women's labor-force participation and seem at odds with the urgent need to increase the workforce to cope with the anticipated consequences of a rapidly aging society.

As a result of the strong expectation in society and within families that women should place a priority on household and family responsibilities, working women often require flexible work arrangements that enable them to juggle these various demands. In general, however, full-time workers are expected to place a priority on their work commitments and there are few concessions to working women. Women who need to work, but who also require flexible schedules that leave time for household duties, are forced to seek part-time employment opportunities since flex-time, work sharing, and similar innovations have not yet become common in Japan.

Non-standard work arrangements account for the overwhelming majority of new jobs in Japan and constitute about one-quarter of all jobs. Unfortunately, such positions offer few advantages for the growing ranks of working women. In assessing the growth of non-standard work and the high percentage of women engaged on these unfavorable terms, Houseman and Osawa (2003: 155) argue that 'public policy has encouraged the growth of part-time employment by providing substantial tax incentives for firms to hire part-time workers and for workers to work part-time.' Between 1992 and 1997, part-time employment accounted for 77 percent of the net growth in paid employment. These non-standard employees have proliferated since the 1990s because they are relatively cheap, wages rise slowly, promotions are rare, benefits are negligible, contributions to government social insurance programs are not required, and termination is easy. They also help offset steep wage increases for the rapidly aging workforce under the seniority wage system. Thus, in order to cut wages and benefits, employers are increasingly hiring part-time or temporary workers, and 80 percent of these part-time workers are women. Significantly, the differences in the tasks performed, and responsibilities assumed, by part-time and regular workers are narrowing. In addition, although one-third of part-time workers are working the same number of hours as full-time workers, they are designated as part-timers purely as a means for their employer to save money. This means that a growing number of non-standard workers, mostly women, are performing similar work to their better-paid full-time colleagues, who also receive social security benefits and enjoy job security. Thus, women looking for flexible jobs to fit around their family responsibilities pay a significant price in terms of lower compensation even if they do the same amount of work as full-time employees.

Recent court cases suggest that women workers are having some success in seeking judicial remedies for such blatant abuses, but they remain pervasive as unions and government officials turn a blind eye to these exploitative practices. The institutionalized exploitation of non-standard workers is tolerated because it helps preserve the pay and perquisites of core employees, mostly men, and is helping battered firms weather the recession. Furthermore, the government is reluctant to embrace the principle of equal pay for equal work, as prevails in Europe, fearing that this would impose too heavy a burden on corporate Japan.

There are signs of change. In 1999 the government banned the employment of dispatched temporary workers for more than one year, in effect forcing firms to either take them on full-time or terminate their contracts. It also appears that the government will introduce changes in its tax and pension regulations that currently penalize working women and encourage them to limit their hours of work and earnings. In 2003 some 12 million women qualified for favorable tax treatment and, along with their employers, did not have to contribute to the national pension scheme because their hours of work are less than three-quarters of regular working hours and they earn less than ¥1.3 million a year. The planned reforms will cut the ceilings to ¥650,000 and one-half of regular working hours, thus eliminating the current tax and pension exemptions for some 3 million women and their employers. It is anticipated that many of these workers will seek to increase their hours of work to offset higher taxes and thereby ease labor shortages. It seems less certain, however, that the government will achieve its goal of raising full-time employment among this group, at least in terms of the higher pay and more secure conditions associated with full-time work. Rather, more of these workers will join the virtually full-time workforce, putting in the hours and taking on the responsibilities of full-time work without the commensurate rewards. In order to dissuade employers from taking this course, and ameliorate the consequences for employees, the government is raising the informal pay target for part-time workers to 80 percent of that of full-time workers from the current level of 60 percent.

This situation is compounded by outdated employment practices and assumptions that all too often see women workers shunted into dead-end jobs. Corporate personnel officers assume that women will marry before they turn thirty and leave the workforce to rear children, returning as part-time workers. The problem is that women are often not given a chance to challenge these assumptions. Since the firm believes that heavy investments in training women workers will not pay off, despite considerable evidence to the contrary, they are not given the same level of training as men. Problematically, the logic of the lifetime employment system and continuous on-the-job-training does not translate well in terms of the lifecycle needs of women workers. The failure to modify this system to accommodate the lifecycle needs and responsibilities of women workers often renders it an impossible or unattractive option for women rearing families. While it is clear that women desire to maintain their careers and return to the workforce after giving birth, the employment and training system discriminates against them. Their skills and potential are squandered, and careers derailed, because of outmoded employment practices designed for men with full-time housewives taking care of the home front. Advocates argue that companies should overhaul employment practices to accommodate the family responsibilities of parents – meaning that pay, rotation, training, and promotions would no longer be based on continuous full-time employment. By eliminating the high career costs of raising families, companies can play a more positive role in supporting families and, in doing so, more effectively utilize, and benefit from, women's potential.

Employment policies designed for men, and based on the assumption that a wife will take care of all domestic duties, make it especially difficult for married women to pursue managerial careers.[26] Despite this, there is evidence that women who work as teachers and civil servants tend to retain and return to their jobs after giving birth and continue their careers. This happens because these professions often have relatively generous and flexible policies enabling women to balance work and family responsibilities (Hirao 2001: 429). This finding suggests that judicious fine-tuning of workplace policies can have a salutary impact on women resuming careers after giving birth. It also indicates that increasing professionalization in the labor market will benefit working women because credentialed professionals such as lawyers, CPAs and MBAs are in a much better position to bargain for similarly generous workplace policies. Moreover, their expertise will allow them to resume rewarding careers after time out for childrearing, rather than return to the workforce on disadvantageous terms as is the case for many educated women at present. To the extent that increasing numbers of educated women can remain in the labor force on more favorable terms as full-time professionals, an improvement in the low returns on women's education in Japan may be in the offing. The increased number of women working as professionals also carries implications for the large male–female wage gap in Japan; in the USA it was the sharp rise of women entering credentialed professions from the 1970s onwards that enabled them to overcome discrimination and sharply narrow the wage gap.

The representation of women in managerial positions in Japan lags well behind other advanced countries.[27] Employers may have opened up managerial track positions for women, but have done little to reform working conditions in ways that would encourage participation by working mothers. Thus, it is not surprising that fewer than 10 percent of managers at Japanese firms are women. In the USA the percentage of women managers has risen from 24 percent in 1985 to 32 percent by 2000, implying that there are no insurmountable gender barriers to assuming managerial responsibilities given the right mix of employer and government policies.

In 2003 a METI study group concluded that Japanese companies employing more women earn higher profits. Foreign managers in Japan have known this for some time and have taken advantage of pervasive gender discrimination by Japanese enterprises to recruit more women and place them in responsible positions. Human resource managers at foreign firms regularly report that they actively seek women in preference to men and have been happy with the results of this informal affirmative action policy. In general, women's language skills are deemed better, and reportedly they show more initiative and are less reluctant to adapt to foreign business practices. While the top male graduates of prestigious universities usually prefer to work for the blue-chip domestic companies, the best women usually do not have such a choice, leaving them receptive to working for foreign firms. In addition, women generally have positive images of foreign firms and have more confidence that they will be judged on their merits and performance, avoiding the systematic gender discrimination that prevails in corporate Japan. The number of full-time employees at foreign firms topped one million in 2002, representing a mere 2.3 percent of the full-time workforce and indicating the limits of this option for many women seeking better career opportunities. However, as the labor shortage worsens and competition for talented women workers rises, foreign standards and practices may come to have a growing influence on corporate Japan.

Women in Japan have a long way to go before achieving equality with men. In 2000, Japan ranked 41 out of 70 countries based on UN criteria for gauging the level of women's participation in society, below El Salvador and

Botswana. In the national Diet, women hold only about 10 percent of the seats, while in the corporate world the 'glass ceiling' is accepted as a fact of life. In terms of wages, nearly 65 percent of women workers earn less than ¥3 million, compared to 15.6 percent of male workers, while 25 percent of men earn more than ¥7 million while only 3 percent of women do so. These income inequalities reflect restricted opportunities and a squandering of women's talents and skills that handicap Japan as a whole. As long as women continue to earn half of what men earn, one cannot expect growth in their productivity because employers have no incentive to use them more effectively, train them, and assign them significant responsibilities; women are thus wasted as cannon fodder for routine tasks.

The returns on education remain lower for women than men because of differences in wages associated with differences in labor-force participation patterns. Of all of the industrialized nations, Japan has the largest wage gap – 50 percent overall, 35 percent for full-time workers – between men and women, and since the mid-1990s it is the only country in the OECD in which this gap is widening. Significantly, the prospects for narrowing the gap appear limited because of the rising proportion of women employed under poorly paid non-standard arrangements as part-time, temporary, or dispatched workers. The labor-force participation pattern of women remains M-shaped, meaning that most working women withdraw from the labor force for child-rearing and then return once these duties decline, usually involving a sustained career hiatus. Upon returning to the labor market, few women return to their previous job and most take on positions with fewer responsibilities and inferior pay. Employment discrimination explains why investment in women's education produces lower returns in terms of employment opportunities and career earnings. Since families know that the return on the education of daughters is lower than for sons, they are inclined to spend more on their son's education.

Although about one-half of women now attend post-secondary educational institutions, slightly higher than the figure for men, more men attend the more prestigious four-year universities. Of course this is a major change from 1960 when only 10 percent of women continued their education after high school. Even now, many women complete their education on graduating from two-year junior colleges or vocational schools. This greater investment in the human capital of sons than daughters has become more pronounced in the 1990s recession, leading to speculation that continued differences in educational attainment will ensure that women's progress in the workplace will be limited. On the other hand, these days more families have only one child, so that daughters' educational desires do not always have to be sacrificed for their brothers. It is also possible that the impending labor shortage in Japan due to shrinking family size will eventually facilitate women's career advancement as they will need to make up for the shortfall in male workers. Moreover, the increasing numbers of professionals with an only daughter may lead to more women pursuing similar careers to take over family practices and/or maintain an equivalent lifestyle. Such developments may make investments in daughters' education more appealing.

It is striking how far women have advanced in certain professions since the 1980s, even if their participation remains relatively low. For example, the percentage of women among those who passed and were hired through the National Civil Service Exam (Category I) rose from 4.5 percent in 1980 to 15.5 percent in 2000. The percentage of female judges rose from 2.8 percent in 1980 to 10.8 percent in 2000, while the figures for prosecutors were 1.2 percent in 1980 and 6.1 percent in 2000, and for lawyers rising from 3.8 percent in 1980 to 8.9 percent in 2000. As of 2000, women accounted for two-thirds of pharmacists and 15.6 percent of all doctors. Looking to the future, in 2000 about one-third of newly certified doctors were women, suggesting a continued erosion of male dominance in the medical profession. It may be true that the percentage of women undergraduates at the nation's two most prestigious universities remains low by international standards – 18 percent at the University of Tokyo and 19 percent at the University of Kyoto – but these levels represent a doubling of the figure for 1980. Clearly the situation in Japan remains well short of the near gender parity at Ivy League universities in the USA, but the significant rise in women's enrollments in top universities both reflects, and is generating, significant social transformations. Younger women have models to aspire to, benefit from the presence of mentors, and, as educational attainment and careers become 'normal,' can count on parents to invest in their education and help them overcome employment barriers. Growing professionalization combined with the looming labor shortage is helping women break through the glass ceiling. Over time, employer policies and attitudes towards women will be influenced by the growing presence of women in the top echelons of the workforce; it will become normal to accommodate women workers' lifecycle needs and expensive – in terms of retention, productivity, and legal actions – not to.

While the future may be brighter, women continue to suffer discrimination in job recruitment. Only in 1999 did newspapers end the practice of posting job openings in separate sections by gender. Most students gather job information and receive invitations for job interviews at employment fairs arranged at their university or school, or at larger events sponsored by job information agencies. Others peruse the readily available job information publications and attend company recruitment sessions. Since the early 1990s, it has been widely reported in the media that many young women have not been able to even get interviews and have been discouraged from applying for jobs by corporate personnel representatives. Although the government has warned against such practices, women contend that they remain commonplace. In the tight job market of recession-hit Japan, companies favor young men, partly because they know that retention rates are higher and also out of a sense that men have a responsibility to provide for their families and thus deserve priority in employment. Women also report that they are frequently asked inappropriate questions at interviews – questions that would not be asked of male candidates – regarding their dating habits, marriage plans, living arrangements, and other personal matters.

Aging society

As Japan shuffled into the new century, it did so as the most rapidly aging nation on earth. As of 1999, there were 21 million Japanese over age 65 out of a population of 126 million. In 2025 demographers expect Japan to have the world's oldest population, as slightly more than 37 million people, nearly one-third of the population, will be 65 or older. Japanese society is rapidly graying due to the drop in fertility, the aging of the baby boomers born soon after World War II, and a sharp rise in life expectancy. Average life expectancy for men increased from 50 years in 1947 to 77 years by 1995, while life expectancy for women rose from 54 to 83 years over the same period. As a consequence of this increased longevity, by 2025 it is estimated that 4.3 percent of the population will be over 85 years old, a five-fold increase from 1965. Correspondingly, those suffering from senile dementia will rise from an estimated 1 million in 1990 to a projected 2.62 million by 2015.

There are growing concerns among experts that society is not yet ready to cope with the burdens and needs of a large elderly population. It is generally agreed that the aging crisis is one of the most serious challenges facing Japan in the twenty-first century as it struggles to balance the needs and interests of the young and old. It is expected that economic growth will slow as the labor force shrinks, savings drop, and the level of business investments and residential construction fall because of a shrinking population. The government also faces a fiscal crisis, and citizens face higher taxes, because of the costs associated with pensions and medical care for the aged. Given the extent of these problems, how is society coping?

Elderly care

The paucity of welfare services for the elderly in Japan is based on the implicit assumption that families will take care of their aging relatives. This assumption is based on the Confucian principle of filial piety and the respect accorded the elderly. This respect is expressed at many levels, including an employment system in which status, power, and wages are closely tied to seniority. Japan is a society where considerable deference is shown to elderly people and their experience is highly valued. Within the family, where patriarchal patterns remain strong, older males are accorded a position of dominance in their household. Given the practical and ideological importance of the family in Japanese society, it is not surprising that the government sees the family as the natural and desirable provider of care for the elderly. This inclination of the government to rely on the family in its social welfare policy is not only cultural; in general, the government has refrained from a generous

Figure 10.2 The number of centenarians is rising in Japan. This gentleman says the secret to longevity is skipping dinner and drinking a big glass of *sake* instead. (Photo: Greg Davis)

cradle-to-grave approach to social services and benefits common in Europe while viable alternatives were in place. Firms have been expected to provide employment security and families to take care of their own, meaning that until the 1990s the government mostly played a limited role in providing the range of social welfare services and benefits common in other advanced industrialized societies.

Widespread public awareness of the inadequacy of the elderly care system in Japan was awakened by the publication of Ariyoshi Sawako's 1972 novel *The Twilight Years*. The novel portrays a working woman at her wits' end trying to balance the competing demands on her time from office and home, and shows how the situation is complicated by the husband's failure to shoulder a share of the burden at home. Since then, more and more women are working and facing a similarly impossible situation. The family-centered approach to elderly care has been critiqued by Yamamoto Noriko (1997: 174), who argues that it is out of step with ongoing changes in the family and social changes affecting women. She asserts that

Figure 10.3 In isolated hamlets depopulated by young people's exodus to the cities, older people like this 75-year-old woman have to fend for themselves. (Photo: Greg Davis)

Japanese caregivers' strong internalization of the societal norms regarding filial caregiving ... is structurally maintained within Japanese society. The norm also has caused the social policy regarding the care of the elderly in Japan to remain heavily dependent on family caregivers, especially females ... Therefore, services to help these caregivers should be expanded in Japan ... The cultural norm of filial responsibility seen in Asian countries including Japan should not be used as a reason for policies that are unduly restrictive to the lifestyle choices of those individuals whose elderly parents happen to be afflicted by physical or cognitive impairments.

Government policies and societal norms, however, continue to place the burden of elderly care on the shoulders of women. Women – already busy as wives, mothers, and workers – are also expected to become nurses for the aged. It is estimated that 85 percent of the elderly receiving care at home in Japan depend on female relatives. This gender-based division of labor ensures that elderly-care responsibilities strongly influence women's careers and their lifestyles. Some women willingly take on this task, internalizing the societal norm because of a feeling of *on* (social debt or obligation). Parents are regarded as having bestowed much upon their offspring, and reciprocating their accumulated generosity is considered natural and a way of assuming the responsibilities that *on* places on one. Some wives live up to social norms by caring for their husband's parents out of the same sense of *on* – the obligations

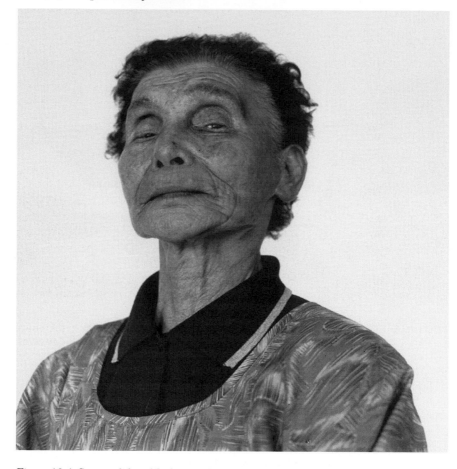

Figure 10.4 Some of the elderly are skeptical about pension and medical care insurance reforms. (Photo: Andreas Seibert/Lookat)

assumed by the husband are internalized by the wife since they are jointly responsible for the extended family unit. Given this situation, however, it is not surprising that many young women are reluctant to marry and thus assume the onerous obligation of caring for their husbands' parents – a trend that reportedly is making marriage especially difficult for eldest or only sons who are expected to take on this obligation. This situation indicates that the patriarchal bias in existing elderly-care policies is partially responsible for the declining proportion of women getting married and thus acts to lower the birth rate.

It has become increasingly apparent to the Japanese that inadequate elderly-care policies are putting families under a great deal of pressure. Moreover, policy assumptions based on traditional expectations are out of sync with recent transformations in the structure of the family. In 1980, nearly 70

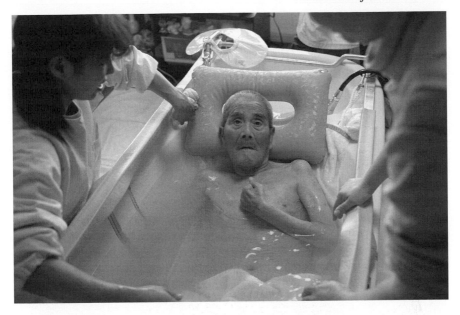

Figure 10.5 Elderly care is a daunting challenge for Japan in the twenty-first century. (Photo: Andreas Seibert/Lookat)

percent of the population over 65 lived with their families, but by the late 1990s this figure had dropped to about 50 percent. In some rural regions that have suffered depopulation because of the migration of young people to job opportunities in urban areas, the percentage of elderly living with their children is even lower. Despite the value society still places on grandparents living with their children and grandchildren, the number of three-generation households has declined from 19.2 percent in 1970 to 12.5 percent in 1995. This significant change in the configuration of the Japanese family, along with rising divorce and non-marriage rates, generates concerns about the failure to develop programs that help families play a significant role in elderly-care policies. Until recently, the family, and especially women, have been largely on their own, burdening them excessively at a significant cost to society.

What has in the past been viewed as a family problem best dealt with at the family level has become a major public policy issue exposing deep fissures in society. The heavy emphasis on home care means that there have not been enough nursing homes for the frail elderly in need of institutional care. In the 1990s the government has belatedly developed policy responses to the shortage of elderly-care facilities and trained home healthcare workers. These new plans emphasize home- and community-based systems that encourage older people to live with a minimum of dislocation and a maximum of independence for as long as possible. Not only is this approach economically prudent, but it also accords with the cultural emphasis on the

Figure 10.6 This generation may have to pay twice as much tax as their parents currently pay to cover rising pensions and medical care of their aged parents.
(Photo: Jeff Kingston)

family as the foundation of the elderly care system – but with a generous
component of public assistance designed to help women escape 'nursing
hell.' In addition, policymakers and care managers recognize that many
elderly have been placed in inappropriate facilities: too many reasonably
healthy people are placed in geriatric hospitals where the level of care is too
high and too expensive. Thus, the government plans call for the construction
of more modern, subsidized nursing-home facilities that provide an assisted
living environment. Progress towards meeting the ambitious targets set by
central government varies by region because cash-strapped local authorities
are expected to assume responsibility for implementing the directives.

The difficulties of instituting elderly care reform result from the volatile
mix of a family-centered ideology, prolonged recession, a bureaucracy
concerned with establishing a sound fiscal foundation for any reform
proposal, and politics. In April 2000, in response to the anticipated costs of
elderly care programs, the government introduced a mandatory nursing-care
insurance scheme for those over the age of 40. Those enrolled in the scheme
pay ¥2,500 a month, plus additional payments levied by local governments.
Under this system, local municipalities dispatch nurses to care for the elderly
at home and set up facilities to provide other care services. It is estimated that
over 2 million elderly are enrolled in the plan as of 2000, bringing relief to

Figure 10.7 Older voters constitute a growing constituency demanding expanded social services. (Photo: Greg Davis)

families exhausted from caring for frail or incapacitated parents. The media
has frequently drawn attention to this 'nursing hell,' generating public pressure on the government to play a more positive role in helping families cope
and to assist women in balancing the competing demands on their time. The
new system is also a belated acknowledgement that insufficient public care
services for the elderly have kept women working on limited schedules or at
home, undermining family finances, interrupting women's careers, lowering
the birth rate, discouraging marriage, and generating friction and stress
within the family.

There is no doubt that healthcare services for the elderly will come under
increasing strain in Japan. The number of those aged 65 or over requiring
some level of nursing care is rising from 2.7 million in 2000 to a projected 3.1
million in 2004, nearly 13 percent of the elderly population. In 2004, about
2.3 million elderly are expected to receive care services at home while the
remainder will receive care at elderly facilities. The nursing care system will
be further strained by the provision that people between the ages of 40 and
64 who suffer from age-related ailments will also be eligible for the service.
By 2025, projections suggest that the system will be required to provide care
for 5.4 million patients. Given the magnitude of the projected demand for
nursing services, there are concerns that many municipalities will be unable
to deliver the level of services outlined in the nursing-care legislation. It
seems certain that these services will require more central government assistance, increased private-sector participation and far higher premiums than
originally planned.

Pension and medical care solvency

Coping with the challenges of a rapidly aging society, in which the number of aged needing care will double by 2025, is rightly described as 'mission impossible.' Japan's demographic time-bomb poses enormous challenges to society and is expected to strain both the medical care and pension systems. Clearly, taxes will have to rise dramatically and benefits will have to be trimmed or constrained in order for society to accommodate the needs and interests of the elderly without sacrificing those of younger generations.

Serious questions are being asked about the viability of the national pension system. Nearly 40 percent of people who should be paying pension premiums into the Kokumin Nenkin (National Pension Plan for the self-employed and unemployed) are not doing so in fiscal 2002, up from 15 percent in 1992.[28] This sharp rise in nonpayment is undermining public faith in the pension system and the ideal of universal coverage. In addition, pension fund investment losses are skyrocketing in a prolonged recession, reinforcing concerns that today's workers won't have much to look forward to. While at the close of the twentieth century there were four workers for every retired person, by 2020 it is estimated there will be only two workers per retiree. This means that if benefits are not trimmed and if eligibility for pensions remains unchanged, pension contributions must double, a taxing prospect for younger Japanese people. In 1997, the pension contribution rate was 17.5 percent – a figure that will have to rise to an estimated 34 percent of basic earnings by 2025 to maintain the current benefit structure. Clearly, this will be an undesirably high burden on the economically active population and will impinge on their quality of life. And, as pension outlays rise more rapidly in Japan than anywhere else in the OECD, by 2020 they could reach some 14 percent of Japan's GDP, nearly triple the average among the English-speaking countries of the OECD and even surpassing the level in some of the continental European nations.

The government's budget woes are worsened by rising medical costs. After age 70, elderly Japanese pay almost nothing for healthcare although spending on this group now constitutes one-third of the entire national health budget. (A small level of co-payment by those over age 70 has been announced in 2003.) Combined pension and medical outlays could rise from 36 percent of GDP in 1997 to 44 percent in 2025, close to the projected OECD average at that time. The sudden worsening of the dependency ratio will force society to make some hard choices in balancing the needs and interests of different generations. As the longevity of the Japanese rises, government benefits are being paid out over a longer period of time to an aging population with expanding needs for medical care.

By the time the baby boom generation (born 1946–55) retires, and the number of retirees per employed person rises considerably, the financial circumstances of the elderly will generate considerable debate. Until the twenty-first century, taking care of the aged through some form of public

Figure 10.8 Older women loaded down with vegetables to peddle in the city. (Photo: Andreas Seibert/Lookat)

funding was considered desirable and affordable. However, as the dependency ratio increases, political confrontation over the level of benefits and qualification criteria for government programs has intensified. In the absence of means testing (determining eligibility for benefits based on an individual's economic circumstances), the benefit structure is regressive because it favors the well-off at the expense of the relatively needy elderly: those who are well established financially usually receive higher benefits because of longer coverage and better pay. Current reform discussions focus on cutting benefits, rationing healthcare and requiring the better-off elderly to pay more for the nursing and medical services they receive. Instituting reform, however, is a difficult process and will not get any easier as older voters will wield considerable power at the polls and can be expected to resist wholesale rollbacks. But given the pressing need for raising revenues and trimming costs, more decisive, timely, and unpopular actions are expected from government.

Policies aimed at economic security for the elderly cannot be considered in a vacuum. Policy analysts point to the dynamic interplay between labor supply, government reforms, and employer policies. Raising the age of pension eligibility represents a real threat to the economics of the aged in the absence of initiatives aimed at providing job opportunities for this labor pool. If the age of retirement is maintained at 60, postponement of access to pensions lengthens the time that retirees must live off their own resources. In this context, post-retirement employment will be needed for the large number of healthy retirees who would prefer working to killing their time and, in any case, need the income. Many firms are eager to retire older workers because their wages are relatively higher, then rehire them on less generous terms, a common practice known as *saikoyoseido*. In 2003 the government is considering tax incentives for firms that employ elderly workers and anti-age-discrimination legislation aimed at protecting their employment rights. It is also mindful that increased employment of older workers will also partially address the impending labor shortage and generate more taxes to pay for the medical and pension costs of their less healthy compatriots.

Even with such cost-cutting and revenue-raising reforms, the impact of higher taxes on younger workers will be severe. It is widely acknowledged that workers in their twenties through forties at the beginning of the twenty-first century will end up contributing more than they receive in benefits; under the current system a typical worker will contribute some ¥60 million in premiums and receive only ¥51 million in benefits. By taxing the young heavily to pay pensions for the old, the government will be overseeing a massive intergenerational transfer of wealth from the relatively poor to the relatively rich. This situation will be untenable, as poorly paid workers living in cramped rental housing balk at providing the pensions of retirees living in their own homes. Nor will they be content to pay higher pension premiums for today's retirees knowing that upon retirement they will receive lower benefits.

Labor shortage implications

The dearth of babies and the rapid aging of society threaten Japan with a labor shortage. By 2010, the government estimates that two workers will retire for every new worker entering the labor force. While it is hard to project what the shape of the future labor force will be like, there is growing concern that this labor shortage will make Japan the land of the setting sun. However, technological changes could rapidly alter this bleak outlook and there is also considerable room for more effectively tapping the pool of women workers in Japan. As we have seen, Japan has in many respects squandered this significant reserve of human capital. However, in order to more fully integrate women into the labor force, attitudes must change, the employment paradigm must be modified to accommodate the lifecycle needs of women, and public policies must be directed to reducing the obstacles to their participation in the labor force. Although this is a daunting agenda, the alternative is a greater reliance on foreign workers.[29] There is a marked reluctance in Japan to accept greater numbers of foreigners in a society that thinks of itself as homogeneous and prizes an imagined ethnic purity. Like everywhere else, Japan suffers from racism and discrimination against foreigners. There is little likelihood in the near future that there will be significant support for accepting a larger permanent foreign population. The current situation allows the government to keep immigrant labor in legal limbo, and thus prevent the emergence of a permanent community of immigrants. It also allows the government considerable discretion in expanding or shrinking the pool of foreign workers depending on business conditions (Douglass and Roberts 2000).

Can Japan do without foreign workers? Although many chauvinists would like to think so, this does not appear likely. There will be a continuing demand for foreign workers if for no other reason than that someone will have to perform the various 3k jobs (*kitanai, kiken,* and *kitsui* – dirty, dangerous, and difficult) that Japanese are unwilling to fill. But of course there are many other types of work performed by foreigners and this should not be forgotten. Foreign workers already play an important role in the Japanese economy and will increasingly be needed to provide services to the elderly and to staff the manufacturing and processing industries. They, along with Japanese women workers, are the solution to Japan's impending labor shortage. Deductions from their wages will also help pay pensions for retirees. It also appears that the high demand for skilled workers in information technology (IT), and the domestic shortage of such talent, is generating pressures to recruit IT professionals from overseas and has led the government to implement visa reforms to facilitate such recruitment. Thus, selectively and on a limited basis, rising demand for foreign workers will ensure some limited accommodation of immigration. It seems highly unlikely, however, that the government will act on recent UN recommendations that it accept 600,000 immigrants per annum, or a total of 17 million by 2050, to cope with the problems associated with its demographic time-bomb. Japan's evident reluctance to accept refugees reveals much about prevailing prejudices.[30] As of 2001, Japan had a mere 3,200 refugees residing within its borders compared to Denmark's 79,284, Finland's 12,728, the Netherland's 152,338, Germany's 903,000, and Italy's 8,571. It is also unclear how the government plans to improve the human rights and living conditions of foreign workers and their families. There seems to be a strong preference in official circles to continue the system of temporary work visas that allows the government considerable discretion over who stays and who leaves.

Prospects

The prospects for Japan seem dismal in many ways and its challenges formidable. The foregoing discussion about changes in the family, gender, aging, and work indicates just how much is changing, how difficult the consequences have been, and how much remains to be done. The security and stability that Japanese have come to take for granted is endangered. The ideology of family and work has been overtaken by events, but the lingering influence of traditional values, ideas, and norms is everywhere evident. This gap between the fading verities and the emerging realities helps explain why this era of transition has been so traumatic and deracinating. While society has been tempted to retreat into denial, the problems affecting the nexus of relations involved in family and work are ever more openly reported and hotly debated. Belatedly, policy reforms and innovations aimed at bridging the gap between traditional norms and contemporary developments in the family and at the workplace are being moved into place.

This is a difficult but revealing time as the government, corporations, and people grope for new answers to existing problems. While it is relatively easy to ascertain what is wrong, solutions are elusive and require more 'thinking outside the box.' This is natural in a society that is becoming relatively more diverse, more open to alternatives, involves wider participation and is becoming more accommodating of the individual. This era of quiet transformation is a time of confusion and slow-motion reforms. It is easy to discount the prospects of reform, especially if one assumes that a reinvigorated civil society will suddenly provide the cure for all that ails contemporary Japan. An ongoing social revolution is reshaping the network of relationships that exist between people and those who govern, those who employ and those they interact with as children, friends, partners, parents, neighbors, and colleagues. In short, this is a period of fundamental social change, an era of transformation that reveals how people are coping with adversity and recasting the world they live in. This is a work in progress and one that reveals a stunning dynamism at odds with conventional views of Japan.

This chapter has charted the impact of social and economic change on and within the family and at work. The traditional family is threatened by a host of changes and burdened with excessive expectations that stem from patriarchal ideals that are increasingly out of touch with emerging realities. The fragility of the family is not a result of declining patriarchy, as conservatives insist, but rather a reflection of the gap between prevailing realities and such outmoded mores. The stresses and frictions generated by this gap, between the way society increasingly is and the way conservative Japanese want it to be, are undermining the family. Today's youth complain that this is a society without dreams, meaning perhaps that it is a society where they cannot dream or have little hope of realizing their dreams. It is a society where their interests are systematically shortchanged in favor of their elders. By insisting on dated norms, conservatives are alienating the individuals who constitute the family and failing to recognize and accommodate the trend towards greater gender equality and more respect for the individual. Households increasingly rely on two incomes out of necessity and pragmatism. Thus attitudes, policies, and practices that assume a woman's place is in the home are no longer viable or desirable. The Japanese family appears to be increasingly dysfunctional because assumptions about how it should function are out of sync with emerging expectations, aspirations, and everyday realities. But while this cognitive dissonance may well persist for some time, perceptions and social norms are slowly being transformed under the impact of everyday reality.

As we have seen, these changing social expectations are impacting with particular force on women, if in unpredictable and contradictory ways. It seems clear that in certain limited ways women's status is gradually

improving and that there is growing concern about women's rights and grievances. The surge in domestic violence reported in recent years does not
reflect a sudden and inexplicable epidemic; what has been a tolerated aspect
of family life is now considered a problem that must be dealt with in order to
strengthen the family. Various government policies and workplace initiatives
are small steps in the right direction in addressing the problems women face
in balancing the competing demands of work and family responsibilities. As
these policies are implemented, expanded and accepted as normal, women's
lives will slowly improve. It is encouraging that steps are being taken to ease
the burdens that were once imposed on families, and on women in particular,
as a matter of course. Despite such progress, much more needs to be done to
support the family. In acknowledging that progress has been limited, it is also
important to recognize that initial positive steps have been taken and these
are generating a momentum, and raising expectations, for more substantive
reforms. Each step along the way may seem insignificant and inadequate, but
cumulatively they represent reform and progress. The flurry of policy
changes affecting the family and employment practices since the mid-1980s
involves legal, ideological, and institutional changes that are promoting
further reforms. While they are not the whole answer, they at least constitute
a beginning and hence are encouraging.

The declining stability of family relationships is taking a toll on Japan,
exposing it to many of the social dislocations common in other developed
nations even though it has done better than many in coping with the social
fallout. The rising rates of divorce, domestic violence, juvenile delinquency,
suicide, truancy, teenage prostitution, drug use, and sexually transmitted
diseases among Japanese youth indicate just how much is wrong with the
family and how wide is the gap between the contemporary reality and the
high expectations embedded in policies and conventional attitudes towards
the family. Given the strong implicit assumption of family stability, the
growing instability of the family is generating unanticipated problems and
uncertainties. These are outpacing what people are prepared for and
straining existing policies and programs. The few hopeful signs that society is
coming to terms with these new challenges are outweighed by discouraging
evidence of lingering denial.

The workplace has also been faced with some shattering changes. The
fading of lifetime employment, seniority wages, and enterprise unionism
strikes at the heart of the ideology of work that has prevailed in postwar
Japan. It has long been acknowledged that lifetime employment applied to
only some 30 percent of the workforce and that enterprise unionism has been
in decline for some time and now involves a mere 20 percent of the
workforce. However, these so-called jewels of Japanese industrial relations
have long had a talismanic importance and appeal. It thus has been
wrenching, for employers and employees alike, to progressively abandon
these potent symbols of Japan, Inc. that have long been a source of pride,
stability and strength. There is also widespread recognition that the

conditions that at one time provided a compelling logic for Japan's employ-ment system no longer prevail. While the costly rigidities of lifetime employ-ment and seniority wages have provided job security, they are no longer affordable because the reciprocal benefits have faded. Benevolent pater-nalism and corporate-based welfare are being jettisoned as unaffordable luxuries in an era when bankruptcies and layoffs have suddenly become commonplace. These changes in the employment system have generated considerable insecurity and led many Japanese people to reconsider their attitudes towards work and the balance between their jobs and private lives. The social contract that characterized Japan, Inc. has been sundered, leaving a disorienting vacuum in society. It remains to be seen what will emerge in the future to provide the cohesion and sense of security people desire.

It appears that the emerging labor paradigm will increasingly shed the arrangements for core workers that are associated with Japan, Inc. and come to more closely resemble the practices that are now standard on the periphery. This means a more flexible system of industrial relations, greater reliance on merit in determining wages and promotions, more job-hopping, and far less job security. There is a strong risk that the fruits of flexibility will not be fully realized because employers are motivated primarily by the need to cut costs. While it is understandable amidst a prolonged recession that cost-cutting is the priority, the potential of greater flexibility for workers, their families, and society is being largely overlooked. More flexible jobs and working hours can help women and men better balance their various respon-sibilities at home and work and participate more equally in rearing children and caring for ailing parents. Work-sharing arrangements can achieve the same results. If the government and employers want to raise the birth rate, more fully tap the potential of women workers and increase tax revenues from them, a more equal sharing of the benefits of flexibility will be essential. As it stands, flexibility is being adopted in a one-sided fashion and in Japan has come to mean hiring cheap part-time workers with little job security. As a result, the benefits are accruing solely to employers.

The Dutch model of work sharing (where two workers divide a job) has generated considerable interest in government, business, and union circles, but despite evidence to the contrary there is still strong skepticism in Japan that such practices are suitable for managers and others in senior positions. Work sharing in Japan has leaned towards reducing hours (and pay) of regular workers and hiring cheaper temporary staff to make up the differ-ence. In Japan, regular workers are motivated to be productive, achieve results, and hit targets, but it is also important to interact with the group and to be seen to sacrifice personal comfort and convenience for the company. Changing such deeply ingrained attitudes will take time. For example, flex-time (arrangement whereby working hours are full-time, but not uniform) has been tried on a limited basis since the mid-1990s; however, in 2002 a number of large companies announced plans to abandon this practice on the grounds that, since it does not involve all employees, it causes inconveniences. There is also a strong reluctance to adopt the principle of equal pay for equal work, as part-time workers can be paid less for doing the same work as full-time workers. The equal pay principle has worked in Europe because part-time workers' productivity has increased enough to pay for it. In order to reduce wage inequalities between part-time and regular workers, Japanese firms would have to deploy their part-time workers more effectively than at present and raise their productivity. However, companies tend to use these workers unproductively, paying low wages and reaping low value-added.

The demographic time-bomb will increasingly generate pressures for modifying existing employment practices in ways that facilitate greater participation of women in the labor force. Given the reluctance to contemplate a large increase in the number of resident foreigners, there is a need to more fully tap the potential contributions of women and this depends on lowering the barriers that exist at present. Given women's lifecycle needs and responsibilities, more flexible working arrangements must become ever more common; they will also influence male work patterns. Innovative policies adopted in the Nordic countries offer possible models and confirm that policies that support the family, help women balance their various roles, and enable them to contribute more productively to their companies are both feasible and beneficial to all involved. The government, employers, and workers have a chance to create a more people-friendly society with family and work norms that better serve individual aspirations, meet public expectations, and accommodate the growing diversity of society.[31]

In 2050 when pundits look back at turn-of-the-century Japan, they will wonder at the hesitant, slow, fumbling moves towards reform that we are now witnessing. But they will also see this as a watershed era when the foundations of transformation were put in place and the verities and assumptions of Japan, Inc. were in the process of fading away, albeit slowly and incrementally. How they assess this third transformation in Japanese history depends on contemporary choices and policy innovations. There has been some encouraging progress in responding to the challenges and problems with which Japanese people are all too familiar. If Japan can build on these foundations of social revolution, broaden participation in society, relieve pressures on the family and diminish patriarchal bias, it can improve on the otherwise rather dismal prospects it faces at the beginning of the twenty-first century. By more fully tapping the talents of all who reside in Japan and breaking down gender barriers to an equal society, Japanese can come to enjoy the fruits of a more vibrant civil society. By moving away from a system where the family has been forced to accommodate and support the rhythms of work towards one in which work accommodates and supports the rhythms of family, the Japanese could greatly improve and strengthen their society. This would be an inspiring legacy for future Japanese people to nurture and build on. Progress towards this goal has thus far been limited, but encouraging reforms and developments bode well for the future of Japan's quiet transformation.

CONCLUSION

Under construction

Japan's nascent civil society

Japan is written off by virtually everyone as an economic basket case and a dysfunctional democracy. Japan's malaise is ascribed to deep-seated economic and political flaws and a lack of decisive leadership. The consensus about its future is equally bleak due to the purported lack of substantive reforms to cope with festering economic problems and the demographic time-bomb.

In the context of this pessimistic consensus, the cautious and measured optimism expressed here about social change in general and civil society in particular may seem wildly euphoric. Just as in the late 1980s when commentators gushed enthusiastically about Japan, now everyone is humming its requiem. Then and now the consensus view is exaggerated and inaccurate. Images of stagnation and gridlock endlessly repeated in the mass media require one to ignore far too much of what is actually happening in Japan in the twenty-first century. Certainly Japan faces immense problems, and the reforms have not gone far enough, but suggestions that it is relentlessly sinking into the abyss are overly pessimistic.

Detailed studies by Katz (2003), Neary (2002), and Maclachlan (2002) provide a more optimistic reading of Japan's pulse beat. Katz expresses confidence that by 2010 or so the economy will begin recovering. Neary argues that the human rights situation has demonstrably improved in the 1990s as a consequence of Japan's increasingly robust civil society. Maclachlan notes that very recent changes have gone a long way in realizing important aspects of the consumer rights movement's agenda, especially in arousing political consciousness in ways that bode well for the future of democracy and civil society. I have sought to supplement these findings by highlighting the various institutional, policy, and legal reforms, propelled by the discrediting of Japan, Inc. and looming demographic problems, that suggest the emergence of a more robust civil society better attuned to the needs and aspirations of contemporary Japanese people.

However, I believe this will be a lengthy and incremental ordeal. The process of laying the foundations of civil society has been a long, ongoing struggle and its habits and patterns will not be acquired overnight. As Maclachlan argues in reference to the consumer rights movement, reform is a

(*Asahi Shimbun*)

slow and cumulative process with numerous setbacks along the way. As I have pointed out, there are remaining obstacles and much unfinished business in realizing a healthy civil society. While these impediments cannot be discounted, nor can we understand contemporary Japan by ignoring how much has been accomplished in a relatively short period of time. Greater transparency and accountability in government and increased participation of people in NPOs and other voluntary activities is already a reality. People are less reverent and beholden to those in authority and are much better informed about the costs of failing to monitor their activities. Because the status quo was so thoroughly discredited by the events of the Lost Decade, the relationship between people and those who govern has fundamentally changed. People are demanding more open government and now have the institutional means, in the form of activist NPOs and the mass media, to exercise and expand newly won legal rights for information disclosure. The mutually reinforcing developments of information disclosure, NPOs, and judicial reforms are creating a momentum favorable to civil society. Surprisingly, this social transformation is being promoted by a broad and diverse array of organizations and groups from across the political spectrum. Some, such as Keidanren, the powerful business lobby, back much of the reform agenda.

Japan's economic implosion and dysfunctional political system are often taken as signs that the reforms have been ineffective, overwhelmed by the sheer magnitude of the nation's problems. Yet the flurry of policy and legal reforms implemented in recent years has gone ahead despite these economic and political difficulties. In this unpromising context Japan has made a promising start by laying the foundations of civil society. Japan is indeed a flawed democracy – and Mulgan (2002) may be right that the structure of political and bureaucratic linkages usually stifles reform – but it is clear that substantive reforms are being implemented that are promoting significant changes affecting the family, the elderly, and relations between citizens and the State, and between employees and employers. These ongoing changes constitute the quiet transformation.

Real and wide-ranging reforms have been driven largely by the sense of crisis that grips Japan. The 1990s served as the wake for Japan, Inc. The system has been irretrievably tarnished, leaving people open to, and eagerly searching for, a new paradigm. Thus, it is not merely a case of rearranging the deck chairs on the *Titanic*; the incremental process of reform is Japan's lifeboat. While these reforms may not revive the Nikkei and root out political corruption, they are reshaping Japanese society in important and positive ways.

As we have seen, the confluence of demographic and economic crises combined with faltering faith in government is propelling a wide array of reforms. The transformation of Japan is partly motivated by a desire to establish a more people-friendly society, but does not only depend on good intentions; few believe that the current system is sustainable or worth preserving. It's not that the powers that be have suddenly become kinder or gentler, but rather they find themselves being overtaken by events and racing to catch up. The train is leaving the station and they are jumping on board. As we have seen, some of these encouraging changes are due to the cumulative efforts of grassroots organizations (information disclosure, NPOs, consumer protection), belated public concerns about marginalized groups (HIV hemophiliacs and lepers), and globalization (judicial reform), while some stem from fiscal woes (downsizing the construction state, empowering NPOs). In many of these cases, odd coalitions ranging across the political spectrum have found common cause in promoting reform.

In looking under the rock of contemporary Japan, it is not hard to see what has gone wrong. However, Japan's significant problems are not relentlessly shaping and determining the future – the public backlash and responses by various actors and institutions are propelling reforms that are taking hold and having an impact. I argue that this Japan, warts and all, is a far more dynamic society than is usually acknowledged. The chapters on hemophiliacs and lepers show how it makes more sense than ever to do the right thing, or at least not go out of the way to do the heinous thing. The discussion of food scandals reflects both the problems and the impact of consumer protection efforts – too weak to prevent bureaucratic and corporate negligence, but now better equipped to force accountability and reform. In twenty-first-century Japan, taboo issues are no longer routinely swept under the national *tatami* mat and are a subject of public discussion. Those in power are discovering that they are no longer immune from public scrutiny and, to some extent, are being held to higher standards of conduct. More politicians are embracing quality-of-life issues and the principle of open government. Rising levels of transparency and accountability are sustaining the reform process. The innovative Japan depicted in these pages reveals what is missing from the consensus view that a stagnant Japan is avoiding necessary reforms and is thus sinking into the abyss. Social change is happening and stimulating Japan's nascent civil society.

In considering the implications and consequences of recent reforms, it is important to step back and examine the process. For example, the realization of national information disclosure legislation took more than two decades. The spread of local ordinances from 1982 over a fifteen-year span built a momentum and created precedents that few would have anticipated at that time. Considered separately, each of these local initiatives to promote transparency in government seemed of little consequence. However, when we consider them together as part of a larger, long-term trend we can now appreciate their significance. Japanese people today are reaping the fruits of these earlier struggles. Similarly, in identifying the municipalities that refused to comply with the national data registry system, Juki Net, it is striking that these are often the same places where citizen groups were most active in the 1970s. The seeds sown then have, three decades later, sprouted into a large campaign of civil disobedience. People are taking their privacy very seriously, defying the government and asserting their civil rights. These two cases are powerful reminders that the consequences of reform percolate only slowly through the polity.

These cases also suggest that those who diagnose the state of Japan's democracy exclusively by taking the temperature of Nagatacho may be overlooking important developments. There is a degree of vitality to Japanese democracy not evident in low voter turnout or the re-election of corrupt politicians. This vibrancy is evident in the election of independent governors, increasing resort to local referendums to challenge government decisions, greater participation in NPOs, grassroots campaigns for open government, and civil disobedience. These gestures form a basis for optimism that the Japanese are not nearly as apathetic or resigned as they are frequently depicted in the press. The Japanese media has also become feistier and has become a leading user and advocate of information disclosure. The media is arousing people to action, uncovering abuses, and facilitating the monitoring of those in positions of authority. To be sure, the press is more beholden than it might be, but in the short period since information disclosure became a reality it has played a vital and positive role. Perhaps more surprising has been the support for information disclosure by the judiciary. Courts are proving to be far more supportive than anyone had anticipated and have thereby generated further momentum for transparency. In addition, some politicians have won elections by embracing open government.

Anyone uncertain about the depth of change experienced in Japan in recent years should consider how far the mighty have fallen. The nation's mandarins, once revered and respected, have plummeted furthest. In a series of scandals engulfing virtually every government ministry, the best and the brightest have been caught with their hands in the till, asleep at the wheel or driving the getaway car. Revelations about negligence, incompetence, malfeasance, and over-generous compensation and post-retirement sinecures have drawn public ire. The age of information disclosure has placed their actions under closer scrutiny and pressured them to meet rising public expectations and standards. The shenanigans of the elite bureaucrats, once tolerated, have now become the public's business. They are being forced to address the crisis in the government's legitimacy that they have spawned.

The myths and taboos of Japan have taken quite a beating in recent years. Issues that never saw the light of day have now become subjects of vigorous media coverage and public debate. Connections between *yakuza*, politicians and bureaucrats are regularly reported. Cherished notions of stable, harmonious families have melted away in the face of widespread reporting on domestic violence, surging divorce and suicide rates, teenage prostitution, and growing challenges to patriarchal bias and gender roles. Corporate Japan no longer enjoys the trust and loyalty it once commanded. It has shed paternalism, made employment less secure, and is guilty of serious and well-publicized ethical breaches. Whistleblowers have shed light on dubious practices while prosecutors have become more zealous in pursuing wrongdoing.

This discrediting of established practices and relationships has led to a reconsideration of the verities of contemporary Japan that has in turn helped to propel the quiet transformation. The crisis in the government's legitimacy resulting from a spate of scandals has become a catalyst for reform. Japan's economic misery, social despair, systemic corruption, and aging society are often cited as proof of Japan's demise. Here they are shown to be vital to Japan's ongoing transformation. The point is not to deny or dismiss the extent of Japan's general malaise, but rather to show how the present crisis is – often unexpectedly – contributing to the forces that are driving its transformation. The foundations of civil society are being laid on the rubble of Japan, Inc.

Japan's civil society is under construction. It is a work in progress that requires careful tending and patience. While the unfinished business of this metamorphosis is substantial, the changes that have occurred over the past decade represent an encouraging start. It is premature either to dismiss the potential of these reforms or to expect that they are the magic cure for what ails the nation. The symptoms of malaise will linger for some time, a legacy of the profligacy of Japan, Inc. This is a transitional era marked by chaos, missed opportunities, half-hearted reforms, breakthroughs, and vigorous resistance from those who stand to lose from reform, transparency, accountability, and a less reticent public.

The potential for improving governance, corporate practices, and the quality of life in Japan is enormous. This will be realized fitfully and incrementally over coming years, a gradual process depending mostly on the actions and choices of the Japanese people. How they respond and partici-pate, who they elect and boot out of office, and how they respond to the demographic and gender crisis will influence the shape and breadth of the transformation. The media and NPOs must also maintain pressure on corpo-rate, political, and bureaucratic leaders to expand transparency while promoting good governance, innovation, and responsive policies. Perhaps the most encouraging development is that the ways and means of the old system have been so thoroughly discredited that there is no turning back; the problems of the present, and those anticipated, are forcing a reinvention of Japan.

Glossary

AIDS Acquired Immuno-deficiency Syndrome. Incurable disease of the immune system resulting from HIV infection that leaves victims vulnerable to various opportunistic infections and diseases.

Amaagari Reference to the not very common practice of corporate employees being hired by ministries that oversee the work of their former employers. Along with *amakudari*, this practice is symbolic of close ties between industry and government.

Amakudari Descent from Heaven. Reference to the common practice of retired senior bureaucrats moving to well-paid, sinecure positions in firms that they dealt with in the course of their government duties. Often criticized as a source of collusive relations between bureaucrats and the firms they hope to join upon retiring.

Article Nine Provision in the Japanese Constitution that bans development of military forces and the resort to war to settle international disputes.

Aum Shinrikyo Supreme Truth Sect. New religion, centered on the teachings of Asahara Shoko, that staged attacks on Tokyo subways in 1995 using sarin gas.

BAD Biological and Antibiotics Division. Section of the Ministry of Health and Welfare responsible for monitoring the safety of blood products when nearly 40 percent of Japan's hemophiliacs became infected with HIV from tainted blood products in the 1980s. Its dual roles in monitoring and promoting industry generated a conflict of interest that was resolved to the detriment of the hemophiliacs.

Borabaito Volunteer work.

BSE Bovine Spongiform Encephalopathy. Popularly known as mad cow disease. Infected cattle develop a progressive brain-wasting disease that can be passed on to humans. The first case in Japan was discovered in September 2001.

Burakumin 'Hamlet people' is the term used to refer to some one million Japanese today, visually indistinguishable from other Japanese, who suffer discrimination in jobs, housing, marriage, and so on because they are identified as being members of this caste. During the Tokugawa era

(1603–1868) this caste became hereditary and was linked to 'polluting' activities such as slaughtering animals.

Dango Bid-rigging among contractors involved in public works construction projects. Symbolizes the corruption, collusion, and orchestration of 'competition' blamed for significantly raising project costs. Cited by foreign contractors as a practice that excludes them.

Diet Parliament in Japan composed of elected upper and lower houses.

Doken kokka Construction state. Reference to Japan's cement industrial complex and vast spending on public works projects carrying implications of environmental devastation and political corruption.

Dorozoku Road tribe. Group of LDP Diet members who lobby for road-building projects and use their political influence to promote the *doken kokka* in general and try to steer pork-barrel projects to their home districts.

Enjo kosai Compensated dating (prostitution) usually between junior- or high-school girls and middle-aged men, often involving sex for money.

Enkai gyosei Partying bureaucrat. Civil servants involved in entertaining as part of their work as in *kan-kan settai*.

Filial piety Confucian virtue of respect for older relatives and one's ancestors that draws on and reinforces patriarchal values.

FILP Fiscal Investment and Loan Program. The so-called second budget (*zaito*) borrowed largely from Postal Savings accounts at low interest rates to supplement the official budget. It is actually nearly five times larger than the official budget and is also less transparent to public scrutiny.

Freeters Free arbeiters, or freelance part-time or temporary workers. This is portrayed rather romantically in the media as a countercultural lifestyle choice, but in reality means that many young people find themselves stuck in dead-end, low-paying jobs with few benefits and no career prospects. The prolonged recession and changing corporate employment practices means many young people, especially high-school graduates, have no other option.

Gaiatsu Foreign pressure. This term refers to the pressures put on the Japanese government by other governments to modify various policies. In some cases, such pressures are actually welcomed as a way to overcome a domestic political impasse that is preventing necessary reforms desired by the government. However, inviting or staging *gaiatsu* as a means of overcoming political inertia has nurtured public resentments about what is portrayed in the mass media as high-handed tactics by other nations, notably the USA.

Gaijin Foreigner(s).

Gakkyo hokai Classroom collapse. Reference to teachers who lose control of their classrooms to unruly students.

Gaman Tough it out. Mental and physical discipline and fortitude.

Generation Slump The Japanese generation aged 18–24 in the late 1990s.

Gengo Imperial system of periodization calculated such that the first year of an Emperor's reign is designated Year 1 and so on: for example, 2003 is Heisei 15, the fifteenth year of Emperor Akihito's reign. Official dates in Japan and even rail passes are commonly based on this system.

Giri Obligation one incurs in accordance with social expectations.

Gyosei shido Administrative guidance. Reference to informal manner in which bureaucrats wield their broad regulatory and discretionary powers to ensure corporate compliance with government goals and policies. Implicit is the threat to use those powers in a manner harmful to those who do not comply.

Habatsu Factions within the LDP.

Haenuki Employees of special public corporations (*tokushu hojin*). They tend to resent the employment of retired senior bureaucrats in *amakudari* positions who do no work for high salaries.

Hakko ichiu Eight corners of the world under one roof. Reference to the imperial ambitions of Japan during the 1930s and 1940s, when it sought to unify Asia under its control, and displace Western colonial powers, through military expansion.

Hanshin Earthquake The Kobe earthquake of 1995. Refers to the name of the region.

Heisei Era of 'achieving of peace' (1989 to present) under the reign of Emperor Akihito.

Hikikomori Socially withdrawn young people who tend to avoid others by staying in their homes. This syndrome is attributed to a combination of problems including bullying and stress at school or the workplace.

Hinomaru National flag with red circle in middle of white background.

HIV Human Immuno-deficiency Virus. A retrovirus discovered in 1981 that in 70 percent of cases leads to AIDS within ten years of onset. In Japan, most cases have been hemophiliacs infected by tainted blood products.

Honne Inner feelings, usually unexpressed because they do not conform to social norms and expectations.

Ie Patriarchal family system that denied women independence and legal rights. The Constitution sought to correct this bias with decidedly mixed results. Many Japanese women today still bridle under what they see as the legacy of this male-oriented system in the home, in society, and at work. Conservatives often blame current social problems on the decline of the *ie* system.

Ijime Bullying is a pervasive practice in society aimed at imposing conformity within a specific group and ostracizing those who do not conform or meet expectations. High-profile suicides among students show this problem to be especially evident in schools.

Iron Triangle Nexus of power involving big business, the bureaucracy, and the Liberal Democratic Party (LDP) said to control Japan in the postwar era.

IWC International Whaling Commission. Established in 1946 to manage world whale stocks. Imposed a moratorium on whaling in 1986 credited with rescuing several species from the brink of extinction. More recently a forum for acrimonious exchanges between pro- and anti-whaling nations divided over the resumption of commercial whaling.

Japan, Inc. Term coined to characterize the close and cooperative – some say collusive – relationship between the government and big business in Japan and the government's preoccupation with promoting economic growth at all costs. Symbolic of the pro-producer and materialist orientation of postwar Japan.

JCLU Japan Civil Liberties Union.

Jinja Honcho National Shrine Association. Major Shinto organization with powerful right-wing political connections.

Jiyu Jinken Kyokai Japan Civil Liberties Union.

Jiyukushakai Mature society. Reference to the contemporary Japanese desire for a focus on quality-of-life issues and a more people-friendly society. Seen as acknowledgement that the economic heyday is over, it signifies a shift in values away from materialistic obsessions of postwar Japan.

Joho kokai Information disclosure. Reference to the movement for more transparency in government and legislation mandating greater disclosure of information gathered and controlled by bureaucrats.

JRC Judicial Reform Council. Developed various proposals that have been transforming Japan's judiciary and the legal profession since 2002.

Juki Net National data registration system introduced in 2002. The absence of a promised privacy law aimed at protecting the data from illicit use led to more than 4 million people withholding their personal information from the network at the time it was launched. This campaign of civil disobedience involves citizens asserting their rights and not meekly submitting to government directives.

Jusen Real estate lending subsidiaries of banks that incurred massive unrecoverable loans in the wake of the bubble, threatening the collapse of the Japanese financial system in the mid-1990s and forcing a government bailout despite strong public criticism.

Kaiware daikon White radish spouts commonly used as a garnish that were the officially designated, however unlikely, source of an outbreak of E. coli food poisoning in 1996.

Kakaku hakkai Price destruction. Reference to price deflation in 1990s and the proliferation of discounting.

Kan-kan settai Bureaucrats entertaining bureaucrats. Reference to widespread practice of prefectural officials lavishly wining and dining central government officials in the hope of gaining a greater allocation of public funds. Revelations about this excessive squandering of public monies discredited bureaucrats and whetted the public appetite for greater information disclosure about how taxpayers' money is spent.

Kanson mimpi 'Revere the official, despise the people', shorthand for bureaucratic arrogance towards the public.

Karashutcho Empty business trip. Reference to common practice of public servants claiming expenses for trips they never made. Revelations about this practice in the mid-1990s discredited bureaucrats and gave momentum to supporters of greater information disclosure.

Karoshi Death from overwork. Symbolizes the distortions imposed by a corporate-centered lifestyle wherein employees are expected to make every sacrifice, and endure every inconvenience, for the good of their employer. In the 1990s the media and government came to pay much more critical attention to this phenomenon, reflecting a general shift in attitudes away from those that prevailed in much of the postwar era. Compensation is now mandated for certified cases.

Keidanren Japan Federation of Economic Organizations. Big-business lobbying organization.

Keiretsu Bank-centered, industrial conglomerates that dominate the Japanese economy, many of which emerged from the prewar *zaibatsu*. The exclusionary business practices and conflicts of interest within the *keiretsu* have come under scrutiny as a source of trade friction, uncompetitive practices, and for contributing to the economic bubble and its aftermath.

Keitai Cellular (mobile) phones. Pervasively used in Japan, where they also provide limited internet access and are frequently used for brief email exchanges.

Keizai Doyukai Japan Association of Corporate Executives.

Kigyo chushinshugi Corporate welfare. Fading notion that corporations have socially sanctioned obligations to workers. This means, for example, that firms would not fire workers even if they did not need them. In general, firms have been reluctant to fire workers and many unneeded workers are still kept on payrolls, reducing competitiveness and slowing recovery in corporate balance sheets. However, this inclination is declining, a wrenching shift that has been widely lamented in Japan. The reliance on corporate welfare has meant that public welfare programs and policies are not well developed.

Kimigayo Your Majesty's Reign. The national anthem, controversial because of its symbolic links to zealous wartime patriotism and apparent reference to the days when the Emperor was absolute monarch. Legally sanctioning this song in 1999 and compelling students to sing it at school assemblies has been a divisive political issue.

Kinken seiji Money politics. Cause of political scandals that have tarnished democracy in Japan and left voters skeptical about party politics.

Koeki hojin Public interest legal persons. Legal status NPOs can apply for that makes it easier for them to function and qualify for tax breaks.

Koenkai Local political support organizations that mobilize voters and funds for politicians.

Kokusaika Internationalization. Concept frequently invoked with mixed results to broaden horizons among Japanese and inculcate a positive attitude for interaction with foreigners and their cultures.

Komeito Clean Government Party. Member of the ruling coalition of parties linked to the Soka Gakkai, a large Buddhist organization.

Koseki Family register maintained over the generations with information about births, deaths, marriages, and so on.

Kozo oshoku Structural corruption. Reference to the tawdry ways and means of party politics in Japan.

LDP Liberal Democratic Party formed by a merger of the Liberal Party and Democratic Party in 1955. Conservative political party that has dominated postwar Japanese politics.

Lost Decade 1990s Japan, when the economy imploded and the postwar system became thoroughly discredited.

Maru-nage Throw it all. Reference to the practice of small local firms winning preferential bidding on local public works projects, taking their cut, and then subcontracting the actual work to national construction firms. Another reason for high project costs.

MBM Meat-and-bone meal. Cattle feed fortified with slaughtered cow carcasses, which is suspected of being a source of BSE (mad cow disease) transmission.

Messhi hoko Self-sacrifice.

METI Ministry of Economy, Trade, and Industry (METI), formerly MITI.

MHW Ministry of Health and Welfare (Koseisho). Now known as the Ministry of Health, Welfare, and Labor (Koseirodosho).

MITI Ministry of International Trade and Industry, now reorganized as the Ministry of Economy, Trade, and Industry (METI).

Monkasho Ministry of Education, Culture, Sports, Science, and Technology. Formerly the Monbusho (Ministry of Education).

Mura hachibu Village ostracism imposed on those who do not meet social expectations in rural Japan. Generally refers to exclusion of those who do not conform.

Nagatacho District in central Tokyo known as the seat of political power.

Narikin Nouveau riche who emerged during the bubble at the end of the 1980s who engaged in conspicuous and often garish consumption fueled by wealth generated by spiraling land and stock prices.

Nasakenai Clueless. Common reference to middle-aged men.

National Citizen Ombudsmen (Zenkoku Shimin Ombudsmen) National network of activist lawyers working to promote, among other progressive causes, transparency and accountability in government through information disclosure ordinances.

Nenko Seniority employment system that has determined wages and promotions, but is now no longer sacrosanct as firms shift towards a more merit-oriented system.

NGOs Non-governmental organizations, usually citizen groups with an international orientation.

Nihon Izokukai Association of War Bereaved Families. Large right-wing organization that maintains close ties with the LDP and advocates unrepentant views about Japan's role in World War II.

Nihon Shohisa Renmei Consumers' Union of Japan.

Nikkeiren Japan Federation of Employers Association. Big-business lobbying organization. Merged with Keidanren into the Japan Business Federation in 2002

Nippon Keidanren Japan Business Federation. Merger between Keidanren and Nikkeiren established in 2002. Big-business lobbying organization.

Nopantsushabushabu Notorious restaurants featuring beef, mirrored floors, and waitresses wearing short skirts and no panties. Wining and dining of Ministry of Finance bureaucrats at such establishments by businessmen under their jurisdiction provoked public outrage in the late 1990s and became symbolic of the collusion between corporate Japan and the government, and the special favors involved.

Nosuizoku Group of LDP Diet members who lobby for agrobusiness interests.

NPOs Nonprofit organizations, usually citizen groups with a domestic orientation.

Nureochiba Sticky wet leaves that are hard to brush off. Negative reference to retired husbands.

On Personal sense of social debt or obligation created in a relationship by a benevolent act.

Oyajigari The hunting of middle-aged men. Reference to attacks on middle-aged men by younger males for money and/or entertainment.

Parasite singles Derogatory term coined in 1999 to refer to young single working people who live at home with their parents. It is mostly used to criticize the lifestyle choices of young women, blaming them for various social and economic problems. This term, and its popularity, reflects a lingering patriarchal bias.

Recruit Large job and educational information company that became symbolic of political corruption due to massive stock-for-favors scandal in late 1980s.

Rengo Largest and most influential umbrella union organization.

Reverse course After 1947, the US Occupation in Japan became influenced by the Cold War between the USA and USSR. Punitive policies were replaced by an emphasis on rebuilding Japan into a showcase for American-style democracy and capitalism. The progressive New Deal policies implemented between 1945 and 1947 were in many cases 'reversed' by more conservative policies. Prior to 1947, SCAP and the Japanese government sought to prosecute right-wing militarists, but after 1947 the government engaged in what is known as the Red Purge, cracking down on left-wing unions and activists.

Romusha Day laborer. Reference to the system of forced labor imposed by the Japanese on local Southeast Asians during World War II, especially in Indonesia. Mostly used on various infrastructure projects where working and living conditions were harsh. It is estimated that more than 1 million *romusha* died from disease, malnutrition, and harsh treatment, belying the ideology of pan-Asian cooperation and liberation that has been used to justify Japan's invasion and occupation of Southeast Asia in 1942–45.

Saikoyoseido Practice of rehiring newly retired employees at a significant reduction in salary.

Salarymen (*sararimen*) Salaried white-collar workers who are often the subject and object of both mockery and respect. Image of hard-working, extremely loyal company employees who place greater emphasis on work than on the family and personal desires.

SDF Self-Defense Forces (*Jietai* in Japanese). The military forces of Japan.

Sebango The eleven-digit number assigned to people under the Juki Net system for storing and accessing personal data. Expected to function like the Social Security number in the USA.

Shinjikai Government advisory councils. Membership often drawn from among prominent people and academia. In general, tend to ratify the proposals and policies prepared by bureaucrats with little input on content.

Shinjinrui New breed. A negative reference by older people to criticize various presumed failings of the younger generation.

Shirukenri The right to know. Legal concept related to information disclosure.

Showa Era of 'peace' (1926–89) under the reign of Emperor Hirohito.

Shufuren Japan Housewives' Association.

Soapland Establishment where men pay for sexual services.

Sodaigomi Large, hard to move garbage that gets in the way. Reference by exasperated wives to retired, often demanding husbands sitting around the house.

Sokaiya Corporate extortionists linked with the *yakuza* who threaten to expose company secrets and disrupt shareholder meetings unless they are paid substantial sums. The government and firms have tried to curb this widespread practice.

Tanshinfunin Solitary transfer. Reference to common practice of a husband relocating to a residence separate from his family due to periodic job transfers. The firm expects the husband to accept any assignment for the good of the company. In many instances the family remains at the existing residence for the benefit of children's education and to minimize disruption related to frequent relocation. However, this corporate practice of creating absentee husbands is seen to place a strain on family relationships.

Tatemae Public behavior conforming to acceptable norms.

Toko kyohi School refusal. Reference to the rising level of truancy among school-age children.

Tokushu hojin Special public corporations that hire many retiring bureaucrats at high salaries in sinecure positions. This is a vast network of semi-governmental, loss-making corporations that depend on massive public subsidies, contributing to government deficits.

Ubasteyama Traditional practice/legend that involved abandoning elderly people in remote mountain areas to die as a way of coping with limited food and allowing younger generation to marry and carry on the family line.

Uyoku Ultra-nationalist groups, linked with mobsters and conservative politicians, that lobby for various conservative issues, usually by blaring martial music and speeches from dark buses decorated with Japanese flags. Resort to threats and actual violence to intimidate and silence progressives critical of their activities or the Emperor system.

vCJD variant Creutzfeldt-Jakob Disease. Brain-wasting disease in humans linked to consumption of beef infected with BSE (mad cow disease). There have been over 100 deaths from this disease in Europe, mostly concentrated in the United Kingdom.

Watari Migratory officials. Common practice by public officials of retiring in succession from a number of positions for the purpose of accumulating retirement allowances and pensions.

Yakugai *Gai* (harm) caused by *yakusho* (government offices) and *yakunin* (government officials). Common term from the mid-1990s reflecting the loss of public confidence in bureaucrats due to various scandals and mistakes involving them.

Yakuza Organized crime syndicates in Japan.

Yoko-suberi Lateral transfer. A job practice among bureaucrats similar to *amakudari*.

Yonigei Running away at night. Service to help heavily indebted households run away from debtors and establish new identities.

Zaibatsu Family-owned industrial conglomerates that dominated the prewar Japanese economy. Initially these were targeted for dissolution by SCAP because they were held responsible for supporting and abetting the 1931–45 military rampage through Asia. However, after the reverse course, SCAP did not aggressively proceed with the dissolution. During the Occupation the ownership and structure of these conglomerates was transformed and the prewar *zaibatsu* became the postwar *keiretsu*.

Zaitech Speculative activities by corporations in land and stock unrelated to core business activities.

Zaito Fiscal Investment and Loan Program (FILP). The so-called second budget borrowed largely from Postal Savings accounts at low interest rates to supplement the official budget. It is actually larger than the official budget and also less transparent to public scrutiny.

Zenkoku Shimin Ombudsmen (National Citizen Ombudsmen) National network of activists and lawyers working to promote, among other progressive causes, transparency and accountability in government through information disclosure ordinances.

Zoku-giin Diet members who act as patrons of particular ministries. Refers to politicians who regularly meddle in policymaking, contract bidding, and regulatory matters on behalf of those who make it worth their while to do so. Diet members develop an 'expertise' in a certain area and form close ties with bureaucrats in the relevant ministry who provide them with information, access, and opportunities to influence policy outcomes for the benefit of their political supporters.

Notes

1 The Lost Decade of the 1990s

1 In Japan, both the standard Western calendar and the gengo system are used whereby the era is given an auspicious name and years are calculated from the date that the reigning emperor, currently Emperor Akihito, ascended to the throne – thus 2003 is Heisei 15. Heisei means 'era of achieving peace.'

2 *Japan Media Review – Wireless Report* is an excellent forum for a discussion about the social implications of internet-equipped *keitai* (cellular phones) in Japan. For example, see Ito Mizuko's posting of March 10, 2003, 'A New Set of Rules for a Newly Wireless Society.' She discusses Howard Rheingold's *Smart Mobs* (Perseus Publishing: NY, 2002) and presents her own views about the social revolution in communications in Japan related to ubiquitous *keitai* usage. Other contributors take a more guarded view about the revolutionary impact of *keitai*; see, for example, Tim Clark, 'Japan's Generation of Computer Refuseniks,' *Japan Media Review*, Wireless Report (March 22, 2003).

3 Neary (2002) also sees the 1990s as a watershed in human rights practices in Japan. His findings corroborate perceptions that civil society is becoming more robust in Japan.

4 Japan, Inc. is a common term used to evoke the corporate-centered, capitalist nature of the Japanese polity in which the government systematically favors producers over consumers and domestic businesses over international competitors. Here it is used as a convenient shorthand for the nexus of practices, arrangements, relationships, networks, institutions, attitudes, policies, and patterns that have prevailed in, and defined, Japan following World War II.

5 See Dehesh and Pugh (1999) for an insightful discussion of the international and domestic factors that caused the bubble.

6 As of April 2003 the Nikkei stock average hovered near 8,000, down from nearly 40,000 at the end of 1989.

7 Estimates of real estate prices, especially during the bubble era, should be treated with caution – they are educated guesses and do not necessarily reflect what the market would bear.

8 The belief that land prices could only rise resulted from the sustained increase in urban land values in postwar Japan. Of course, there were pronounced cycles in land values prior to the late 1980s bubble that corresponded with loose monetary policies, leading to significant volatility in urban land prices in 1961, 1974, and 1980. In general, however, for those who bought and held, it was hard to go wrong in stock and land investments in this era. This explains why banks readily loaned vast sums of money for questionable schemes with little credit risk analysis; land was considered solid collateral – despite excessive valuations – because its value had always risen and it was assumed that any drop in land prices

signaled a buying opportunity rather than a logical correction. Thus the myth that land prices always rise and are immune to business cycles was a powerful factor in triggering the asset bubble.

9 The recent bursting of the US stock market bubble, especially in the technology sector, demonstrates the proclivity for a herd mentality and a collective amnesia about the effects of previous bubbles. It is important to bear in mind that the Japanese asset bubble was driven by corporate speculation. The proportion of Japanese households owning stocks was 8.5 percent in 1985, 9 percent in 1990, 6.4 percent in 1995, and 6.4 percent in 1999; the comparative figures for the USA were 13 percent in 1985, 12.5 percent in 1990, 18.7 percent in 1995, and 24.2 percent in 1999. The relatively low figures for Japan help explain why the asset bubble and its collapse have not been as catastrophic as one might expect. However, households that borrowed to buy real estate during the bubble era have been badly hit by collapsing values and negative equity in their houses or apartments.

10 In response to clear signals from Washington favoring a cheap dollar, Japanese institutional investors unloaded significant portions of their dollar-denominated investments in stocks and bonds and reinvested much of this money in yen-denominated investments at home. This was a significant development as capital flows from Japan to the USA had risen from only $5 billion in 1970–71 to $75 billion between 1985 and 1988, accounting for 3.6 percent of Japan's GDP. This surge in capital outflows occurred in the context of internationalization of global finance and the financing of US deficits by a recycling of Japanese trade surpluses in the form of investments.

11 Hartcher (1997) attributes this monetary easing to pressure from the Ministry of Finance, which was reluctant to use fiscal measures such as tax cuts to stimulate domestic demand.

12 Japanese firms affiliated with the same *keiretsu* or core bank often invest in one another's shares to prevent takeovers and insulate management from stockholder pressures. These were stable, long-term relationships that were designed to minimize volatility in stock prices and maintain control of ownership within the *keiretsu* by significantly limiting the amount of a firm's stock that traded on the market. Thus, the general surge in demand for stocks beginning in 1987 had an amplified impact on stock prices. In the 1990s these relationships have unraveled to some extent in response to mounting financial pressures.

13 The government also had a vested interest in raising asset prices as it facilitated, and rendered more profitable, the privatization of public-sector enterprises such as Japan National Railways (JNR) and Nippon Telegraph and Telephone (NTT) during the 1980s.

14 Annual surveys conducted by the Prime Minister's Office indicate that more than 90 percent of Japanese claim to be middle class.

15 Huge disparities in wealth already existed, and the myth of the middle class sat uncomfortably against prevailing realities. However, the sudden emergence of a class of conspicuous consumers drew extensive media attention, stirred jealousies and undermined the social cohesion nurtured by the cherished myth of equality.

16 The impact of the economic malaise on families, including suicide, is discussed in Chapter 10.

17 On the influence of *sokaiya* see Szymkowiak (2001).

18 See Dower (1999) and Bix (2000) regarding the decision to exempt Hirohito from prosecution and testifying before war crimes tribunals, and his importance to the USA in promoting their reform agenda. In cooperation with the Japanese government, the USA cultivated an image of Hirohito as a peace-loving, powerless puppet of the military who bore no responsibility for Japan's wartime

excesses. These scholars argue that failure to hold him accountable made it easier for Japanese in general to avoid taking responsibility for the war.

19 See Schaller (1985), Cohen (1987), Finn (1992), and Takemae (2002) for a discussion of the 'reverse course' in the US Occupation of Japan. This began in 1947 and signaled the abandonment of many progressive political and economic reforms in favor of relying on the conservative business and political elite to quickly rebuild Japan. See Dower (1999) for a fuller discussion of the social history of the Occupation and the lively interplay between occupier and occupied.

20 See Tanaka (1998) for a thoughtful assessment of these atrocities.

21 See Havens (1987) for a discussion of the impact of, and responses to, the Vietnam War in Japan. Ienaga (2001) sheds light on his role as a pioneer in the battle against the Ministry of Education's censorship of textbooks. Hein and Selden (2000) offer a comparative study of the issues of textbook censorship and selective war memories.

22 Over the entire postwar era there have been Japanese military veterans who drew attention to Japan's grim record all over Asia in 1931–45, but until the 1990s their voices and experiences were largely ignored, discredited or pushed to the periphery.

23 McCormack (2000) is especially good on this subject.

24 Fujioka Nobukatsu, Kanji Nishio, and Kobayashi Yoshinori are prominent in this camp.

25 This issue is taken up in Chapter 9.

26 See Murakami (2001) for a collection of interviews with victims of the subway attack by one of Japan's leading novelists.

27 In 2003 the court handed down suspended sentences to the six company executives responsible for the processing operations in Tokaimura that led to the accident and fined their company, JCO, ¥1 million ($8,000). This token punishment reflects the way in which corporate interests in Japan, as in other countries, remain insulated from meaningful standards of accountability.

28 In 2003, the Nagoya High Court ruled in favor of plaintiffs residing in the vicinity of Monju eager to mothball the trouble-plagued plant; this has postponed plans to restart the reactor. This landmark decision is the first victory by a citizens' group in a nuclear power plant lawsuit. The government is appealing the verdict, in which the judge agreed with the plaintiffs that fundamental design and safety flaws justify nullifying the original approvals to build and operate the reactor. This unexpected ruling is expected to bolster similar legal challenges around the nation and create new obstacles for proponents of nuclear energy.

29 In 2003, all seventeen of the nuclear power-plant reactors run by Tokyo Electric Power (TEPCO) were shut down as a consequence of the record-falsification scandal. Local government officials were angered to learn of the record falsification and criticized the opaque management of these facilities in their towns. Although one town council passed a non-binding resolution to shut down the local power plant permanently, central government and the nuclear industry hold the legal trump cards in any showdown.

30 In late 2002, I had chance encounters with two men working in the nuclear power industry. An industry official treated me to a tirade against the media for blowing the issue out of proportion while indicating no remorse or embarrassment about the cover-up or failure to follow established procedures. From his perspective as an expert, the reported problems constituted no safety threat and thus there was no need to alarm a public already prey to 'irrational' fears about nuclear power. The other man, a consultant, readily admitted that the media had revealed only the tip of the iceberg and that the practice of falsifying inspection and repair records is widespread. In his view there is more concern among industry and

government officials over sensational media exposés than about nuclear mishaps and the public interest. He added that the exposure of the whistleblower by government officials to industry counterparts is exactly the sort of problem created by overly close ties between bureaucrats and those they oversee. While supporting greater reliance on nuclear energy, he noted that the cult of secrecy and disastrous public relations have unintentionally fanned opposition to the industry and made it difficult to win the public's trust.

31 See Bowen (2003) on Japan's political malaise and the ways in which political corruption undermines democracy. Significantly, many of the key reforms detailed in the following chapters are being achieved despite dysfunctional party politics and the corrosion of democratic practices and institutions described by Bowen. The success of citizen groups and NPOs in challenging existing practice and policies, and promoting reforms – with the support of powerful actors including Keidanren, a more feisty press and judiciary, and some politicians and bureaucrats – indicates that the health of Japan's democracy cannot be judged solely on taking the temperature of party politics. Paradoxically, fundamental legal and institutional reforms are happening while the structural corruption that Bowen laments continues. Democracy may not be happening in Nagatacho, but this does not mean that it isn't happening elsewhere in Japan and in different ways that are effectively bypassing or selectively mobilizing support in the Diet and ministries. Watching citizens oppose the government's national data registration system, demanding transparent government by using information disclosure legislation, electing anti-party-machine governors around the nation, initiating referendums, and suing the government over issues ranging from visits to Yasukuni Shrine to nuclear power plants (often with the support of volunteer-staffed NPOs), raises serious doubts about his assertion that Japan is a *shigata ga nai* (it can't be helped) society where a passive citizenry is allowing democracy to wither.

32 Mulgan 2002 analyzes the causes of failed reform in Japan and argues that the structure of the policymaking process, involving complex linkages between the ruling party and the bureaucracy, is weighted against reform. She shows how Prime Minister Koizumi's economic reform agenda was effectively stymied. Her pessimism about the prospects for reform seems exaggerated given the significant policy reforms already achieved, and detailed in the following chapters, that have made their way through the system and past the gatekeepers.

33 Critics such as Katz (2003) argue that the failure of the government to shut down the zombie companies that cannot repay their debts is worsening the non-performing loan problem, causing deflation, and making life difficult for sound firms, because troubled companies will cut prices in order to generate enough sales revenues just to stay afloat. Others argue that vested interests are the chief enemies of reform. There is an assumption among critics that market-oriented prescriptions for what ails Japan are the only alternative. However, Japan's policymakers are wary of market forces and reluctant to embrace economic orthodoxy and the painful consequences it would entail. They believe that shutting down major employers will swell unemployment, swamp an inadequate social safety net, depress consumption, worsen deflation, and increase fiscal deficits. The critics debate whether Japan's policymakers are hostages to vested interests, merely inept, paralyzed or pragmatically muddling through. Katz argues that the government will be forced to jumpstart the economy by closing down the zombie debtors, thus easing deflation, encouraging new businesses, and channeling capital more efficiently. Resolution of the non-performing loan problem, he argues, is a precondition for recovery. He anticipates sharp gains in productivity from the adoption of industry best practices in low productivity

sectors. He also advocates an opening of markets to imports as a way to sharpen competition, spur innovation, and raise productivity.

34 The 1999 hit film *Kinyu Fushoku Retto Jubaku* (Jubaku: The Archipelago of Rotten Money) dealt with the same nexus of corruption depicted by Kurosawa, albeit in a less subtle fashion, showing that the same themes persist despite the changing times.

35 For more information on levels of foreign direct investment into Japan see: www.meti.go.jp/english/information/data/cFDIJapane.html (accessed April 6, 2004).

36 Apparently not by his employees, however. When I mentioned Ghosn's positive media image to the wife of a Nissan employee I know, she replied that her husband and his coworkers despise Ghosn and consider him cold-hearted and uncaring about the misery he has caused by shutting factories and firing employees. To them it is especially galling that he is lionized for what they view as a betrayal.

37 In Japan, nonprofit organizations (NPOs) are usually focused on domestic issues while non-governmental organizations (NGOs) are engaged in internationally oriented activities. The new legislation facilitates the establishment of both.

38 On subsequent 'research' visits I learned that the proprietor rents 'space' on Rakuten Ichiba, Japan's most popular internet shopping mall. He is charged ¥50,000 ($400) a month to be featured on the site and pays a 4 percent commission on sales exceeding ¥1 million ($8,000) each month. He says that 50 percent of his sales come from this portal while his own website generates another 10–20 percent of his business, indicating just how important the internet is to his small business.

39 Camel Cigarettes in 2003

40 Neary (2002) argues that Japan's Korean community is suffering less institutional discrimination since the 1990s in a context of generally improving human rights practices in Japan.

41 The Tokugawa government (1603–1868) made *burakumin* into a hereditary caste for those engaged in 'polluting' activities such as slaughtering animals. Although castes were officially abolished in the nineteenth century, *burakumin* have remained a distinct lower class facing a high degree of discrimination.

42 See Chapter 10 for a discussion of these demographic imperatives and their implications.

2 Information disclosure

1 See www.freedominfo.org for an excellent collection of papers and useful links regarding freedom of information issues and case studies.

2 See L. Repeta, 'Japan – Breaking Down the Walls of Secrecy: The Story of the Citizens' Movement for an Information Disclosure Law,' July 2002, available at www.freedominfo.org (accessed April 6, 2004).

3 See L. Repeta, 'The Birth of the Freedom of Information Act in Japan: Kanagawa 1982,' MIT Japan Program Working Paper 03–01, September 2003 available at www.freedominfo.org (accessed April 6, 2004).

4 See Crenson and Ginsberg (2002) for a compelling and sobering discussion of how citizens have been sidelined in American politics in a process they refer to as 'downsizing democracy.' Their findings suggest caution in assessing the potential of information disclosure and other legislative reforms in nurturing civil society. For a detailed analysis of freedom of information in Japan and how it compares with the USA see L. Repeta and D.M. Schultz, 'Japanese Government Information: New Rules for Access – The 2001 Information Disclosure Law, and

a Comparison with the US FOIA,' July 2002, available at www.freedominfo.org (accessed April 6, 2004).

5 *Asahi*, May 29, 2002.
6 *International Herald Tribune*, June 17, 2002.
7 Although new privacy legislation enacted in 2003 omits the controversial intrusions on media freedom, elements of the bill are still seen as too ambiguous and could be broadly interpreted in ways that have nothing to do with protecting citizens from snooping into their personal information. Under the law proposed in 2002, a reporter interviewing a politician involved in a bribery scandal would have been forced to get permission to use such information. Under the new bill, such permission is no longer required and punitive sanctions have been dropped. The government has also enacted a related bill designed to protect personal data held by central government offices. This bill introduces penalties for government employees who pass on personal information to third parties without just cause. Private firms are also subject to penalties for unauthorized use of personal data. Concerns about adequate safeguards remain, as do suspicions about the government's use of data collected under the Juki Net system. The media has given a lukewarm reception to the new legislation, welcoming the revisions affecting journalism while expressing concerns about vague provisions that could permit government intrusion on civil liberties.
8 *Japan Times*, June 15, 2002.
9 *Asahi*, June 7, 2003.
10 Municipalities such as Suginami and Yokohama that are at the forefront of the Juki Net resistance have a long tradition of progressive citizens' movements, suggesting connections between current developments and activism in the 1960s and 1970s.
11 In May 2003, Suginami-ku followed the Yokohama model in allowing citizens to choose whether to join Juki Net. As of 2003, only two of the original six municipalities maintained a full boycott of Juki Net, but resistance to plugging into the network remains powerful despite considerable national government pressure.
12 *Aera*, August 12–19, 2002.
13 *Japan Times*, August 28, 2000.

3 Building civil society: NPOs and judicial reform

1 See, for example, Howard French, 'Japan's Shrunken Role: Is It Permanent?,' August 12, 2002, *International Herald Tribune*.
2 The Meiji modernization was crafted by an oligarchy dominated by former samurai from Satsuma and Choshu, who implemented their program under the unassailable aegis of the Emperor Meiji. The reforms of the Occupation era were enacted by a coalition of American and Japanese technocrats and reflect robust debate between the two groups. As a result of the indirect nature of the Occupation, the Americans relied heavily on Japanese bureaucrats to implement their agenda, offering considerable leeway to dilute, alter, or stall reforms. Although a vigorous public debate was conducted over these reforms in Japan, SCAP was an autocratic body and measures were imposed without the compromises and concessions characteristic of democracy. See Dower (1999) and Takemae (2002) for comprehensive assessments of how policies were devised and implemented during the Occupation, and Gordon (2003) for the Meiji era.
3 McCormack's views about war memory, national identity and constitutional revision are reflected in national debate but are largely rejected by national leaders. However, his views about the construction state, farm policies, 'resortification,' and unsustainable environmental policies have become

embedded in the rhetoric, and to some extent positions, of those in power and are regularly featured in the national press.

4 See Yamamoto 1998 for a discussion of how state–NPO relations have evolved in response to perceived needs.

5 See the Introduction to McCormack (1996) for an incisive analysis of the bureaucratic blunders and mindset that exacerbated this natural disaster and undermined the government's credibility.

6 I am indebted to Ogawa Akihiro, a doctoral candidate at Cornell University who conducted fieldwork in a Tokyo NPO 2002–03, for this insight. He focuses on what he terms the 'colonization' of NPOs by the government and how bureaucrats orchestrate participation, set agendas, and control from above what is ostensibly a grassroots movement. In his view, the volunteer movement is largely controlled and supported by the government while *shimin dantai* (social activist groups), usually associated with NPOs and NGOs elsewhere in the world, have been shunted aside. This conscious peripheralization of social activists from the sanctioned volunteer movement suggests that the potential for critical scrutiny of government by NPOs is being stifled. However, government obstruction does not mean that NPOs are unable to exercise a monitoring function and support transparency and accountability. Certainly, the government remains suspicious and fearful of social activists, but an ability to control some NPOs does not mean that it can manipulate all of them nor prevent unintended consequences. Many activists will not develop partnerships with government and will continue to challenge official efforts to sideline them. Indeed, this helps explain why such a high proportion of NPOs have not sought official recognition despite the legal and financial advantages. In addition, savvier citizens can cope with bureaucrats and effectively challenge how the volunteer sphere is defined and functions: not all of the 'colonized' are meekly submitting to the 'colonizer,' and they now have more weapons at hand to resist co-optation, assert their agendas and influence society.

7 The government proposal in March 2003 to curtail tax exemptions for public-interest corporations (*koeki hojin*) demonstrates the NPO movement's vulnerability to bureaucratic interference. A number of high-profile scandals involving businesses that have fraudulently claimed not-for-profit status have led the government to express concern about abuse of the full or partial exemption from corporate taxes of 30 percent. However, the proposed reforms mean that NPOs are at risk of losing the limited tax benefits that they currently enjoy and facing increased financial strains. Making it easier for NPOs to secure tax-exempt status is a crucial, but as yet unrealized, reform.

8 *Japan Times*, September 28, 2000.

9 In 2002 the two major business associations, Keidanren (Japan Federation of Economic Organizations) and Nikkeiren (Japan Federation of Employer's Associations), merged and are now known as Nippon Keidanren (Japan Business Federation).

10 This initiative reflects concerns about youth 'tuning out and turning off,' media coverage of their antisocial behavior, and a broader debate about the role of education in instilling the virtues of good citizenship. The participation of young volunteers in the Kobe relief effort has failed to dispel deep-rooted doubts about today's youth and their lack of the basic values cherished by their elders.

11 *AERA*, a weekly magazine published by *Asahi* newspaper (December 9, 2002), recommends readers improve the quality of their lives by volunteering.

12 These statistics were presented by Barnett Baron, Asia Foundation, at the Symposium on State–NGO Relations in Japan, the USA, and Europe held in Tokyo on May 27, 2002.

13 China is also promoting a vast expansion in the number of lawyers and has

assisted Temple University in opening up a law program in Beijing. However, there is no official numerical target for legal professionals,
14 Keizai Doyukai 1997, as cited in Sato 2002: 77.
15 See Upham (1987) for discussion of informal conflict-resolution procedures in Japan.
16 Out of the roughly 45,000 applicants in 2002, nearly 10,000 were women, the highest percentage ever. As in the USA, professional degrees are seen as the key to personal autonomy and the most effective means to overcome barriers to promotion and discrimination that impede women's career advancement in other fields.
17 In late 2003 an advisory panel submitted plans for a high court specializing in patent disputes to be based in Tokyo that will handle all such court cases nationwide. The aim is to ensure consistent rulings and speedy proceedings. The new court will hire experts to assist judges in dealing with complex cases. In recent years Japanese companies have become more aggressive in initiating legal proceedings to protect IPR against international and domestic infringements. The prolonged recession has spurred firms to more fully exploit the value of IPR portfolios through licensing and royalty arrangements. See Taplin 2003.
18 In October 2003 a government taskforce proposed that four 'citizen judges' work alongside three professional judges at trials although the final number is still being debated prior to submission of enabling legislation in 2004. This system is similar to the lay judge system operating in France and Germany, except in Japan citizen judges would also exercise the same authority as professional judges in determining verdicts and sentencing those who are convicted. The proposal calls for participation of citizen judges in trials involving the possibility of death sentences, life imprisonment, and in those in which a deliberate criminal act results in death.
19 *Japan Times*, November 13, 2002.
20 An editorial in the *Asahi* (September 12, 2003) points put that the loser-pays principle might in fact make courts less accessible to individuals and frighten them away from initiating civil suits because of the possibility that they would have to cover the legal expenses of the sued party. In a situation where the government and corporations enjoy inordinate advantages in gathering and blocking access to evidence and information in damage suits, citizens have good reason to doubt victory and thus may be reluctant to assume the risk of covering all legal expenses. Thus, the *Asahi* suggests further reforms that will level the playing field and warns that 'It should not be forgotten that the whole point of judicial reform is to create a situation in our society in which people do not need to feel they have no recourse when they believe their rights have been violated.' The *Asahi*'s misgivings about the principle of 'loser pays' are not so much a condemnation of the reform, but a reminder that it is but one step in the process.
21 *Asahi*, July 18, 2002.
22 These aspiring lawyers were previously paid, but with the vast expansion in the numbers of clerks and budget cuts, payment for this work is no longer an option.

4 Rogues and riches: the bureaucrats' fall from grace

1 *Yomiuri Shimbun*, editorial, December 29, 1996.
2 To set the record straight, documents made public as a result of an information disclosure request indicate that, in recent years, the most expensive wine purchased by the Ministry of Foreign Affairs were two cases of 1989 Château Lafite Rothschild for ¥65,800 (about $520) a bottle. In general, the ministry's wine purchases are concentrated at the end of the fiscal year in March when unspent monies are pooled and used for bulk purchases. Exhausting the annual budget in

this way was designed to prevent budget cuts in the following year. In March 1999, ¥10 million was spent on 1,800 bottles of wine for an average of ¥5,550 (US$44) per bottle, a fairly steep price even by Tokyo standards.

3 Ito (1997) and Kuge (2001) have published independent exposés of wasteful practices, excessive allowances, and the blurry line between public and private monies, raising questions about the incompetence and mismanagement endemic to the diplomatic corps.

4 However, Freeman (2000) criticizes the media's collusion with ministries and politicians, arguing that the national newspapers often maintain a conspiracy of silence. But she does point out that the weekly magazines have played an important role in providing an outlet for investigative reporting and exposés about wrongdoing in high places.

5 In 1996 incoming FDI in Japan was a paltry $200 million but has since risen dramatically. In 2002 FDI was $9 billion, about one-sixth of the FDI flowing into China in that year. By any measure FDI remains very low, but the size does not determine the impact; foreign investments in the relatively small bank Shinsei (formerly the Long Term Credit Bank) and Renault's controlling stake in Nissan have had a tremendous impact on attitudes and business practices. What used to be unthinkable or impossible in Japan, Inc. is now becoming normal and seen to be beneficial.

5 Downsizing the construction state

1 Interview in *Japan Times*, April 25, 2002.

2 In 2003 Japan Highway (JH) admitted that there was a secret balance sheet showing that the public corporation had a massive negative net worth as of March 2001. This secret accounting was reported in a whistleblowing article written by a ranking JH executive in the monthly *Bungei Shunju* (August 2003), but the existence of this report was initially denied by JH officials. The secret balance sheet contradicts the rosy financial picture in the official balance sheet released in June 2003, initially rejected by auditors, showing assets exceeding debts by ¥5.76 trillion. The secret account indicates that the corporation's negative net worth stood at ¥617.5 billion. It is alleged that the secret balance sheet was hidden out of fear that it would justify drastic cuts in future expressway construction. The president of JH, Fujii Haruho, was sacked from his job in 2003 after being implicated in the cover-up and for obstructing privatization of the entity. This scandal illustrates the difficulty of gaining reliable financial information from public corporations and the minefield that awaits privatization.

3 *Asahi*, July 25, 2001.

4 Following his ousting as governor, Tanaka was able to run for re-election because prefectural law required a new election.

5 *Asahi*, August 30, 2001

6 *Japan Times*, June 2, 2002

7 See Kidder 1998; Kidder and Miyazawa 1993.

6 Bad blood: the betrayal and infection of Japan's hemophiliacs

1 For a discussion of patients' rights in Japan and changing medical practices, see Neary (2002).

2 For detailed discussions of Unit 731 see Gold 1996; Harris 1995; Tanaka 1998.

3 The US subsidiary of Green Cross had alerted the company's Osaka headquarters in late 1982 about the possible links between blood transfusions and HIV infection.

4 One of the defendants died while appealing his sentence. The two surviving

defendants succeeded in having their sentences reduced on appeal in 2002; the judge explained the reasons for his decision: 'The defendants have each visited and apologized to the family of a victim, and have each paid ¥30 million in a settlement with company shareholders.' Both have since appealed to the Supreme Court for a suspension of their sentences.

5 Matsushita is one of the two surviving defendants mentioned in note 4. He was convicted of professional negligence and sentenced to two years in prison; this sentence was subsequently reduced to eighteen months. As of 2003 his appeal continues.

6 Suzuki is quoted in the *Japan Times*, September 29, 2001. In 2002 the Diet passed legislation stipulating the government's responsibility for ensuring blood product safety and securing sufficient domestic supplies of blood products.

7 In 2003 Dr. Abe won a libel case against Sakurai. The judge overturned a lower court decision and ruled that she had defamed Abe by stating that he had intervened to delay the approval of heat-treated blood products and had asked for contributions from drug firms in an apparent quid pro quo. The court ordered her to pay damages of ¥4 million (Abe had asked for ¥10 million), but she has appealed the ruling.

8 Green Cross, blamed for numerous cases of AIDS in Japan by selling HIV-tainted blood products, merged with Yoshitomi Pharmaceuticals Industries Ltd. in 1998, which then merged with Mitsubishi-Tokyo Pharmaceuticals Inc. in 2001 to create Mitsubishi Pharma. This is one of the companies being sued.

9 The government approved the import and production of fibrinogen in Japan in June 1964. Although the United States revoked its approval for fibrinogen in 1977, the Japanese government failed to take any measures until a mass outbreak of hepatitis C occurred in Aomori Prefecture in 1987, apparently stemming from the use of fibrinogen.

7 Dignity denied

1 *Japan Times*, May 28, 2001.
2 Three decades later, when reporter Calvin Sims visited this site, only 229 patients remained. *New York Times*, July 30, 2001.
3 *Japan Times*, March 22, 2000.
4 *Japan Times*, May 12, 2002.
5 *Japan Times*, March 22, 2000.
6 *Sankei Shimbun*, June 1, 2001.
7 *Japan Times*, May 12, 2001.
8 *Japan Times*, May 19, 2001.
9 Dr. Sakaguchi recounts his experiences as a medical professional in his celebrated book *Takenoko Isha* (Bamboo Shoot Doctor) (2001).
10 *Mainichi*, May 18, 2001.
11 *Mainichi*, May 23, 2001.
12 *Mainichi*, May 25, 2001.
13 *Japan Times*, May 26, 2001.

8 Mad cows and ocean cockroaches

1 The ninth case announced in November 2003 is troubling in that the infected bull was born after the government ban on use of meat-and-bone meal (MBM) to fortify cattle feed. This means that either the ban on MBM use is not fully effective or that there is another source of BSE transmission.
2 In this case it appears that the Farm Ministry's inept handling of the crisis also failed to protect the producers' interests.

3 As of March 2003 there were still seventeen prefectures lacking adequate personnel and facilities to conduct the mandatory BSE tests, including major beef production centers such as Hokkaido and Kagoshima. In Hokkaido, it is estimated that only about 5,000 out of the 40,000 cattle supposed to be tested for BSE were tested in 2003. Under a special measures law passed in 2002, carcasses of all cattle at least two years old that die from illness or accidents must be tested for BSE. This is based on the European experience that such cattle are 20 times more likely to be infected with BSE than beef cattle raised and slaughtered for human consumption.

4 Nearly 10,000 people nationwide were infected with 0157 in the summer of 1996 and 11 died. In Sakae city there were 6,300 cases and 2 deaths.

5 Despite publicly blaming the E. coli outbreak on *kaiware daikon*, the government's rapid introduction of new standards for slaughtering cattle in August 1996 suggests an official awareness of the fact that E. coli originates in cattle intestines. It was clear that many people infected with E. coli in the 1996 outbreak had not eaten *kaiware daikon*.

6 As director of the livestock industry bureau in 1996, Kumazawa issued a non-binding 'administrative guidance' instructing farmers to refrain from feeding cows MBM. This policy permitted continued use of MBM in Japan at a time when it seemed the probable cause of BSE transmission in Europe.

7 In response to the scandals and to limit the damage to milk sales, the core business of Snow Brand, the company launched a new brand called Megmilk packaged in distinctive bright red cartons. This packaging is quite different from the old blue/white/red milk cartons with the snowflake symbol and is clearly intended to sever ties with a tainted past. Consumers I spoke with had no idea that the new Megmilk is connected to Snow Brand. This rebranding strategy, along with Snow Brand's dominant market position, are expected to soften the financial fallout of the scandals. It is interesting that most of the banks and government ministries have also rebranded themselves since the 1990s, taking on new names that suggest they are also trying to cover their tracks and links with past failures and discrediting scandals.

8 In October 2003 the Board of Audit, a government oversight agency similar to the General Accounting Office in the USA, announced that it saved taxpayers ¥2 billion by uncovering inflated subsidies calculated by the Farm Ministry for the beef buyback program. Yet again questions were raised about how seriously the Farm Ministry takes its watchdog responsibilities.

9 Stephen Hesse, *Japan Times*, June 27, 2002.

10 As cited in the *Japan Times*, May 23, 2002.

11 See Komatsu (2002) for a spirited defense of whaling.

12 In the mid-1990s the risks of PCBs were highlighted with the publication in the media of a photograph comparing a carp taken from the PCB-rich Tama River and an uncontaminated specimen. The dissected healthy carp had testes five times the size of the withered genitals on the Tama specimen, perhaps one of the reasons the government and researchers have taken this issue seriously, especially in light of the fertility decline in the human population. In 2000 the Health Ministry tested the ubiquitous *bento* box lunches on sale at kiosks all over the nation and found relatively high traces of PCB contamination that was traced to the plastic gloves worn by food preparers. However, rather than issue an immediate public health advisory, the ministry contacted the Bento Association and gave them six months to solve the problem. When this story became public knowledge, the media was highly critical, castigating the ministry for failing to mend its ways and placing the interests of producers ahead of consumers yet again. This reaction may explain the ministry's more proactive response to PCB contamination in the case of whale meat.

9 One hand clapping: currents of nationalism in contemporary Japan

1 In August 2003, Japan demonstrated its tentative commitment to, and general ambivalence about, overseas military operations, less than one month after the Diet authorized, amidst considerable controversy, the dispatch of SDF troops to Iraq. The day after the UN headquarters in Baghdad was bombed (August 19, 2003), the Japanese government postponed the mission indefinitely. The evident dangers and strong public opposition forced the government to reconsider its participation in the occupation of Iraq. Finally, in early 2004, despite public misgivings, a small contingent of troops was dispatched to Iraq both to curry favour with the Bush Administration in dealing with the threat from North Korea and to advance the neo-con agenda in Japan. There is a robust public debate calling for revision of the Constitution and the abolition of Article 9, a provision that ostensibly bans Japan from having the large military it now maintains. Some liberals support this goal because they see that Article 9 is observed in the breach anyway and thus want to put into place detailed security restrictions that will specify what the Constitution does and does not allow, in preference to the ad hoc policies that cumulatively have rendered Article 9 virtually irrelevant.

2 The emergence of such activist movements in Korea and Taiwan in the late 1980s reflects democratic political transformations that ended much of the authoritarian repression of political activism in these nations during the Cold War era. In Japan, one often hears questions about why demands for redress have been so long in coming, and complaints edged with contempt that these 'victims' are only interested in getting reparation money from Japan now that it is a rich nation. These Japanese, echoing government attitudes, evince little appreciation for the shame felt by former comfort women that has made it difficult for them to step forward, nor for the importance of an official acknowledgement of past atrocities, sincere acts of atonement, and demonstrations of contrition that go beyond cash payments. Aside from the reflection of greater political openness, the rising chorus of demands can also be interpreted as a last chance for something resembling justice for these aging women. Interestingly, PM Kim Young Sam undermined Japanese attempts to portray the comfort women as 'blackmailers' by rejecting monetary compensation and declaring that the Korean people would prefer an accurate historical accounting of this era based on open access to Japanese archives. It is also significant that only a handful of the former comfort women accepted the compensation offered by the Asian Women's Fund. Most rejected this offer of money because they saw through the subterfuge that it involved. This ostensibly privately funded organization established by the Japanese government (and to a large extent funded by it) was designed to give the impression that Japanese firms were voluntarily stepping forward to right the wrongs of the past. However, it was seen as a disingenuous and transparent attempt by the Japanese government to avoid an official admission of wrongdoing and responsibility. China also experienced upheavals in the late 1980s associated with economic reforms that created more political space for reparation movements, at least until the Tiananmen crackdown, that also served as a safety valve for growing disenchantment with the consequences of these reforms. In addition, artful orchestration of public demands for redress and displays of anti-Japanese sentiments have proven diplomatically useful for Beijing.

3 See Dower (1986), Friend (1988), Goto (1997; 2003), Ienaga (1968), and Marshall (1995).

4 As depicted in the British film *Bridge Over the River Kwai* (1957). Ironically, the decrepit railway near the Thai–Burma border has become a featured tourist attraction for Japanese tour groups visiting Thailand.

5 For a comprehensive discussion of Indonesian *romusha* see Sato 1997.

6 The year 1978 marked 33 years after the end of World War II, corresponding to the Buddhist 33 *kaiki* (anniversary) tradition of reconciliation with the souls of the dead known as *mizumi nagasu* (literally, throw into the water, referring to the casting aside of troubling conflicts and problems), akin to the Western concept of 'forgive and forget.' This tradition was cited by the Yasukuni Shrine spokesman, Kannoto Jujin, as the reason for the enshrinement of the fourteen war criminals in a 1986 interview cited in Nishikawa (2000).

7 Not surprisingly, many Korean and Taiwanese families whose relatives died while serving in the Imperial armed forces do not want to be associated with what they perceive as a symbol of Japanese aggression. They are angry that, despite the Japanese government's failure to pay pensions to immediate family survivors, it has placed the names of these deceased soldiers, 40,000 in all, at Yasukuni to honor them as 'gods' without requesting permission to do so. Some of these families have lobbied and sued, without success, to 'dis-enshrine' the souls of their deceased relatives from Yasukuni. The courts have argued that these dead soldiers have become 'public persons' and their relatives thus have no choice in the matter. Ironically, while these colonial conscripts remain under Japanese control even after death, Japanese prime ministers reserve the right to decide if and when they are 'public persons' when visiting Yasukuni Shrine.

8 On Kodama's role in the formation of the LDP see van Wolferen (1989) and Whiting (1999). The role of the CIA in funding the establishment of the LDP, in collusion with Kodama and the mob, was first revealed by the *New York Times* of October 9, 1994.

9 Nonaka announced his retirement from politics and did not run for office in the November 2003 elections.

10 Chidorigafuji is an ideal alternative except for the fact that it is not legally recognized as a cemetery and thus the interment of soldiers' remains there has been illegal, a point often raised by those who favor retaining Yasukuni Shrine as the nation's war memorial and cemetery for the war dead. In a bid to secure this status, in 2002 a new war museum was opened on the shrine grounds at Yasukuni. Across the street, the Showa Museum, which opened in 1999, also devotes considerable space to war-related displays depicting the ravages of war experienced in Japan. This museum was also at the center of considerable controversy during the planning stage because an organizing committee rejected suggestions to include exhibition space related to the suffering Japan inflicted on its neighbors during the war.

11 To this end, the government has proposed a revision to the basic education law in March 2003 that is designed to emphasize the cultivation of patriotism among students.

12 The implications and legacies of 'race war' between the USA and Japan are analyzed in Dower 1986. Pan-Asian sentiments notwithstanding, Japanese racial contempt also played a significant role in the Sino-Japanese War (1937–45).

10 Social transformations: family, gender, aging, and work

1 The rising number of abused children taken from their families is overloading existing child protection institutions. Advocates point out that these impersonal and overcrowded institutions lack properly trained staff to provide abused children the individual counseling and treatment they need to cope with their physical and emotional trauma. In the absence of such treatment, many of the adolescents who leave these institutions fail to reintegrate into society and often end up in gangs, prostitution or jail. See Goodman (2000) for a discussion of child protection institutions and child welfare mechanisms in Japan.

2 In recent years, there have been approximately 125 cases a year of wives

murdering their husbands in Japan. Inoue Maya, an activist who runs a feminist counseling service in Kyoto, reports that the courts have come to look more favorably on legal defenses based on long-term abuse by these husbands. This is a well-established defense for battered women accused of murdering their spouses in Western countries. However, in Japan women typically receive fairly lengthy prison sentences (seven years or more) in such cases, and are not exonerated as is often the case for battered wives in Western countries.

3 Although violence against women is a longstanding social problem in Japan, as a 'taboo' subject it has received little publicity. By reporting such statistics the government seems to be trying to rectify this omission and place domestic violence on the nation's social agenda.

4 In 1985 women accounted for 9.3 percent of those who passed the bar exam while in 2000 this figure rose to 27.2 percent.

5 *Sunday Mainichi*, May 26, 2002.

6 Postponing divorce also gives the children a chance to establish themselves, in terms of employment and marriage, so that many women wait to divorce in order to lessen the impact on their loved ones.

7 *Shukan Bunshun*, August 19, 2002.

8 *Japan Labor Bulletin*, October 2002.

9 *Japan Times*, August 31, 2000.

10 Nonetheless, despite such cultural values suicide also carries a social stigma.

11 *Newsweek*, August 20, 2001: 13.

12 Neary (2002) discusses the human rights problems of the mentally ill in Japan and the abysmal care they generally receive. He argues that there are some signs of improvement in the treatment of mental illness, reflecting broader improvements in human rights practices and civil society in Japan during the 1990s.

13 In 2003 the government reported that less than one half of paid holidays in 2001 were actually taken by employees, while unions report that nearly one half of workers are obliged to work unpaid overtime (*sabisu zangyo*), averaging 30 hours a month. These reports indicate that work practices have not changed substantially despite widespread recognition of overwork-related health problems. According to the quasi-governmental *Japan Labor Bulletin* (January 1, 2003: 2), 'the poor utilization of paid holidays may be attributable to an atmosphere in the workplace which makes it difficult to take holidays as the recession continues and many companies undertake restructuring measures.' Workers are thus fearful that if they take their holiday entitlements, or refuse requests for unpaid overtime, they may be seen to lack the proper zeal and risk losing their jobs. In terms of ideological change, it is interesting to observe that the low utilization of paid holidays is ascribed to negative job pressures, whereas in the past such an attitude was extolled as symbolic of workers' dedication.

14 In fiscal 2000 (April–March) there were 85 recognized cases of *karoshi*, rising to 143 in 2001 and 115 in the first half of 2002 . In addition to the relaxed criteria, the rise in *karoshi* is attributed to increased workloads for remaining staff in firms that have curbed hiring and encouraged workers to take early retirement. It is estimated that 20 percent of employees work 80 or more hours of overtime a month, the key criterion for judging cases of *karoshi. Japan Labor Bulletin* (February 1, 2003).

15 It appears that greater use of *keitai* may be contributing to a decline in personal computer literacy as many youth opt for the simpler, cheaper, and smaller cellular phones for email and internet surfing. Thus, reports that more than half of Japanese use the internet need to be understood in the context of the scaled-down, Japanese-language, mini-web built for cellphones. Due to the availability of pre-selected content, *keitai* users do not develop the level of information-gathering skills common among PC net surfers. Some commentators compare this passive

approach to information gathering and media access to patterns inculcated in the educational system. In their view, it is mistaken to assume that *keitai* endow users with the kind of media literacy offered by PCs, which provide direct access to alternative news sources and multiple one-to-many channels for opinion expression. Although 17 percent of Japanese households (about 8.3 million) have broadband connections to the internet as of 2003, cellphones appear to be the communication tool of choice for Japanese youth. Given that youngsters from the age of 9 often commute more than 30 minutes each way to school by train, *keitai* are a convenient way to stay in touch with friends and family. They fill the need for intimate communications rather than broadening horizons over the unmediated web. See Tim Clark, 'Japan's Generation of Computer Refuseniks,' *Japan Media Review*, Wireless Report (March 22, 2003).

16 There have been media reports of desperate parents who have resorted to killing their children because they can no longer cope with their violent behavior.

17 Interview with the artist October, 2002.

18 The film *Bounce Kogal* (1997) shows the role of cellphones in arranging liaisons with clients and illustrates the blasé attitude of young girls to a practise depicted as relatively commonplace.

19 Editorial in the *Japan Times*, November 5, 1999.

20 In 2002 it became possible for women to petition the family court to either retain or reclaim their maiden names with full legal sanction; however, this is a time-consuming and expensive process that is not seen as an effective remedy and imposes a requirement on women that men do not face.

21 For an analysis of the politics of abortion and the Pill see Norgren (2001).

22 The declining birth rate – 4.54 in 1947 to 2.1 in the 1960s to 1.32 in 2002 – reflects the rising number of single women (the government estimates that one out of seven women born in 1980 will never marry) and a preference for smaller families. Smaller family size is a consequence of higher average length of education for women and rising levels of labor-force participation by them. In 1975 the number of women working outside the home was approximately 12 million, rising to 20 million by 1993 and 27 million by 2001. The low birth rate symbolizes the failure of both government and corporations to implement policies and practices that would help women reconcile their multiple roles and make giving birth a less daunting and costly option.

23 In June 2003 former Prime Minister Mori Yoshiro asserted that childless women do not deserve public pensions: 'The government takes care of women who have given birth to a lot of children as a way to thank them for their hard work. ... It is wrong for women who have not had a single child to ask for taxpayer money when they get old, after having enjoyed their freedom and had fun.' Harsh media criticism of Mori's gaffe indicates that such views are out of step with the times.

24 Maternity leave with full pay is policy in Spain (16 weeks), Germany (14 weeks), and France (16–26 weeks). In Sweden, those who take maternity leave receive 80 percent of their pay for up to 78 weeks. See Clearinghouse on International Developments in Child, Youth, and Family Policies, Columbia University.

25 *Japan Times*, January 4, 2002.

26 See Haruka (2001; 2003). She bleakly asserts that Japanese women have three choices: have no career and get married; abandon a career and get married; or plan a life without men. Popular writers such as Haruka are tapping into a rich vein of frustration among working women.

27 For a cross-national comparison of gender empowerment measures see the UNDP website: www.undp.org/hdr2000/english/presskit/gem.pdf.

28 Japan has three main categories of national pension schemes: 1) *kosei nenkin* for company employees; 2) *kyosai nenkin* for civil servants and employees of public and quasi-public entities; and 3) *kokumin nenkin* for farmers, and self-employed

and unemployed workers. For the first two categories, pension contributions are deducted directly from salaries while those enrolled in the *kokumin nenkin* must arrange payments themselves. Part of the reason for the steep rise in non-participation in the *kokumin nenkin* system is the sharp reduction in exemptions; in 2002 the number of people who were exempt from paying any premium was cut in half, but only 14.5 percent of those who lost their exemptions paid into the pension program in fiscal year 2002. All citizens must pay pension premiums from the age of 20, regardless of employment status, but nearly half of those in the 20–24-year-old age cohort did not pay into the system in fiscal 2002. The rise in the delinquency ratio in the *kokumin nenkin*, the largest of the national pension schemes, has a negative impact on the company employees' pension plan, *kosei nenkin*, because the latter's funds are used to pay the minimum amount promised to all pensioners. When more people fail to pay into *kokumin nenkin*, the *kosei nenkin* system provides funds to make up the difference. Civil servant pension funds are sequestered and thus insulated from the growing problem of delinquency.

29 Lie (2001) discusses the critical role of foreign workers in the Japanese economy and the lingering reluctance to either acknowledge this situation or recognize the ethnic heterogeneity of contemporary Japan. This cognitive dissonance is a significant obstacle to developing better policies for foreign workers and ethnic minorities resident in Japan.

30 According to the *Japan Times* (May 3, 2003), 'Japan is notorious for its closed door to people seeking refugee status. From 1989 to 1997, only two applicants a year were successful, and only 19 annually from 1998 to 2002. Last year, refugee status was granted to 14 foreigners, while 250 people applied for the first time for refugee status.'

31 It is telling that Okuda (2003), the chairmen of Keidanren, advocates just such a transformation in employment practices and societal priorities.

Bibliography

Alexander, A., 'What Happened to Japan's Economy in the 1990s?,' *Japan Economic Institute Report*, 27A (July 14, 2000): 1–12.

—— , *In the Shadow of the Miracle: The Japanese Economy Since the End of High-Speed Growth.* Rowman & Littlefield, New York, 2002.

Ariyoshi, S., *Twilight Years.* Kodansha, Tokyo, 1984 [1972].

Awaji, T. (translated by Keisuke Mark Abe), 'HIV Litigation and its Settlement (in Japan),' *Pacific Rim Law and Policy Association*, 6(3), 1997: 581–605.

Bix, H., *Hirohito and the Making of Modern Japan.* Harper Collins, New York, 2000.

Boling, D., 'Access to Government-Held Information in Japan: Citizen's "Right to Know" Bows to Bureaucracy,' *Stanford Journal of International Law*, 34, winter 1998: 1–45.

Bornoff, N., *Pink Samurai.* Grafton, London, 1991.

Bowen, R., *Japan's Dysfunctional Democracy: The LDP and Structural Corruption.* M.E. Sharpe, Armonk, 2003.

Brinton, M., *Women and the Economic Miracle: Gender and Work in Postwar Japan.* University of California Press, Berkeley, 1993.

Broadbent, J., *Environmental Politics in Japan: Networks of Power and Protest.* Cambridge University Press, Cambridge, 1998.

Buruma, I., *The Wages of Guilt: Memories of War in Germany and Japan.* Farrar Strauss Giroux, New York, 1994.

Campbell, J., *How Policies Change: The Japanese Government and the Aging Society.* Princeton University Press, Princeton, 1992.

—— , 'Administrative Reform as Policy Change and Policy Non-Change,' *Social Science Japan Journal*, 2(2), 1999: 157–76.

Chang, I., *The Nanking Massacre.* Basic Books, New York, 1997.

Cohen, T., *Remaking Japan: The American Occupation as New Deal.* Free Press, New York, 1987.

Condon, J., *A Half Step Behind: Japanese Women of the 1980s.* Dodd, Mead, New York, 1985.

Cook, A. and H. Hayashi, *Working Women in Japan: Discrimination, Resistance and Reform.* New York State School of Industrial and Labor Relations, Ithaca, 1980.

Crenson, M. and B. Ginsberg, *Downsizing Democracy: How America Sidelined Its Citizens and Privatized Its Public.* Johns Hopkins University Press, Baltimore, 2002.

Curtis, G., *The Japanese Way of Politics.* Columbia University Press, New York, 1988.

—— , *The Logic of Japanese Politics: Leaders, Institutions and the Limits of Change.* Columbia University Press, New York, 1999.

Dehesh, A. and C. Pugh, 'The Internationalization of Post-1980 Property Cycles and the Japanese "Bubble" Economy, 1986–1996,' *International Journal of Urban and Regional Research*, 23(1), March 1999: 147–64.

Douglass, M. and G. Roberts (eds), *Japan and Global Migration: Foreign Workers and the Advent of a Multicultural Society*. Routledge, London, 2000.

Dower, J., *War Without Mercy*. Pantheon, New York, 1986.

—— , *Japan in War and Peace*. New Press, New York, 1993.

—— , *Embracing Defeat: Japan in the Wake of World War II*. W.W. Norton, New York, 1999.

Drucker, P., 'In Defense of Japanese Bureaucracy,' *Foreign Affairs*, 77, September/October 1998: 68–80.

Eades, J., T. Gill and H. Befu (eds), *Globalization and Social Change in Contemporary Japan*. Transpacific Press, Melbourne, 2000.

Emmott, B., *The Sun Also Sets: Why Japan Will Not Be Number One*. Simon & Schuster, New York, 1989.

Feldman, E., 'HIV and Blood in Japan: Transforming Private Conflict into Public Scandal,' in E.A. Feldman and R. Bayer (eds), *Blood Feuds: AIDS, Blood, and the Politics of Medical Disaster*. Oxford University Press, Oxford, 1999: 59–93.

—— , 'Blood Justice: Courts, Conflict, and Compensation in Japan, France, and the United States,' *Law and Society Review*, 2000a: 651–701.

—— , *The Ritual of Rights in Japan: Law, Society and Health Policy*. Cambridge University Press, Cambridge, 2000b.

Field, N., *In the Realm of the Dying Emperor: Japan At Century's End*. Vintage, New York, 1993.

Finn, R., *Winners in Peace: MacArthur, Yoshida and Postwar Japan*. University of California Press, Berkeley, 1992.

Fogel, J., *The Nanjing Massacre in History and Historiography*. University of California Press, Berkeley, 2000.

Freeman, L., *Closing the Shop: Information Cartels and Japan's Mass Media*. Princeton University Press, Princeton, 2000.

Friend, T., *Blue Eyed Enemy: Japan Against the West in Java and Luzon*. Princeton University Press, Princeton, 1988.

Fujino, Y., *Inochi no Kindaishi (Modern Being)*. Kamogawa Shuppan, Kyoto, 2001.

George, T.S., *Minamata: Pollution and the Struggle for Democracy in Postwar Japan*. Harvard University Press, Cambridge, 2001.

Gill, T., *Men of Uncertainty: The Social Organization of Day Laborers in Contemporary Japan*. State University of New York Press, Albany, 2001.

Gluck, C. and S. Graubard (eds), *Showa: The Japan of Hirohito*. W.W. Norton, New York, 1992.

Gold, H., *Unit 731: Japan's Wartime Human Experimentation Program*. Yen Books, Tokyo, 1996.

Goodman, R., *Children of the Japanese State: The Changing Role of Child Protection Institutions in Contemporary Japan*. Oxford University Press, Oxford, 2000.

Gordon, A. (ed.), *Postwar Japan as History*. University of California Press, Berkeley, 1993.

—— , *The Wages of Affluence: Labor and Management in Postwar Japan*. Harvard University Press, Cambridge, 1998.

—— , *A Modern History of Japan*. Oxford University Press, Oxford, 2003.

Goto, K., *Returning to Asia*. Ryukei Shyosha, Tokyo, 1997.

—— , *Tensions of Empire*. Ohio University Press, Athens, 2003.

Greenfield, T., *Speed Tribes: Days and Nights with Japan's Next Generation.* Harper Collins, New York, 1994.

Grimes, W., *Unmaking the Japanese Miracle: Macroeconomic Politics 1985–2000.* Cornell University Press, Ithaca, 2001.

Haley, J., *Authority Without Power: Law and the Japanese Paradox.* Oxford University Press, Oxford, 1991.

—— , 'The Myth of the Reluctant Litigant,' *Journal of Japanese Studies,* 4, summer 1978: 359–90.

Hall, I., *Cartels of the Mind.* W.W. Norton, New York, 1997.

—— , *Bamboozled: How America Loses the Intellectual Game with Japan and Its Implications for our Future in Asia.* M.E. Sharpe, Armonk, 2002.

Harris, P.B. and S.O. Long, 'Husbands and Sons in the US and Japan: Cultural Expectations and Caregiving Experiences,' *Journal of Aging Studies,* 13(3), fall 1999: 241–68.

Harris, S., *Factories of Death: Japanese Biological Warfare, 1932–45, and the American Cover-Up.* Routledge, London, 2001.

Hartcher, P., *The Ministry: The Inside Story of Japan's Ministry of Finance.* Harper Collins, Sydney, 1997.

Haruka, Y., *Kekkon Shimasen!* Kodansha, Tokyo, 2001.

—— , *Hybrid Woman.* Kodansha, Tokyo, 2003.

Hasegawa, K., 'The Organization and Activation of the Civil Sector: Rapid Development During the Lost Decade,' *Social Science Japan,* 23, April 2002: 5–7.

Hashizumi, Y., 'Gender Issues and Japanese Family-Centered Caregiving for Frail Elderly Parents or Parents-in-Law in Modern Japan,' *Public Health Nursing,* 17(1), January/February 2000: 25–31.

Hatch, W. and K. Yamamura (eds), *Asia in Japan's Embrace: Building a Regional Production Alliance.* Cambridge University Press, Cambridge, 1996.

Havens, T., *Fire Across the Sea: The Vietnam War and Japan.* Princeton University Press, Princeton, 1987.

Hein, L. and M. Selden (eds), *Censoring History: Citizenship and Memory in Japan, Germany and the United States.* M.E. Sharpe, Armonk, 2000.

Hicks, G., *The Comfort Women.* Yen Books, Tokyo, 1995.

Hirao, K., 'The Effect of Higher Education on the Rate of Labor-Force Exit for Married Japanese Women,' *International Journal of Comparative Sociology,* 42(5), 2001: 413–33.

Hirokawa. R., *Yakugai AIDS no Shinso (Report on Drug-Induced AIDS).* Tokuma Bunko, Tokyo, 1996.

Houseman, S. and M. Osawa, 'Part-Time and Temporary Employment in Japan,' *Monthly Labor Review,* October 1995: 10–18.

—— , 'Part-Time Employment in the United States and Japan,' in J. O'Reilly and C. Fagan (eds), *Part-Time Prospects.* London, Routledge, 1998: 232–51.

—— , 'The Growth of Nonstandard Employment in Japan and the United States: A Comparison of Causes and Consequences,' in *The Growth of Nonstandard Work Arrangements: A Comparison of the United States, Japan and Europe.* Upjohn Institute, Kalamazoo, 2003.

Hurd, M. and N. Yashiro (eds), *The Economic Effects of Aging in the US and Japan.* University of Chicago Press, Chicago, 1997.

Ienaga, S. (translated by R. Minear), *Japan's Past, Japan's Future: One Historian's Odyssey.* Rowman & Littlefield, Lanham, 2001.

—— , *The Pacific War, 1931–1945: A Critical Perspective on Japan's Role in World War II*. Random House, New York, 1968.

Inoguchi, T., 'Japanese Bureaucracy: Coping With New Challenges,' in P. Jain and T. Inoguchi (eds), *Japanese Politics Today*. Macmillan, Melbourne, 1997.

International Public Hearing Report (ed.), *War Victimization and Japan*. Toho Shuppan, Osaka, 1993.

Ishida, H., *Social Mobility in Contemporary Japan*. Stanford University Press, Stanford, 1993.

Itagaki, T., 'Kan Naoto Stirs the Health Ministry,' *Japan Quarterly*, 43(3), July–September 1996: 24–9.

Ito, P., 'Japan: The Interaction of "Weak Feminism," a Low Birth Rate, and an Aging Society,' in S. Michel and R. Mahon (eds), *Child Care and Welfare State Restructuring: Gender and Entitlement at the Crossroads*. London, Routledge, 2001.

Ito, T., *Owarai Gaimusho Kimitsu Joho (Humorous Secrets of the Foreign Ministry)*. Asuka Shinsha, Tokyo, 1997.

Iwai, S., *The Japanese Woman: Traditional Image and Changing Reality*. Free Press, New York, 1993.

'Japan and AIDS: What, us?,' *The Economist*, September 4, 1993: 37.

Johnson, C., *Japan: Who Governs?*. W.W. Norton, New York, 1995.

Jolivet, M., *Japan – The Childless Society?*. Routledge, London, 1997.

Katz, R., *The System that Soured – The Rise and Fall of the Japanese Miracle*. M.E. Sharpe, Armonk, 1998.

—— , *Japanese Phoenix*. M.E. Sharpe, Armonk, 2003.

Kawada, E. and Y. Yasuda, *Ima Yakugai AIDS Wa Atarashi Tatakaihe (New Developments in Drug-Induced AIDS)*. Kamogawa Shuppan, Tokyo, 1998.

Kawano, S., 'Sakurai Yoshiko Somusho no Teki' (Interview with Yoshiko Sakurai, Enemy of the Ministry of Home Affairs), *AERA*, August 12–19, 2002: 15–17.

Kerr, A., *Dogs and Demons: Tales from the Dark Side of Japan*. Penguin, London, 2001.

Kidder, R.L., 'Disasters Chronic and Acute: Issues in the Study of Environmental Pollution in Urban Japan,' in P. Karan and K. Stapleton (eds), *The Japanese City*. University of Kentucky Press, Lexington, 1998.

—— and S. Miyazawa, 'Long-Term Strategies in Japanese Environmental Litigation,' *Law and Social Inquiry*, 18(4), 1993: 605–27.

Kingston, J., *Japan in Transformation, 1952–2000*. Longmans, London, 2001.

Kitamura, T. *et al.*, 'Frequencies of Child Abuse in Japan: Hidden but Prevalent Crime,' *International Journal of Offender Therapy and Comparative Criminology*, 43(1), 1999: 21–33.

Kobori, K., *Yasukuni Jinja to Nipponjin (Yasukuni Shrine and the Japanese)*. PHP Kenkyu Senta, Tokyo, 1998.

Komai, H., *Foreign Migrants in Contemporary Japan*. Trans Pacific Press, Melbourne, 2001.

Komatsu, M., *Kujira to Nihonjin (Whales and Japanese)*. Seishun, Tokyo, 2002.

Kondo, D., *Crafting Selves: Power, Gender and Discourses of Identity in a Japanese Workplace*. University of Chicago Press, Chicago, 1990.

Konishi, T., *Domestiku Baiorensu (Domestic Violence)*, Hakusuisha, Tokyo, 2001.

Kuge, Y., *Taishikan Nanka Iranai (Embassies Are Not Needed)*, Gentosha, Tokyo, 2001.

Lam, A., *Women and Japanese Management*. Routledge, London, 1992.

Levkof, S., 'Graying of Japan: Choju Shakai,' *Ageing International*, 26(1/2), summer–fall 2000: 10–24.

Lie, J., *Multiethnic Japan.* Harvard University Press, Cambridge, 2001.

Lifton, R., *Destroying the World to Save It: Aum Shinrikyo, Apocalyptic Violence and the New Global Terrorism.* Metropolitan Books, New York, 1999.

Long, S.O. (ed.), *Caring for the Elderly in Japan and the United States.* Routledge, London, 2000.

Machimura, T., 'The Urban Restructuring Process in Tokyo in the 1980s: Transforming Tokyo into a World City,' *International Journal of Urban and Regional Research,* 16(1): 114–28.

Maclachlan, P., 'Protecting Producers from Consumer Protection: The Politics of Products Liability Reform Japan,' *Social Science Japan Journal,* 2(2), 1999, 249–66.

—— , 'Information Disclosure and the Center-Local Relationship in Japan,' in S. Smith (ed.), *Local Voices, National Issues: The Impact of Local Initiative in Japanese Policy-Making.* Monograph Series in Japanese Studies, no. 31, University of Michigan Press, Ann Arbor, 2000: 9–30,

—— , *Consumer Politics in Postwar Japan: The Institutional Boundaries of Citizen Activism.* Columbia University Press, New York, 2002.

Marshall, J., *To Have and Have Not: Southeast Asia's Raw Materials and the Origins of the Pacific War.* University of California Press, Berkeley, 1995.

Marshall, J., 'Here Comes the Judge,' *Social Science Japan Journal,* April 2002: 8–13.

Masujima, T., 'Evaluating Administrative Reform: An Insider's Report,' *Social Science Japan Journal,* 2(2), 1999: 215–28.

Matsubara, A. and H. Todoroki (translated by R. Forrest), *Japan's Culture of Giving. Coalition for Legislation to Support Citizens' Organizations.* Coalition for Legislation to Support Citizens' Organizations, Tokyo, 2003.

McCormack, G., *The Emptiness of Japanese Affluence.* M.E. Sharpe, Armonk, 1996 (revised 2001).

—— , 'Nationalism and Identity in Post-Cold War Japan,' *Pacifica Review,* 12(3), October 2000: 247–63.

McVeigh, B., *Japanese Higher Education as Myth.* M.E. Sharpe, Armonk, 2002.

Mencimer, S., 'The Baby Boycott,' *The Washington Monthly,* June 2001: 14–19.

Miyamoto, M., *The Straitjacket Society: An Insider's Irreverent View of Bureaucratic Japan.* Kodansha International, Tokyo, 1994.

Miyazawa, S., 'The Politics of Judicial Reform in Japan: The Rule of Law at Last?,' *Asian-Pacific Law and Policy Journal,* 2001: 89–121.

Mochinaga, K., 'What I Didn't Know about AIDS,' *Japan Echo,* 23(3), autumn 1996: 18–24.

Morishita J., *Naze Kujira wa Zasho Suru no ka? (Why Do Whales Run Aground?).* Kawadeshobo, Tokyo, 2002.

Mulgan, A.G., *Japan's Failed Revolution: Koizumi and the Politics of Economic Reform.* Asia Pacific Press, Canberra, 2002.

Murakami, R., *The Bubble: What Could That Money Have Bought?* Shogakukan, Tokyo, 1999.

—— , *Underground.* Vintage, New York, 2001.

Murphy, R., *The Weight of the Yen.* W.W. Norton, New York, 1996.

—— , 'Japan's Economic Crisis,' *New Left Review,* January/February 2000: 25–73.

Naff, C., *About Face: How I Stumbled onto Japan's Social Revolution.* Kodansha, Tokyo, 1994.

Neary, I., *Human Rights in Japan, South Korea and Taiwan.* Routledge, London, 2002.

Nikkeiren (Japan Federation of Employers Association), *Creating a Dynamic and Appealing Society*. Nikkeiren, Tokyo, 1999.

Nishikawa, S., *Tenno no Jinja Yasukuni Kyokasho ni Kakarenakatta Senso* (Part V) (*The Emperor's Yasukuni Shrine: The Untold Story*). Nashi no Kisha, Tokyo, 2000.

Nishio, K., *Kokumin no Rekishi* (*People's History*). Sankei Shimbunsha, Tokyo, 1999.

Nonoyama, H., 'The Family and Family Sociology in Japan,' *The American Sociologist*, fall 2000: 27–41.

Norgren, T., *Abortion: Before Birth Control: The Politics of Reproduction in Postwar Japan*. Princeton University Press, Princeton, 2001.

Nottage, L., *Product Safety and Liability: From Minamata to Mad Cows*. RoutledgeCurzon, London, 2004.

Ohtake, F., 'Aging Society and Inequality,' *Japan Labor Bulletin*, 38(9), July 1999: 5–11.

Oizumi, E., *Property Finance in Japan: Expansion and Collapse of the Bubble Economy*. Discussion Papers in Urban and Regional Economics, no. 82, Series C, vol. 5, University of Reading, Reading, 1993.

Okuda, H., *Ningen o Kofuku ni suru Keizai: Yutakasa no Kakumei* (*Towards a People-friendly Economy: The Revolution for Well-being*). PHP, Tokyo, 2003.

Osawa, M., 'Working Mothers: Changing Patterns of Employment and Fertility in Japan,' *Economic Development and Cultural Change*, 36(4), 1988: 623–50.

——, *Atarashi Kazoku no tameno Keizaigaku* (*Economics for the New Family*). Chuo Koron, Tokyo, 1998.

Ozawa, I., *Blueprint for a New Japan*. Kodansha, Tokyo, 1994.

Pekkanen, R., 'Japan's New Politics? The Case of the NPO Law,' *Journal of Japanese Studies*, 26(1), winter 2000: 111–48.

——, 'Molding Japanese Civil Society: State-Structured Incentives and the Patterning of Civil Society,' in F. Schwartz and S. Pharr (eds), *The State of Civil Society in Japan*. Cambridge University Press, Cambridge, 2003.

Pempel, T. (ed.), *Uncommon Democracies*. Cornell University Press, Ithaca, 1990.

——, *Regime Shift: Comparative Dynamics of the Japanese Political Economy*. Cornell University Press, Ithaca, 1998.

——, 'Tokyo's Little Italy,' *The International Economy*, May/June 2000: 34–7, 55.

Raymo, J., 'Later Marriages or Fewer? Changes in the Marital Behavior of Japanese Women,' *Journal of Marriage and the Family*, 60, November 1998: 1023–34.

Reader, I., *Religion in Contemporary Japan*. Macmillan Press, Basingstoke, 1991.

——, *A Poisonous Cocktail? Aum Shinrikyo's Path to Violence*. Nordic Institute of Asian Studies, Copenhagen, 1996.

Repeta, L., 'Local Government Disclosure Systems in Japan,' *National Bureau of Asian Research*, 16, October 1999.

——, 'Changing the Guard on the Provinces: A New Platform for Hard Times,' Speech at the conference *Energizing Japanese Politics: New Tools for Citizen Participation*, April 2001. Japan Information Access Project (US–Japan Friendship Commission).

——, 'Birth of the Freedom of Information Act in Japan: Kanagawa 1982,' MIT Japan Program Working Paper 03-01, September 2003.

Richardson, B., *Japanese Democracy: Power, Coordination and Performance*. Yale University Press, New Haven, 1997.

Richie, D., *Inland Sea*. Weatherhill, Tokyo, 1971.

Roberts, G., *Staying on the Line: Blue Collar Women in Contemporary Japan*. University of Hawaii Press, Honolulu, 1994.

Ruoff, K., *The People's Emperor: Democracy and the Japanese Monarchy, 1945–1995.* Harvard University Press, Cambridge, 2001.

Sakaguchi, C., *Takenoko Isha (Bamboo Doctor)*. Kobunsha, Tokyo, 2001.

Sakurai, Y., *AIDS Hanzai Ketsuyu-byo Kanja no Higeki (The Tragedy of AIDS Hemophiliac Patients)*. Chuo Koron, Tokyo, 1994.

——, *Yakugai AIDS Muzai Hanketsu -Doshite Desuka? (Why was the Verdict on Drug-Induced AIDS Not Guilty?)*. Chuo Shinsho, Tokyo, 2001.

Samuels, R.J., *Machiavelli's Children: Leaders and their Legacies in Italy and Japan.* Cornell University Press, Ithaca, 2003.

Sato, I., 'Judicial Reform in Japan in the 1990s: Increase of the Legal Profession, Reinforcement of Judicial Functions and Expansion of the Rule of Law,' *Social Science Japan Journal*, 5(1), 2002: 71–84.

Sato, S., *War, Nationalism and Peasants: Java Under the Japanese Occupation 1942–45.* M.E. Sharpe, Armonk, 1997.

Saso, M., *Women in the Japanese Workplace.* Shipman, London, 1990.

Schaller, M., *The American Occupation of Japan: The Origins of the Cold War in Asia.* Oxford University Press, Oxford, 1985.

Schlesinger, J., *Shadow Shoguns: The Rise and Fall of Japan's Postwar Political Machine.* Simon & Schuster, New York, 1997.

Schoppa, L., 'Japan the Reluctant Reformer,' *Foreign Affairs*, 80(5), September/October 2001: 76–90.

Schultz, D., 'Japan's Information Disclosure Law: Why a Law Full of Loopholes is Better than None,' *Law in Japan*, 27(128), 2001: 128–83.

Shimada, H., *Japan's 'Guest Workers': Issues and Public Policies.* University of Tokyo Press, Tokyo, 1994.

Starr, D., *Blood: An Epic History of Medicine and Commerce.* Alfred A. Knopf, New York, 1998.

Stockwin, J., *Governing Japan: Divided Politics in a Major Economy.* Blackwell, London, 1998.

Stronach, B., *Beyond the Rising Sun: Nationalism in Contemporary Japan.* Praeger, Westport, 1995.

Szymkowiak, K., *Sokaiya: Extortion, Protection and the Japanese Government.* M.E. Sharpe, Armonk, 2001.

Takemae, E., *Inside GHQ: The Allied Occupation of Japan and Its Legacy.* Continuum, London, 2002.

Tamamoto, M., 'A Land Without Patriots: The Yasukuni Controversy and Japanese Nationalism,' *World Policy Journal*, fall 2001: 33–40.

Tanaka, N., *Yasukuni no Sengoshi (Yasukuni in the Postwar Era)*. Iwanami Shoten, Tokyo, 2002.

Tanaka, Y., *Hidden Horrors: Japanese War Crimes in World War II.* Westview Press, Boulder, 1998.

Taplin, R. (ed.), *Exploiting Patent Rights and a New Climate for Innovation in Japan.* Intellectual Property Institute, London, 2003.

Toer, P.A., *Mute's Soliloquy.* Hyperion East, New York, 1999.

Upham, F., *Law and Social Change in Postwar Japan.* Harvard University Press, Cambridge, 1987.

Vogel, E., *Japan as Number One.* Tuttle, Tokyo, 1980.

van Wolferen, K., 'Japan Analyst Urges People to Take Their Political Life Seriously,' *Tokyo Business Today*, January 1992, 46–7.

—— , *The Enigma of Japanese Power.* Macmillan, London, 1989.

Wakamiya, Y., *The Postwar Conservative View of Asia.* LTCB International Library Foundation, Tokyo, 1999.

Werner, R., 'Japanese Foreign Investment and the "land bubble",' *Review of International Economics,* 2(2): 166–78.

Whiting, R., *Tokyo Underworld.* Pantheon, New York, 1999.

Wood, C., *The Bubble Economy: The Japanese Economic Collapse.* Charles Tuttle, Tokyo, 1993.

Yamada, M., *Parasaito Singuru no Jidai* (*The Era of Parasite Singles*). Chikumashobo, Tokyo, 1999.

Yamamoto, N., 'The Continuation of Family Caregiving in Japan,' *Journal of Health and Social Behaviour,* 38(2), June 1997: 164–76.

Yamamoto, T. (ed.), *The Nonprofit Sector in Japan.* Manchester University Press, Manchester, 1998.

Yamauchi, N., *Nonpurofito Ekonomi* (*Nonprofit Economy*). Nippon Hyoronsha, Tokyo, 1997.

—— , *NPO Deetabukku* (*NPO Debate*). Yukihaku, Tokyo, 1999.

Zenkoku Shimin Ombudsman, *Renraku Kaigi, Nihon Wa Sentaku Suru* (*Conference Report on Disclosure in Japan*). Kyoiku Shiryo Shuppankai, Tokyo, 1998.

Internet links

www.asahi.com/english/english.html (*Asahi* newspaper)

http://pages.britishlibrary.net/bridgetojapan/ (Daiwa Foundation (UK) Information Resources)

http://coombs.anu.edu.au/asia-www-monitor.html (Australian-hosted Asian information resource site)

http://freedominfo.org (Website focusing on freedom of information issues, including Japan and other links)

www.japanfocus.org (Writings about Japan and Asia)

www.japanreview.net/index.htm (Reviews of books on Japan)

www.japantoday.com (Daily news with searchable archive)

www.jcer.or.jp/eng/index.html (Japan Center for Economic Research)

http://jguide.stanford.edu (Resources on Japan)

www.jpri.org (Japan Policy Research Institute)

http://joi.ito.com (Provocative personal website on contemporary Japan)

www.mainichi.co.jp/english/index.html (*Mainichi* newspaper)

www.mofa.go.jp (Official website of Ministry of Foreign Affairs)

www.newsonjapan.com (Current news on Japan culled from various sources)

http://nias.ku.dk (Nordic Institute of Asian Studies)

www.ojr.org/japan/home/section.php (Japan Media Review)

www.sentaku.co.jp/en/news/text07.htm (Japanese monthly magazine)

http://web-japan.org/stat/index.html (Japanese government statistics)

www.yomiuri.co.jp (*Yomiuri* newspaper)

Index

Page numbers in italics indicate illustrations

politicians: construction industry
128–30, 144–6
pornography: child 273
porpoises 223
Portugal: BSE 213
postal system 127, 133, 153–4
post-retirement positions *see amakudari*
powdered milk: BSE crisis 204, 205
POWs (Allied prisoners of war) 234
Pramoedya Anata Toer 232, 235
pressure groups 42
price destruction (*kakaku hakka*) 37
Pride 233
privacy 48–9, 57–60; Juki Net 60–5
privatization 119, 154–5; *amakudari*
107–8; construction projects 125;
highway construction 127, 132–9;
Post Office 127
productivity 35
Products Liability Act (1994) 86
projections: *doken kokka* 139–40
property assets 5
prostitution 26, 39; child 273
protesters: Iraq war *229*
public apologies *see* apologies
public debt 135
public disenchantment 23, 24–5
public ethics 25–8
public safety: nuclear energy 17–20
public spending 117; construction
industry 123–5, 152
public trust 157

quality of life 37–9, 122

racism 300
racketeers (*sokaiya*): corporate 12
radiation 19
radish sprouts 204–5
Railtrack Group: UK 135
railways: network 134; travel costs 155
Ramsar Convention on Wetlands 147
Rape of Nanking 14
Raymo, J. 279
reactors: nuclear energy 17–18
Reader, I. 17
real estate 5, 6, 9
real-estate lending institutions (*jusen*)
8–9, 96
recession 1–41
reclamation: land 147–50
reconciliation 247
Recruit scandal 23–4
reforms 306–8, *307*; 1990s 2–4;

amakudari 106–7; domestic violence
261–2; educational 268; judicial
85–94; pension 286–7, 299–300;
political 20–2; taxation 286–7;
textbook 233, 241, 243–4
refugees 301
relocation: of industries 122
repackaging scam 207–9 *see also* false
food labeling
Repeta, Lawrence 46, 49, 51, 54
report: BSE outbreak 199–200
reservoir dams 140–3
restaurants 38
restructuring 53–4
retailers: traceability 211–12
retirement: divorce rates 263; early 31;
post-retirement employment
299–300
revelations: war record 230–2, 235
'revolving door' 100
Richie, Donald 185–6
right-wing political parties: Europe 228
risk assessment: lack of 8
risk management 210–11
river bank: concrete *123*
roads: building *see* highway
construction; privatization *155*;
revenues 138–40
'road tribe' politicians (*dorozoku*) 125,
127
Roberts, G. 39, 301
romusha (day laborer) 234
rule of law 85, 86, 88, 119
rural districts: road building 136
rush hour *26*
Russia: whaling 220

Safety First 222
safety procedures: nuclear power 18–19
Sagawa Kyubin scandal 23, 24–5
Sakaguchi Chikara 191, *194*, 195
Sakai Wakamatsu 93
Sakurai Yoshiko 64, 173
salaryman *7*, 269
Samuels, R.J. 22, 128
Sanbanze wetlands 147
sarin gas attack 16–17
sashimi (raw fish) 38
Sato, I. 88
scandals 42, 129; bureaucrats 97–8;
government 2 *see also* BSE outbreak;
Hansen's disease case; Minamata
Schlesinger, J. 23
Scientific Feed Laboratory 204